D1283881

NEW GUINEA

NEW GUINEA

CROSSING BOUNDARIES AND HISTORY

CLIVE MOORE

University of Hawai'i Press | Honolulu

© 2003 University of Hawai‘i Press
All rights reserved
Printed in the United States of America
08 07 06 05 04 03   6 5 4 3 2 1

Library of Congress Cataloging-in-Publication Data
Moore, Clive.
New Guinea: crossing boundaries and history / Clive Moore.
   p. cm.
Includes bibliographical references and index.
ISBN 0-8248-2485-7 (hardcover: alk. paper)
1. New Guinea—History.   I. Title.
DU739 .M66 2003
995—dc21   2003002471

University of Hawai‘i Press books are printed on acid-free
paper and meet the guidelines for permanence and durability
of the Council on Library Resources.

Production Notes for Moore / NEW GUINEA

Cover and Interior designed by April Leidig-Higgins.
Text in Monotype Garamond.
Composition by Copperline Book Services, Inc.

Printing and binding by The Maple-Vail Book
   Manufacturing Group.
Printed on 60 lb. Text White Opaque, with insert on
   80 lb. glossy.

Table of Contents

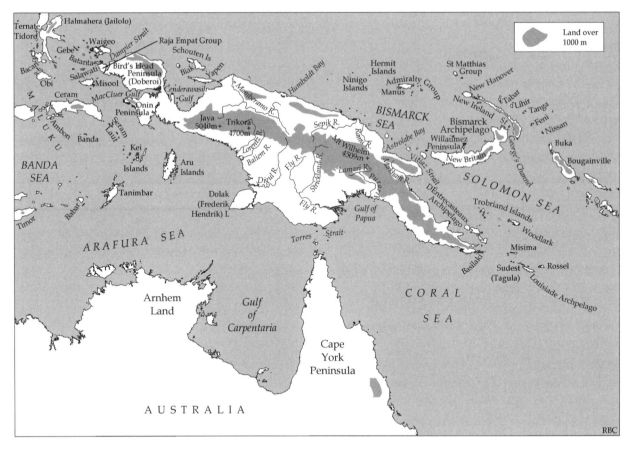

New Guinea

Maps

Preface

Nothing is more depictive of New Guinea than the stunning bird-of-paradise, a unique and beautiful bird species that occurs only in New Guinea and adjacent islands. Called *kumul* in Pidgin English and *cenderawasih* in west New Guinea, they hold a prominent place in traditional culture and are widely valued for their extravagant plumage. New Guinea, the second largest island in the world, is also quite unique. For at least 40,000 years, humans have moved around and through New Guinea, giving the island a history back to the very beginnings of the modern human race.

Conceptualizing the long span of human history in New Guinea is a difficult, daunting task. While visiting Canberra when this book was nearly complete, I was taken aback by the negativity of a colleague who dismissed my lengthy struggles to master the literature as a waste of time. She said that without the skills of an archaeologist there was no sense trying to connect the history of New Guinea before contact with the wider world to that of the last few hundred years. I beg to differ. Two things seem to me to have been very wrong about the way the history of New Guinea has been written. Almost all of the histories, whether by archaeologists, linguists, geographers, or historians, divide the island in half, concentrating on the Dutch-Indonesian west or the German-British-Australian and now independent east. We find another anomaly in the Torres Strait Islands, incorporated into Queensland since the 1870s and often ignored in histories of New Guinea, as if they were no longer contiguous to the New Guinea mainland. Likewise the border between the Shortland Islands and Bougainville which divides the Solomon Islands. There is also an intellectual disciplinary divide: archaeologists usually turn to the ancient past without dealing with the present, while historians give undue emphasis to the last few hundred years.

There have been very few attempts to treat the history of New Guinea as a whole. The earliest such histories concentrated on European exploration. In 1884, Dutchman A. Haga published *Nederlandsch Nieuw Guinea en de Papoesche Eilanden: Historische Bijdrage, c. 1500–1883* (vol. 1, c. 1500–1817; vol. 2, 1817–1883), covering the political claims of the Malukan Sultans over New Guinea, and European exploration of New Guinea. During 1909–1912 Arthur Wichmann, a geographer involved with exploration in west New Guinea, published *Entdeckungsgeschichte von Neu-Guinea* (History of the discovery of New Guinea), which comprised the first two volumes of a series entitled *Nova Guinea: Uitkomsten der Nederlandsch Nieuw Guinea Expedities* (Results of Netherlands New Guinea expeditions). The most significant of these early texts is the three-volume *Nieuw Guinea: De Ontwikkeling op Economisch, Sociaal en Cultureel Gebied, in Nederlands en Australisch Nieuw*

Guinea (New Guinea: Economic, social and cultural development in Dutch and Australian New Guinea), published in Dutch during 1953–1954 with short English-language summaries of each chapter. Many archaeologists have attempted to write overviews of human settlement on Sahul (the early continent that included Australia, Tasmania and New Guinea), and of New Guinea as an island over the last ten thousand years, but they seldom extend their histories into the early years of European contact. Three books have been influential in showing me that my course was the correct one: Gavin Souter's *New Guinea: The Last Unknown* (1963), an accessible historical overview of recent centuries; J. L. Whittaker, N. G. Gash, J. F. Hookey, and R. J. Lacey's superb compendium, *Documents and Readings in New Guinea History: Prehistory to 1889* (1975); and Matthew Spriggs' authoritative *The Island Melanesians* (1997). These authors leap across centuries, disciplinary divides, and political boundaries in a manner that I admire and hope to emulate.

Ridding one's mind of boundaries is one necessary step. Another is to use all possible methodological and disciplinary means to explore New Guinea's present and its past. Travel in the region has been important. The best macro view is certainly that gained from an airplane, crossing the coasts and traversing the spine, passing along the length of the island or from coast to coast. The huge equatorial island can never be seen in its entirety, although views across the central mountains to the coasts are possible in the east and west. In the Highlands, lines of green mountain ranges stretch over the horizon and huge rolling valleys unfold, a breathtaking vision first revealed to the outside world in the 1920s and 1930s. Looking down from 10,000 meters, it is easy to see why the Baliem Valley is usually called the Grand Valley. The coasts shimmer in the heat, mangroves and sand beaches blending out into turquoise reefs. Not until I flew from Misima to Alatau over the southern Louisiade reefs did I realize what an impenetrable barrier they presented to ships moving north up the Australian coast, forcing use of more easterly routes. Nor until flying high above the flat wetlands around the Trans-Fly, which soon reveals the impenetrable waterlogged region, could I see clearly why the area is unlikely to ever support a large population.

I have pursued all types of printed sources, including images. The best micro-views come from early sketches and etchings, and photographs by visitors onwards from the 1880s, who tried to capture what was a fast-changing lifestyle even then. New Guineans peer out from these posed shots, dressed in wonderful *bilas* (ornamentation) but little else. Today, they no longer dress as they once did, except on ceremonial occasions. Indeed, modern women competing in Port Moresby's "Hiri Hanenamo Queen" competition usually apply their face tattoos with felt pens, and at the Goroka or Mt. Hagen shows the face paints likely came from supermarkets or local trade stores. Nonetheless, the Huli of Papua New Guinea's Southern Highlands still wear wigs decorated with yellow daisies, the Dani of Indonesia's Irian Jaya (Papua) Province wear their penis gourds, and at any coastal village near Port Moresby, old Motuan women still have body and facial tattoos—wonderful, partial views of the past.

Personal involvement is another factor. I spent most of my undergraduate years

studying the history of Island Southeast Asia, with no inkling of how useful this would be thirty years later in writing this book. My first connections with Melanesia were through my doctoral studies on Australia's South Sea Islanders, the descendants of indentured laborers brought to Queensland during the final four decades of the nineteenth century, some of whom were from the island archipelagos of Papua New Guinea. My first direct experience of Melanesia was during fieldwork in 1976 on Malaita, the largest and most populous of the Solomon Islands. In 1981, I left Townsville for Port Moresby to teach at the University of Papua New Guinea, remaining there until 1987, returning for a short period in 1993, and again in 2000–2001 as a consultant to Papua New Guinea's Office of Higher Education. Twenty years on from my first days on the Waigani campus, I completed this history of all of New Guinea, east and west, straddling the two modern-day regions of Southeast Asia and the Pacific. Twenty-five years of involvement with Melanesia and its inhabitants has provided a good apprenticeship, although I remain in many ways a novice. New Guinea's immensely complex history has been my overwhelming fascination as I have sought to understand it, and to refine my knowledge into one book.

The size of New Guinea and its adjacent archipelagos, the complexity of a 40,000-year time span, and its thousand indigenous languages, several lingua franca, and three European languages, all present the historian with unique challenges. New Guineans had no writing system until they recently adopted that of the West, and in attempting a history that seriously addresses the millennia before European influence I have journeyed into the territories of archaeologists, geographers, linguists, and anthropologists. I believe that disciplinary frontiers are meant to be crossed in quest of the long *durée*. Hopefully, the light of a skeptical historian shines through it all.

The book is divided into eight chapters, along with an Introduction that places New Guinea into the wider context of discourses on Melanesia, emphasizing interlocking exchange systems and associated human interchanges as the invisible strength that unites the diverse ethno-linguistic groups. The chapters proceed chronologically, beginning with the environment and people from 40,000 to around 5,000 years ago, the period when humans first began to move through New Guinea and Melanesia. At the end of that time period, agriculture and settlement patterns began which were direct precursors of those existing in recent centuries. Chapter Two looks at cultural spheres and trade systems as they have developed over the last 5,000 years, the period during which the Austronesian migrations occurred and there was increasing contact in west New Guinea with Asia's early metal-using cultures. Chapter Three deals with west New Guinea and its connections with the Malay world, particularly the *sosolot* and *kain timur* exchange systems that linked the area to the Malukan Islands. The fourth chapter covers the history of early European exploration and exploitation of New Guinea, beginning with the Portuguese and Spanish in the 1520s, then turning to later Dutch and English interests, through to the first European attempts at settlement in the west onwards from the late eighteenth century. Chapters Five and Six explore the intensification of outside contact during the nineteenth century, including shipping routes after the advent of the Australian colonies, as well as the arrivals of traders, whalers, Christian missionaries, gold miners, and scientific expeditions, and exploitation of the labor reserve. In Chapter Seven I examine patterns that emerge from early coastal contact, and the early contacts with inland peoples during the late nineteenth century and the first half of the twentieth century, and I attempt to interpret the reactions of New Guineans to these intrusions. The final chapter concentrates on the twentieth-century colonial period, examining economic, social, and political changes, leading through to decolonization and independence in the east and incorporation into Indonesia in the west. Undoubtedly, some readers would prefer more detail on the twentieth century, but I have chosen not to privilege the modern era. Clearly, the last fifty years have been crucial in shaping contemporary New Guinea, but a large and easily available supporting literature on this period already exists, and to overemphasize the last fifty to one hundred years would undermine the book's argument that New Guinea has a 40,000-year history.

Having said all this, I hope that New Guineans will forgive my shortcomings and that they will take up the challenge to write their own histories of New Guinea.

Acknowledgments

I have accumulated many debts over the twenty years it took to research and write this book. Much of my research took the form of a wide trawl of secondary sources, and I am grateful to all of those who went before me, creating and smoothing the path. My early research was funded by the University of Papua New Guinea, and I appreciate the services of the staff of the University's Michael Somare Library. I also used the British New Guinea records in the Papua New Guinea National Archives. Key individuals can be singled out from this period: James Griffin, Les Groube, John Waiko, Jean Kennedy, Joe and Vero Mangi, Edgar Waters, Ann Turner, and Lohia Raka. Each was a source of inspiration in some way, and their continuing friendship is appreciated.

After moving to the University of Queensland in 1987, I received funding from that institution and the Australian Research Grants Council. The library's staff remained patient over many years as I sought materials. I also used the records of the Queensland State Archives. I am indebted to my colleagues in the History Department within the School of History, Philosophy, Religion and Classics, and to the School for funding preparation of maps and photographs. Jennifer Harrison assisted with information on Australian convicts. Bryan Jamison worked as a research assistant on the project for one year. Serena Bagley beat recalcitrant endnotes into shape. Particular mention is due to Kay Saunders and Robert Cribb for their intellectual support and friendship. Robert Cribb read a draft of Chapter Three, and also expertly prepared the maps. Ian Lilley cast a critical eye over my prehistory chapters, and Greg Poulgrain gave advice on Chapter Eight. My colleague Max Quanchi, based at neighboring Queensland University of Technology, was constantly available as a sounding board on New Guinea, reading and commenting on drafts of the manuscript. This is a far better book because of his efforts and I thank him sincerely.

Terry Crowley of Waikato University assisted with advice on linguistics. Glen Tauliso, District Officer, Misima, hosted me when I was collecting information of the wreck of the *St. Paul* and the death of W. B. Ingham. Nicholas Coppel provided details on urban population levels in Papua New Guinea. Garth Wong and Grant Tebbutt have always been ready to share their extensive knowledge of Papua New Guinea, and Len Davidson read a final draft of the manuscript.

In the Netherlands, I owe two considerable debts of gratitude. Foremost is that to Bob and Nettie Hering in Stein for their help with translations of Dutch sources on New Guinea and for their hospitality and encouragement. Bob Hering first taught me Southeast Asian history at James Cook University in 1971 and was responsible for my initial interest in Indonesia, particularly the Maluku and Irian Jaya regions. His multidisciplinary approach is probably responsible for my attitude that disciplinary boundaries only exist to be crossed. Jeroen Overweel also provided his home as my Amsterdam base and freely shared his expertise in west New Guinea archival sources. Denny Lim provided my Port Moresby base in 2002, and to him I dedicate the book.

At the University of Hawai'i Press, Pamela Kelley, Ann Ludeman, and their team created a book out of a manuscript. My particular thanks go to David Akin, whose knowledge of Melanesian anthropology and history supplemented his skillful editorial work. My thanks also to the two anonymous reviewers, whose comments were helpful in my rewriting of the original manuscript.

I remain responsible for all errors and interpretations.

Introduction

Interpreting Melanesia

‧‧‧

The Region

NEW GUINEA

It is stating the obvious to say that New Guinea is an island, but this has been its main governing characteristic over the last ten thousand years, as humans have flowed through the region. As Greg Dening suggests, constant movement is part of the way both environment and human society were created there. However, New Guinea was not always an island, and for most of the time humans have lived there, the "island" was joined to Australia. Even so, until recent times New Guinea was too big to be conceived of as a whole by its inhabitants, who lived in small-scale societies each intimately linked to local areas, with only limited regional geographic knowledge. It is also doubtful that the early visitors from the west—Malay and Chinese seamen and traders—had any concept that New Guinea was one island, as they seem seldom to have ventured past its western and central coasts, very rarely reaching its eastern extremities.

The island and its peoples had no one name. Over recent centuries, "Onin" and "Haraforas" were used fairly consistently as names for west New Guinea and its peoples, although only the word "Papua" is uniquely descriptive of the whole island and its inhabitants. The names "Papua" and "New Guinea" have been used in several contexts. Early European visitors remarked on the physical similarity between the indigenous peoples of Guinea in west Africa and the peoples of the Maluku (Moluccan), Timor, and Flores Islands, as well as those of the large landmass to their east. Ynigo Ortiz de Retes, while noting that the Maluku people called their neighbors "Papuas," on 20 June 1545 chose to name the land "Nueva Guinea" when claiming possession for the Spanish Crown. "New Guinea" eventually was adopted for the whole island, and as the name of European colonial divisions. The west became part of the Dutch East Indies (1828–1949), and then a separate Dutch colony (1949–1963). The northeast became German New Guinea (1884–1921, under Australian military control 1914–1921), then a League of Nations Mandated Territory, converted to a United Nations Trust Territory administered by Australia (1921–1975). The southeast was first known as British New Guinea (1884–1906), then the Australian Territory of Papua (1906–1975). After the Pacific War

Every islander has had to cross a beach to construct a new society. Across those beaches every intrusive artefact, material and cultural, has had to pass. Every living thing on an island has been a traveler. Every species of tree, plant and animal on an island has crossed the beach. In crossing the beach every voyager has brought something old and something new. The old is written in the forms and habits and needs each newcomer brings. The new is the changed world, the adjusted balance every coming makes.
—Greg Dening, Islands and Beaches, 1980, 31–32

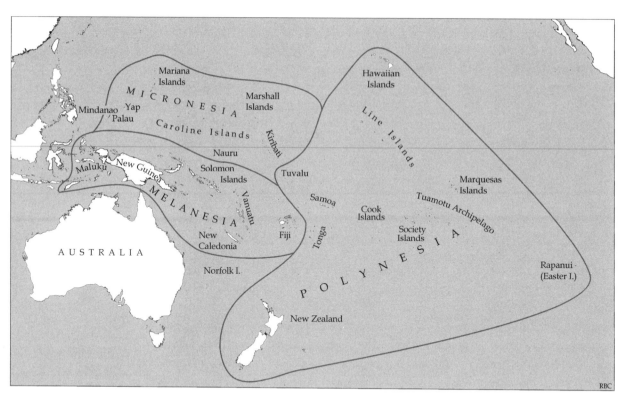

New Guinea and
the Pacific

interregnum, both eastern territories were administered as a single unit by Australia, known as the Territory of Papua (and) New Guinea from the late 1940s until 1975.

The term "Papua" or "Papuas" was already in use in the fifteenth century when the Portuguese adopted it as an identifier for the peoples of Halmahera and the other Maluku Islands. It was also used to describe the Raja Empat Islands and the Bird's Head (Vogelkop, Mejprat, or Doberai) Peninsula region of New Guinea, appearing on early seventeenth-century European maps.[1] When Australia took over British New Guinea the colony was renamed the Territory of Papua, and Papua Barat (West Papua) was chosen in 1961 as the new name for west New Guinea, anticipating an eventual handover by the Netherlands. The name continues to be used in several ways, including as an identifier for a major linguistic category and within the title of the independent nation of Papua New Guinea. In the west, Papua is part of the names of the liberation movement *Organisasi Papua Merdeka* (OPM or the Free Papua Movement) and the Papuan Presidium Council. Indonesia's Irian Jaya Province was renamed Propinsi Papua (Papua Province) in 2001, although this new name has not yet been totally accepted in Indonesia.

"Onin" was also used fairly widely to describe the southern side of the Bird's Head Peninsula, a far larger area than today's Onin Peninsula, and also as the descriptor for the tens of thousands of New Guinea peoples enslaved into the Malay world. The term "Haraforas" is used throughout nineteenth-century texts to describe the inland people of northwest New Guinea and other inland peoples in the eastern Malay Archipelago. According to G. W. Earl's 1850s findings, the word is a variation of *alfores* or *alforias*, a Portuguese term signifying freed men or manumitted slaves. The root *fora* means "out"; therefore, the term *alfores* came to be applied to tribes from beyond the influence of Portuguese coastal settlements in India and the East Indies. Earl noted that *arafura* was first used on sailing instructions published in 1837, and he claimed to have suggested to the hydrographer of the British Admiralty that the name be used for the sea between Timor, New Guinea, and northern Australia. The closest equivalent east Indonesian word, which may actually be the correct origin of the term, is *halefoeroe*, meaning "wilderness" in the language of north Halmahera.[2] The name "Irian Jaya" is a creation of the 1940s: *irian* is a word from the Biak language meaning "to rise," and *jaya* is the Malay term for "victorious."[3]

MELANESIA

European scholars tried to classify the peoples of Oceania, not realizing that migrations into the region had occurred over tens of thousands of years, and that recent settlement patterns and supposed racial characteristics were not always the best keys for understanding the distant past. It was much like contemplating model ships in glass bottles: wonderful to look at, but one has to wonder how on earth it was managed. In 1756, Charles de Brosses suggested the divisions "Magellanic," "Australasian," and "Polynesian." Polynesia was then being used to describe an enormous area of the South Pacific Ocean, and was too broad a label to be very useful. Later, nineteenth-century European scientists and geographers, challenged by the enormous diversity they were encountering in the Pacific Islands, classified the islands and their inhabitants into three regions which they thought were coterminous with human "races": Melanesia, Polynesia, and Micronesia. This was really justified only for Polynesia, where the islands had been peopled only recently by Austronesian migrants who were phenotypically quite homogenous. J.S.C. Dumont d'Urville and D.M.G.L. de Rienzi used the Greek word *melos* (black), referring to the dark skin color of the inhabitants, as the basis of their classification *"Melanésie"* in the 1830s, but they had no understanding of the time-depth of human migrations into the area. Nor did they comprehend the implications—for humans, flora, and fauna— of the existence of the ancient continent (which archaeologists call "Sahul") that had united Australia, Tasmania, and New Guinea until around 10,000 years before. Today, "Melanesia" has become a geographic and cultural shorthand description for the inhabitants and the chain of large mountainous islands beginning in the west at the Maluku and Timor-Flores region adjacent to New Guinea, progressing southeast through New Guinea, the Solomon, Santa Cruz, Torres, Banks, and New Hebrides Groups, to Fiji and New Caledonia.[4]

"Melanesia" is a convenient geographic construction which has become a reality in the decolonized southwest Pacific. The peoples living there describe themselves as Melanesians and conceptualize their future as part of Melanesia. However, "Melanesians" exhibit enormous physical and cultural diversity, and there is a lack of correlation between physical appearances, their languages, and their migratory origins. Melanesia was peopled over tens of thousands of years by multiple migrations coming out of Asia, a process further complicated by numerous back-migrations. Dark skins, tight curly hair, and emphasis on root-crop cultivation are not unique identifiers. Grouped together as Melanesians one finds the light-skinned, golden-haired lagoon-dwellers of Malaita in the central Solomon Islands, the tall blue-black-skinned people of Buka in the northern Solomon Islands, and the short-statured brown-skinned Huli or Engan wigmen of the south and central New Guinea Highlands. Tight curly hair is fairly typical, but in some areas, particularly noticeable in southeast New Guinea and in the Massim (the islands off the eastern tail of New Guinea), hair is wavy, not tightly curled. Subsistence patterns vary, from total reliance on the coasts, lagoons, and the ocean for sustenance, to peoples high in the central valleys of New Guinea, once dependent solely on swidden agriculture and hunting. Highlanders knew of the seacoast only as a remote source of the shell valuables and sometimes salt which reached them along trade routes. There are also neighboring dark-skinned peoples in Micronesia and the Malay Archipelago, and some inhabitants of Philippines and Indonesia also depend on root crops for their subsistence. Differences are most marked on the outer fringes of Melanesia. For instance, the Fiji Islands in the south fit only marginally within Melanesia, and they seem to have been first settled by the ancestors of the Polynesians. Culturally and genetically, Fijians owe as much to Samoans and Tongans as to their Melanesian neighbors in Vanuatu or New Caledonia. Polynesians, more recent Austronesian migrants, also inhabit many of the outlying islands in eastern Melanesia, part of the small-scale back-migrations that have occurred since the first movements south and east.

Despite its imprecision, the term "Melanesia" has survived and strengthened as a convenient ethnic and geographical classification, one used by Melanesians and non-Melanesians alike. Partly this is because of two more recent historical influences that have unified the region. Firstly, all areas of Melanesia share a similar colonial history, despite the islands having been divided between several European nations. Administrators, traders, and missionaries of the colonial period employed the concept, most accepting that Melanesians were of a lower human order in terms of a "Great Chain of Being" and, later, within various models of social Darwinism. Melanesians themselves, then, have adopted a Western racial category from the 1830s, one amplified by academic studies of Melanesia beginning with the work of R. H. Codrington and W.H.R. Rivers in the 1890s and 1900s, by long-established European attitudes toward "natives," and by colonial government policies prefaced on racism.[5] Secondly, as Melanesia moved from colonialism to independence, the inhabitants consciously identified themselves as "Melanesians," indigenizing the concept and divorcing it from any element of inferiority. Bernard Narokobi's 1970s conceptualization of the "Melanesian Way"—a typical cultural way of behaving—was broadly, although rather uncritically, accepted in Papua New Guinea and elsewhere in Melanesia.[6] The creation of the Melanesian Council of Churches and the Melanesian Spearhead Group among South Pacific Island nations provides evidence of this supposed racial unity. In late 1997, Solomon Islands' Prime Minister Ulufa'alu suggested a future Melanesian Federation that would override the region's national (but actually European-created colonial) boundaries.[7]

"Melanesia" has gained credence because it conveniently describes both a geographic area and the people, who appear to have much in common but who share no discrete history independent of surrounding territories. Almost since its coinage, the term has been slowly deconstructed. Australia was initially included within Melanesia, but was soon removed when it was reclassified as a continent, and the lifestyles of its indigenous peoples were found to have little in common with their Melanesian neighbors. Melanesia's boundaries were readjusted to merely touch Australia at Torres Strait and Cape York. More recently, academics such as Marshall Sahlins, Bronwen Douglas, and Nicholas Thomas have discussed, clarified, and reassessed the use of this 1830s terminology that groups such diverse peoples into one broad geographic region.[8] The implications of a "Melanesianism" existing in the sense that Edward Said has explored "Orientalism" have yet to be expounded.

ISLAND MELANESIA

"Island Melanesia" refers to the chain of archipelagos, islands, atolls, and reefs forming the outer bounds of the sheltered oval-shaped Coral Sea. It begins at the Admiralty Group northeast of New Guinea and extends south to New Caledonia, gently curving outwards to encompass the Coral Sea, virtually from the Equator to the Tropic of Capricorn, bounded on the west by the Australian coast. The high islands fringing New Guinea—the Bismarck[9] and Louisiade Archipelagos, the D'Entrecasteaux, Woodlark, and the Trobriand Groups—extend from the landmass eastward 500 km. Then, beginning opposite the tail of New Guinea and extending south for 1,500 km, comes the double chain of Solomon Islands from Buka and Bougainville down to the Santa Cruz Group. Moving further south Vanuatu (the Torres, Banks, and New Hebrides Groups) continues the chain down to the Loyalty Islands and New Caledonia.

Island Melanesia is often depicted as a separate geographical, cultural, and historical unit quite distinct from New Guinea. The argument is sound enough for Island Melanesia south of the Santa Cruz Group, but it has little relevance to human migrations which over the last several thousand years have moved back and forth through the archipelagos adjacent to east New Guinea.[10] Island Melanesians are not a "race" by any conventional use of that term—what connects them is that they inhabit a set of islands east of New Guinea and Australia. Island Melanesia also lacks geographic unity, because it is not really one chain. Substantial gaps occur on both sides of the Santa Cruz Group, and Fijians in the southeast are marginal both geographically and culturally. The same argument applies to the inhabitants of Timor and Halmahera in Maluku, west of New Guinea, where in recent centuries constant contact with, and eastward migration by, Malay peoples has weakened similarities with nearby New Guineans. Further, Torres Strait Islanders blend with Australia's Aborigines, and Melanesian influences dominate the Strait and reach well down the coast of northeast Australia as far as the Whitsunday and Cumberland Island Groups opposite present-day Proserpine and Mackay.

Many archaeologists and prehistorians now argue that the term "Melanesia" (along with "Polynesia" and "Micronesia") should be abandoned as an inappropriate legacy of European colonialism and racism which has no bearing today, to be replaced by a distinction only between "Near Oceania" and "Remote Oceania." Roger Green has been the strongest advocate of this division, and he draws a divide in Island Melanesia between the central Solomon Islands and the Eastern Outer Islands (including the Santa Cruz Group). North of the line is Near Oceania, to the south is Remote Oceania.[11]

Discourses on Melanesia

In earlier centuries, Europeans often deterministically equated culture and behavior with perceived racial categories. Melanesians were typically described as savages, and always as inferior to their Polynesian neighbors. In the nineteenth century, after the ravages of (previously unknown) epidemic diseases, introduced through contact with traders, missionaries, government officials, and labor recruiters, they were depicted as a dying race.[12] Thus, colonial concepts of race were tied intimately into colonial ideology and practice. Edward Said sees the "Orient" as part of the structure of power by which the West triumphed over their Asian colonial territories—peoples grouped together and represented by outsiders, who wished at the same time to manage and control them. "Melanesia" represents a similar mode of Western discourse supported by "institutions, vocabulary, scholarship, imagery, doctrines, even colonial bureaucracies and colonial styles."[13] While acknowledging criticisms of Said, his "Orientalism" thesis can be adapted to craft a similar thesis of "Melanesianism" from past and present constructions that have imaged, delineated, governed, and exploited Melanesia. This can be seen in the visual construction of Melanesia—in the art of early voyages and the photography of missionaries, expeditions, and colonial officials early in the twentieth century. Literature, fiction, and travelogues also constructed a place called "Melanesia."[14]

Overlaying this early history we find a more recent colonial and post-colonial history which links New Guinea and Island Melanesia with the Malay Archipelago (Indonesia), the Torres Strait, and Australia. The middle chapters of this book focus primarily on the early period of European intrusion into New Guinea and its adjacent archipelagos to the east and west between the sixteenth and the nineteenth centuries. While we must remain aware of geographic and indigenous cultural divisions, and that the last five centuries cover only a fraction of the tens of thousands of years during which humans have lived in New Guinea, and that effective colonialism only began in the 1880s and 1890s, this 500-year period was crucial to creating modern New Guinea.

Pacific historiography, suggests historian David Chappell, "is, in a sense, the last colonial frontier, a kind of dysfunctional family reunion. Whom should the next generation believe: the paternalistic ex-colonizer or the unleashed native?"[15] How does one come to terms with the writing of history in the Pacific? During the last half-century, Pacific history has progressed from a "fatal impact" genre that saw Islanders as passive, helpless victims of colonialism, through "Islander-centered" but still largely expatriate-authored studies which restored indigenous agency, leading into the contemporary writings of indigenous nationalists who stress postcolonial pan-Pacific sentiments. Earlier nonliterate Islanders have left little evidence through which we might interpret their feelings and actions during periods of gradual change, or when they confronted massive changes brought by colonialism. We have access mostly to fragments of the experiences of foreigners who lived amongst them. How can expatriate historians listen to, assess, and present the indigenous voice, which moves to a different rhythm from conventional Western scholarship? Dancing, singing, chanting, and oration may be understood differently by indigenous historians and audiences, and certainly they are quite distinct from scholarly books with reference notes and bibliographies. Today's Oceanic peoples quite rightly desire to tell their own stories, recount their own histories, in their own ways, from their own "speaking positions," challenging the insider/outsider dichotomy. But are their versions of the far past likely to be any more accurate than those of outsiders?

An immense literature on New Guinea in several languages precedes this book. Thousands of individual primary and secondary sources underpin the present text in terms of narrative and chronology, explanation and interpretation. The different chapters use and pursue different methodologies depending on the matters under examination. Resourceful empirical scholarship enables an adequate historical interpretation. Modernist influences on the writing of history suggest the possibility of using traces of consciousness from a variety of sources to get a sense of Melanesian, Asian, and European perceptions, aspirations, and understandings of changing social hierarchies in New Guinea. Postmodern thinking leads us to analyze the power relations that determine why one set of meanings, rather than another, are hegemonic. An "indigenous voice" can add substance and interpretation. Government reports, maps, literature, art, photographs, records left by maritime and land explorers, missionary hagiographies, newspaper accounts, recent archaeological, linguistic, anthropological, and historical accounts, mixed with indigenous oral testimony, tempered by a degree of friendly skepticism and personal involvement with the region over the last quarter-century have all been used to piece together this interpretation of the history of New Guinea and adjacent islands. The advantage of this long-term overview approach is that many observers, regardless of whether they were sixteenth-century explorers, nineteenth-century missionaries, or modern archaeologists and historians, have dealt only with one small region of this amazingly diverse group of hundreds of societies. My task here has been, whenever possible, to soar above New Guinea, looking for overarching patterns and meanings.

European and Asian explorers and traders, European missionaries, and colonial officials reported and interpreted what they saw in the Pacific within the limits of their understanding of science, race, religion, and morals. European first encounters took place between the early sixteenth and mid-twentieth centuries, a time of enormous changes in European self-perceptions and understanding of the rest of the world. The Age of Discovery—the fifteenth and sixteenth centuries—quickly dispatched existing limited European concepts of cosmology, geography, and demography. Other conventions still held to by the first Europeans who reached the Pacific Islands were influenced by concepts left over from the Middle Ages and by Renaissance thinking. They viewed human cultural development as evolutionary, moving from primitive beginnings to city life. Europeans were self-confident about the superiority of their civilization, and determined to spread Christianity and exploit newly discovered natural resources. Scientific and philosophical advances in the eighteenth century made some difference to educated thinking, but native peoples in Asia, Africa, the Americas, and the Pacific remained largely curiosities, the inferior end of a grand European-appropriated world plan.

Pacific peoples' knowledge bases were limited geographically and cosmologically. They viewed time not as linear but as cyclical and episodic. The religious concepts of Oceanic peoples were integrated into all aspects of social and economic life. All elements in the cosmos were alive and worked together, and land was bound to cosmology through sacred sites and ancestral heroes. The spirit world is timeless—part of the present, it links the past to the future, recognizing no sense of chronology beyond immediate annual cycles in nature. There was no unified belief in spirits. Ancestral and local area spirits all needed to be propitiated to ensure fertility and renewal. While the past tense has been used in this description, for many Pacific peoples this religious and spiritual world continues relatively unchanged into the present. Garry Trompf, in his *Melanesian Religion*, advises against trying to define the spirit world exactly: "one 'feels into' one's cosmos and its inhabitants through an organic process, with paradigmatic moments of disclosure into cultural secrets at initiations, until one knows what to *do*, rather than possess speculative knowledge for its own sake. It is far more important to learn whether the deities are supportive or harmful, and need offerings of the confident or apotropaisms of the nervous, and whether they are ethically neutral . . ."[16] Retribution against enemies, revenge, and reciprocity were all central to life. Religious specialization was normal, although not always through clearly designated priests. Dreams, visions, and trances were integrated into everyday religion. Trade, too, had a ritual component and was not simply a commercial transaction. Particular local areas or houses were extremely sacred, and to enter uninvited or to desecrate these areas brought swift, violent repercussions. Early European visitors usually had no understanding of the taboos they were breaking, sometimes arrogantly and deliberately, but just as often by what they viewed as normal actions or through curiosity.

There were also fundamental differences between Asians, Europeans, and Oceanic peoples in the etiquette of first encounters and ongoing relations with foreigners. All Pacific peoples belong to cultural-linguistic groups. They are divided into social categories and relate to each other in a coded way that includes established reciprocal rights and obligations. Initially, outsiders tended to be dealt with by applying the same social mechanisms. Europeans, for their part, accustomed to their own nation-states, judged small-scale societies as inferior, and they could not comprehend unity forged through legitimizing myths which established the shape of Pacific cosmologies and governed social orders. The intruders also failed to appreciate either the binding strength of short- and long-distance trade, or that relationships were governed by historic practice and preordained ways of behaviors that were legitimized through much wider cosmological beliefs.

There is an extensive literature on the dynamics of transactions between Pacific peoples and foreigners, but crucial aspects of these exchanges are often ignored. Insufficient attention has been paid to the articulation of foreigners, their goods, and diseases within indigenous populations, their economies, societies, and religious beliefs. Little account has been taken of the androgynous nature of the introduced artifacts (in that they were largely free of gender restrictions), and to some of their less obvious sources (such as shipwrecks), which must be taken into calculation in considering the impact of foreign influences.

Artifacts, Trade, and Exchange

Studies of artifacts have concentrated either on their social function as part of an exchange system, particularly exchange relations and concepts of gift-giving, or on the description and cataloguing of the objects, neglecting their wider functions. As Maureen MacKenzie notes in her study of string bags and gender in New Guinea, there is still a need for a theoretical framework that: "allows the object to be considered in relation to the technological, social, economic, political, ideological and historical systems of which it is an integral part. That is, a framework which would enable one to see how the object becomes constructed as a social form endowed with culturally specific meanings, and to then allow an interpretation of that cultural form which includes indigenous understandings."[17] MacKenzie warns that culture cannot be reduced to isolated components, and that material culture items should be examined in relation to the particular structures and processes through which they were created. There is always an integrated relationship between the culturally constructed processes of production and consumption. Objects, like people, pass through transformations. Their identity is not fixed, and changes occur depending on use. Goods that are utilitarian in one place might become valuable items in another, or sacred objects in yet other places. Gender-specific artifacts or sacred objects can become mere curios in the hands of visiting collectors, or personal treasures decorating the homes of foreigners, quite unlike their original sacred forms.

Artifacts are combined with raw materials and food stuffs within exchange networks, with a multitude of variables. Canoe hulls, pots, shell ornaments and valuables, wooden bowls, drums, bows and arrows, bird plumes and pelts, obsidian, ochre and paint, tobacco, sago, taro and yam, dog teeth and pig tusks (and the whole animals) were traded through a series of interlocking trade systems. Trade in labor and services was limited, although some societies traded "slaves" captured during fighting or as part of ritual exchanges. Exchanges of women in marriage also helped bind neighboring trade systems. Foods and more utilitarian items usually remained within closed systems, while more valuable items were the medium of long-distance trade. Thus, raw shell from Rossel Island on the outer extreme of the Louisiades could end up manufactured into armshells in the Gulf of Papua, and, theoretically at least, the same valuables could end up in Maluku. Pearlshell from Torres Strait passed north into the Highlands and south into Australia, and red feathers from New Guinea were traded north through Yap to Palau in Micronesia. Much-valued obsidian was traded over thousands of kilometers through the Pacific Islands from several sites in islands off eastern New Guinea.[18] Trading networks linked island to island and the islands to the coast of the New Guinea mainland, ran all along the mainland coast, and seeped into the hinterland and deep into the central mountains beyond. How ancient are these long-distance trade systems? Around the coasts they may well be as old as human settlement itself—at least 40,000 years. However, they are thought to have become more extensive and elaborate during recent millennia. Voyaging corridors and long-distance trade carried obsidian and presumably more perishable items over thousands of kilometers.

We know that humans have lived in the New Guinea Highlands for at least 25,000 years. Seashells were traded into the Highlands as long ago as 9,000 years ago, but the importance of pearlshell as a trade item may only date back a few thousand years. When the first Europeans made their way through the huge central Highlands valleys in the 1920s and 1930s, much of the pearlshell available was in the form of broken bits, sometimes pieced together, and whole shells were rare and treated with great care. Cowrie shells were also much sought after. Pearlshell was in short supply even in the east. In Papua New Guinea's Western Highlands it was available only in small quantities, much of it broken.[19] Trade routes crisscrossed the Highlands and linked to the coast. Aletta Biersack has described the complex trade patterns in the Papuan Highlands during the decades directly after first contact in the 1930s.[20] In the Porgera and Paiela areas shells and pigs were traded for opossum skins, spears, shell nosepieces, and salt from saline springs.[21] The Porgera received cowries, pearlshells, and axe blades from the east which originated on the south coast, and for these they gave hand-drums, pigs, bird feathers, and cassowaries. These in turn were traded west for stone axes from Mt. Hagen. They also imported shells from the Waka Enga in the southeast, salt from salt springs in Taro Enga to the east, tree oil from the Lake Kutubu region, and pigs from the Waka Enga, the Huli, and the Duna. In Ipili trade with the Huli, salt was traded south, while pigs, oil, and colored earths used in self-decoration moved north. Huli received slate from Porgera in return for cowries, and obtained salt (originally manufactured by Engans) and stone adzes and axe blades (probably from Mt. Hagen) from the Enga, Paiela, and Porgera peoples. Tari people exchanged body oil for gold-lip and cowrie shells and pigs. These Highland groups also traded with their Highlands-fringe neighbors. For example, the Simbu traded with the Mikaruan-speaking Daribi people of the Karimui Plateau, and the Huli traded with the peoples around Lake Kutubu and Mubi River for much-prized black-palm bows, tree oil for body decoration, cassowaries, and sago flour, giving in return pigs, pearlshells, and stone axe blades. This movement of material culture items was accompanied by marriages, migrations, linguistic hybridization, and mythic and ritual connections.[22]

The political units of Melanesia were constructed from a thousand ethno-linguistic areas, linked by interlocking trade systems radiating from cultural spheres, and often also by marriages and aggressive raiding that moved along the same exchange "roads" and "passages."[23] Europeans thought that Melanesia lacked regular government, and depicted the small-scale societies as each isolated from the other. They failed to realize that Melanesian society was constructed on the basis of close relationships between descent, language, and territory, and reciprocal exchange "roads" and "passages," rather than on large and permanent territorial entities. New Guinea exchange networks—such as the *hiri* and *kula* in the southeast, the *tee* and *moka* of the Highlands, or the *kain timur* in the Bird's Head, and the *sosolot* network around Onin—linked generations and territories through material culture exchanges, intermarriage, ideology, and technology transfers.

Movement is related to trade. Before the diaspora that came with colonialism, local territories formed and transformed over decades and centuries. Melanesians migrated within local territories, as well as from valley to valley, or island to island. Today, it is not unusual for a family to have two places of residence for ceremonial or subsistence reasons, or for individuals to move from one area to another using kinship connections. After marriage a wife usually moves to her husband's village, but continues to visit her own family at intervals. Tree crops, such as *ngali* Canarium almond nuts, are harvested seasonally, and in the past shell and obsidian valuables and other wealth items were exchanged continuously. The articulation of all of these necessitated movement by individuals and groups, often over several weeks or even months. Early European visitors regularly observed trading parties on large multi-hulled vessels, or lone small sailing canoes moving between islands and along the mainland coasts, trading and sometimes raiding.

The invisible "government" of precontact Melanesia consisted of such interlocking exchange systems and associated human interchanges. The "roads" and "passages" along which these exchange systems operated also had magical significance, and were deeply embedded in the religious fabric. Complex trading networks allied peoples from quite different cultures and ecological zones. Roderick Lacey, a historian of the Enga from Papua New Guinea's Highlands, suggests that three patterns of journeys occurred: First, goods that flowed along routes over sea and land: "These journeys thus opened socioeconomic channels along which generations of traders have travelled. Journeys for exchange and trade, over land and sea, and across barriers of environment and culture join with the epic movements of creators, and bearers of innovation, emphasising Papua New Guinea's ancient history of ebb and flow."[24]

Lacey's second pattern of journeys is that of people as migrants and traders. Descent groups moved over long distances. Warfare, sorcery, disputes over land and sea rights, and over foods such as pigs and fish, jealousy within marriages, or the distribution of items at ceremonial feasts, all led at times to social disruptions and consequent mobility. So did larger ungovernable forces such as epidemic disease and natural disasters. Lacey notes that these traditions of migration remain important because they "are significant to people's heritage, for the knowledge transmitted through generations in legend, song, chant, and dance constitute their basic legal, political, social, and economic charters. It is on this basis that the rights and obligations of lineages are defined within communities and both access to and use of specific resources and territories are defended."[25]

Lacey's third journey pattern concerned *rites de passage*, when males and females were initiated, publicly transformed from children into adults. Youthful bachelors were often secluded, initiated, and purified, in the process learning about sacred objects and knowledge. There were many variations: Even today Huli youths in Papua New Guinea's Southern Highlands still enter seclusion to grow their hair for the ornate wigs that they wear constantly as adults; Orokolo boys from Elema in the Gulf of Papua were usually initiated twice, but some as many as four times, in bull-roarer ceremonies. Many communities practiced homosexual initiations, believing that semen was needed for boys to grow to manhood.[26] Girls and women also underwent initiations, but usually to a lesser extent than males. Their equivalent times of seclusion and learning revolved around menstruation, conception, and birth. Lacey employs Enga as his example for *rites de passage*, where he says initiates' dreams were the source of new knowledge which they communicated to their families: "Cast in highly compressed and elaborately symbolic language, these songs conveyed wisdom and insights about the community and its destiny that had been acquired from dreams experienced during seclusion on the ridge tops. Through these rites the youths had been transformed into mature men, brave warriors, productive husbands, efficient cultivators, and effective negotiators in exchange transactions."[27]

These journeys and transformations were interlinked and never ending, all different and yet the same. It is my intention in this study to extend Lacey's Engan journeys to all of New Guinea and its adjacent archipelagos. Disintegration or expansion in any section of the great trade network necessarily affected the wider structure. Into this dynamic system came foreigners, who failed to understand its complexity, or that exchanges depended on local political, economic, and cultural needs, not on the demands of strangers.

Trade in all its forms is a key mechanism of the imperial process, although, as Nicholas Thomas points out, our concern should be with entanglement rather than presuming colonial penetration.[28] Asian and European outreach imposed a foreign web over indigenous foundations, which began to draw New Guinea's coastal and island people first into the periphery of long-distance Asian tribute-seeking and barter-trade, and then into European capitalism through trade and as a labor force. In the process, rights of suzerainty were established, followed by colonial control. New Guinea's people responded to this intervention in ways useful to their own societies. This is illustrated not only through their use of introduced material culture items and exchanges of labor, but also their use of shipwrecks and their adoption of human flotsam—castaways—into their social networks. By attacking visitors and ships, cargos and crews, and also by supplying artifacts and natural history specimens to collectors, and even tourists onwards from the 1880s, Melanesians were able to accumulate new types of wealth before permanent colonization. These strategies provided shortcuts to possessing the foreigners' wealth without working directly for them. My contention is that before the nineteenth century and the arrival of large numbers of permanent foreign settlers, the earlier introduction of both foreign individuals and artifacts brought about shifts in the regional prominence of coastal, and to a lesser extent inland descent and language groups, and also transformed gender relations. But these alterations to the contours of power were not unique—they merely continued a process that had begun 40,000 years earlier.

Not every material item was for sale to foreigners, but in most cases the contact strategy was based on a desire to obtain European or Asian goods, and to incorporate the foreigners and their possessions into local kin networks. During early contacts, coastal people paddled out to the visiting ships, sometimes waving green boughs, a practice often interpreted by Europeans to signify peace. At the same time they offered trade or gifts, in the same way they would with any strangers, hoping to anchor the new relationship with ritual exchanges. Sometimes, either not desiring or perhaps failing to incorporate the strangers into the world they knew, New Guineans resorted to aggression, only to be thoroughly trounced by superior weaponry. Peaceful trade was the most common and productive way to get what they wanted. European explorers, whalers, traders, missionaries, government officers, and Asian and Pacific Island traders, all had to negotiate and exchange every time they wanted to engage labor or purchase basic foodstuffs. Peaceful trade and sale of labor were the major points of contact with foreigners. Early trade items included beads, nails, fishhooks, knives, axes, mirrors, and cloth, but seldom larger items. Usually, New Guineans wanted iron, but their tastes became more refined over the decades. Nails and hoop iron were soon rejected in favor of steel axes, tomahawks, and knives. Tobacco was another major trade item demanded from Europeans, although it is unclear how wide its use was before foreigners entered the area. We do know that it had already been spreading along indigenous trade routes for some hundreds of years.[29]

Prehistorians have noted the complex dynamics of the circulation of new wealth,[30] but most anthropologists and historians have not taken sufficient account of the "entangled objects." Foreign observers tried to depict these indigenous societies as they supposed they operated before contact, but they were observing communities that were never static and had probably altered significantly over previous decades. Trade in Melanesia has parallels in other areas of the Pacific. Pacific historians are used to pondering alliances and warfare in New Zealand (Aotearoa), and the impact of Tongan tribute and control over much of the central South Pacific, the power plays of the Kamehamehas in Hawai'i and the Pomares in Tahiti, or of Cakobau in Fiji prior to the establishment of European enclaves. However, not enough attention has been paid to the changing dynamics of power among the indigenous peoples of Melanesia on the eve of colonization.

A key challenge for cross-cultural studies in the Pacific is to understand the motivations of indigenous peoples there when they have dealt with foreigners and their artifacts. How did Pacific exchanges systems alter, and how did trade routes become modified when they entangled with foreign artifacts and people? Changes in social roles were closely related to this process. Gender balances in particular were altered significantly during the colonial encounter by new buyers, production for seasonal and regional markets, and the availability of new trade items.

Through a complex mix of movement and trade, large amounts of Asian and European manufactured goods entered Melanesia's short- and long-distance trade cycles. This began much earlier in the west than in the east, because of long-term links there with the Malay trading region. The entry of goods into eastern New Guinea and Island Melanesia came only in the second half of the nineteenth century, with new trade goods moving via old trade routes by the 1870s and 1880s, joining more traditional items along the coasts. James Chalmers, of the London Missionary Society, traveled with the Motu on a *hiri* trade voyage from Hanuabada village, Port Moresby, to the Gulf of Papua in 1883, and recorded that: "Now they go in these trading voyagers much better equipped than formerly, taking with them tomahawkes, knives, beads, looking-glasses, red-cloth, and tobacco."[31] The products of nineteenth-century industrialization had become entangled in the "roads" and "passages" of Melanesia. Foreigners were beginning to presume the right to rule the bodies and minds of Melanesians. But the peoples of New Guinea and adjacent islands continued to adapt their lifestyles, just as they had always done, while maintaining integrity and continuity.

Environment and People

40,000–5,000 B.P.

....

Environment

LANDSCAPE

As geographer Richard Bedford indicates, describing New Guinea and Melanesia is not a simple task. Even the shape of New Guinea is unusual—it is often metaphorically likened to a great prehistoric bird flying west into the Malay Archipelago, hovering above northern Australia, spread from Arnhem Land to the east coast, about to perch uneasily atop Australia's Cape York. It is the largest island in the world after Greenland, at approximately 900,000 square kilometers, and is part of a chain of substantial tropical islands that stretch from the Asian mainland into the Pacific Ocean, and south to Fiji and New Caledonia. Between southern New Guinea and Australia's north is one of the world's major sheltered channels, a tropical sea between two shores and open at both ends. The Timor, Arafura, and Coral Seas, filtered through Torres Strait, have served as a corridor from Asia to the Pacific over several thousand years. Shallow, sheltered embayments, the largest of which is the Gulf of Papua, are fed with sediment and fresh water from surrounding sluggish rivers until they pump silt out from New Guinea's coast. The north coast is more exposed, and the island's east and western ends are extended by smaller neighboring islands. Island-hopping along New Guinea's coastlines and off-shore islands provided the main pathway from Asia into Oceania.

New Guinea's coastal climate is hot and wet, graduating to snow on the highest mountains. The spine, almost continuous from New Guinea's head to its eastern tail where the great island meets the Louisiade Archipelago, is magnificently high in the center where Indonesia and Papua New Guinea meet. Papua New Guinea's highest mountain is Mt. Wilhelm (4,509 m) in the Western Highlands, while Puncak Jaya (5,040 m) in Indonesia's Papua Province is the island's highest point. On some edges of the Highlands bare windswept slopes stretch for kilometers, while other areas earn their nickname of "broken bottle country" with almost impenetrable craggy limestone canyons. These brought considerable grief to early government patrols, and must have been equally devastating to all humans who traversed them. The Lakeplain *(Meervlakte)* and the Van Rees Mountains separate the Maoke Range of the central Highlands of northwest New Guinea from

It is difficult to generalize about indigenous societies in Melanesia: the exception seems to be the rule in this part of the world.
—Richard Bedford, *Perceptions, Past and Present, of a Future for Melanesia*, 1980, 13.

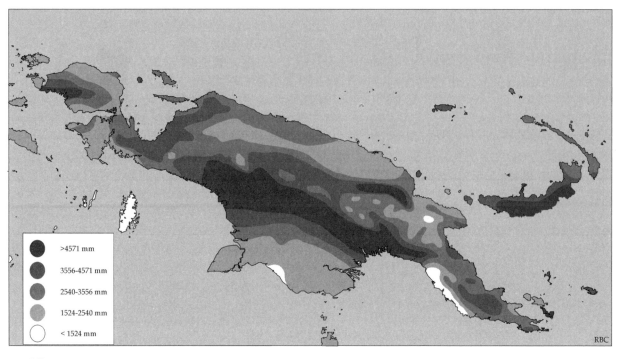

Rainfall

the coast. These correspond to the flood plain of the Sepik River and the Torricelli, Adelbert, and Finisterre Mountains in northeast New Guinea. The Lakeplain is drained by the Mamberamo River, which divides into two, flowing east and west, each fed by tributaries descending from the central Highlands. On the slopes of peaks and in the high fertile valleys are alpine herb fields and moss forests, pines and oaks beginning lower down. At lower levels there are jungles, coastal savanna, swamps, and beaches, surrounded by mangroves and fringing reefs. Open plains capable of supporting large populations are found in the central valleys and around coastal rivers such as the Ramu and the Markham on the northeast coast. The huge Sepik and Fly Rivers, both navigable for several hundred kilometers, connect to myriad tributaries that flow down north and south from the central massif. In the southwest, the smaller Digul River is a similar system that drains south of the central mountains.

Water constantly glints in a multitude of rivers and creeks, waterfalls, and rapids. On the southern shore, vast lowlands extend along almost one-third of the island. Much of the coast is cloaked by mangroves, a food-rich but often inhospitable environment, but the dark green is cut in places by white or black sand beaches reached through passages in the surrounding reefs.

Here and there along New Guinea's northeast coast and adjacent islands are volcanoes decked with clouds, serving with earthquakes as a reminder that the island's north side rubs (geologically-speaking) up against the larger Pacific Plate. Melanesia as a whole straddles the Pacific "Ring of Fire," and volcanoes and earthquakes are common—close to thirty volcanic areas form an arc along New Guinea's northeast coast and down through Island Melanesia to Vanuatu. Papua New Guinea alone has fourteen active volcanoes, while Indonesia's Papua Province has none. Several Melanesian eruptions in recent centuries have been global catastrophes, rating with the Santorini, Vesuvius, and Krakatau eruptions. When west New Britain's Mt. Witori exploded about 3,500 years ago, the eruption was so large that it was seen, and possibly heard, over most of eastern New Guinea and northern Island Melanesia. Much of central New Britain would have been rendered uninhabitable for at least a year. As surrounding people fled, they became a new wave of migrants flowing out into Island Melanesia. Archaeologists postulate that since there is no evidence of Lapita-ware on New Britain before this eruption, Lapita migrants (see below) may have taken advantage of the exodus from the Bismarcks to establish themselves there.[1] Another eruption on New Britain in about 536 A.D. is thought to have caused a haze recorded as far away as the Mediterranean Sea. Volcanoes on New Britain's Gazelle Peninsula have also erupted more recently: in 1888 (killing several hundred people), in 1937 (killing over 500), and one in 1994 that mercifully caused only three deaths. The Long Island eruption that took place on New Guinea's north coast in the seventeenth century remains in legend as "the time of darkness" when ash covered vast areas of central New Guinea and blocked out the sun for days. An unexpected 1951 eruption of supposedly dormant Mt. Lamington, near Popondetta, killed almost 3,000 people. New Guineans have learned to live with their volcanoes, wary of their ferocity but thankful for the replenishing fertility of their ash deposits.[2] Seismic activity over thousands of years may be one reason why some Melanesians migrated to safer regions of their island world.

CLIMATE

The climate in New Guinea varies enormously with the height and breadth of the island. Located near the equator, with its mountainous terrain, the island's climate is dominated by the subtropical high pressure system and the intertropical convergence zone, always tempered by an oceanic influence and modified inland by altitude. All around the island temperatures are high near the coast, with monthly averages fluctuating within fairly narrow limits: 25°C to 27°C seasonal temperature shifts are not considered important, since average daily ranges can be greater than average seasonal ranges. The climate does cool when the east monsoon blows, caused by comparatively low temperatures and dry air, for instance near Port Moresby and Merauke. Winds are not usually strong, but during the monsoon season the prevailing winds are often violent, making coastal navigation quite difficult. Cyclones form in the Coral and Solomon Seas during the summer months, and move southwest, creating havoc around Island Melanesia and northern Australia. Temperatures descend rapidly as one moves inland into the high mountains, at a rate of approximately 0.6°C for each 100 meters until 1,500 meters, after which the fall is 0.55°C for each 100 meters. The Highland valleys of the interior are pleasantly cool during the day and chilly at night, and frosts sometimes occur in agricultural areas. Permanent snow cloaks the highest peaks and perennial small glaciers survive in central west New Guinea. Rainfall is abundant, but with significant variations within local areas: Port Moresby receives less than 1,000 mm each year, while 7,000 to 8,000 mm totals are normal in the central mountains.[3]

New Guinea sits within the larger chains of islands that is Island Melanesia, consisting of hundreds of large and small islands surrounded by reefs, spread north to south over 3,000 kilometers of ocean. After New Guinea, the largest island is New Caledonia's Grande Terre, 400 kilometers long but only 30 kilometers wide, and several others are 100 to 200 kilometers in length. These islands are dominated by high central mountains, and the land often rises abruptly from narrow coastal plains, reaching 1,000 to 2,000 meters. The climate in Island Melanesia is similar to that of coastal New Guinea. Oceanic influences dominate the weather patterns, and rainfalls are commonly around 3,000 to 3,500 millimeters a year, although there are some distinctly drier areas such as the coastal plains around Honiara on Guadalcanal. The north-south axis is long but entirely tropical, extending from two degrees south of the equator to the Tropic of Capricorn, twenty-two degrees south. Except with altitude there is little decrease in temperature, and seasonal variation in rainfall is slight, although as one moves south through Island Melanesia wet and dry seasons become more distinct.[4]

BIOGEOGRAPHIC BOUNDARIES

The geographic description just presented applies to the last several hundred years, but it does little justice to New Guinea as part of the great continent of Sahul and the large islands that were once the dominant presence in Melanesia, nor to the identifiable biogeographic boundaries that have played a significant role in human settlement. The 100 to 200 kilometer-wide Wallacea area separates Sunda (the old Asian continent) from Sahul (New Guinea, Australia, and Tasmania). This barrier affected the movement of animals, plants, and humans. "The Wallace Line," the western boundary of Wallacea, is a meeting place for the flora and fauna of Sunda and Sahul. The large placental mammals of Asia, many of which were hunted by humans, never crossed the divide, and the fauna of the eastern Malay Archipelago is impoverished. New Guinea, benefiting from its midway position, has the richest and most varied Pacific biota, acting as the heartland for flora and fauna found throughout the rest of the Pacific Islands. New Guinea's vertebrate fauna is basically the same as Australia's, although many of its snail, insect, and bird faunas are of Malaysian origin. New Guinea's flora has a small Australian content but is predominantly Indo-Malaysian in origin. Because Australia and New Guinea were once linked, many of their animal forms are related; for instance, the same carnivorous marsupial mammals are found both in New Guinea and Tasmania.

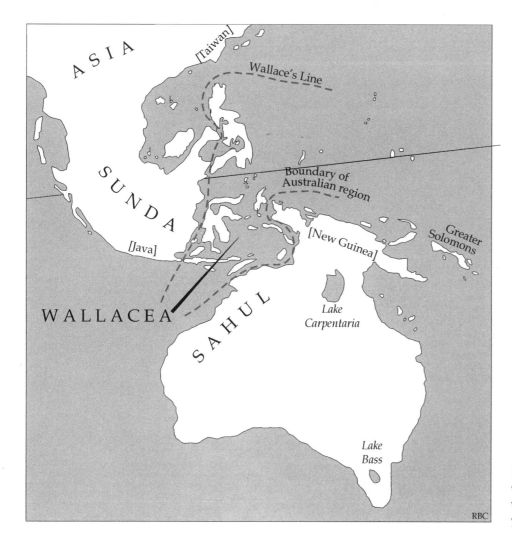

New Guinea and the western Pacific during the last Ice Age, 17,000 years ago

For much of the Pleistocene (the geological era until 10,000 years ago), sea levels were at least forty to seventy meters lower than today's, and the Great Barrier Reef off eastern Australia marked the eastern coast of Sahul. Another large low island existed between Sahul and New Caledonia. The Arafura Sea between Australia, New Guinea, and the eastern Malay Archipelago did not exist; Sahul's mainland extended out to include the Aru Islands. The high mountains and huge valleys in the north of Sahul were much colder than they are now, and this would have discouraged migrations and settlements into the center of what is now New Guinea.

Other biogeographic boundaries can be found between New Guinea, Island Melanesia, and remote Oceania. The Bismarck Archipelago just east of New Guinea was never part of Sahul, separated by another permanent waterway that inhibited movement of many terrestrial species. The further one moves east, past the Bismarcks and the Solomon Islands, the more impoverished is the natural environment for the needs of sustaining human life. This must be taken into account when we envision the human migrations entering remote Oceania between 30,000 and 3,000 years ago. While it is now clear that modern humans successfully colonized the Bismarck Archipelago and the north and central Solomon Islands 30,000 to 20,000 years ago, it was the Lapita migration 3,000 years ago that first crossed the 450 kilometer-wide water barrier which separates the last archipelagos of eastern Melanesia from those of western Polynesia. The final movements took their descendants—now known as Polynesians—into the most easterly of the Pacific Islands, north to Hawai'i, out to Rapanui (Easter) Island, and south to Aotearoa (New Zealand).

RECENT CLIMATIC AND TOPOGRAPHIC CHANGES

The last ice age was at its peak around 25,000 to 15,000 years ago. Quite rapidly, perhaps over only one or two centuries, temperatures fell by around eight degrees Celsius. As already noted, New Guinea's mountainous areas were once much colder than today. Tree lines were lower and grasslands extended higher, up to the moss forests. Worldwide, so much water was held as ice, particularly in huge polar ice caps, that sea levels fell remarkably around Sahul, exposing large coastal areas once under water, or leaving very shallow seas and swamps. Mountains above 3,600 meters would have been permanently covered in snow and ice until around 9,000 years ago. Even though northern Sahul, close to the equator, generally remained quite tropical, subalpine grasslands would have covered huge areas.

Then, about 15,000 years ago, global warming caused temperatures to rise quickly, leaving only small pockets of ice and snow on the highest peaks, and the glaciers began to retreat toward their present minimal forms.[5] Sea levels rose again 10,000 years ago, taking oceans to their highest point in the last 70,000 years and permanently covering many reefs and coral islands which grew too slowly to keep up with the rising waters. The low-lying, swampy plain between New Guinea and Australia flooded to become the Arafura Sea, the bed of which is now 50 meters below present sea level, suggesting that it would have begun to flood about 11,000 years ago. Eventually the remaining isthmus between Cape York and New Guinea also slowly became submerged, until around 8,000 years ago only the present-day chain of Torres Strait Islands remained, final remnants of the join in the old Australia-New Guinea landmass.[6]

Sea levels stabilized at the present levels around 6,000 years ago, and only in the last 2,500 years have reef growths been sufficient to allow atolls and sand cays to reemerge. This process created the atolls paralleling the Solomon chain, which were soon populated by back-migrating Polynesians, the reefs between New Caledonia and Australia (perched on the submerged island), and the reef barrier along the Queensland coast and out into the Louisiade Archipelago off eastern New Guinea. Many early coastal settlements would have been washed away in this period, and it is only on land areas that are rising, such as the Huon Peninsula, that we can expect to find evidence of coastal settlements more than 6,000 years old.

During this time, humans were living in Sahul, surviving by adapting to the rapid changes, some of which would have been evident over just one or two generations. The coast of the modern New Guinea landmass was created over approximately four millennia, between 15,000 and 9,000 years ago. By then, the megafauna had disappeared, and drainage systems had been introduced in the Highlands, indicating large-scale cooperation between groups. Ancestors of present-day New Guineans now began to increase in numbers and to make their mark on the island. They moved through the islands east and west of New Guinea and to a lesser extent south into Australia, leaving a linguistic trail that marks the beginning of modern New Guinea history.

People

DIVERSITY

Before colonial partition in the nineteenth century, two to three million people lived in Melanesia. There has been constant migration into and through the region over tens of thousands of years. Newly arriving peoples were absorbed into the wider population, while pockets of isolation resulted in an astounding range of physical appearances and languages. The inland peoples of New Guinea remained within their mountain domains and had little direct contact with the coast, but on smaller islands there was always interaction between coastal and inland people. Despite their diversity, the people of Melanesia are distinctive in several ways, and this helps explain early nineteenth-century attempts to classify them as a single racial/cultural unit. All inhabited a region consisting of chains of substantial mountainous islands, beyond the influence of the major Asian religions and cultures and on the outer fringes of European exploration and knowledge. Their physical appearance, though varied, was different from their neighbors to the east and west. And Melanesians were primarily root-crop agriculturalists, further distinguishing them from most of their Malay neighbors to the west (who are grain growers), and from Australian Aborigines (who are nonagricultural).

Today we know what Dumont d'Urville and De Rienzi did not—that the first human settlements in Melanesia were ancient, having occurred more than 40,000 years ago in Sahul, 35,000 to 30,000 years ago in the northern island chains, and 4,000 years ago in the south, with drainage systems and simple agriculture beginning in the New Guinea Highlands 6,000–9,000 years ago.[7] Situated on the outer fringe of the Malay world, Melanesians were on the far edge of human migration. By the time they were classified as one Melanesian "race," Europeans had developed firm ideas about racial hierarchies, graded from light- to dark-skinned. Scientific opinion, just emerging from the strictures of biblical knowledge and exactly calculated dates for the creation of the human beings, could only envisage the peoples of the "black islands" as near the bottom of the human chain.[8]

Several fairly distinct population-groupings have been formulated based on genetic and blood-group data. DNA research indicates that there were five original populations in northern Melanesia: Austronesian-speaking peoples of the Bismarck Archipelago and the southeast coast of New Guinea, indicating a chain of settlement from the mainland to the archipelago; Austronesian-speaking and Non-Austronesian-speaking peoples of New Guinea's north coast; New Guinea's Highlanders; Non-Austronesian speakers from New Britain and southern New Guinea; and the peoples of the northern Solomon Islands. We also know that there has been extensive intermarriage between groups along the divide between Island Melanesia and New Guinea.[9]

Estimates of the number of inhabitants of Tasmania, Australia, New Guinea, and Island Melanesia just prior to European contact can only be conjecture, but a figure of three to four million seems plausible. Douglas Oliver suggests, conservatively, 2,830,000: two million as the pre-European population of New Guinea and nearby islands; 390,000 for what he terms "Island Melanesia" (the Admiralties to New Caledonia, excluding the Polynesian Outliers); and 140,000 for Fiji. Matthew Spriggs suspects that Oliver's estimate for Island Melanesia is far too low, and his calculations suggest that one million inhabitants might be closer to the mark.[10] We do not know how fast populations have grown over the last 40,000 years, but Les Groube's analysis of the role of malaria as a population regulator suggests that increases in the tropics were always slow.[11] Furthermore, increased regular contact between the Malay world and western New Guinea during recent centuries may have introduced epidemic diseases such as smallpox, which would have acted to further counter population increases.

MIGRATIONS INTO SAHUL

Settlement of Australia and New Guinea began when they were one landmass (Sahul), and reliable dates for human occupation of northern Australia extend to 55,000 years ago. Given the speed with which the dates have been pushed back over the last two decades, archaeologists may find earlier evidence of human occupation in New Guinea, but even 40,000 years of occupation, a conservative estimate, is an enormous period of time.[12]

When first human settlement occurred, the Pacific Islands were much larger, and many were linked together. At its greatest extent about 20,000 years ago, Sahul covered approximately ten million square kilometers.[13] At the same time, Island Melanesia—in reality the northern tops of an undersea ridge stretching as far south as New Zealand—was far more substantial than today's islands. When the first humans traveled to Sahul, they used some form of watercraft to cross the 70 or 80 kilometers of deep sea between the two continental shelves. Once on northern Sahul, migrants were able to travel around the coast, or walk across the lowlands (today covered by the Arafura Sea) between New Guinea and Australia. The last remaining links from this old continent are the Kei and Aru Islands and the islands of Torres Strait, which remain easy stepping-stones between Australia and New Guinea.[14] Movement into Island Melanesia was by necessity different —a deep sea trench separated Sahul and what is now the Bismarck Archipelago, meaning that watercraft were required to travel between east New Guinea and the islands.

There are of course great unsolved mysteries in the history of Melanesia. In scientific terms, Australia's and Tasmania's Aborigines are Australoid and part of the Australo-Melanesian lineage which includes Melanesians. It has been suggested that the first inhabitants of Sahul held some relationship with the early Javanese *Homo erectus* population, but today most experts agree that they came from a rapid expansion of *Homo sapiens* —modern humans who came out of Africa through one migration route via Southeast Asia into Sahul. There were probably multiple waves of immigrants, and there may be a relationship between Australo-Melanesians and the Negritos of Southeast Asia.[15] Other puzzles involve the timing and motivations of early migrations, and the type of watercraft people used, first to reach Sahul out of Island Southeast Asia, and then to move out into Island Melanesia. With sea levels 40 to 70 meters below present-day levels, the water gaps between Sunda's outer islands and Sahul would have been around 90 kilometers, and 140 to 175 kilometers between Sahul, the Bismarck Archipelago, and on to the northern Solomons. The earliest dates for human use of Gebe Island off the Bird's Head in the west, 33,000 years ago, fit well with research indicating 40,000 years of habitation on the Huon Peninsula.[16] The watercraft of 40,000 years ago were probably primitive bamboo rafts or sewn-bark canoes, rather than the sophisticated sailing craft we now associate with Melanesians.

By way of comparison, we need to remind ourselves that there is no evidence of human capacity to cross the Mediterranean Sea until about 10,000 years ago, which makes early Pacific migrants quite extraordinary. Originally, it was thought that these first sea crossings were rare and probably accidental, but during the 1990s Geoffrey Irwin and others argued that early voyages were deliberate, frequent, and probably two-way, the first controlled sea travel anywhere in the world.[17] Archaeological research tells us that humans lived on New Britain 35,000 years ago, on New Ireland 33,000 years ago, on Buka in the northern Solomon Islands 29,000 years ago, and on Manus at least 10,000 years ago.[18] Reaching Buka (at that time joined to Bougainville) 180 kilometers away from New Ireland, may have been achieved using Nissan and Feni Islands as stepping-stones, or by launching out into the unknown off New Ireland. The migration to the Admiralties involved a 200–230 kilometer voyage over several days, a far more dangerous feat than the shorter voyages through the Bismarcks or to Buka. Between 20,000 and 10,000 years ago, several species of New Guinea's wild animals and plants were introduced into the Bismarck Archipelago and the northwest Solomon Islands, indicating deliberate human manipulation of their environment in the late Pleistocene. *Canarium* almond trees were introduced from further north, and a possum *(Phalanger orientalis)*, a wallaby *(Thylogale brunii)* and a rodent *(Rattus praetor)* were introduced to the Bismarcks from New Guinea during the Pleistocene.[19]

There appear to have been two distinct phases in the settlement of the northwest Solomon Islands. The first occurred at some time prior to 29,000 years ago, coming from the west out of the Bismarck Archipelago. The second phase was during the time of the Lapita "homeland" in the Bismarcks, 3,000 to 2,000 years ago, relating to the movement of speakers of Austronesian languages. The antiquity of the Buka/Bougainville and other western Solomons peoples is also evidenced by their dark skin color, a characteristic not found in the neighboring peoples in the Bismarcks or the central Solomon Islands. Genetically, they are a distinctive biological cluster, but linguistically, they speak both Austronesian and Non-Austronesian languages, the latter linked to languages spoken in areas of New Britain, New Ireland, and Rossel, the most easterly island of the Louisiade Archipelago. The northwest Solomons is also the only area in the Solomon Islands where pottery was manufactured after the Lapita period, continuing into recent times.[20]

Population pressures, escape from epidemic diseases, local seismic and vulcanological activity, curiosity, and accidents; all could account for the migratory voyages.[21] Travel by rafts between nearby islands probably led to accidental voyages further into the southern ocean. Even today, unplanned drift voyages in small canoes during the monsoon season sometimes carry Pacific Islanders hundreds or even thousands of kilometers away to other islands, an indication of what undoubtedly occurred tens of thousands of years ago. Roger Green suggests that the invention of simple oceangoing rafts, refined into shaped-rafts, came during the late Pleistocene, and that their use in Sunda began some 50,000 years ago: "This occurred neither solely by accident nor was it enforced. People found they could now transport themselves to those islands they could see on the horizon, and they began to do so. Moreover, they continued to do so until all of Ancient Near Oceania was settled."[22]

These first settlers were probably hunter-gatherers who used a flaked-stone tool kit, then common throughout Southeast Asia, New Guinea, and Australia. Perhaps because of the limited fauna available to hunt, a social need for communities to become more sedentary, experimentation with plants, or even population pressures, slowly, they began to cultivate wild crops, which led to domestication of tubers, vines, and nut trees, and to rudimentary irrigation and drainage. Taro, banana, yam, sago, breadfruit, coconut, pandanus, tree-nuts, and edible leaves were the agricultural staples of the first colonists. Although animal numbers dwindled once migrants crossed into Island Melanesia, there was fauna available as food, changing in type from the more plentiful placental mammals of Sunda, to marsupials in Sahul. Coastal peoples also used sea resources, with a focus on accessible reefs and lagoons. Agricultural advances depended on the migrants' abilities to clear rain forests, at least by ring-barking and burning. Waisted stone axes from the

Huon Gulf terraces of northeast New Guinea—the oldest known artifacts—seem to have been used for forest clearing. They have been dated by their position in ash layers as having been deposited between 40,000 and 60,000 years ago.[23] Evidence from the last 20,000 years indicates that there was deliberate human transporting of animal and plant species from one area to another, actively shaping the environment. This indicates a transition from an earlier economy to the beginnings of what existed when Europeans first intruded a few hundred years ago.

The Melanesians' stone tool kit was slowly refined during their millennia of residence. Beginning with large waisted axes such as those found on the Huon Peninsula, there was a steady decrease in size and increasingly fine manufacture. The waisted axes of New Guinea and Australia—so far only found at Yuku and Kosipe in New Guinea, in the Pioneer Valley at Mackay (Queensland), and on Kangaroo Island (South Australia)—may be a Sahul invention independent of Asian influences.[24] We know that exchanges of stone tool resources were occurring 20,000 years ago through long-distance movements of obsidian. There are four known obsidian sites in eastern Melanesia, in New Britain, the Admiralties, Fergusson Islands off Goodenough Bay in east New Guinea, and the Banks Group in Vanuatu. Obsidian from the New Britain site at Talasea/Mopir was being traded as far west as the Sepik-Ramu River basin, and east as far as Nissan Island between New Ireland and Buka Island. There have also been two isolated finds of Talasea obsidian in Sabah on Borneo, and in Fiji. Obsidian-stemmed tools, probably dating back 3,500 years, have been found along the north coast of New Guinea. Similar tools made of chert (flint-like quartz) flakes have been found on New Britain dated at approximately one thousand years earlier, and blood and plant residues on them indicate multipurpose uses. The Lapita migrants at about this time also introduced their own distinct stone adze kit and pottery.[25]

Another Melanesian mystery is the origins and use of stone mortars, pestles, and figurines found in the New Guinea Highlands and neighboring islands in the Bismarck Archipelago. Highlands' examples have been dated back 3,000 to 3,500 years, but present-day inhabitants deny any connection with them, claiming only that the stone artifacts have magical connotations. Some experts suggest that these artifacts were introduced by seafaring people with knowledge of agriculture, who used stone to grind grains or ochre, and to crack seeds and nuts, perhaps indicating a widespread but now unrecognized cultural tradition linking the Highlands with the islands to the northeast.[26]

HUNTING THE FAUNA

Tim Flannery's *The Future Eaters* provides a very readable account of the early history of Sahul and its flora, fauna, and peoples. He argues that humans were the most successful carnivorous predators on Sahul, managing to kill off all of the land-based fauna larger than themselves. Although Sahul's species were nowhere near the size of now-extinct species elsewhere on the planet, the earliest humans would still have had quite a task to capture and kill the large carnivores, herbivores, and insectivores. Sahul once had around sixty mammal species which weighed in at more than ten kilograms, among them two or three carnivores now extinct: a 40–60 kilogram marsupial lion *(Thylacoleo carnifex)*; the Tasmanian tiger *(Thylacinus cynocephalus)* which survived until recent times; and a 40 kilogram giant rat-kangaroo *(Propleopus oscillans)*. Two smaller carnivores have survived: the 5–8 kilogram Tasmanian devil *(Sarcophilus harrisii)* and the slightly smaller spotted-tailed quoll *(Dasyurus maculatus)*. There is no evidence of these cat- or fox-like predators in the New Guinea end of Sahul, except for the thylacine *(Thylacinus)*. There were also very formidable seven-meter goannas *(Megalania prisca)*, each weighing over a ton, several now-extinct freshwater crocodiles *(Pallimnarchus* and *Quinkana fortirostrum)*, and a 100 kilogram python-like snake in southern Australia *(Wonambi narracoortensis)*.[27] These carnivores fed on the many herbivores and insectivores, an array of echidnas, marsupials, flightless birds, and tortoises, which were spread and largely coexisted through all Sahul habitats. The largest were 2,000 kilogram diprotodons (roughly one-third the size of an elephant, but looking like a wombat), ranging down to large kangaroos weighing 200 kilograms and echidnas at around 20–30 kilograms. A 100 kilogram panda-like animal once roamed the Highlands, and 50–100 kilogram diprotodons *(Maokopia ronaldi)* once lived at alpine and glacial tundra levels in the mountains of west New Guinea. (By way of comparison, today's largest Australian kangaroos, the red and gray, only weigh up to 90 kilograms.) Two hundred-kilogram horned turtles plodded along, large flightless birds resembling emus and cassowaries roamed about, flamingoes cavorted on inland lakes, huge eagles flew circles in the sky, and large mallee fowls nested in mounds. Smaller species coexisted with the giants, providing a great range of animals and birds for humans to hunt.[28] Some species became extinct, but in many cases smaller related species remain.

New Guinea shares much of Australia's flora and fauna, but its northerly position allows more influence from the Malay Archipelago, and its terrain allows far more diverse habitats. Flannery attempts to categorize New Guinea's diversity, noting that research is inadequate and that "numbers should be doubled to get a realistic estimate": "An idea of its extraordinary richness can be gained from the following comparisons: it supports 210 species of mammals, only 35 less than the much larger Australia; the Papuasian region supports 840 bird species, against 750 from Australia and its nearby islands. Furthermore, it supports about 300 reptiles and 220 frogs, against Australia's 750 reptiles and 250 frogs."[29] Although we lack detailed evidence, it is clear that this megafauna overlapped in time-span with humans by at least 10,000 years, and possibly much longer. Flannery concludes that the number of megafauna species in New Guinea was more limited than in southern Sahul. Because the dense jungle environment was not suited to large animals, and at lower elevations most animal life exists in treetops, New Guinea has perhaps lost only ten species of large animals since humans arrived 40,000 years ago.[30]

Just as intriguing as postulations about the number of species and their distribution through New Guinea are questions of why the megafauna died out and whether humans played a role. Certainly the megafauna disappeared after humans arrived. By way of comparison, we know that during the last millennium Polynesian migrants to New Zealand, although already agriculturalists, had to adapt their skills and crops to the much colder conditions. In the meantime, they became dependant on hunting for subsistence, and in less than 1,000 years they cleared many species of birds from New Zealand. Similarly, early humans in Sahul may have managed to kill off the tamest megafauna during the first few millennia after they arrived, but human numbers would have been low and no evidence of bones in large kill sites has yet been found. Extinctions could have been climate-related, but if so, why did it occur relatively simultaneously across the diverse environment from dry central Australia to wet tropical New Guinea? When combined with a natural dwarfing of species over tens of thousands of years, and perhaps the effects of human-controlled fires in clearing natural habitats, humans, as efficient omnivore-predators, certainly could have been instrumental in causing the extinction of all of the larger animals, land reptiles, and birds in Australia and New Guinea. However, the "overkill" hypothesis has few supporters among archaeologists. Many suggest that natural ecological change caused the extinctions, and doubt that humans were able to conquer the megafauna, some of which would have been more than a match for them.[31]

Whatever the reasons for their demise, no large species remained as candidates for domestication, in the way elephants, horses, and buffaloes were harnessed for transport, agricultural, or warfare in other parts of the world. Thousands of years of hunting animals, reptiles, and birds, of all sizes, must have remained the mainstay of human existence before agriculture developed in New Guinea.[32]

EARLY AGRICULTURE

As noted, tools probably used for forest clearance 40,000 years ago have been found on the Huon Peninsula. Forest clearance was taking place at Kosipe in the southeast Highlands 30,000 years ago, adjacent to high-altitude pandanus swamps, and in the Baliem Valley in the west 32,000 years ago.[33] Waisted blades or hafted axes were in use at Kosipe 25,000 years ago, and a stemmed axe of the same vintage has been found at Nombe, 400 kilometers northwest. New Guinea was much colder at this time—3° to 7°C below present temperatures—with much more glaciation and a tree line 1,700 meters below present levels. The climate did not approach that of today until about 15,000 to 9,000 years ago, a shift that enabled permanent settlement of higher altitudes in the Highlands.[34] Before extensive human settlement and forest clearance, the Highlands were thick with birds, giant rats, small marsupials, and arboreal animals like possums and tree-kangaroos, and fruit bats. Before they began to introduce agriculture, the earliest settlers exploited these food supplies. Humans were living in upland environments by 12,000–15,000 years ago, and New Guinea's Highland valleys were certainly occupied 10,000 years ago, when shell valuables were being traded up from the coast.[35]

Like long-range watercraft and sea travel, intensive irrigated agriculture is another early first for Melanesia, although when it was introduced is open to debate. Evidence of the construction of drainage channels is usually taken as indicating the beginning of an agricultural economy and the abandonment of rock shelter-based living for settled village life. Drainage systems in the Wahgi Valley's Kuk Swamp (in Papua New Guinea's Western Highlands Province) date back 9,000 years. Research by Jack Golson and his colleagues suggests that Kuk Swamps were first drained 9,000 years ago, partly to facilitate a wild food economy, although the earliest drainage channels may not be artificial nor directly connected with forest clearance. The network expanded around 6,000 years ago — a surer date for the beginning of agriculture — and continued in use until about one century ago. Initially, the drainage ditches were uncoordinated, but then about 2,000 years ago they became a network — a tight drainage grid. There are indications of other drainage systems in Western Highlands Province, which could have been duplicated in lowland and coastal areas, and perhaps in the Bismarck Archipelago. Because the Kuk site came into use as soon as the climate was suitable (at the end of the Pleistocene), perhaps we should be looking for manipulation of warmer coastal swamps at even earlier dates.[36]

The only agricultural sites in the world as old as 9,000 years ago are in Mesopotamia, Indochina, and Central America.[37] Based on excavations of rock shelters, shell midden sites, and bone accumulations, most archaeologists are not convinced that we should presume a steady evolution of Melanesian agriculture from 9,000 years ago, and prefer a cautious interpretation which has agriculture beginning about 6,000 years ago, followed by gradual intensification and integration of inland and coastal activities.[38] The first unambiguous evidence of agriculture comes from 6,000 to 5,000 years ago, with intensive horticulture and pig-raising only certain over the last 2,000 years, intensifying during the last 1,000 years.[39]

The dating of tree crops was pushed back during the 1990s. The earliest evidence of an arboriculture in New Guinea is a date of 14,000 years ago in the Sepik-Ramu Basin for the important species *Canarium indicum*. Species of pandanus were domesticated in the Highlands by 10,000 years ago, and *Cocos, Canarium, Pandanus, Aleurites, Areca catechu,* and *Pometia pinnate* have been dated to more than 5,000 ago years at Dongan on New Guinea's north coast.[40] It is not clear which were the first root crops grown. Certainly they were not the now ubiquitous sweet potato *(Ipomoea batatas)*, which can be dated as a Portuguese-linked introduction that arrived no earlier than the sixteenth century, via Island Southeast Asia, originally out of South America. (There remains a possibility that sweet potatoes were imported into Polynesia 600 to 1,000 years ago, but there is no known link through to New Guinea.) Nine thousand years ago, the cultigens were probably indigenous greens and *Australimusa* bananas, with Southeast Asian tubers such as taro *(Colocasia esculenta)* and *Dioscorea* yams (in drier areas) being introduced 6,000 to 2,500 years ago. Thereafter, taro became a monoculture until supplemented finally by sweet potato. Although taro and yam are usually presumed to be of Southeast Asian origin, which would indicate migrants carried them to New Guinea thousands of years ago, there remains a possibility that cultivated taro is indigenous to New Guinea.[41] Since the 1970s, ethnobotanist Douglas Yen has challenged the belief that plant domestication occurred only in Asia and Southeast Asia, and has presented evidence for quite independent plant domestication in New Guinea.[42]

NON-AUSTRONESIAN LANGUAGES AND MIGRATION

Melanesia looks less like a united cultural region when one considers its languages. It is the most linguistically complex and diverse region on earth, with more than one thousand different languages, broken down into as many dialects, none of which were in written form. These languages developed over thousands of years as communities moved from one area to another, or were separated by uninhabited areas and by natural boundaries such as mountains, valleys, swamps, and islands. The enormous time period—40,000 years—during which languages have split partly explains their huge number. Linguists estimate that there are approximately 205 languages spoken in Indonesia's Papua Province and more than 750 spoken in Papua New Guinea, 150 of these spoken by fewer than two hundred people.

Some linguistic unity can be restored to the bewildering diversity by a division of the indigenous languages into two quite distinct types. The first is the more recent "Austronesian" languages, which are related to the spread of the Lapita culture-complex (discussed in the next chapter) and have a comparatively simple structure. The second type is the "Non-Austronesian" or "Papuan" languages, which dominate New Guinea's interior and are marked by greater structural complexity and antiquity. The latter are not all related, as the Austronesian languages are; rather they are grouped together by the negative trait of not being Austronesian. Although they are the oldest identifiable languages in Melanesia, none of them are necessarily of direct descent from the languages of the area's first humans of 40,000 years ago.

Today, the majority of the peoples of New Guinea and the adjacent islands to the east and west speak one of some 750 Non-Austronesian languages. Their speech communities are usually larger than their Austronesian counterparts, averaging around 10,000, although Simbu and Engan, the two largest, each have over 300,000 speakers. The largest grouping is the Trans-New Guinea Phylum, which occupies most of the New Guinea mainland, and includes 365 languages in Papua New Guinea and 251 languages in Papua Province. The latter has several languages with more than 40,000 speakers: Western Dani, Grand Valley Dani, Ekagi, and Biak-Numfor. The West Papuan Phylum, with twenty-four member languages, is located entirely in west New Guinea. The East Papuan Phylum contains twenty-eight member languages, sixteen of them in Papua New Guinea, and is concentrated in the islands east of the New Guinea mainland.[43]

In the 1970s and 1980s, Stephen Wurm hypothesized a common origin for the Trans-New Guinea Phylum, which if true would link two-thirds of the Non-Austronesian languages. Wurm and others believe that it is possible to trace the relationship between

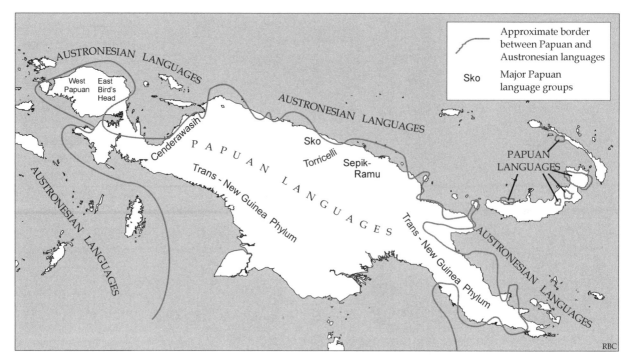

Languages

these languages, and they hypothesize separate groups entering New Guinea at different times many thousands of years ago. Out of favor for many years, Wurm's view is now undergoing a renaissance. Linguist Andrew Pawley suggested in a 1997 review that there is more consistency and connection between the Trans-New Guinea Phylum than previously supposed, and that they may be the ancestral languages of the migrants who introduced agriculture into the Highlands.[44] His colleague William Foley is more cautious, and argues that our present state of knowledge is still too incomplete to be confident about wider relationships. He ventures no further than to say that on the basis of present knowledge they belong to at least sixty different language families, and adds that there are another couple of dozen languages which are isolates, not clearly linked to any other language.[45]

New Guinea's archaeologists and linguists suggest distinct but slowly drifting movements of people from west to east over at least 40,000 years, as migrant groups moved through the island and on to neighboring islands. In 1975, four linguists, Wurm, Laycock, Voorhoeve, and Dutton, rather bravely attempted to reconstruct the linguistic prehistory of human migration into New Guinea. Today, most archaeologists and linguists would be more circumspect, merely suggesting that the Non-Austronesian languages developed amongst populations that had been *in situ* for thousands of years, subsequently expanding to new regions of New Guinea, and east and west to neighboring islands, after the development of a taro-based agriculture system in the central Highlands.

Advance parties would have gone ahead scouting, collecting information and relaying it back to the main migrant groups. Ian Lilley, trying to explain pre-Lapita and Lapita migrations in the Bismarck Archipelago, suggested that we also think in terms of trade diasporas, whereby trader-scouts would have begun the process, followed by settlement of spatially dispersed trader communities that eventually became culturally distinct from the communities in which they lived.[46] Certainly this is what Maluku traders did as they moved around and settled at key spots on the Bird's Head Peninsula during the last few hundred years. Migrations may also have leapfrogged, passing up closer areas for sites they thought more propitious. For land migrations, this could have occurred because of a favored mountain path, or finding an exploitable natural commodity or food supply, or the friendly or hostile reaction of local people met on the way. For sea migrations, difficult seas, a sheltered anchorage, access to fresh water, or some mishap that necessitated going ashore could account for a particular direction of travel. These rather quixotic patterns, thus established, might then have become well-defined migration routes for later generations. Once kinship and trade links were established, relationships directed the migration flows, traditions of past migration becoming the forward driving force. As well, because of the lengthy time period involved, we must also consider back-migrations. A scenario of one-way west-east migration, in trickles and bursts over 40,000 years, without any return movements east-west, is highly unlikely.

It is easier to suggest what might have motivated the migrations than to determine exactly their pattern. Movements through and around New Guinea seem to have increased about 15,000 years ago, intensifying again 5,000 years later.[47] The 1975 paper by Wurm, Laycock, Voorhoeve, and Dutton suggests four migrations: a very early migration from the west, of unspecified geographic origin, still detectable in the form of substrata in some present-day phyla; a second early migration moving into north Halmahera through the Raja Empat Islands, then into New Guinea's Bird's Head Peninsula and deep into the island. These first two language movements, which can be regarded as ancestral to the Trans-New Guinea Phylum, seem to have crossed in the neck of the Bird's Head Peninsula perhaps 15,000 to 10,000 years ago, intermingling and spreading into the central Highlands of what is today Papua New Guinea. From there they moved south into the Trans-Fly, north to the Markham Valley, through to the Huon Peninsula, with some outreach into the southeast tail of New Guinea and into the Bismarck and Louisiade Archipelagos, displacing earlier language groups. Evidence of the distribution of waisted axes, typical of the Non-Austronesian cultural tradition rather than that of the later Austronesians, would seem to add substance to this interpretation. Based on current archaeological evidence, most of the Non-Austronesian languages in Island Melanesia are found only in areas settled prior to 10,000 years ago, during the Pleistocene era before global warming ended the last Ice Age.[48] One language group is anomalous, however—that of the Reef and Santa Cruz Islands in the southern Solomon Islands, which were not settled during the Pleistocene. Presumably these Islanders represent later displaced language groups from the New Guinea mainland, who moved from the eastern tip to Rossel Island in the east of the Louisiade Archipelago, then further out to the Solomon Islands, reaching the Santa Cruz Group only in the last few thousand years. At about the same time, Austronesian language-speakers arrived in the area.[49]

The third much more recent migration followed, perhaps around 5,000 years ago. Backed by the findings of archaeologist Peter Bellwood, Wurm and his colleagues suggested that this third migration is also ancestral to the large Trans-New Guinea Phylum. They hypothesize that it entered via Timor, Alor, and Pantar Islands, moving from Onin Peninsula into east New Guinea along the north coast, filling uninhabited areas and also displacing other early groups who sailed into the eastern islands as far south as the Santa Cruz Group.[50] Then a fourth movement, independent of the Trans-New Guinea Phylum, but probably just preceding it, may have entered the mainland at the center of the north coast. This might be the ancestral form of what is now classified as the Sepik-Ramu Phylum, which moved south into the Highlands, continuing east into the Solomon Islands.

The pattern of migration suggested above is conjectural, but it does at least give a picture of the complexity of the movements which occurred over tens of thousands of years.[51] In *The Papuan Languages of New Guinea*, Foley suggests some regional scenarios. There are three large language families in the central Highlands—Papua New Guinea's Eastern Highlands, Simbu, and Enga—their people well-adapted to the Highlands environment and using sophisticated high-altitude agricultural techniques that indicate some millennia of occupation. The Eastern Highlands language family has clear genetic links further west in the Highlands and to the Huon languages, but it also contains Austronesian loan words, indicating some geographic proximity to later migrations, the most likely link being at the Markham Valley. The Engan family has few links to the Eastern Highlands languages and contains more Austronesian loan words. Foley suggests, very tentatively, a possible Engan origin in the Sepik basin. The Simbu, one of the largest modern linguistic and cultural groups in New Guinea and the largest in Papua New Guinea, have no potential genetic links outside the Highlands. They occupy the earliest agricultural sites, which suggests that they might be the original settlers, or at least have a time depth of around 3,000 years.

Using a hypothesis suggested by Pamela Swadling, Foley also creates a scenario for the recent history of the Sepik-Ramu basin, which was submerged 5,000 to 6,000 years ago when the sea reached its present height, leaving a huge salt-water inlet. To the south were the foothills of the mountains in the central Highlands, and to the north the lower mountains of the Prince Alexander and Torricelli Ranges. Water runoff from these mountains gradually silted up the inlet, creating the present floodplain about 2,000 years ago. Five millennia ago, the inundation would have caused large-scale population disruptions as people were forced to move to higher ground. Swadling's hypothesis is that this movement away from the Sepik-Ramu inlet became mixed with Highlands refugees being pushed onto the upland fringes and the emerging flood plain by more dominant High-lands language families. At the same time Austronesians arrived and found the large shallow inlet to their liking. The result was that 4,000 years ago a mixing of languages occurred that we may never unravel.[52]

. . . .

New Guinea emerged as a marginal outer edge for dislocated migrant people from Island Southeast Asia. But if one examines all of the evidence, the island clearly hosted an affluent human society many thousands of years before the same could be said of Southeast Asia. Sahul's people practiced large-scale hunting and gathering, tree-cropping and tree-cultivation. They were sailors capable of moving long distances. They perfected fire-stick farming and developed complex agricultural practices, including drainage and irrigation. The introduction of agriculture in central New Guinea either preceded by a few thousand years or was contemporaneous with agriculture in Southeast Asia. Such was the strength of the core culture of New Guinea and Island Melanesia that later Austronesian migrants only managed to have a peripheral affect, with their colonization limited to the coasts. The next chapter builds on this pattern of migrations through New Guinea over tens of thousands of years, and links it to more recent developments of languages, cultural spheres, and exchange networks.

2 Cultural Spheres and Trade Systems
The Last 5,000 Years

Austronesian Languages and the Lapita Culture Complex

That the people of present-day New Guinea have so many characteristics in common can be partly explained by the existence of trading networks which led to the exchange of ideas and attitudes as well as goods.
—John Dademo Waiko, personal communication, Brisbane, October 1999.

John Waiko, Papua New Guinea's first indigenous Professor of History, and more recently Minister for Education, and then Foreign Affairs, is from Binandere in Oro Province. Brought up in a remote village, he did not begin school or learn English until he was eleven. Waiko was educated in two cultures, and as Minister for Education he constantly stressed the need to continue using vernacular languages in education. His doctoral dissertation was written in both English and Binandere, to satisfy the demands of both the Australian National University and his village elders, whom he regarded as his most important examiners. In Binandere, a *tugata* is the introduction to a speech, when the speaker establishes himself, his identity, and his social position in the clan, and gives a brief outline of the subject. It would be embarrassing if someone else introduced the person. Having attracted attention by rattling his spatula against his lime gourd and clearing his throat, a man begins: "'I am a grandson of so and so, my father is X of Y clan and I live at Z village. No one but me is about to talk.' In this way the speaker introduces himself through his grandparents, from whom his knowledge is derived, and through his parents and relatives who are his mentors. The *tugata* is important in two ways. The audience must know from the beginning the identity of the speaker and the sources of his information because without that they will turn their backs on him, a certain sign that they think he knows little about his topic. He has failed to establish his authority over his subject and his right to a hearing."[1] Waiko's people speak a Non-Austronesian language, but to their north and south on the mainland, and across the Solomon Sea on New Britain, more recent Austronesian language communities surround the Binandere.

The last great change in Melanesia, before the intrusion of Europeans, was the arrival of the Austronesian language speakers and the associated Lapita culture complex. The name "Lapita" comes from an archaeological site in New Caledonia, characterized by a highly distinctive style of earthenware used by agricultural people. The ancestors of these Pacific settlers are presumed to have migrated out of Asia or Island Southeast Asia. While we know Austronesians' originated on the Asian mainland, approximately 6,000 to 7,000 years ago, from the rice-growing cultures of southern China or Indochina, prehistorians and linguists remain divided regarding their specific origins. Some reconstructions of the Proto-Austronesian languages suggest an origin around Taiwan, and migration east by the Proto-Malayo-Polynesian branch. Others point to the Thai-Kadai and Austroasiatic groups of languages spoken in Thailand, Laos, Cambodia, and parts of southern China and Malaysia as the closest external relatives. More recent evidence suggests an origin around Wallacea, or along the voyaging corridor between Wallacea and the Solomon Islands.[2] What ever explanation is correct, Austronesian language-speakers continued to move east through Island Southeast Asia into the Pacific Islands.

Lapita is a relatively low-fired non-kiln style of pottery, and is thought to have originated in eastern Indonesia. It displays distinctive decorative motifs, with finely carved, toothed, or dentate stamps that include parallel lines and curves, eye-designs, rope and arcade motifs, rectangular meanders, interlocking Y's, and indented circles.[3] For archaeologists, however, Lapita has represented much more than another variety of pottery, because the original Lapita migrants seem to have also brought other material and cultural artifacts with them. As listed by Spriggs, these are: "domestic animals, quadrangular adzes, polished stone chisels, various shell ornament types, rectangular houses (some on stilts), large villages, language, and probably aspects of boat technology, tattoo chisels, pearl-shell knives, trolling hooks and various stone-artifact classes."[4] Their village sites were characteristically built along beaches or on small offshore islands, enabling them to exploit marine resources in adjacent lagoons and reefs, while at the same time clearing gardens close by on the coast for root and tree crops. These Lapita people brought with them domestic pigs, dogs, and chickens, as well as a range of nut trees and other domesticated plants.

Their arrival in Maluku 5,000 years ago greatly altered the existing culture of this transitional area, wedged between the Malay/Austronesian peoples and the earlier migrant stock of Sahul living on New Guinea and Australia. The people of Maluku physically resemble both the Asian and Austroloid types, and in both northern and southeastern Maluku, not only Austronesian but also older Non-Austronesian languages are spoken. Cultural forms brought by the Austronesians eventually came to dominate in Maluku, and the two cultures have intermingled over the centuries and now share common elements.[5] Hunting and fishing was supplemented with pig and chicken breeding, and agriculture began with tuber, banana, coconut, and sago palm cultivation, and swidden methods derived from dry rice cultivation. The Austronesians also introduced their particular style of ceramics, the material culture items just mentioned, and canoes using outriggers. These outrigger canoes are today ubiquitous, and their arrival must have revolutionized people's mobility. New house styles were also introduced, with raised floors on piles, decorative gable finials, and saddle-backed roofs with outward-sloping gable ends, exhibiting a boat symbolism now deeply imbedded in Malukan culture. Rock art on the Kei Islands south of the Bird's Head, estimated to be 2,000 to 2,500 years old, depicts warriors on boats and figurative signs. Society became more hierarchical, more conscious of status, and developed three clear categories: important leaders, freemen, and slaves. *Ikat-*

making (weaving), which has great symbolic significance in Maluku, probably developed at about this time.[6]

Austronesian migrations continued moving east, into huge Cenderawasih (Tjenderawasih) Gulf 4,000 years ago, skirting along New Guinea's north coast but never penetrating far inland, and reaching the Bismarck Archipelago around 3,500 years ago. Austronesian settlement on the New Guinea mainland was quite marginal, probably because of the prior development of agriculture and arboriculture, and the already substantial inland population, which left the Austronesian migrants no real incentive to expand into the landmass. Rather, they skirted along the coasts, establishing a few pockets of settlement but never making much impact. Only two Lapita sherds have been found on the New Guinea mainland, one at Aitape on the north coast and one on a neighboring island.[7]

There are now more than 300 Oceanic Austronesian interrelated languages, two-thirds of which are found in the extreme east of the New Guinea mainland and in Island Melanesia.[8] The Central Austronesian languages, which include those of the Lesser Sundas and Maluku (except for Halmahera), spread into west New Guinea as far as the Mamberamo River east of Cenderawasih Gulf. The Austronesian languages of Halmahera and New Guinea west of the Mamberamo are classified as Eastern Austronesian. Oceanic Austronesian languages begin in east New Guinea, reaching down through the Solomons and Vanuatu, out into the Pacific to Polynesia, as far as New Zealand and Rapanui (Easter) Island. Austronesian languages in northeast New Guinea probably originated in the Bismarck Archipelago around Vitiaz Strait, thought to be the first major stopover in the west-east migration. Austronesians sailing small craft caught by southeasterly winds would have been blown along the central north coast, which, along with serendipity, may explain why the earliest evidence of Austronesian settlement in east New Guinea is in the inner curve of the Bismarck Archipelago. These islands caught them like a ball in a baseball catcher's glove, halting the easterly journeys. Back migrations followed later along the central north coast of New Guinea.

Most linguists accept the "Oceanic hypothesis," that all the Austronesian languages in Oceania east of a line drawn north/south through the western Pacific are descended from a single proto-language, designated as Proto-Oceanic. The line cuts through Micronesia between the Mariana Islands and Palau, and through New Guinea at 138° east longitude (just west of Jayapura). The New Guinea mainland has two Austronesian-speaking subgroups: those around south Halmahera and Cenderawasih Gulf, and the Oceanic group further east. Proto-Oceanic is subdivided into Proto-Admiralty, Western Oceanic, and Central/Eastern Oceanic. Western Oceanic is further divided into three groups: Meso-Melanesian, around New Britain and New Ireland; the Papuan Tip, in the archipelagos directly off the tail of New Guinea and around the southeast coast; and the North New Guinea linkage, around Vitiaz Strait and Huon Gulf, with possible connections west as far as Sarmi and Jayapura. Linguists Lynch, Ross, and Crowley define a clear center for each group: for Meso-Melanesian this is around the Willaumez Peninsula on New Britain, and for the North New Guinea subgroup the center is around Vitiaz Strait.

The third center is the Papuan Tip, which they suggest had a period of shared history with the North New Guinea linkages, inferring that the first Papuan Tip speakers moved southeastwards down the New Guinea coast from Huon Gulf.[9]

Although trade networks already existed, the Lapita people seem to have extended them considerably. Obsidian mined at Talasea, on New Britain's Willaumez Peninsula, was carried as far as Fiji in the south and Sabah in Borneo in the west. Obsidian from Fergusson Island is present in a Lapita site in the Reef/Santa Cruz Islands, and obsidian from Lou Island in the Admiralties found its way as far south as present-day Vanuatu.[10] Their pottery-making, stone and shell adze use, and quite different economy based on agriculture marks them as distinct from the peoples already living in Island Southeast Asia, New Guinea, and Island Melanesia. The first settlements to reach out into Remote Oceania were connected to this culture. Lapita sites begin in the northwest in the Admiralties and New Britain, arch over 4,000 kilometers through the main central and southern Melanesian archipelagos, and bridge the accepted ethnographic divide between Melanesia and Polynesia, to Tonga and Samoa in the southeast. The earliest Lapita sites in the Bismarck Archipelago, from Arawe Islands off southwest New Britain, date from about 3,300 years ago. Similar sites in the Vitiaz Strait and just west of the Willaumez Peninsula date from around 2,700 years ago. The earliest sites in Tonga and Samoa have the same age range, suggesting an exceptionally fast dispersal of people across more than 4,000 kilometers in 300 to 500 years, or some fifteen to twenty-five human generations.[11]

Research during the 1990s suggested that ground-stone, shell-tool, ceramic, horticultural and efficient sailing technologies had emerged in Melanesia well before the Lapita peoples arrived. There is no evidence of the Lapita culture complex west of Manus in the Admiralty Group, which may mean that the Bismarck Archipelago is its real "homeland." If we couple this with the evidence of New Britain obsidian being imported into Borneo 2,000 years ago, it suggests that we should be thinking of a two-way movement between west and east. There is of course the possibility that Austronesian-speakers actually began to enter Melanesia much earlier than our physical proof—the appearance of Lapita pottery and associated items—indicates. However, this still would not imply that the resident populations did not have access to the above technologies, which may only have been modified when they came in contact with Lapita peoples.

Several questions are relevant to this argument. Why do we find a word for sugarcane in Proto-Austronesian, the ancestral language reconstructed by linguists and spoken in Fujian (coastal China) and Taiwan 6,000 years ago, when botanical evidence suggests that the plant was first domesticated in western Melanesia? Are there Austronesian languages in Melanesia that predate the Lapita migrations? Some archaeologists suggest that there may have been a "voyaging corridor of trade" which extended from western Melanesia to eastern Indonesia, perhaps linked to Taiwan and China, well before the first evidence of Lapita pottery.[12]

Do we need Lapita migrations out of Southeast Asia to explain technological developments in Melanesia several thousand years ago? Recent evidence from the Bismarck

Archipelago increasingly points to local adaptations and long developmental sequences. Yet the foundations of the Polynesian languages are linked to migrants connected to the Lapita culture complex, and ultimately with Southeast Asia. There has been considerable debate as to whether the Lapita style of pottery arrived in Melanesia with immigrant Austronesians, or rather evolved in the Bismarck Archipelago, based on the pottery styles of pre-Austronesian peoples. Although the extent of local Bismarck influence on what is recognized as the Lapita culture complex is much disputed, the truth is probably that the development of the Lapita culture complex involved early interaction between immigrant Austronesians and already established inhabitants of the islands, and an incorporation of earlier traditions. The Bismarck Archipelago and the north and central Solomon Islands had already been settled for around 20,000 to 30,000 years when the new wave of migrants arrived. Obsidian was already being traded over long distances, edge-ground tools were in use, and shell was being worked into ornaments and fish-hooks. Given the antiquity of agricultural systems, tree-cropping, and long-distance inter-island exchange in New Guinea and northern Melanesia, the new arrivals probably interacted with the highly diverse regional cultures and languages of the longer-established inhabitants.[13] However, this interaction is unlikely to have been on equal terms, given the social, economic, and political dynamics of Austronesian/Lapita movement south out of the Bismarck Archipelago.

Since the archaeological Lapita Homeland Project of the 1980s, the importance of the Bismarck Archipelago to the Lapita culture complex has been unassailable. Archaeologists disparage the "express train theory" which suggests that Austronesian-Lapita migrants sailed quickly around New Guinea on an Austronesian express canoe that did not stop at local stations, arriving in the unsettled southern Pacific Islands with their Southeast Asian-ness still intact.[14] The evidence now points to their loitering for a long period in the Bismarck Archipelago, certainly long enough to absorb local artifact and cultural traditions. Several centuries' residence on New Guinea and in northern Melanesia before the migrations continued south cannot be ignored. As Jim Allen nicely states:

> Many Melanesian Lapita sites continued in use for many centuries and show developmental sequences, particularly in ceramics. In addition, there are now scores of Lapita sites known throughout thousands of kilometers of the Melanesian island chain. Thus the demographics (specifically unknown but generally imaginable) needed to sustain a single Lapita migration, which also left in its wake many culturally distinct and enduring villages, alone indicate the improbability that Southeast Asian people arrived in what is now Western Polynesia unchanged linguistically, genetically or culturally. The notion that Lapita colonists remained separate from incumbent Melanesian populations as they progressed eastwards is also denied by Lapita sites in Melanesia, which show evidence of interaction in the presence and transportation of local raw materials such as obsidian.[15]

How many times major migrations occurred, moving south out of the Bismarcks, or north into Micronesia, is also unclear. Based on archaeological evidence relating to incised and applied relief pottery styles found in the Solomon Islands, Vanuatu, New Caledonia, and Fiji, there is the possibility that there was a second southward movement of people out of the Bismarck area. Or, alternatively, says Spriggs, "the changes may represent the continuation of the Lapita exchange network in attenuated form, with cultures in contact producing changes in pottery style 'in sync.'"[16] Perhaps languages can provide a more substantial clue. Lynch, Ross, and Crowley divide the Central/Eastern Oceanic language subgrouping into five families. The Southeast Solomon family begins south of Santa Isabel and extends down to Sa'a/Ulawa/Ugi, at which point they split, southward to Makira and northward through Malaita. Utupua and Vanikoro is the smallest subgroup, consisting of the six languages spoken in the Santa Cruz Group. Below this is Southern Oceanic, which includes the languages of Vanuatu and New Caledonia. Then, extending west to Rapanui Island and Hawai'i, comes the Central Pacific linkage, including the Fijian dialect network, that of Rotuma, and the geographically widespread Polynesian family. The last of the five is Micronesian, the family of languages spreading from Nauru, Kiribati, and north through the Marshall and Caroline Groups. Several paths north through either Malaita, northern Vanuatu, or Manus have been suggested, with Lynch, Ross, and Crowley favoring northern Vanuatu.

One last question: did proto-Melanesian Lapita migrants visit Australia? It is almost insulting to suggest that peoples capable of sailing out of Asia, west to Madagascar, east to Hawai'i and Rapanui Island, and south to New Zealand, somehow missed knowing that New Guinea was a large island separated by a narrow strait from a large southern land. Tim Flannery argues that there is evidence which links them to northern Australia.[17] There may also be links between Non-Austronesian languages in the west and those along New Guinea's south coast. In the 1980s, C. L. Voorhoeve put forward a hypothesis of contact between Non-Austronesian north Halmahera in the Maluku Islands and the central coast of southeast New Guinea, connecting Halmahera, the Aru Islands, the Kiwai at the mouth of the Fly River, and the Elema (Kerema or Toaripi) further east in the Gulf of Papua. Voorhoeve interpreted these links as suggesting that Non-Austronesian traders were also moving along the predominantly Austronesian long-distance trade routes.[18] Perhaps Austronesians also managed to reach northern Australia, traveling through Torres Strait and south along the east coast, or they may have come down outside the Great Barrier Reef, finding their way through passages to the coast. If they did, they left no linguistic evidence: the Aru Islands Austronesian languages are not directly related to those of New Guinea's southeast coast, which are linked to the migration along the north coast. Austronesians could also have sailed west from southern Melanesia or Polynesia, landing on the Australian coasts south of the reefs. There is no proof, but the likelihood of visits somewhere on the Australian coast seems very high.

M. D. Ross suggests that along the New Guinea north coast the closest non-Oceanic relatives of the Western Melanesian Oceanic languages (spread from Sarmi on the north coast, through the Bismarck Archipelago and south to the Louisiades and Santa Isabel) are those around Cenderawasih Gulf and south Halmahera. Ross believes that Vitiaz Strait is the homeland of the Western Melanesian Oceanic languages, rather than, as others have suggested, further west around Sarmi and Humboldt Bay. The linking path between Cenderawasih Gulf and Vitiaz Strait, perhaps by way of small settlements along the coast or on offshore islands, may have been obliterated from the archaeological record.[19] Austronesian languages in the Louisiades and around the southeastern coast of New Guinea seem to have developed out of migrations originating from the Bismarck Archipelago. Archaeological evidence offers some support for this hypothesis, as it suggests that around 2,000 years ago a number of settled communities appeared along the southeast coast, all involved in long-distance trading. Based on evidence from ceramic and adze styles, as well as maritime technology, it is thought that they were closely related to the Lapita culture complex migrants of the western Pacific.[20]

There has also been back-migration from earlier Austronesian movements as far south as present-day Vanuatu. Independent Austronesian migration, not closely associated with the New Guinea migrations, proceeded direct to central Vanuatu. By 4,000 years ago, they had expanded through most of Vanuatu, before moving back north into the Solomon Islands, finally settling in New Britain and on parts of the south coast of New Guinea.[21] The modern Solomon Islands nation (the archipelago minus Bougainville and Buka, which are now within Papua New Guinea) has more than sixty distinct languages, the majority of which belong to the Austronesian family. When these Austronesian migrants reached the Solomons, around 4,000 years ago, they would have found earlier settlers who spoke Non-Austronesian languages. The East Papua Phylum includes languages on Vella Lavella, Rendova, and New Georgia in the western Solomon Islands, and Savo and the Santa Cruz Group to the south. As with New Guinea, in the Solomon Islands there is no correlation between the geographic location, physical appearance, and languages of ethnolinguistic groups.[22]

Interdisciplinary evidence, relating to blood types, material culture items, the introduction of pigs, and deliberate distribution of food crops, strengthens the linguistic scenario of possible past ethnolinguistic group migrations. But there are pitfalls to attempting to simplify the complexity of the process. Three final examples of the linguistic intricacies involved will suffice. There is a great deal of evidence of Austronesian and Non-Austronesian transfers of loanwords and structural features in the New Guinea area. In recent millennia, when the Trans-New Guinea Phylum speakers moved into the Markham Valley on New Guinea's north-central coast, they met up with newly arrived Austronesian speakers.[23] This conjunction caused mingling of Austronesian loanwords in Trans-New Guinea Phylum languages and also stimulated extensive further migrations, including one back to the west as far as Timor. As well, M. D. Ross has shown that the Lamasong and Madak Austronesian language-speakers of New Ireland once spoke a Non-Austronesian language, and though they abandoned that language, they have assimilated elements of it of into their present languages.[24] Lastly, recent small migrations, like those from the D'Entrecasteaux Archipelago to west New Britain in the nineteenth century, have thoroughly shuffled prior language communities.[25] Like so many aspects of New Guinea and Melanesia, trying to simplify any description of 40,000 years of human migration, trade, and habitation is fraught with difficulties.[26]

Cultural Spheres

Although the region's linguistic complexity is awesome, four mitigating factors need to be stressed. First, New Guinea and adjacent islands have seen constant change over tens of thousands of years as different language groups replaced each other, intermingled, or engaged in regular contact, and because of this, Melanesia's small-scale societies possessed cultural mechanisms that enabled them to cope with change and diversity. They were capable of adjusting religious rules to enable movement away from ancestral shrines and heartlands, allowing them to migrate and live among different peoples.[27] Second, as a result of the small size of most ethnolinguistic groups, and their great diversity, most people in New Guinea speak three or four languages that they use in different circumstances, and neighboring languages are linked by loanwords. In this way, Austronesian and Non-Austronesian languages were interrelated. This makes the diversity more manageable, but a third point—that only a few languages were used as lingua franca—made intergroup communication even easier. Before the introduction of several modern lingua franca,[28] most intergroup and interregional communications were accomplished by individual cross-linkages, and in extreme cases people communicated using sign languages.[29] Fourth, establishing firm boundaries between social, linguistic, or ethnic groups is always difficult, particularly when the traffic across boundaries is constant and large-scale. Rather than 1,000 distinct groups, New Guinea is best conceived as divided into a few large cultural spheres.

Various attempts have been made to classify Melanesians into large subgroupings on the basis of, for instance, languages, exchange cycles, or patterns of leadership. By far the most straightforward has been the "cultural sphere" concept which divides New Guinea into a series of lowland, mid-altitude, and Highland spheres, separated by frontiers rather than hard boundaries, each with core and fringe areas, based on human population density and distance from centers. David Hyndman and George Morren Jr. argue that the "culture-area is an obsolete concept" which fails to "denote adequately the dynamic relationships of New Guinea culture history and demographic and environmental change":[30] "Spheres have frontiers rather than boundaries. Frontiers describe the zones in which spheres meet and compete or, through occupation, reduce uncontested margins. Within a sphere, contiguous segments are linked or separated (as the case may be) by marriage, mobility, migration, trade, exchange, alliance, warfare, ideological differences and similarities, co-operative demonstrations, competition and conflict. Changes at the center, particularly demographic ones, ramify to the periphery. . . . On the island of New Guinea, spheres sometimes correspond to culture areas identified on ethnolinguistic grounds, but this is generally difficult to demonstrate in Melanesia where the location and territorial integrity of indigenous peoples had been disrupted by the invasion of hierarchically organized states."[31]

The core lowland spheres, some incorporating contiguous islands, cover an environmentally diverse zone from the coast to foothills up to 500 meters, and comprise approximately 30 percent of the island. In west New Guinea, the core lowland spheres are the central Bird's Head, the Raja Empat Group and Onin Peninsula, Cenderawasih Gulf, the lower Baliem River on the southwest coast, Humboldt Bay and the Lake Sentani area, and the upper Digul River west of the Indonesia-Papua New Guinea border.[32] In east New Guinea the core lowland spheres are the Middle Sepik, Huon Peninsula, Orokaiva, and the southeast coast. Hyndman and Morren suggest that the average population density in the lowlands was sixteen to thirty persons per square kilometer, although a few areas (Middle Sepik, Arapesh, Iatmul, Abelam, and Wosera) carried up to 200 people per square kilometer.[33] Subsistence in lowland areas was based on sago production, with taro as the main root crop, supplemented by banana and yam in the dry season. Areas lacking substantial sago stands coincided with areas of low population such as the Mamberamo River basin in the northwestern lowlands, and the large area north of the Aramia River in the southern lowlands. Key lowland spheres were also centers for ritual and trade, and depended on specialized production and exchange.

The Highlands denotes the valleys of the central cordillera, especially areas above 1,500 meters, and is divided into three spheres: the western sphere in Indonesia's Papua Province, centered on the Baliem (Grand) Valley and the Paniai Lakes; the central sphere focused on the Sepik source basin and the Sibil Valley; and the eastern sphere, consisting of eight huge valleys from the Tari-Koroba to the Airono-Aiyura. These central valleys carry high population densities, often more than 100 persons domiciled per square kilometer. Over the last several thousand years, Highlanders have used their fertile valleys to conduct the most intensive agriculture and pig breeding in New Guinea, and have deployed the bounty toward developing complex festivals and exchanges. Within the last 300–400 years, the introduction of sweet potato has allowed cultivation at much higher elevation than was possible with taro (which grows best below 1,500 meters), leading to dramatic population increases. Sweet potato has multiple advantages over taro: It provides higher caloric yields per acre, which assisted growth of communities, and it provides better pig food which allowed expanded use of the animals for food, ceremonies, and exchange. Sweet potato can be replanted repeatedly before a swidden has to be fallowed, and production is less labor-intensive because the more complete ground cover reduces the need for weeding. The plant is also less susceptible to blights and other diseases, is more frost resistant, and can be stored for longer periods. The mid-altitude fringe occupies 40 percent of New Guinea, forming a distinct ecological zone between 500 and 1,500 meters that is rich with food resources. Population densities here range from eight to sixteen persons per square kilometer.[34]

There are several major interlocking core and fringe lowland spheres along the southern coast of Indonesian's Papua Province and Papua New Guinea. Furthest west are the peoples of the Bird's Head, and the Asmat centered on the Baliem River, both with substantial populations. Much less populous are the alluvial flatland territories of the Marindanim, a lowland fringe cultural sphere spread from the eastern side of Dolak Island down to the Indonesia-Papua New Guinea border and the Trans-Fly area. The neighboring sphere to the east is the Trans-Fly, which extends from west of the border along to the Fly River, down into Torres Strait, and east to the Fly River delta. The next coastal sphere includes the Kiwai, Purari, and Elema peoples in the immense delta lowlands of the Gulf of Papua.[35] To the east are linguistically distinct ethnolinguistic groups of Austronesian origin, centered on the Motu around Port Moresby: the Roro and Mekeo, then the Western and Eastern Motu. The Motu were quite central to trade in the southeast. They were connected to their Highlands-fringe neighbors the Koitabu and Koiari, and in recent centuries they traded annually with the Elema to supplement their food supplies in the dry season. They also traded east to the Hula-Aroma area. Next came the southeast sphere, where the Mailu operated a long-distance trade network along the tip of eastern New Guinea, which connected with the Louisiade Archipelago, the D'Entrecasteaux Group, and the Trobriands to the north. The famous *kula* trade system dominated exchange in the southeastern archipelagos.[36]

Trade Systems

These cultural spheres continue around the northeast coast, where, once more, linking trade exchanges dominated. The importance of trade systems, the invisible web that links together all New Guineans, was raised in the Introduction. Similar cultural spheres and trade systems to those in the south existed along the north coast. Research in the Vitiaz Strait between New Britain and New Guinea indicates that after an initial Lapita presence in the area, 2,700 to 3,300 years ago, there was probably a break in the production of pottery and trade for around 1,000 years, until post-Lapita trade networks began to operate. Ian Lilley's research suggests that Vitiaz post-Lapita ceramic-production resumed about 1,500 to 1,600 years ago, and that about 1,000 years ago there was an expansion in pottery manufacture and trade both to the east and west of the Strait: "Austronesian-speakers dispersing from a homeland in the Vitiaz region leapfrogged the area between the Huon Peninsula and Karkar Islands to settle on the Sepik coast or adjacent islands such as Manam. Within the next couple of centuries, the area they had initially avoided was then filled-in by pottery-manufacturing speakers of Austronesian languages related to theirs."[37]

There are three distinctive pottery wares. There is also evidence of movement of New Guinea mainland pottery and New Britain obsidian across the Strait. Lilley suggests that at the time of first European contact, a super-trade system encompassed the entire seaboard of northeastern New Guinea, stretching from Astrolabe Bay (present-day Madang) around the Huon Peninsula to the Huon Gulf and reaching out to west New Britain. This super-system was composed of three systems which, even though each group probably saw themselves as the most important trading center, actually overlapped and interconnected. The Bilbil system, centered on Astrolabe Bay, reached west to Karkar Island. The Siassi system operated around Umboi Island between Vitiaz and Dampier Straits, linking the Huon Peninsula to west New Britain. The third system, operated by the Tami, was concentrated around Huon Gulf.[38] They made regular voyages in large twin-masted canoes, all of similar design, and thereby linked several hundred communities. The Tami did not trade directly with the Bilbil, but through intermediaries among the Siassi their wares were exchanged along the Rai Coast, particularly pig-tusk and snail-shell ornaments, coconut shell products, and hourglass-shaped *kundu* drums. In return, they received fish and garden products. The Bilbil made pots and canoes, trading them along the nearby coast and into the larger exchange network. They traded out to Karkar Island to their northwest, but had no direct contact with the Siassi to the east, although the Siassi trade area overlapped with that of the Bilbil along some 160 kilometers of the Rai Coast. The Siassi environment provided little scope for agriculture, but the Islanders were expert craftsmen, fishermen, and sailors. They became consummate traders, connecting the resources of the mainland with those of New Britain. Using sailing canoes made of logs from Umboi Island, they carried red ochre and obsidian to New Guinea, and ferried clay pots, palm wood bows, and *bilums* (string bags) from the mainland to New Britain. They also transported highly valued wealth items such as dogs and pigs, dog-tooth ornaments, and curved boars' tusks. Trading cycles could entail multiple voyages and take years to complete, as Thomas Harding explains:

> A typical sequence might have begun with various low-value goods, some of which, like coconuts and pandanus mats, were produced locally, while others, such as red ochre and sago, were acquired in exchange with Umboi communities. The low-value goods—that is, goods low in value at their point of origin—were then converted into high-value items—clay pots, ornate wooden bowls, dogs, and ornaments of teeth and shell. Thus, mats were exchanged for pots on the New Guinea mainland, the pots being exchanged later on for pigs, for example, in New Britain. Bowls, pots, dogs, and ornaments were exchanged for pigs at various localities, and some additional pigs were received in payment for services as ceremonial dancers, services the Siassi performed at the invitation of prominent leaders of the port communities. Many of the incoming pigs were reserved for ceremonious distribution.[39]

Trade systems developed into an invisible network that bound together all peoples on New Guinea, and linked them to the surrounding archipelagos. The coastal networks linked all offshore islands through trade to the mainland, but the coast, with its maritime products, is just as firmly connected to the hinterland and the central mountains. Annual long-distance expeditions were planned for months, and relied on changing wind directions to drive the multi-hulled canoes back and forth along the coast, weighed down with pots, wooden plates, shields, and drums. Informal day-to-day trade was continuous. On the Rai coast (around Madang), the inland Ngaing peoples brought bowls and bark cloth down to the coast, returning with fish, salt, dry coconuts, pots, and other valuables.

As long as 10,000 years ago, cowrie and other shell valuables were being traded 90 kilometers into the New Guinea Highlands, and flakes of obsidian reached the Highlands 5,000 years ago. Within the Highlands, by 1,500 to 2,500 years ago, there was organized quarrying and intra-Highlands trade of valuable stone axes. Goods moved across the northern coastal ranges as well as along the coast. Products from Huon Gulf and the Markham Valley entered the Siassi trade system across the Finisterre Range, just as goods from the Highlands entered the Tami and Bilbil systems via the Markham, Ramu, and Gogol Rivers.[40] Evidence suggests an intensification of these elaborate trading systems over the last 1,000 to 2,000 years.

On current evidence, pearlshells seem to have been traded into the central Highlands for at least 3,000 years. Initially, only slivers of shell were used as nose and ear pendants. The more recent trade in shells ground into crescent-shape probably dates back a mere two hundred years on the southern Highlands fringe and appeared in the central Highlands only in the final decades of the nineteenth century. This may have had as much to do with European influence in Torres Strait as with any fully indigenous process. When Europeans first entered the central Highlands in the 1920s and 1930s, pearlshell was present only in small quantities. Even broken pieces were treasured. But the Europeans flew in large quantities of pearlshells and cowries to pay Highland laborers, and this lead to tremendous inflation in the shells as a medium of exchange. It also caused a reversal of established trade hierarchies since those who had once received shells from peoples closer to the coast now became shell suppliers to those same peoples, who were now farther away from the new, European source of shells.[41] Although no longer a major item of exchange in the Highlands (overtaken during recent decades by cash, and consumer items such as beer and trucks), pearlshells in some areas continue to be incorporated into ceremonial exchanges and used as ornamentation.

Through trade, coastal pot-makers supplemented their dry season food resources and acquired valuables that could not be produced locally. The Bilbil Islanders traded their pots for root crops produced by local coastal people, and also exchanged them for valuables in the wider super-system around to the Huon Gulf. They formed intricate inheritable "brother" relations with their trading partners from hundreds of kilometers away. Trade of all types helped construct the social infrastructure which matured in New Guinea over the last one or two thousand years. Peter Lawrence's description of the Bilbil trading system of the Rai coast could equally be applied to the *kula* of the Massim, or the *hiri* trade along the coast of southeast New Guinea: "For the formal trade, the Madang groups assembled canoes, which they loaded with pots and valuables. They made for the Rai Coast, putting in at all villages from Singor to somewhere east of Wab. When the fleet was known to be at sea, Sengam, Gira, and Som prepared to receive it. They got any additional bowls or bark cloth they needed from their Ngaing partners. When the canoes reached each port, hosts and guests danced in each others' honor and exchanged wares. The visitors were entertained with feasts. In these formal exchanges, Rai Coast seaboard and Madang island groups took the lead. They tended to patronize the inland peoples, who were not expected to participate, although they were always free to do so."[42]

Thomas Harding, who studied the Siassi system in the 1960s, provided the following vivid picture of the way trade was the fabric that bound together New Guinea's small-scale societies in any one region, always overlapping with neighboring regions:

> Connected to the maritime trading centres by overseas trade routes were dozens of coastal villages, the ports of the canoe traders. The coastal ports, in turn, were linked to the communities of the interior through direct relations with one or more groups of hinterland middlemen. In some areas middlemen were absent, and coastal peoples dealt directly with inland villages.
>
> A port community, with its hinterland, formed a local trading sphere. The people of the ports thought of their hinterlands less in terms of bounded territories than in terms of proprietary interests in economic relations with a number of interior communities. The numerous local trading spheres making up the larger system varied in size and population (although averaging a few thousand villagers), and they varied also with regard to items traded and the urgency of exchange (e.g., some coastal ports depended on the interior for imports of food).[43]

Along these coastal trade routes, a pattern of fortified hilltop villages and trade links was obvious when Europeans first passed by: the fortified villages of Vitiaz Strait and west New Britain probably have around 1,000 years of continuity. At Talasea on New Britain's Willaumez Peninsula, the source of valuable obsidian, the pattern of fortification goes back 2,000 years.[44]

In New Guinea and wider Melanesia, trade networks were at the very core of human existence. Trade languages developed over centuries, supplemented by extensive multilingualism. Tukang Besi (Malay for "blacksmith"), an Austronesian language from southwest Sulawesi, was spoken in pre-pidgin form around the Bird's Head, particularly at Fakfak. A simplified version of Onin, another Austronesian language, was widely used around the south of the Bird's Head, often understood passively, but not actively spoken. Similarly, Iha, an Austronesian language, was spoken throughout the far west of the Bird's Head. The language of Geser, a small trading island at the east of Seram, was understood from Banda to Fakfak and east to the Kei Islands. Various other languages, particularly Tor and Ekari (Wissel Lakes), were used as trading languages in pre-European times, as was Biak-Numfor. The latter was originally from Biak Island above Cenderawasih Gulf, and was probably the most widely understood in west New Guinea. There it was used as a lingua franca from the Mamberamo River in the east, around the huge gulf, and along the north coast of the Bird's Head out into the Raja Empat Islands. Four pre-European contact pidgin languages have been reported from east New Guinea: three

Mekeo trading languages (Imung, Ioi, and Maipa), and the Siassi trading language from the north coast. The languages of Koriki, Elema, and the Motu were also used for long-distance coastal trade along the south central coast. The situation along the south coast of eastern New Guinea was similar, with considerable interchange between Non-Austronesian and Austronesian languages. Motu, from around Port Moresby, was used along trade routes, although it seems to have grown in importance after the 1890s as a means of communicating with foreigners. At about the same time, Hiri Motu developed as a pidgin language, having been used initially by the British New Guinea police.[45]

The number of commodities available for exchange controlled the level of trade. The social structures of key trading communities were not markedly different from those of their neighbors, although some key trading communities were less able to sustain themselves through agricultural production. Often these became dependent on imported staple foods, particularly sago, which could easily be stored and carried over long distances. Middlemen who re-traded goods were essential to most networks, but nowhere did such middlemen emerge in distinctive occupational roles, which might have led to more hierarchical control, as occurred in Asia's agrarian and maritime economies.[46]

Trading systems generally exhibit variations over time. For example, material goods in demand from one area at a particular time might not remain in demand in another region. Cautiously, we can say that New Guineans have always lived in small social units based on kin and linguistic affiliations, linked by the invisible economy of trade. Trade here functioned as a regulator of society, in much the same way that organized government did in other parts of the world. We cannot claim that trading systems existing in recent centuries have direct prehistoric connections. Nor is there any suggestion that increasingly complex trading cycles are necessarily an early stage in the evolution of protostates. But in New Guinea long- and short-distance trade was the main link between communities, and New Guinea trade also had ritual and religious elements that linked the physical world to cosmology.

Connections with Asia's Metal-Using Cultures

At the same time as the Austronesians were moving around New Guinea's coasts, another significant material culture change was taking place in the west. Based on limited but tantalizing evidence, we can hypothesize that the north coast of New Guinea was briefly drawn into Bronze Age trading systems, when a small number of so-called Dongson artifacts were traded into New Guinea, possibly bartered for bird-of-paradise pelts and plumes. This may have occurred two thousand years before metal of Asian and European manufacture became ubiquitous all around New Guinea, in the late nineteenth century. Clear markers of the Early Metal Phase, in the form of pottery, and copper and bronze items at jar burial sites, exist in isolated areas of the Philippines and Indonesia, dated for one Philippine site at 2,300 years ago. Several authorities mention large Dongson bronze kettledrums and axes found in the Lesser Sunda Islands, the Maluku Islands, and west New Guinea, datable to about 2,000 years ago. Bronze axes and spearheads, together with other objects of Dongson type, have been located in surface finds on the Bird's Head Peninsula, but they cannot be dated accurately. Early glass beads and bracelets (possibly of Chinese origin) have been found at sites along New Guinea's north coast, of an age commensurate with Dongson influences.[47]

Maluku seems to have been part of an extensive Asiatic trade network dating back 2,500 years, reaching out from present-day south China via the Lesser Sunda Islands and the southern Philippines. Large bronze drums have been found at various locations in Maluku, including eight places in the east of the Group: on the islands of Leti, Luang, Tanimbar, and Kei, the latter two directly south of west New Guinea.[48] Limited Indonesian trade in New Guinea slaves, cloves, nutmegs, sandalwood, bird-of-paradise plumes, and obsidian was in progress 2,000 years ago, and this may have drawn bronze objects into the trading network as far east as the Admiralty Group. Exactly when the drums reached Maluku and west New Guinea is a matter of contention. They may have been traded into the region long after the demise of the Dongson culture in Vietnam, almost certainly by Indonesians, or they may even have been manufactured in Indonesia. Many bronze artifacts have been found halfway along the north coast around Lake Sentani, which was connected through trade links, via Humboldt Bay, to the Admiralty Group.[49] Lou Island in the Admiralties, at the northern end of the Bismarck Archipelago, has long been a base for production and trade of obsidian. This may explain a three-gram bronze/tin object found in 1985 on Lou Island in ash beds deposited 2,100 years ago. Allied to the Lou Island bronze/tin find are pieces of double-spouted pottery of the same age, almost identical to finds in Borneo.[50] All of New Guinea's bronze/tin objects are clearly imports from Island Southeast Asia as there is no evidence of any metal-working technology in New Guinea itself until much later, and then only in west New Guinea.

Since the Han Dynasty (206 B.C. to A.D. 221), the Chinese had encouraged the development of Central Asia overland trade routes carrying silks, furs, iron, lacquerware, bronze and glass objects, mirrors, and ceramics. The port of Guangzhou (Canton), became an important commercial center. During the Sung Dynasty (A.D. 960–1279), disturbances brought migrants with knowledge of ceramic technology south to Guangzhou. With the disruption of overland routes through Central Asia, the southern Chinese ports achieved unprecedented importance, as vessels laden with ceramics and manufactured metal objects traveled along the Southeast Asian maritime paths.[51] The furthest eastern extreme of these trade routes was probably New Guinea.

The early slave, spice, bird-of-paradise, and sandalwood trades from this period included the Maluku Islands and presumably also the western end of New Guinea. There are also other links between Melanesia and Island Southeast Asia, which likewise indicate early but not yet fully understood connections. Motifs on shell and stone objects in southeast New Guinea, and on stone mortars and pestles in the central Highlands, indicate possible Asian Bronze Age influences. Betel nuts and pigs seem to have reached New Guinea from Southeast Asia about 5,000 years ago. The Southeast Asian back-strap loom is used to weave abaca fibers in parts of Micronesia, on some of Melanesia's outlying islands, and in the Santa Cruz Group.[52] As mentioned earlier, New Britain obsidian has been found as far west as two sites in Borneo. Pottery that appears to be related to that of the Early Metal Phase in Indonesia and the Philippines has been found at Collingwood Bay and the Trobriands, and burial jars in the Massim region (the islands off eastern New Guinea) may relate to the same ceramic complex. And, finally, the small piece of bronze/tin found on Lou Island in the Manus Group provides another tiny hint that metals were traded around east New Guinea.[53]

More than 2,000 years ago, people along the northern coast of New Guinea and east to the Bismarck, Trobriand, D'Entrecasteaux, and Louisiade Archipelagos, were on the edge of the Asian trading system, and therefore on the outermost periphery of the Euro-African-Asian world system. The extent of the early introduction of metals around the west coast of New Guinea, both through trade and primitive smelting, probably has been underestimated. Some of the supposed "stone age" people of west New Guinea were certainly using iron as long ago as the early seventeenth century, shaping the metal with Malay forges. These forges, used in the Philippines and Indonesia for the last 2,000 years, smelt copper, tin, and zinc, making bronze and brass as well as some limited working of gold and silver. They were also used to shape iron into agricultural and war implements, but they did not produce sufficient heat to cast the metal. Malay forges are worked by two wooden cylinders that are usually made from large bamboos approximately one meter high and fifteen centimeters wide. Each piston of these double-piston bellows has a nozzle that holds small pipes that are connected to the clay-made chamber where heating or forging takes place. To maintain the heat inside the chamber, air is pumped manually from the pistons, passing through the smaller pipe and increasing the temperature tremendously. Cast iron was being manufactured in China 2,700 years ago, in the Philippines 2,000 years ago, and in Borneo 1,400 years ago. Ian Hughes suggests that the Timorese may have been receiving enough metal tools, 2,000 to 3,000 years ago, to begin phasing out stone tools.[54]

Metal-working was introduced into west New Guinea by itinerant Malay boat crews. Metal forges were operating in 1606 at what seems to have been Triton Bay, when Prado and Torres found Chinese porcelain, small amounts of iron goods, and cane bellows with a nozzle of clay for working iron. Thirty years later, there is a record of west New Guinea coastal tribes using iron spear tips, indicating rudimentary iron-working.[55] In 1767, Philip Carteret found the people of Pegun Island, 190 kilometers off the Bird's Head, to be more fond of iron than any other Pacific people he had encountered.[56] When John Forrest visited Dorei in Cenderawasih Gulf in 1775, the use of iron tools was spreading along the eastern side of the huge gulf, and he observed that the trade was not sustained further along the northwest coast of New Guinea.[57] Dumont d'Urville, explorer and coiner of the term "Melanesia," found primitive forges operating at Dorei Bay in 1827, with stones, iron ballast, or a broken anchor used as an anvil. The specialist technology was known to only a few families, but was well established and had come from Gebe Island, between Halmahera and the Raja Empat Group.[58] They were manufacturing rings, bracelets, and ear ornaments from copper and silver obtained through trading. In addition to their traditional weapons, they used imported metal swords and chopping-knives, and manufactured iron heads for their arrows. Iron axes were in use to clear garden land and to make canoes.[59]

In 1850, Lieutenant G. F. De Bruijn Kops described the state of metal manufacture and use at Dorei Bay:

> They understand the art of smelting iron. In some houses I saw bars of iron, and smiths-bellows, as well as some parangs, klewangs, and points of fish spears, which they had made themselves, and which, however rude, appeared to be well fitted for use. They however give the preference to articles manufactured elsewhere and brought by vessels. The bellows is like that of natives elsewhere and consists of two hollow pieces of bambu with suckers of feathers . . .
>
> They are acquainted with the art of working in copper and silver, in which they manufacture their ear and other ornaments, bracelets, rings, &c. And give them many different shapes. The silver is derived from the Spanish dollars which they received from the French vessels *Astrolabe* and *Zelee* in exchange for bartered articles.
>
> The trade is small and consists principally in tripang, tortoiseshell, massooi bark and mother o' pearl, which they give in barter for lue cotton, sarongs and other cloths, copper-wire, knives, parangs, different kinds of iron-ware and colored glass beads, the large kind of which are in most demand. Each one trades for himself, and for that purpose they repair their prahus to islands a long way off even as far as Timor, from whence a parahu returned during our stay.[60]

It is not possible to say how much earlier this technology was available, but the evidence of metal use runs against the standard image of New Guineans as having pre-metal cultures.

Contemporary New Guinea Society

New Guinea's coastal people were usually maritime-focused, subsistence traders, sailors and navigators of renown. They used small and large single-hull river canoes, and single- and double-outrigger ocean-going sailing canoes, some of them multi-hulled and up to twenty meters in length. Coastal peoples, and those further inland, were also tropical agriculturalists, planters of yam, taro, sweet potato and banana. Domestic pigs were another essential food source and a valuable exchange item. New Guineans were bowmen of great skill, and also fought and hunted with spears, clubs, axes, and shell and bamboo knives. Over the last several hundred years—the limited period for which we have reliable information from outside observers and indigenous oral testimony—New Guineans have lived in upwards of 1,000 small-scale language-and-territory-based units with no overarching political unity, and political units ebbed and flowed over the centuries. Political boundaries sometimes exactly duplicated language and dialect areas, but in other cases political alliances joined contiguous language and dialect areas, or deadly enmities occurred between close neighboring villages speaking the same language. There were always cultural spheres that linked wider regions, as well as close relationships between descent and territory.

Melanesian leadership styles have often been contrasted unfavorably with the more formal hereditary chieftainships of Polynesia. But Melanesian forms of leadership are actually extremely diverse. In the Papua New Guinea Highlands the bigmen of the Mendi, the Melpa, the Mae-Enga, the Kyaka, and Baruya peoples prosper through exchange of material wealth which goes well beyond ceremonial exchanges such as the *tee* and *moka*, to exchange of women and the flow of bride wealth engendered. As Maurice Godelier suggests, one feature of these interior bigman societies is "the absence of male and female initiations and the presence of male cults of the spirits of fertility, wealth, and success in exchanges."[61] Other leadership systems operate quite differently, from the warrior *(mambri)* system of Biak, the clan-chief *(ondoafi)* system of the Humboldt Bay lowlands, to the *raja* system of the Fakfak area and the Raja Empat Islands adjoining west New Guinea, to the chiefly systems of the Trobriand Islands off east New Guinea, or the prominent chiefs and sorcerers of the Roro-Mekeo of the southern New Guinea coast. Jean Guiart's 1990s reassessment of land tenure and hierarchies in southern Melanesia suggested that the distinctions between Polynesia and Melanesia are more theoretical than real, and that our academic interpretations of Pacific rank, leadership, and land-owning have owed much to Western concepts. Guiart suggests that we must take into account personal names as signifiers of social status and affiliation to land, as well as the pragmatic flexibility in island life that subverts our best laid theories.[62]

Formal leaders are usually male, although the influence of women, particularly older women, was always strong in discussions and decision-making. Like concepts of leadership, gender can also be difficult to typify. Belief in the dominance and high status of men, in contrast to the submissive, lower status of women, is widespread in Melanesia, but gendered oppositions are permeable, not rigid. As Marilyn Strathern argues, personal relationships are composed through debts to others, both males and females. Gendering as "masculine" or "feminine" through social life is more significant than being "sexed" as male and female by virtue of biological anatomy. In Melanesia, gender is more than a language relationship with others. It extends to artifacts, events, and processes, which may also be gendered as masculine and feminine, as well as to same-sex and cross-sex relationships. Many communities do observe pollution taboos, and their women often live separately during menstruation and birth, and living quarters and family units do often operate through various degrees of separation of the sexes. Men usually do dominate public and political roles, but women also exercise influence, which they often exert through less-visible, private realms, by producing and providing food and wealth, and by bringing up children.[63]

If male leadership and gender differences are constant features of Melanesian society, so is movement. Over many thousands of years, ethnolinguistic groups have seeped along the coasts, between islands, and through inland valleys—movements not obvious to the casual observer, occurring as they do over generations and centuries. Some tribal groups have remained reasonably stable in one location for several hundred years, while others have been aggressive, expansionary, and highly mobile. Groups could become refugees when they fled seismic activity, droughts, or obstreperous neighbors. Villages moved site reasonably frequently, and territories altered in size. One striking example is the movement of Tolai people from central New Ireland to New Britain over several recent centuries, a migration which began after volcanic eruptions on the Gazelle Peninsula decimated the population there, clearing the way for Tolai colonization. Other recent migrations have occurred on the New Guinea mainland, such as population movements to higher altitudes in the Highlands consequent to the introduction of the sweet potato over the last four hundred years, or the movement of the Marind-anim out of southeast Dutch New Guinea into the Fly River delta area during the second half of the nineteenth century. Movement within territories was also common. Descent groups' oral traditions are full of tales of movements from site to site within their own terrains, motivated by population pressure, quarrels, wars, sorcery, and famine. Two-place residence was common, to facilitate the harvest of seasonal crops, the utilization of localized resources (such as the best stone for axes and spear points), or the exploitation of seasonal fishing grounds or tree crops. During a lifetime, individuals changed their primary dwelling on numerous occasions. In so doing, they constantly shifted gardens, and built a series of houses at the different sites.

The habitation of coastal and lowland New Guinea intensified during the last 3,000 to 4,000 years, most obviously over the last millennium. The consensus view among archaeologists is that the evolution of agricultural and trading systems over the last thousand years enabled Melanesian societies to develop more complex forms of organization. There is also an unwelcome association in this argument, a presumption that systems based on achieved status are simpler, an evolutionary stage of social organization which in mature form becomes hereditary. Part of the cultural baggage of this thinking is a racial hierarchy that placed Melanesians at a lower evolutionary point within a world scheme. Certainly, during pre-colonial and colonial contact between Europeans and Melanesians, European thinking was shaped by belief that the Pacific Island peoples were on the same rung on the evolutionary scale as Neolithic societies, just below Bronze Age societies, and many rungs below the civilizations of Europe and Asia. Even the argument that the Lapita culture complex was the real stimulus for extensive agriculture and trade networks has unwelcome connotations. Ian Lilley and others argue convincingly that complex organization arose in western Melanesia at around the same time as the dispersal of Austronesian-speaking peoples out of Asia. Austronesian-speakers in Melanesia, and those that moved onward to colonize Polynesia, may have further developed "a weakly stratified social order derived from western Melanesia before systematic changes there produced more egalitarian societies." Lilley postulates a "nascent stratification pivoted on canoe building and ownership, control of both voyaging per se and associated practical and ritual knowledge, and, through these things, control of trade. . ." The absence of social complexity can be seen as "the exploration of adaptive avenues other than general-evolution's one-way route leading from bands through chiefdoms to states."[64]

People joined together in gardening, fighting, fishing and hunting, water control, and building projects. Through trading, they reached out to surrounding communities, and dialect and language groups. Authority in Melanesia was very localized, although leaders in any area were linked by exchange relationships over long distances. Today, individual New Guinea communities continue to share complex histories relating to mobility, divisions and regrouping, alliances and wars. Regarding such histories, Binandere historian John Waiko suggests: "To clan members this is essential knowledge, for the behavior of people can be partly predicted through an awareness of past relationships. Those setting out on a journey or planning a feast carefully reassess all relevant associations, but even the most detailed knowledge does not bring security."[65] The details of one clan's "history of fusion, division, and travel can be fitted into a much broader pattern of movement and relocation within Binandere territory that can be traced over a distance of at least 130 kilometers."[66] The Binandere are like all New Guineans, in possessing an inner core of knowledge covering relationships and history, which spirals out through alliances fashioned through previous links of war, trade, and marriage links. Nowadays this knowledge includes relations of education, religion, business, and politics that connect people to each other, to their Province, and ultimately to modern nation-states.

Australia and Torres Strait

Finally, we need to address New Guineans' relationships to Australia. New Guinea was once the northern mountains of Sahul, and Australia's "Aborigines" (first inhabitants), were once the southern section of the same Sahul people. As with New Guinea, the first human settlement in northern Australia is confirmed as having occurred at least 40,000 years ago. Australia has a distinctive flora and fauna, much of it is closely related to that of New Guinea. The flora has three distinct components: the largest, distinctively Australian; a small cold-climate flora in the southeast and Tasmania, with connections to New Zealand; and a Malaysian-Melanesian flora which is limited to Queensland. North Queensland maintains many characteristics that relate more closely to New Guinea than to the rest of Australia. As Roger Green notes: "the moist, palaeo-tropical, coastal margin of north-eastern Queensland can be included in the Papuan sub-division of the Oriental Region, though the Australian element here is much stronger."[67] Australia's fauna is like an exaggerated form of that in New Guinea, except that it also included now-extinct giant marsupials that were present when humans first arrived. Early humans entering northern Australia would not have had to make any major cultural adaptations, but innovations certainly became necessary once they entered the drier central and colder southern regions.

From about the same time as Australia physically separated from New Guinea, 8,000 years ago, there is evidence of new and widespread stone technologies in Australia. This "small-tool tradition," with backed artifacts, has been dated to at least 8,000 or 9,000 years ago, with flaked adzes/chisels and hatchets, points, and backed blades appearing in widespread cultural assemblages all over mainland Australia during the following few thousand years.[68] These innovations, although not considered as a "package" (to use Green's phrase), begin to mark Australia's people as separate from those of New Guinea. A relationship of these technological changes to new migrations from Island Southeast Asia is often suggested, but remains unproved and unlikely. There must have been some new migrations to Australia around 3,000–4,000 years ago when the dingo (Australia's domesticated native dog) was introduced, either from southern mainland Asia or from Southeast Asia, and over recent centuries Makasan traders from Sulawesi made annual trading visits to northern Australia, some northern Aborigines returning with them. Torres Strait always remained a route from Melanesia into eastern Australia, directly from the north and from the west, with possible connections to Seram-Laut and southwest coastal New Guinea.[69]

Ten to twenty thousand years ago, when linguists suggest there was a great deal of migration through New Guinea and the islands, the same must have been true of the land now under the Arafura Sea, the Gulf of Carpentaria, and eastern Australia, out to what is now the Great Barrier Reef, as ethnolinguistic groups moved between what became New Guinea and Australia. Over a long period, however, northern Australians became quite distinct from their Melanesian neighbors. Australia's Aboriginal people obtained their foods and other necessities mainly by collecting and hunting, using spears and spear-throwers rather than bows and arrows. Like the Melanesians, they lived in small kin- and language-based units. Aborigines used watercraft on the rivers, creeks, and in coastal waters, but their canoes were smaller than those of Melanesians, mainly made from tree bark, and their voyages were far shorter. The continent is vast, and over tens of thousands of years Aborigines spread across it, some living in quite dry or cold regions in the south and center, the largest numbers remaining around the coast, with the heaviest concentrations of all in the southeast, particularly along the Murray River system and in the tropical north. The climate of northern Australia is affected by annual monsoons that necessitate large seasonal changes in lifestyles, although the temperature is never very cold.

The total eighteenth-century population of Australia and Tasmania is now usually estimated to have been in the vicinity of three-quarters of a million people. Linguists conclude that there were around 250 languages in 1788, almost all of which are genetically related and came from one common proto-Australian language. Eighty-five percent of the languages form a coherent group named Pama-Nyungan. The other fifteen percent, known as Non-Pama-Nyungan languages, spread across the north from the Kimberlys to the Gulf of Carpentaria. Highly conventionalized sign languages were also used, and word-tabooing was observed, along with separate sacred vocabularies.[70] Although there are physical similarities between peoples in the highlands of islands to the north (such as Timor) and northern Australians, there is no indication of links with other languages directly to the north across the Timor, Arafura, or Coral Seas, suggesting that the Australian languages have been separated for so long that all linguistic evidence of any putative relationship has eroded away.

There are several Aboriginal cultural spheres in northern Australia, neighboring New Guinea: the Kimberley in the northwest, bordered by the Fitzmaurice and Wagait areas, which extend into Arnhem Land; northeast Arnhem Land; the area on the west and south of the Gulf of Carpentaria; east and west Cape York; and the wet rainforest area below, along the Queensland coast down to the headwaters of the Burdekin and the Fitzroy Rivers over the ranges from Mackay. Although Melanesians and Australian Aborigines once shared the same landmass, they are not a continuous population and undoubtedly have different multiple origins out of Asia over tens of thousands of years. Only at two points was there any substantial connection with the outside world in modern times: the relatively recent Makasan connection with Arnhem Land and the Gulf of Carpentaria (described in the next chapter); and the permanent connection between Melanesia and Australia at Cape York through Torres Strait.

Jeremy Beckett aptly described the Torres Strait Islands as "stepping stones in a two-way genetic and cultural traffic."[71] For tens of thousands of years the land bridge between Australia and New Guinea was repeatedly inundated by water, reemerging when sea levels lowered. The first sea channels through Torres Strait were created between 8,500 and 6,500 years ago. The area that is now Torres Strait was once a vast area of swamp and seasonally waterlogged plains, dissected by sea channels. Today's islands are thought to have looked much the same for the last 4,000 to 5,000 years, and to have been inhabited for some thousands of years. The present Islanders, by their own traditions and linguistic and material culture evidence, came originally from New Guinea, probably at least 2,000 to 3,000 years ago.[72]

Torres Strait Islanders speak two unrelated languages. Meriam Mir, which belongs to the eastern Trans-Fly Phylum, is the language of eastern Torres Strait. Kala Lagaw Yo, formerly called Mabuiag (or Kalaw Kawaw Ya on Saibai Island), the language spoken in the western Torres Strait Islands, is Aboriginal Australian in origin but includes some Non-Austronesian elements connecting it to New Guinea. Although there are many vocabulary links between eastern and western languages, the lack of a shared language indicates the absence of recent sustained contact. Cape York's Uradhi languages, which stretch from the tip of the Cape south 160 kilometers to around Port Musgrave and Cape Grenville, are more closely related to the southern Paman subgroup than they are to Kala Lagaw Yo.[73]

Characteristics of the northern Melanesian culture reach down onto Cape York and along several hundred kilometers of the east Queensland coast. Culture-heroes straddle Cape York and the adjoining coast of New Guinea, and there are similarities between initiation ceremonies. Sleeping platforms, hollow communal smoking pipes, cylinder ear ornaments, and methods of preserving the dead all were still in use around the Archer River on Cape York in the 1920s and seem to have originated in New Guinea.[74] During the nineteenth century, single-outrigger canoes of New Guinea design were in use as far south as the Whitsunday and Cumberland Islands off Proserpine and Mackay.[75] Generally, however, modern northern Aborigines have had more in common with their southern kin than with New Guineans. While conditions for establishing tropical agriculture were auspicious in northern Australia, there is no evidence that cultivation ever occurred. The seeming advantages of adopting New Guinea technology were apparently not sufficient to justify an economic revolution in horticulture and material culture. Only on Cape York and in Torres Strait did Melanesia and Aboriginal Australia meet and meld, producing a smooth transition and interdependence in trade and ritual between north and south.

As Nicholas Thomas points out in *Colonialism's Culture*, European ideologies of conquest from the fifteenth to the eighteenth centuries were couched in terms of religion rather than race. Race and racism, earlier embedded in a narrative of natural history, did not become part of the driving engine of colonialism until the nineteenth century, when Europeans and Asians began substantial trade and colonization of Australia, New Guinea, and surrounding islands.[76] These outsiders had very limited knowledge of New Guinea, really only what they could experience, fleetingly, around the coast. Their attempts at explaining the immense cultural complexity, and their own preconceived ideas about race, resulted in various conflicting classifications of peoples in hierarchies based on race—often decided purely on the basis of skin color—rather than on cultural, linguistic, or genetic elements. This led to substantial misunderstandings of culture, territories, and concepts of power. The intruders from other parts of the world never comprehended the complex but limited cosmologies of the indigenous peoples. European and Asian concepts of productivity, race, class, gender, and religion, bolstered by their technical superiority, meant that they would soon collide with the established Melanesian cultural systems.

West New Guinea and the Malay World

Early Malay Archipelago Trade

Alfred Wallace was certain he had discovered an exact boundary between the Malay and Melanesian peoples, although the distinction was not quite as clear as he supposed. This chapter examines early encounters between west New Guinea and the outside world—the links with their neighbors in Island Southeast Asia, and the reaction of the "Harafora" (the "inlanders") or "Papua," the names which Malay visitors gave to New Guinea's indigenous peoples. Long-term commodity exchanges and ceremonial connections, particularly through the *sosolot* and *kain timur* trade complexes, linked west New Guinea to Maluku. Conflict and accommodation between indigenous and foreign trade is a continuing theme in this and the following chapters, which together deal with Malay and European incursions into New Guinea.

The Malay and Melanesian worlds blend together over several hundred kilometers of ocean and islands. The conceptual separation of the Pacific from Southeast Asian cultures and polities, particularly on the margins, owes far more to the European mania to classify and tidy than to absolute cultural or racial boundaries. The peoples of this island region have never been inhibited about exchanging commodities, genes, and ideas. If we consider their connections over tens of thousands of years, it is obvious that they were originally one population, divided by multiple overlapping migrations and complex intergroup exchanges. The northwest continental shelf of Sahul ended just beyond where the Bird's Head Peninsula is today, although some of the Australasian flora and fauna continue over into Maluku and Sulawesi. The original inhabitants of Timor and Maluku were closely related, physically and linguistically, to those of New Guinea. The west New Guinea coast is only 100 to 200 kilometers from neighboring lands to the west and south. The distance between the Bird's Head Peninsula, the bulbous western tip of the New Guinea mainland, and Halmahera (also called "Jailolo") in northern Maluku, or Seram in southern Maluku, is similar to that separating southern New Guinea from Cape York, Australia's northernmost point. Although the spread of the Maluku Archipelago does not offer such clear stepping-stones as the islands of Torres Strait, it does allow easy access from the west.

New Guinea is situated on the eastern edge of ancient Asian trade networks. Premod-

A careful examination convinced me that these people are radically distinct from all the Malay races. Their stature and their features, as well as their disposition and habits, are almost the same as those of the Papuans; their hair is semi-Papuan—neither straight, smooth, and glossy like all true Malays', nor so frizzly and woolly as the perfect Papuan type, but always crisp, waved, and rough, such as often occurs among the true Papuans, but never among the Malays. Their color alone is often exactly that of the Malay, or even lighter. . .
—Alfred Russel Wallace, Djilolo [Jailolo] village, Halmahera Island, 1858 (in Wallace 1869, 323).

ern maritime exchanges in Southeast Asia date back to the second century A.D., when merchants from the northern Malay Peninsula and the south coast of Vietnam began to participate in trade between India and China. Onwards from the second century, trade extended into the Java Sea and east to the outer islands, including Maluku. Srivijaya, a maritime state based in southern Sumatra, powerful from the seventh through to the early eleventh century, thriving on trade with China, controlled the Strait and Malay Peninsula, encompassing an area from the mouth of the Irrawaddy River to Borneo and Java. Chinese records from 724 and 872 A.D. mention that *"jěnggi"*[1] were sent by the King of Srivijaya to the Chinese imperial court. These were black slaves, possibly from New Guinea. Sung dynasty twelfth- and thirteenth-century maritime trade included items such as cloves and parrots from Maluku, obtained as re-exports from Java and Sumatra.[2]

Borobudur, the great Buddhist monument in Java, was constructed during the eighth century, and its reliefs contain depictions of fuzzy-haired men and women who may be from Maluku or New Guinea. Mid-fourteenth-century references to Kwanin and Seran, in Prapantja's epic poem Desawarnyana (Nāgarakrtāgama), suggest that the Java-based Majaphait empire made claims of suzerainty over Wanin (Onin Peninsula) and Seran (Seram, in the southeast of the Maluku archipelago, including the Kowiai region east of Onin in west New Guinea), or at the very least that west New Guinea was known to Majapahit scholars.[3]

After the decline of Srivijaya, two maritime commercial zones emerged. First, the Java Sea zone flourished in the eleventh and twelfth centuries, involving Chinese traders with links into the southern Philippines, north Borneo, and Maluku. A second zone, centered on the Bay of Bengal, reached out to India and into the islands of Southeast Asia.[4] The focus changed again at the end of the fourteenth century, when Melaka (Malacca) was established, aided to some degree by Chinese Ming dynasty patronage. Modern commerce began in 1511 when the Portuguese took control of Melaka and almost immediately established a spice-trade monopoly in Maluku.

The Spice Islands and Islam

Maluku—the Spice Islands—a few hundred kilometers off the western end of New Guinea, were on the outer edge of the Banda and Sulu Seas zone, and integral to outer Island Southeast Asian trade networks. There are no known written sources that provide direct information on Maluku until the fifteenth century, although other evidence suggests that a mutual barter trade was built up in the island group during the thousand or so years before reliable records begin. Before European intervention, the largely Austronesian people of Banda, Ambon, and northern Maluku lived for safety in fortified villages on precipitous heights, growing tubers and dry rice. But they also depended on imports of sago produced on Seram, the Kei and Aru Groups, and from Sula and Banggai Islands in the west, which they obtained through trading their cloves, nutmeg, and mace. Rice was also imported, usually from Javanese ports.

Ternate and Tidore were apparently uninhabited until around 1250, visited only by casual clove-gatherers.[5] People of Maluku traveled by fast-moving *kora-kora*, large canoe-like ships with raised ends, up to forty-five meters long, each propelled by oarsmen sitting on double outriggers. The Maluku Islands were not a political state, although people lived in larger social units than those of New Guinea. Leonard Andaya suggests that their unity came through common commitment to "legitimizing myths which established the physical and cosmic parameters of their world and the social orders within it."[6] The mythological center of Maluku was in the north, based at Ternate, Tidore, Bacan, and Jailolo village on Halmahera. These centers developed societies that were more monarchical than those in southern Maluku. Each leader was "basically the head of a clan whose influence did not extend far beyond the boundaries of the royal settlement."[7] The Ternate state came to control the coasts of Seram, Ambon, and north Sulawesi, while Tidore controlled the Raja Empat Islands, Seram-Laut, and neighboring areas on New Guinea.[8]

Specific islands became known for specialist items—Kei Islands for their boats, Kisar and Luang for fabrics, Banda and other islands for their nutmeg, the Aru Islands for birds-of-paradise, pearlshell, and pearls. Slaves were obtained and traded throughout Maluku and from New Guinea. Nico de Jong and Toos van Dijk describe the scene: "Inhabitants from the island of Kisar, for instance, traded very profitably in slaves and spices with the inhabitants of the surrounding islands. They also sailed to Timor and even to Malacca, where they traded their cargo for high profits. In 1643, when the sultan of the northern Moluccan island of Ternate heard about the great wealth of Kisar, he sent an invasion fleet to the islands to capture many precious treasures."[9]

Traders from southern Sulawesi shipped exotic products and Asian manufactured goods to eastern Maluku, to barter for spices, copra, marine products, slaves, and bird-of-paradise pelts.

The clove tree is native to only four Maluku islands: Ternate, Tidore, Makian, and Bacan.[10] The nutmeg tree, producing a nut and red filament mace comes from only one island, Banda.[11] There is evidence of Maluku cloves being used in Mesopotamia (modern Syria) 3,700 years ago, in the Chinese court 2,300 years ago, within the Roman Empire at least 1,900 years ago, and by the aristocracy of Europe a thousand years ago.[12] Quantities of Indian pottery have been found on Bali, dated at between 150 B.C. and A.D. 200, but no Indian goods have been found in Maluku."[13] Few Chinese traders entered Southeast Asia until the Sung Dynasty (A.D. 960–1279), as they concentrated their efforts on Manila in the central Philippines, and ports around Java and the Gulf of Thailand. Local boats of shallower draft brought the spices to these ports. Although some Chinese junks were sailing annually directly to Maluku in the mid-fourteenth century, the Chinese withdrew from competition with the Javanese in Maluku later in the century, satisfied to purchase their spices from the Chinese, Arab, and Javanese traders at Javanese ports, or in later centuries from Malacca.[14] There were two types of external trade out of Java: the India-China trade in spices and other luxury items, and an export-import trade in rice to

Maluku and other parts of the archipelago in exchange for spices and cloth. Java's success in the international spice trade was based on a mutual dependency between Java and the other islands. Java produced surplus rice, which enabled the inhabitants of the spice islands to concentrate on spice production rather than food production, buying Javanese rice with their cloves, nutmeg, and mace.[15] Arab traders called the islands *jazirat-al-mulk* (the land of many kings), which with Portuguese pronunciation became Moluco or Moluccas (Maluku), and was used to describe the entire "Spice Islands," from Ambon and Seram, to Ternate, Tidore, and Halmahera.[16] The main trade route to the Maluku Islands came via Banda, which acted as *entrepôt*, obtaining cloves from Ternate and Tidore and other small islands in the north. Banda also produced nutmeg and mace, to such an extent that the islands had to import food supplies, even rice and sago, the latter produced in Kei and Aru, the most eastern of the Malukan Islands, and on the west New Guinea mainland.

Exactly which Chinese and Malay Archipelago goods were passed on to west New Guinea via Maluku at this early stage is difficult to estimate. The eastern route to Nanhai (the South Seas) through the Philippines, to Borneo, Sulawesi, and Maluku, was known by early Chinese traders, and access became easier with improvements in navigation and shipbuilding during the Tang Dynasty (A.D. 618–907). By the tenth to twelfth centuries, the center of commerce in southern China was at Guangzhou (Canton), the distribution hub for ceramics, various textiles, and lacquerware which were traded for exotic goods from Nanhai, such as pearls, turtle-shells, the feathers and pelts of kingfishers, parrots, and birds-of-paradise, and scented woods and spices. By the fourteenth century, the seat of government had moved south to Hangzhou (in Zhejiang Province), and the center of trade shifted to the neighboring coastal provinces of Fujian and Guangzhou. Kilns proliferated, sustaining the expanding overseas market in mainland and Island Southeast Asia. One century later, porcelain from these kilns had been traded as far away as Egypt, the Middle East, and Japan, as well as into the central and southern Philippines. Thai pottery from kilns at Sawankhalok in the fourteenth and fifteenth centuries, as well as some Sukhotai pieces, reached the Philippines during the fifteenth and sixteenth centuries. Mindanao certainly had received Chinese porcelain by the fifteenth century.[17] Trailing south from Mindanao, and beyond Sarangani Island, a string of islets bridge the waters across to Sulawesi and Maluku. Southern Mindanao is only 600 kilometers away from northern Halmahera, which suggests the possibility that porcelain could have passed from this direction through Maluku to New Guinea, four hundred years ago. Old Chinese plates are still used in marriage exchanges in central Maluku, and even broken pieces are valued, calling to mind the fragments of pearlshell so much sought after in the New Guinea Highlands before great quantities of whole shells were introduced by Europeans.[18] Porcelain traded into west New Guinea was similarly prized.

While Austronesian migrants were moving around the New Guinea coast 5,000 to 2,000 years ago, the eastern boundary of the Asian commercial zone, operating through a rudimentary trading corridor, stretched along the north coast as far as the Bismarck

Archipelago. Non-Austronesian linguistic evidence appears to suggest long-distance trade links stretching from Halmahera along New Guinea's south coast to Torres Strait and the Trans-Fly.[19] The natural products of the eastern Malay Archipelago contrast with those of the west, and a substantial trade grew up based on the exchange of their respective products. The Raja Empat Islands, the Bird's Head, and Onin acted as a transitional region between Asia and Oceania, exploited for its human and natural resources. Malay Archipelago rulers had a prominent share in trade and shipping, or promoted their interests with the help of foreign traders. Earlier connections are really conjectural, but it is clear that since about the fourteenth century west New Guinea has been firmly linked into wider Malay Archipelago trade complexes, particularly through the introduction of metals and cloth, and the export of humans into slavery.

The heartland of early clove growing was located in Ternate and Tidore, and nearby Moti, Makian, and Bacan Islands. The people here share a common linguistic heritage with the inhabitants of the western end of New Guinea.[20] The native languages of Tidore and Ternate are from the West Papuan Phylum, although the people's cultural heritage is predominantly from western Indonesia. Languages, myths, migrations, trading, raiding, and kinship intertwine in the links between New Guinea and Maluku. Biak Island and Raja Empat myths give prominence to special connections with Maluku. In more recent times, possibly 500 years ago, the Biak Island culture-hero Gurabesi, of Austronesian ancestry, is said to have married a daughter of a ruler of Tidore, their lineage providing the first four rulers for the Raja Empat Islands.[21] Some of the Raja families, particularly on Misool, had special relationships with the people of Onin.[22] Warriors from Salawati and Misool Islands, and Fakfak on the Onin Peninsula, are known to have raided as far afield as Seram, Ambon, and Halmahera. Marriage links were still maintained in the nineteenth century: in 1825 one of the wives of the Raja of Kilwari on Seram-Laut was from Ati-Ati of the New Guinea mainland.[23]

The trade-based hierarchical society of Maluku was suited to conversion to Islam, a religion introduced into the archipelago along established trade routes which thrived in the cosmopolitan ports. Although there is evidence of Islam in Java since the eleventh century, the religion did not become a significant force in the Maluku Archipelago until the fifteenth century. Javanese inland states, particularly Majapahit, exported rice to eastern Indonesia, mainly to Maluku, in return for the spices for which the islands were famous. Merchants from the north coast of Java were among early converts to Islam because of their wider trade connections, and they dominated the trade. With their agents they carried Islam to the Maluku and the west New Guinea coast. The first important convert was probably a leading Tidore chief around the 1470s. Islamic trading influence seems to have reached Ternate earlier, but it made slow progress there until a Moslem trader influenced a local ruler, who then traveled to Java to convert in 1495 and married a Javanese noblewoman. Within the next twenty years there was also an Islamic ruler at Jailolo (Gilolo), a kingdom on the northern arm of Halmahera.

Ternate and Tidore are small neighboring volcanic islands in a zone of frequent earthquakes just off the west coast of Halmahera. It suited both sultanates, and later the Dutch, to exaggerate the extent of their territorial claims, particularly in New Guinea.[24] Ternate became the most powerful of the Malukan sultanates, with authority in the south over Ambon, Banda, Seram, Buhu, and the Lesser Sundas, and west as far as Buton, Pose, and the Toraja region of Sulawesi, as well as in northern Halmahera and the Uliassa Islands. Tidore rule was more limited, extending to southern Halmahera, eastern Seram, Seram-Laut, and the fringe of west New Guinea. Tidore claims of suzerainty over the Bird's Head of west New Guinea (for all practical purposes the largest island in the Tidore domain) predated their conversion to Islam, and the Malukan sultans controlled local leaders, who collected tribute for them. Nowhere is this more apparent than in the Raja Empat Islands off the western tip of New Guinea, where Rajas were resident on Misool, Salawati, Waigeo, and Batanta Islands. The Sultans of Bacan were subservient to Tidore, and they too had direct influence on the coastal fringe of the Bird's Head. A mixture of Malukan settlers and local converts lived in Islamic trading enclaves on the west New Guinea coast and adjacent islands.

Trade with West New Guinea

Perahu (sailing boats) from Makasar, Timor, Seram, Aru, Ambon, Ternate, and Tidore, and later Chinese junks, made regular trading trips to islands adjacent to the west and north New Guinea coast, and along the south coast as far as Triton (Etna) Bay.[25] The massoi-bark trade process was described to G. E. Rumphius in about 1685:

> The native traders live on the island Sacca iha and trade the *massooi*, which they obtain from natives of the mainland with the Ceram Lauters. The natives of the coast have to obtain the *massooi* from the natives who live in the mountains.
>
> The inhabitants of New Guinea are all tall, ugly and deformed, not so much as a result of nature, but mainly due to their own practices, such as cutting open their nostrils which are splintered with a bit of wood so that you can look right down their throat. . . . You can't trust them and they murder and steal, so that the Ceram Lauters are forced to trade with them from a distance.
>
> The natives place the *massooi* on the beach, the bundles placed on top of each other. The most courageous appear on the scene and with signs explain what they like to have in return for their *massooi*. The articles given in return for their goods consist of swords, hatchets to peel the *massooi*, poor quality rugs, sagobread, rice and black sugar, although rice and black sugar has to be given first before the natives are willing to get the *massooi* from the forest.[26]

Despite conforming to standard New Guinea trade-at-a-distance methods when dealing with foreigners, the Seramese were generally rapacious in their treatment of the New Guineans. They were also responsible for introducing Islam. A 1705 description, by Dutch Burgomaster Witsen, explains this as a ploy to exert control, although in fact he was describing the complexity of the *sosolot* exchange of women, which bound west New Guinea to Maluku: "The Ceramers are subjects, and likewise allies, of the Dutch Company, and for the most part expert sailors; and by them, and none else, is the coast of New Guinea visited. The inhabitants of New Guinea have for many years suffered from the treachery and murders of this people, who, not by force of arms but by cunning have subdued the Papoos [Papuans]. Under the cloak of friendship they take their women (in which they are not very choice) for wives, and the children thus born, being very carefully instructed in the Mahomedan faith, are easily able to control these simple inhabitants of the woods. By this connection the Ceramers, having gained the attachment of the women, always know how to escape the evil intentions which, for all that, the Papoos cannot restrain themselves from trying to put into practice against their visitors."[27]

One hundred and fifty years later, Alfred Wallace traveled from Makasar to the Kei and Aru Islands by *perahu*, a voyage similar to thousands that followed the same route over hundreds of years: "They leave Macassar in December or January at the beginning of the west monsoon, and return in July or August with the full strength of the east monsoon . . . It was a vessel of about seventy tons burther, and shaped something like a Chinese junk . . ." The crew consisted of about thirty men: the captain and his deputy, four "steersmen" who controlled the two large rudders, ten Chinese and Bugis ("slave debtors, bound over by the police magistrate to work for him"), and young men from Makasar and the adjacent coasts and islands.[28] Similar to other trade of this type in the Malay Archipelago, the New Guinea trade concentrated on high-value items. Traders came searching for a variety of exotic produce: slaves, cockatoos, lorikeets and crowned pigeons, bird-of-paradise plumes and other bird pelts and plumes, bêche-de-mer, pearls, turtle-shells, and ambergris. Ornamental goods, edible birds' nests, tobacco, long and round nutmegs, and massoi, pulasari, and rasamala fragrant barks were sought for sale as cosmetics and medicines in Java and Bali, and even as far away as India and China through the wider trade networks.[29] These items formed part of *sosolot* exchange and ritual networks that tied Seram and other Malukan islands to coastal west New Guinea, and coastal to inland areas. A huge variety of incoming trade items are mentioned in historical records. Chinese porcelain and glass earrings were being traded to the Schouten Islands above Cenderawasih Gulf in 1615.[30] These were joined by more exotic imports in later centuries, and in the 1820s the well-to-do on Satawait Island and in the Aru Islands were receiving elephant tusks obtained from Banda traders, who in turn purchased them from Melaka, Batavia (Jakarta), and Singapore. The tusks came from Siam, Cochin-China, and latterly from Africa. Along with brass gongs, large porcelain dishes, and Javanese wooden chests, the tusks were used as bride wealth payments and in other ceremonies.[31] Etchings published in the mid-nineteenth century clearly show the extensive use of imported cloth, weapons, and utensils.

Pamela Swadling's *Plumes from Paradise* provides an extensive account of the place of birds-of-paradise—the forty-five species of birds belonging to the family *Paradisaeidae*—

in the Asia-New Guinea trade system. Swadling postulates that the famous birds, which are found no further west than Maluku, were known in Asia 5,000 years ago, and that their trade may, perhaps, be responsible for the first introduction of pottery, betel nuts, and pigs on to the New Guinea mainland along long-distance trade routes. As agriculture intensified and proto-states developed in the foothills above major rivers on the Southeast Asian mainland, some 2,000 to 2,500 years ago, the birds and their plumes may well have become symbols of wealth. Swadling goes so far as to suggest that some of the designs on Dongson bronze kettledrums illustrate humans decorated with plumes. Her interpretation is that there was a decline in contacts between Southeast Asia and west New Guinea by about A.D. 250, and that over the next hundred years the plume trade was replaced by Asian interest in spices and sandalwood.

This plume trade probably never ceased, but rather simply contracted as plumes became restricted to use by great rulers such as those of Srivijaya and Majapahit, who also sent bird-of-paradise plumes as tribute to the Emperors of China. When the Portuguese and Spanish arrived early in the sixteenth century, they reported that bird-of-paradise pelts were being traded as far away as Persia and Turkey. In 1521, the ruler of Bacan Island presented Magellan's expedition with two preserved bird-of-paradise pelts, some slaves, and cloves as gifts for the Spanish Emperor. Charles V. Swadling's text is accompanied by photographs of treasured bird-of-paradise plumes being worn by the king and senior officials of Nepal in the first half of the twentieth century, illustrating one manner in which the plumes were used by Asian royalty.[32]

The use of New Guinea slaves within the Asian trade system, too, is traceable over hundreds of years. One consequence of New Guinea's position on the periphery of established trading centers in the Malay Archipelago was the development of trade calculated in terms of human lives. The Dutch Constitutional Law of 1818 forbad international commerce in slaves, and the internal Indies slave trade was outlawed in the 1860s. Nonetheless, there is evidence that Onin slaves continued to be exported to Bali and Java in the 1870s; and anthropologist Jelle Miedema reports that a slave trade was still operating in the interior of west New Guinea in the 1960s, when Papua Province was being incorporated into Indonesia.[33]

The full historic and geographic extent of east Indonesian trade with west New Guinea is difficult to estimate. Occasional exploratory voyages and trade connections occurred over the last millennium, in the south possibly as far east as Torres Strait and in the north at least as far east as Humboldt Bay, the Sepik coast, and the Hermit and Ninigo Islands. Regular Asian trade was reaching out to Maluku by the fourteenth century, intensifying onwards from the sixteenth and seventeenth centuries, at the same time as, but seemingly independent of, the first European settlements in the Maluku and other islands off west New Guinea. The ferocious Dutch quest for monopoly caused migrations out of eastern Indonesia into west New Guinea waters during the eighteenth century. Nineteenth-century accounts suggest that as the indigenous spice, slave, bêche-de-mer, bird-of-paradise, and pearlshell trades developed, there was an accompanying steady movement of Malay peoples to islands such as Timor, Seram, Misool, and Aru, which forced earlier Melanesian inhabitants further inland, to other islands, or onto the New Guinea mainland.[34] During the later decades of the nineteenth century, Malay traders were infiltrating the north New Guinea coast, east as far as the Huon Gulf, much to the consternation of German New Guinea officials who did not know how to control the influx.[35]

Although Maluku had a long history of trading spices to Java and Sumatra, often in the form of tribute to major states such as Srivijaya and Majaphait, it was cloves, nutmeg, and pepper exports that made the islands such a sought-after colonial prize. Until the eighteenth century, the European colonies in Island Southeast Asia were merely trading bases, competing with each other and equivalent indigenous trading states. But the arrival of Spanish, Portuguese, Dutch and English trading companies, and the colonial states that followed them, brought a major economic change, causing the Islamic trading states in the outer islands (such as Ternate and Tidore) to decline. European trading companies operated in much the same style as these Asian states until the Dutch established monopolies. Through a system of restricted cultivation, the Dutch Vereenigde Oostindische Compagnie (VOC, or East India Company) was able to dominate the north coast of Java toward the end of the seventeenth century, and soon after had established a ruthless monopoly over the Maluku spice trade.

West New Guinea and adjacent islands were linked to the Maluku commercial world. The Raja Empat Group was within the sphere of the Sultans of Tidore and Bacan, as were the coast and islands of Cenderawasih Gulf. Alfred Wallace visited Waigeo Island in the Raja Empat Group in 1860, and he described the inhabitants as a "mixed race" from Halmahera and New Guinea:

> many of them had taken Papuan wives from Salwatty or Dorey, while the influx of people from those places, and of slaves, had led to the formation of a tribe exhibiting almost all the transitions from a nearly pure Malayan to an entirely Papuan type. . . . Very few of them take the trouble to plant any vegetables or fruit, but live almost entirely on sago and fish, selling a little trepang or tortoiseshell to buy the scanty clothing they require. Almost all of them, however, possess one or more Papuan slaves, on whose labour they live in almost absolute idleness just going out on little fishing or trading excursions, as an excitement in their monotonous existence. They are under the rule of the Sultan of Tidore, and every year have to pay a small tribute of Paradise birds, tortoiseshell, or sago. To obtain these, they go in the fine season on a trading voyage to the mainland of New Guinea, and getting a few goods on credit from some Seram or Bugis trader, make hard bargains with the natives, and gain enough to pay their tribute, and leave a little profit for themselves.[36]

On Salawati Island, adjacent to the tip of the Bird's Head Peninsula, coins were in use as currency as early as 1825. The Maluku islands close to southwest New Guinea (Seram, Seram-Laut, Goram, Kei, Tanimbar, and Aru) were on various occasions controlled by the Sultans of Tidore or Bacan, although at other times acting fairly independently. They controlled much of the trade with the southern New Guinea coast east as far as Dolak

Island, including the *kain timur* trade on the Bird's Head.[37] As Jan Pouwer states: "It is difficult to overestimate the direct and indirect effect of these contacts. They led to wars, depopulation, migration, and the exchange of great numbers of prisoners of war and slaves by eastern Indonesian and local traders and dignitaries. All kinds of commodities, from small copper cannons to choppers, textiles, beads and ear-rings travelled from the coast to the interior."[38]

An insight into the extent of Asian trade with New Guinea can be gained by examining the well-researched bêche-de-mer (trepang or *Holothurioidea*) and turtle-shell trade carried out to Arnhem Land in Australia by Bugis from Makasar in southern Sulawesi, along with fishermen from Sumbawa Island (east of Flores). Makasan voyages to northern Australia are usually said to have begun sometime between 1650 and 1750 (although radiocarbon dates indicate possible earlier contact). Certainly by the initial decades of the nineteenth century, a fleet of around fifty Bugi *perahu* was visiting Australia each year, carrying 1,000 to 2,000 men. In the 1820s, when Britain was attempting to begin settlement in northern Australia, one estimate of the trade's value was between £180,000 and £240,000 annually, measured at the point the smoked bêche-de-mer was sold to Chinese traders in the East Indies.[39] The Makasans sailed down with the northwest monsoon (from March to November), cruised along the north coast and sometimes the west and south coasts of the Gulf of Carpentaria (occasionally blown east as far as Torres Strait), collecting bêche-de-mer, turtle-shells, pearlshells and pearls, timbers and fish. They then returned to Makasar with the southeast trade winds. When Matthew Flinders visited small islands in the southwest corner of the Gulf of Carpentaria, in November and December 1802, he was puzzled to find evidence of trees felled by iron axes and fragments of Asian material items: "Indications of some foreign people having visited this group were almost as numerous as those left by the natives. Besides pieces of earthen jugs and trees cut with axes, we found remnants of bamboo lattice work, palm leaves sewed with cotton thread into the form of such hats as are worn by the Chinese, and the remains of blue cotton trowsers."[40] Some months later, Flinders' puzzle was solved when his expedition came across six Makasan *perahu* at Gove Peninsula near the western entrance to the Gulf. They were part of a sixty-*perahu* fleet which had sailed from Makasar in the northwest monsoon two months before, then divided into groups of five or six vessels to seek out and process bêche-de-mer. The man in charge of the group encountered by Flinders, Probasso (in Makasan, Pu' Baso'), had made six or seven similar trips to Australia over twenty years, carefully recording Port Jackson as the origin of Flinders' voyage.[41]

Local Aborigines assisted in the collection and preparation of the bêche-de-mer, compensated with trade items such as food, tobacco, alcohol, and cloth.[42] Whenever the monsoon failed, the Makasans did not visit Australia. Their visits ceased altogether in the first years of the twentieth century when the South Australian government fostered a local bêche-de-mer industry, and the new Australian Commonwealth's White Australia Policy denied them further access.

Makasans brought with them knowledge of European colonialism from their own experiences with the Dutch. They introduced hundreds of loanwords into northern Aboriginal languages, and left genetic evidence of their dalliances with local women. Some
Aborigines voyaged back with them across the Banda Sea to the Sulawesi, although not
as slaves as was the pattern in New Guinea.[43] Aru, the most eastern of the Malukan Islands, is one of the ports through which Makasans passed on their way to and from Australia. The same islands are integral to the Maluku-Onin trade route, which raises the intriguing possibility of Aborigines from Arnhem Land, traveling back with the Makasans,
perhaps also reaching southwest New Guinea. Taking the Sulawesi-Arnhem Land statistics as a bench mark, along with what we know of foreign trade agents who lived permanently on the west New Guinea coast, it seems reasonable to presume that the west coast
must also have been visited every year in recent centuries by several hundred Malay and
Chinese traders and fishermen.

Sosolot Exchange: Slavery as Trade

The word "slavery" conjures up images of human beings owned as property and living
in oppressive conditions. But the word is also used more widely to cover situations that
cannot be readily equated with chattel slavery. Its use in the Malayan and Melanesian
worlds stretches meanings to include far more flexible states of bondage, which may indeed be transitory, allowing an individual to move from abject bondage to a position of
power over a lifetime. Having said this, it is still the most appropriate term available in
English.

The importance of unfree labor in traditional Melanesian societies has generally been
underestimated. Men, women, and children became slaves as captives in warfare, or after
having sought asylum, or sometimes as punishment for crimes they committed. It is unclear from the literature how widespread slavery or adoption of captives was, but in the
Western Solomon Islands and the Bismarck Archipelago "slaves" were regarded as assets, used in agricultural and domestic service, and as sexual partners, while among the
Marind-anim of southern New Guinea approximately one in seven adults were captives/
adoptees gained during head-hunting raids into the Trans-Fly.[44] In west New Guinea,
slaves were traded to Maluku and further afield along with other valuable items. The
sosolot exchanges reaching into west New Guinea were driven by the population clusters
along the eastern and southeastern coast of Seram, and by the people of the Seram-Laut,
Goram, and Watubela Archipelagos. Although these exchanges shared many features
with Melanesian trade more broadly, they were essentially exploitative, taking advantage
of the disparate nature of the region's ethnic and linguistic groups, but at the same time
connecting such groups.[45] Unfree labor was an economic and social reality, its importance probably exaggerated in west New Guinea by the use of tens of thousands of humans over hundreds of years as essential trade items, linking Melanesia to the Malay

Archipelago. The trade in humans for Asian and European manufactured goods changed the material cultures and economies of west New Guinea, a process similar to that which occurred in Island Melanesia during the nineteenth-century labor trade there.

The full extent of this slave trade is difficult to estimate—it predated any European presence, though it continued for many years after Dutch emancipation laws were passed in the 1860s, after which, in theory, the Sultan of Tidore was forbidden to extract slaves.[46] Slaves were an indigenous trade commodity, and they also became part of the European colonial economy. We can take as a large urban example Batavia, where over several centuries slaves were the majority population within the city walls. A substantial rate of import was needed to maintain supply because of high death rates and frequent manumissions, and because slaves did not live in family units and thus were not self-reproducing. Batavia imported about 1,000 slaves each year during the seventeenth century, and 3,000 per year during the eighteenth century. In 1673, Batavia's population of 27,068 included 13,278 slaves. As Batavia increased in size, so too did the number of slaves. From the end of the seventeenth century until the 1770s, during any one year there were between 25,000 and 30,000 slaves in Batavia.[47]

The first Dutch attempt to control the human trade from New Guinea was a treaty signed at Onin in 1678 which fixed the price of slaves and regulated their supply to VOC bases on Banda and Ambon.[48] The majority of Java's slaves came from Sulawesi and Bali, but each year for several centuries hundreds of New Guinea slaves—children and adults —were transported east into the Malay Archipelago, usually never to return. The slave trade was substantial. The earliest Portuguese, Spanish, Dutch, and English voyagers also regularly purchased slaves from New Guinea, or were presented with them as gifts.

Anthony Reid suggests that attitudes to slavery must be rethought and extended beyond the specific moral associations it had for nineteenth-century European reformers. There were many categories of captured aliens and it was often possible to move up the social ladder of the new society. The slave category becomes most clear-cut on the interface between two cultures,[49] which was the case between Melanesia and the Malay region. As Reid points out, in Southeast Asia, unequal relationships can be both cooperative and intimate, and early family structures were broader and more open. He concludes that, "The various systems of bondage encountered during the last eight centuries of recorded history, including those we recognise as slavery, are indigenous developments having their origin in a characteristically Southeast Asian acceptance of mutual obligation between high and low, or creditor and debtor."[50]

Slavery was a terrifying and often violent institution, sometimes with calamitous results for individuals involved. Jean Taylor, writing on the social world of seventeenth-century colonial Batavia, makes quite clear that most "slaves died in servitude, undernourished, ill-housed, and ill-clothed. Punishments were harsh, the most ferocious reserved for striking an owner or overseer."[51] Even so, it would be wrong to depict all west New Guinea slaves as stolen away and brutally treated. Dutch female immigration to the Indies was not encouraged in the early centuries, which meant female slaves were much sought after, becoming concubines for all ranks and lawful marriage partners for low-ranking employees. In the 1850s, New Guinea slaves at Dorei Bay and in Maluku sometimes married influential Malays, or were promoted to positions of considerable trust. Slaves were also used as dowry payments and some seem to have been well-treated.[52] Enslaved humans were integral to the functioning of the trading networks of the region. We can take our lead from research into the system of indentured labor current in eastern Melanesia in the nineteenth century, where historians now generally believe that a combination of kidnapping and willing enlistment occurred, with the emphasis on voluntarism. As was the case there, we must suppose that in west New Guinea, too, there was some degree of Melanesian community and individual agency within the traffic in human beings.

New Guinea slaves were valuable property. Slave prices seem to have doubled between the 1820s and 1850, when De Bruijn Kops estimated the value of a slave at between twenty-five and thirty guilders[53]: "A slave is the standard of value throughout the western parts of New Guinea, as is the case with a musket at Timor and the neighboring islands, so that when the price of any article is said to be so many slaves, it is intended to mean the value of a slave in blue and red calico or other articles of trade, all of which bear a fixed proportionate value. It is therefore, like the 'pound sterling,' an imaginary standard of value."[54]

Villagers often found their small-scale societies claustrophobic and welcomed a chance to get away. Life as a New Guinea slave in Maluku, Bali, Java, or Sulawesi was not always a repressive experience. Slave men in households engaged in many different crafts and retailing ventures on their master's account, and worked as valets, guards, and musicians. Those in public service built canals, laid roads, and erected new buildings. Some were paid a small wage in addition to rations, and when slaves were converted to Christianity owners often released them from bondage as an act of piety. At the very least they were exposed to several new languages; they worked alongside slaves from across Dutch Asia and most had a speaking knowledge of both Malay and Dutch, if not also Portuguese. Nevertheless, few ever returned to New Guinea to incorporate this new knowledge into their old communities.[55]

New Guinea societies operated through reciprocal exchange relationships, obedience, and obligation. Trade in goods and humans (through marriage alliances or *sosolot* slavery) acted as the link between cultural spheres, and cosmology supported patterns of long- and short-term movement. Unfree labor in its various forms was allied to basic tenets in wider Melanesian trading and belief systems—it was not an alien imposition. Therefore, west New Guinea slavery should not be viewed only through Western notions of economics and commerce. For example, the *sosolot* trading relationships contain elements of ceremonial exchange. Some west New Guinea peoples were forced into slavery, in the chattel meaning of the word, but for a variety of reasons it could be expeditious for a community to place one or several of their number into slavery, for middlemen to arrange the exchanges, or for an individual to "enlist" as a slave. Understanding the *sosolot* and *kain timur* exchanges further expands our thinking on slavery and unfree labor.

The Kain Timur Trade

The slave trade went hand-in-hand with the *kain timur* (imported woven cloth) trade that was prominent in the center of the Bird's Head Peninsula. The *kain timur* exchanges reached the peninsula via the south and were centered on the Ayamaru area in the interior, extending around the entire northern coast of the Bird's Head. The Raja political system was connected through to the *sosolot* exchanges, and operated throughout the Raja Empat Archipelago, around contiguous areas of the Bird's Head and down along the Onin-Lascar and Onin-Kowiai coast. New Guinea peoples—for instance the Ekari of the Wissel Lakes or the Dani of the Baliem Valley—practiced intensive agriculture and pig production, which most anthropologists suggest are necessary for the rise of classic bigman political systems. However, in the Bird's Head the political system operated around *kain timur* exchanges. There, the prominence of bigmen and war leaders was based not only on agriculture of animal husbandry, but also on trade in slaves with their neighbors to the west and the cloths received in return. As outlined in discussions of leadership patterns in the previous chapter, bigmen leadership styles vary considerably, and exchange of exotic goods is a regular aspect of leadership in many bigman systems throughout Melanesia. While slavery is not usually considered in these leadership models, trade in humans is another kind of exchange and fits well within classic Melanesian leadership models.[56]

The *kain timur* complexes, which included the exchange of women of differential values, seem to have arisen within a context of inter-community competition relating to their regional origins, warfare, and slavery. Cloth was acquired in exchange for slaves captured in the interior areas, and bigmen competed for prominence by controlling the movement of women and cloths. In return for their participation, they received *sarung batik* (printed cotton from Java), *kain timur*, brass wire, swords, steel chopping-knives and axes, porcelain cups and bowls, basins, rugs, glass beads, armlets, tobacco, rice, and many other kinds of Asian and later European hardware and food. The earliest written sources we have that mention slaves being traded for *kain timur* are from the sixteenth century, indicating that at least a rudimentary form of the trade existed four hundred years ago. In early times, centers of slave export were found along the lower reaches of the Kais, Kamundan/Ayfat, Wiriagar/Aimau, and Sebjar Rivers. Jelle Miedema describes the path that the trade took: "From there, the trade agents went upstream to trade and raid in the hinterland, particularly the upper Inanwatan or Aytinyo area (the southern Ayamaru area). It is important to note that slaves were not simply exported. In the interior of the Bird's Head they were also much sought after as reserve capital and cheap labor . . ., or as cheap marriage-partners and a means to enlarge a small kinship group . . . However, the exportation of slaves can in general be regarded as a mechanism resulting in the importation of *kain timur*."[57]

Over hundreds of years, imported cloth was distributed through the Bird's Head Peninsula by this trade, which used *kain timur* for bride wealth and other ceremonial exchanges. Cloth became the major material item used in exchanges of women between descent groups. Miedema suggests three stages to this trade: initially male and female slaves were exchanged for *kain timur*; then *kain timur* was used to obtain wives; and finally free women were forced into marriages with outsiders to obtain *kain timur*. The rise of the *kain timur* bride wealth system disrupted "sister" exchange between neighboring descent groups, leading to the abandonment of direct woman-for-woman exchange.[58]

The people distinguished between *kain pusaka* (heirloom cloths) and *kain jalan* (wandering cloths, suitable for exchange). Genealogies reflect women being purposefully married to outside groups to afford access to *kain timur*. This trade complex was exceptional for three reasons: first, it was based on trading humans, not on production of surplus food or shell valuables; second, it involved trade in imported valuables; and finally, it relied on slaves from the south and central areas of the Bird's Head, rather than from the north, which altered the nature of the ethno-linguistic groups in that area. Trade agents were based permanently on the south coast, working as middlemen between the bigmen in the interior and the slave traders. Important among the latter were the *Raja-Raja* (kings) of Rumbati, Patipi, Kokas, and Arguni, each of whom had his own *sosolot* area of influence. Miedema argues that the *kain timur* trade acted like a wedge driven into the culture of the hinterland: "migrations—triggered off by raids and slave-trading along the south coast—resulted in a decrease of intertribal contacts along a west-east axis, and at the same time in an increase of contacts along (semicircular) south-north axes in the eastern part as well as the most western part of the Bird's Head . . ."[59]

Two large and quite recent changes to the ethnolinguistic groups of the Bird's Head Peninsula relate to this trade. First, over several centuries, trade-agents—new middlemen—established bases on the coasts. After the Dutch abolition of slavery in the 1860s, these traders, deprived of their sources of power on the coast, moved inland, using their hold on valuables, particularly the *kain pusaka*, to marry into descent groups, thus ensuring their continuing hold over land and power. Second, Miedema suggests that the *kain timur* trade system changed gender conceptions in the favor of women, as they became increasingly pivotal in intertribal marriage relations. Miedema supports Daryl Feil's argument (based on Papua New Guinea Highlands exchange systems) that the west New Guinea exchange of cloth altered gender relations. Women were central to these exchanges: there were cloths specifically for women, and women were consulted in the logistics of arranging marriages.[60]

Evidence presented in Chapters Two and Three suggests that parts of coastal New Guinea were on the periphery of the world-system 2,000 years ago. We do know that some indigenous working of metals in Malay forges was occurring on the west coast at least 400 years ago, but it was not until the nineteenth century that iron, initially old barrel-hoop iron obtained in barter with Europeans, became much in demand for reworking as adze blades.

Traders, facilitated by Austronesian language links, and in recent centuries using the Malay language and a few New Guinea lingua franca, had been moving through Maluku to New Guinea over an unknown number of centuries. A speculative argument can be made to suggest that as early as the eighth century, New Guinea slaves may have reached China via Srivijaya. Malays certainly had explored the coasts of the western half of New Guinea and may well have reached the eastern end along the north coast, by accident or design.[61] In the fourteenth century, the Java-based Majapahit empire made claims of suzerainty over limited areas in west New Guinea, but this was probably rather fanciful aggrandizement, based on the vague geographical knowledge of Majapahit scholars, and bolstered by a little indirect trading through the Maluku rulers. The later sultanates of Ternate and Tidore in northern Maluku made more realistic claims, based on their continued extraction of slaves and tribute, and their trade in nutmegs, medicinal barks, and bird pelts from a few places around the west New Guinea coast.[62]

West New Guinean involvement in the trading networks of the Timor, Banda, Seram, and Arafura Seas certainly existed well before the arrival of the Spanish and the Portuguese in Maluku early in the sixteenth century. Within this period of increasing contact with Europeans, Onin Peninsula traders were well-organized, and capable of trading the products of New Guinea—both goods and lives procured from the surrounding coast —with the Chinese and Malay traders operating out of Halmahera, Seram, and the Sulawesi.[63] Traders at Onin were competing with Seramese traders, and some converted to Islam. It is not possible to know if these were recently arrived Malay traders who married into local communities, or indigenous New Guineans. The manner in which the *kain timur* trade developed indicates that these trading families may once have come from Maluku, but equally that when they married locally their children became indigenous to New Guinea. On the north side of west New Guinea, the people of Dorei in Cenderawasih Gulf were included in the Maluku trade sphere, and coastal villages controlled the trade of Asian goods to inland groups. Small supplies of iron and other foreign trade goods trickled in to the inland peoples from both sides of Bird's Head Peninsula, supplementing their local exchange regimes.

This and previous chapters have challenged the idea of an isolated "stone age" New Guinea. West New Guinea—particularly the Bird's Head and Onin regions, and the adjacent Raja Empat Group and Cenderawasih Gulf—was as much part of the Malay sphere of trade and influence as were other outlying areas of Island Southeast Asia. Just as west New Guineans adapted new material possessions, ideas, and concepts to their needs, so too they incorporated the Malay presence for their own purposes. The basic argument put forward here is that trade is the essential mechanism that has bound New Guinea's peoples together over many thousands of years. The relationship between west New Guinea and Maluku were based on ceremonial and material exchanges that were part of this process.

4

West New Guinea

European Trade and Settlement, 1520–1880

Early European Incursions: Portugal and Spain

Confronted by what was different, exotic and to them bizarre, as well as bewildered that their own 'natural' world was now unnatural and all their obvious symbols were meaningless, they played out their own cultural systems in caricatured charades. When they tried to describe what they saw, they themselves were revealed naked.
—Greg Dening, *Islands and Beaches*, 1980, 19.

Europeans began to explore the further corners of the world from the fifteenth century onward. In doing so they found very different cultures, which made them confront their own, ripping away some of their most cherished beliefs while reconfirming others. The existence of *Terra Australia Incognita*, the southern continent, had long been postulated, based on the writings of classical authors such as Ptolemy and Pliny the Elder, and the more recent stories of Marco Polo and Luigi Varthema. Cartographers had added vague outlines of the continent to their maps long before European navigators began to sail around New Guinea and Australia. Although European contact with the region began early in the sixteenth century, not until a century later did the Spanish realize that New Guinea was separate from Australia. It was the middle of the seventeenth century before Tasman confirmed the same information for the Dutch, and the seventh decade of the eighteenth century when Cook proved it for England. Not until well into the nineteenth century were the entire coasts of New Guinea and adjacent islands charted. The inland areas were among the last unknown settled regions on earth, so difficult was the terrain, and some peoples were not contacted until the 1950s and 1960s.[1]

New Guinea, its adjacent islands and their peoples are seldom highlighted in the history of European exploration of Asia and the Pacific. Painstakingly piecing evidence together from maps, globes, logs, and early books, historians have followed various voyages as they wander the oceans, and often divide them chronologically, or by the nationalities of the navigators. Geographic themes are also employed, but if the concentration is on the lengthy search for *Terra Australia Incognita*, the focus is on Australia, not New Guinea. The subject of this and following chapters is the gradual process by which European navigators explored, commercially exploited, and incorporated New Guinea and the islands to its east and west into empires. They came into contact with its peoples from the decks of ships, on beaches and in coastal villages, and up the lower reaches of sluggish coastal rivers. Dening, in his *Islands and Beaches,* suggests that in this process the Europeans often felt as if they had been stripped naked, that their established symbols and codes had been rendered meaningless. Because the chapters which follow are based largely on European evidence, they concentrate on the points of view of the outsiders, but these same observers, often quite inadvertently, give us evidence of indigenous behavior. Indigenous "voices" are difficult to discover, but they have been included wherever possible. The records of these encounters provide us with the earliest detailed views of New Guinea and New Guineans. Some of these interactions were fleeting, spasmodic and, given that they occurred generations apart, almost irrelevant. Others, such as those in St. George's Channel between New Britain and New Ireland, Torres Strait, the Raja Empat Group, Onin Peninsula, or Cenderawasih Gulf, were constant, and brought about tremendous changes in the surrounding societies.

European exploration of New Guinea in the sixteenth century was the province of the Spanish and the Portuguese, an outgrowth of their attempts to monopolize the Maluku spice trade. At that time, the only outside power to have even a peripheral political influence on New Guinea affairs was the Sultanate of Bacan, an island adjacent to southern Halmahera. The Bacanese were subservient to the Sultans of Tidore, and held sway in the Raja Empat Islands, especially on Misool.[2] Both Spain and Portugal had ambitions to control the Spice Islands, but their inadequate cartographical knowledge and navigation techniques meant that neither knew exactly where the islands were in relation to papal bulls and the 1494 Treaty of Tordesillas, which had drawn a line around the globe, dividing it between the two Iberian kingdoms.

Portugal was the first European nation to have direct contact with New Guinea. After capturing Melaka (Malacca) in 1511, Alfonso d'Albuquerque sent Antonio d'Abreu and Francisco Serrão to the Spice Islands. They returned with accounts of people of a totally different race from the Malays, but the Portuguese did not set foot on New Guinea themselves, and relied instead on Javanese and Malayan maps, stories from local traders, and their own observations of New Guinean slaves in Maluku. Maps by D'Abreu's pilot indicated the existence of "Papoia," a large island to the east of the main Spice Islands. Possibly this meant Halmahera, or even the Raja Empat Group (which were also known as the Islands of Papua), but he was probably trying to depict the western end of New Guinea.[3] Portuguese ships began paying regular visits to Maluku, although no permanent settlement was attempted until 1522, when, through an alliance with Ternate, they established a fortified permanent settlement. The Sultan could only see advantages: the Europeans were visiting traders like the many Asian groups with whom he dealt; surely their presence would only strengthen his position in Maluku. What he did not realize was that they intended to take over his economic monopoly and to Christianize his people.[4]

In 1512 the Portuguese reached Banda, at that time the *entrepôt* for the spice trade of all of eastern Indonesia, and they found local leaders less pliable than the Ternate Sultan. Initially, the Banda elite refused the Portuguese permission to build a fort, but they did enter into a treaty. Banda's *kora-kora* dominated the trade between Maluku and Melaka, and Banda's traders had an advantage over those in northern Maluku because prevailing wind patterns allowed them to travel west more quickly via the Sunda Chain.[5] Javanese and Malay traders sailing out of Java, Bali, Nusa Tengarra (the chain of islands from

Lombok to Timor), and the Indian subcontinent visited the Banda *entrepôt*, trading textiles and rice for spices, and they met traders there from Kei and Aru who were in constant contact with west New Guinea. Islam spread along this trade route, reaching out into northern and eastern Maluku onwards from the fifteenth century. Within a few years, New Guinea was named on Portuguese maps, and in 1513 it was noted by Tom Pires in his *Suma Oriental*. The first Portuguese voyage to actually reach New Guinea was that of Jorge de Meneses, Portuguese Captain-designate of Maluku in 1526. His ship was caught in a storm and blown 600 kilometers east of Halmahera into what may have been Cenderawasih Gulf. De Menses and his crew spent some months during 1526–1527 at "Versija," which may have been Waigeo in the Raja Empat Group, but more likely was Biak Island. He confirmed what the Portuguese had found in 1511: the large island was known locally as "Papuwah."[6]

The Spanish also began trading in cloves. In 1521, when the two remaining ships from Magellan's fleet arrived in Maluku, they were welcomed by Sultan Mansur of Tidore, who hoped to build up the same type of relationship that Portugal had with Ternate. Cortés, ruler of Spanish Peru, sent expeditions in 1525 and 1527 to try to wrest control of the spice trade away from the Portuguese,[7] and a return voyage in 1528 captured three local men at what was probably Murai, an islet off Manus' southwest coast. They subsequently joined the voyage to Guam, Mindanao, Maluku, and back along the north New Guinea coast to Manus in 1529. The one surviving Manusian learnt Spanish and was converted to Christianity, but he was killed by his own people while swimming ashore.[8]

The first European sojourners in New Guinea seem to have been seven survivors from a 1537 Spanish expedition, whose ship disintegrated off Cenderawasih Gulf's Schouten Islands. The commander, De Grijalva, was murdered by the crew, who then got their comeuppance when they were enslaved, sold to the Portuguese, and ransomed back to the Spanish several years later. Voyagers out of the Americas during the 1540s collected information about the north New Guinea coast, including in 1545 De Retes, who named the mainland "Nueva Guinea" because he perceived a physical similarity between the inhabitants and those of Guinea in Africa. At the Hermit-Ninigo Groups canoes visited the ship, and the people were described as good-looking, light-skinned, and courageous, and their canoes as particularly well made. De Retes also described New Guinea as a "big island," and although the discovery of its insular status is usually credited to Torres in 1606, several maps from the second half of the sixteenth century show a strait between New Guinea and Australia, perhaps indicating that Torres was aware of the Strait that now bears his name.[9]

Soon after the first decade of Iberian incursion, the Maluku Sultans realized their error, and attempted to expel the infidel with the assistance of their allies in the Raja Empat Group. This 1534–1535 uprising was put down, and the Portuguese seized large quantities of natural products in compensation. Then, in 1570, the Portuguese unwisely murdered their host, Sultan Hairun of Ternate, which was enough to ensure Ternate,

Tidore, and Bacan united to overwhelm the Portuguese and force their temporary withdrawal to Ambon, resulting in a higher profile for Tidore. Sultan Bab Ullah later attempted to normalize relations with Portugal, and allowed them to build a fort at Tidore.[10] By the final decades of the sixteenth century, the well-established Asian trade pattern in Maluku had been altered irreparably. The Spanish allied themselves to Ternate, and, because they had not gone to the expense of establishing a permanent settlement in the islands, they could offer far better prices than could the Portuguese. Philip II's ascension to the Spanish throne in 1556 brought an alteration in Spanish policy, which in turn led to Spanish settlement in the Philippines in 1565 and the discovery of a satisfactory north Pacific route to the Americas, which lessened interest in the Spice Islands. Then, in 1580, Philip II seized the Portuguese Crown, unifying the two Iberian kingdoms until 1640, after which protracted warfare eventually forced Spain to recognize Portugal's independence in 1668. Competition between buyers continued in Maluku during the remainder of the sixteenth century, driving up prices and leading to planting of more spice trees. Private Asian trade continued despite Portuguese threats to impose a monopoly, but whereas the Portuguese and Spanish were content to continue bartering for spices, the Dutch, who followed them in the early seventeenth century, transformed the trade into one based on cash payments.

The motivation for Iberian exploration east of the Maluku Islands was their search for mythical sources of the biblical King Solomon's gold and other valuable natural products such as pearls and aromatic medicinal barks. In 1567, Spanish ships left Peru to search for the golden islands of Solomon and the antipodean continent that Europeans conjectured must exist in the southern hemisphere, though its relationship with New Guinea was unclear. Mendaña did find a string of islands that he named after King Solomon, but not his gold. He returned there almost thirty years later to colonize the Santa Cruz Group, but died in the attempt.[11] A decade later, Mendaña's former chief pilot, Quiros, set out to colonize the southern continent. He mistook Santo Island for a corner of a great southern landmass, and there established the short-lived New Jerusalem colony. The fleet later became separated, with Quiros heading back to Mexico while Torres sailed north with two ships along the southern coast of New Guinea. Sketches from the pen of second-in-command Prado are among the earliest pictorial records of New Guinea. In July 1606, the ships encountered Sudest (Tagula) the most southerly of the Louisiades, then sailed along the reefs until they reached the New Guinea mainland at China Strait. Prado described the people they saw around Sideia and Basilaki Islands as light-skinned, and naked apart from coconut-matting midriff-wraps. Their foods were yam, fruit, coconut, pork, turtle, and fish, they kept dogs, pigs, and turtles in their villages, and they manufactured fishing nets, clubs, shields, and small spears. Sketches were made at Mailu in southeast New Guinea, in Torres Strait, and in southwest New Guinea, and the artist carefully differentiated skin color, appearance, tattoos, apparel, weapons, and shields. Prado was responsible for a particularly bloody massacre at the fortified village on Mailu

Island, the largest skirmish of the voyage. The initial peaceful intentions of the landing party were misunderstood. First they were ambushed in a narrow passage, then attacked from canoes, and finally stoned from cliffs. Torres' party retaliated by slaughtering men, women, and children, kidnapping fourteen children, and ransacking the fortress.[12]

More extensive exploration continued around west New Guinea. Details that survive from a 1580s Portuguese voyage have preserved a picture of the convolutions of trade and politics. Travel was via the swift *kora-kora* craft that, powered by banks of up to 200 oarsmen, could cover 70–80 kilometers a day. Seram-Laut and Misool merchants were trading with Onin Peninsula for slaves, massoi bark, and gold. In the south of the Raja Empat Group, the Raja of Misool lived in a village of 4,000 people, built over a lagoon at Tomulol Bay. The peoples of the island's interior manufactured sago starch, an important export. Misool's people obviously had ready access to gold. The Raja presented one Portuguese traveler with a heavy gold chain, the general population wore gold ornaments, and there was a great deal of gold for sale. The gold, along with cloth, iron gongs, and slaves, was obtained through *kora-kora* fleets raiding the island of Seram-Laut, the inhabitants of which the Misool ruler considered to be his vassals (although their view of the relationship was quite different).

Seram-Laut is at the center of a small archipelago contiguous with eastern Seram, and at this time it was under Tidore's influence. With a population of several thousand, it rivaled nearby Banda as the region's richest and leading trading port. The village was divided between eight leaders, each with equal powers. The light boats of Seram-Laut merchants could maneuver around reef complexes that frightened Europeans in their heavier-draft ships, and they roamed the entire eastern archipelago as far as Java, Bali, and Sulawesi. Seram-Laut traded for gold, cotton and other textiles, amber, wax, and iron, some of which found their way to Onin ports where they were exchanged for slaves and massoi bark, the oil from which was much favored by Javanese as a medical ointment. The island's gold supplies were deposited in four treasuries, central funds drawn upon when war fleets had to be raised from nearby Seram. Although the island was constantly preyed upon by Misool's marauding *kora-kora*, their trading ventures were so lucrative that the merchants were able to pay ransoms whenever they were captured by raiders. Miguel Roxo de Brito, the Portuguese visitor mentioned above, was told that: "there was no Seranho who had not been caught five times, and we don't want to be vassals as long as we possess sails [with which] to earn our living by trade, because we can buy our liberty with our merchandise."[13]

The main Seram-Laut settlement was guarded by a stone fort equipped with guard towers and small arms. Forty years later, the fortifications were more than three meters thick and high, having been extended after the merchants began having to deal with European predations. In 1632–1633, when the Dutch Governor of Banda was planning to conquer Seram-Laut, the inhabitants managed to stay his hand with a payment of 200 slaves and three kilograms of gold.[14]

On Batanta Island in the north of the Raja Empat Group, the Raja of Waigeo diplomatically ingratiated himself with his Portuguese guest, expressing a fervent interest in Catholicism and supposedly accepting the overlordship of Phillip II. He also accompanied De Brito across the narrow Sele Straits to the New Guinea mainland and around Onin Peninsula, where they met armed resistance: "The people of this region are all black, like those in Guinea, and they are all traders; they [go to] trade in a kingdom on the equator, called Sekar, where there is a village with an important market where black slaves are traded: here the people of Onin buy [slaves], which they sell in Serdanha [Seram-Laut]. The Serdanhos, since they are very wealthy, buy them and take them to the island of Kidang [off Seram-Laut] as labor for their gardens. It is [a] certain [fact] that there are Serdanha *yndios* [of Malay appearance] who own a thousand black slaves, who produce much sago bread, which they accumulate in order to sell to the Javanese; and [these] trade it for nutmeg and mace in Banda, because [the Bandanese] lack a staple food."[15]

Further into MacCluer Gulf (Bintuni Gulf) were people of mixed Malay and New Guinea ancestry who traded pearls and beeswax for export. At one place, a large group of warriors tried to stop De Brito and the Raja's party from landing, and at another a fleet of canoes was drawn up in battle formation until they were scattered by arquebuses. The Raja could communicate with this fleet, perhaps indicating that they were familiar with the Biak lingua franca from Cenderawasih Gulf, and had traveled south for ceremonial or trading purposes. The major export of the region was massoi bark, the main wealth item was iron gongs obtained in raids and from ransoming captives from Gebe Island, midway between Waigeo and the eastern arm of Halmahera. The Raja's informants also described the mutineers from De Grijalva's expedition, when the *San Gerónimo* was wrecked in Cenderawasih Gulf in 1537, and claimed that three captives still remained. Onin was a prosperous region, producing a surplus of sago starch along with an assortment of domestic animals—chickens, pigs, goats, and *kerabau* (buffaloes)—and fish. Gold was plentiful, and was worn as earrings and necklaces that the people claimed to have gained from groups further east around the peninsula. Seram-Laut traders regularly visited the region, trading iron implements and Malay *keris* (swords and daggers) for massoi bark.

De Brito and the Raja retreated for recuperation to prosperous Notan Island, which was within the Raja's territory. When the voyage continued they were joined by the Raja of Misool, and they traveled to Seram-Laut and along the north coast of Seram, visiting several villages of several hundred people. There they received news that the Sultan of Ternate had sent a fleet to lay siege to Portugal's fortress at Ambon.

Tidore and Ternate Islands, the seats of the main Halmahera Sultanates, feature in illustrations that show the original forts and harbors, the *kora-kora* fleets, and the sumptuous galleys of the Sultans. Ambon, Banda, Seram, and Seram-Laut were also depicted with quite substantial harbors and fortifications. At Ambon, Castle Victoria had been built by the Portuguese in 1580, and it dominates a 1617 sketch showing the structure surrounded by plantations of clove and coconut trees. Half a century later, Ambon had a substantial port city with a church, town hall, hospital, warehouses, and market. Other sketches show the *kora-kora,* and Malay garb of the warriors from Gebe Island, an essential base in the Maluku trade network.[16]

Though the area had been included within the Spanish realm, it was the Portuguese who managed to monopolize the spice trade during most of the sixteenth century, continuing to reduce the local influence of Javanese and Malayan commerce. They constructed further forts, on Kisar and the eastern Aru Islands. Portuguese loanwords found their way into the Maluku-Malay lingua franca, but overall neither the Portuguese nor the Spanish, or their Catholicism, made much impact on Maluku or western New Guinea. Only on neighboring Timor did the Portuguese leave an indelible cultural mark—it remained their colony until the Indonesians took it by force of arms in 1975, only to reluctantly relinquish it themselves in 2000.

Dutch Exploration and Trade

If the sixteenth century belonged to the Iberian kingdoms, the seventeenth was dominated by the Dutch, who made their first visits to Maluku in 1599. Their Vereenigde Oostindische Compagnie (the voc, or the Dutch East India Company) began operations in 1602, and took over the existing Dutch presence in Maluku, also being interested in the economic potential of the southern continent and its northern neighbor, New Guinea. Almost immediately, the Dutch began to battle the Iberian kingdoms for supremacy in the Spice Islands, and they wrested Ambon from the Portuguese in 1605. The Dutch, wanting to establish links with New Guinea, sent a ship to Banda and Seram in 1602 to inquire about establishing trade. Willem Schouten reported back negatively; nevertheless his voyage was the first of many the Dutch sent to explore New Guinea and the southern continent. The Bantam factory dispatched the *Duyfken,* which called at the Kei and Aru Islands before reaching New Guinea at Dolak Island. Unknowingly, Willem Janszoon then sailed to Australia, reaching what he thought to be a gulf (the western edge of Torres Strait) before sailing south down the west coast of Cape York. This was the first documented European sighting of Australia, a few months before Torres and Prado sailed through Torres Strait in 1606. After nine of the crew died in skirmishes with Aborigines, the *Dufken* retraced the same route home, and Janszoon conveyed a gloomy picture of the prospects and the people.[17]

As Dutch hegemony strengthened in the Malay Archipelago, their explorations around New Guinea increased, providing quite detailed reports on New Ireland and its outliers. Merchants from the Dutch city of Hoorn tried to break the voc monopoly by establishing the Australische Compagnie, which sent two ships, the *Eendracht* and the *Hoorn* west across the Pacific. Landings were made on the east coast of New Ireland during 1616, where the local people were described as black-skinned with tattoos. They chewed betel nut, wore rings through their septums, and built substantial canoes. Continuing along the northeast coast, the two ships passed between New Ireland and New Hanover, sighting the Tabar, Tanga, Lihir, Feni, and Nissan Groups, and observing canoes that probably came from Tabar. In early July, the ships reached the Admiralty Islands, presumably the first Europeans to visit the area since Saavedra's expeditions of 1528–1529. From there they sailed along west New Guinea, landing at the Schouten (Biak and Eilanden) Islands above Cenderawasih Gulf, and also at the Raja Empat Group, before continuing to Batavia. Chinese porcelain seen at the Schouten Islands indicated contact with foreign traders. Jacob Le Maire and his captains (brothers Willem and Jan Cornelisz Schouten) were not enthralled by the peoples they met, but the expedition proved that New Guinea did not extend east as far as the Bismarck Archipelago. The accidental destruction of the *Hoorn* by fire in December 1615, and the confiscation of the *Eendracht* in Bantam in October 1616, brought an end to the venture.[18]

Overall, the early European impressions of New Guinea were negative. The most useful information was gathered from around the Bird's Head and Onin, although even there uncertainty would remain about a possible passage between Cenderawasih and MacCluer Gulfs until Jacob Weyland on the *Geelvink* charted the former in 1705. That same voyage captured the first New Guineans to reach Europe. Weyland kidnapped three young men from Jobi and Kui and took them to Batavia, where one of them was drawn by the famous traveler and painter Cornelis de Bruyn. The trio was then transported to Amsterdam, where their portraits were painted once more. They settled there, too frightened to attempt a return to Batavia or New Guinea because they feared being sold as slaves once they reached the Indies. One eventually worked as a carpenter in a shipyard.[19]

The voc continued to receive reports—from ships accidentally sailing too far east across the Indian Ocean en route to Java, and from expeditions out of Batavia and Ambon—of the existence of a large southern continent.[20] In 1622, when forty-six survivors from an English ship wrecked on the southwest New Guinea coast reached Batavia, the Governor-General was shocked out of complacency and further Dutch expeditions were launched. The next year, the governor of Ambon sent two yachts to search for commercial possibilities east of the Kei and Aru Islands. At Aru they formally recognized the authority of local *orang kaya* (leading merchants) in exchange for exclusive trade privileges. This voyage, under Jan Carstensz, continued further along the coast of southern New Guinea, and at one point sighted something remarkable: the snowcapped mountains which were to remain beyond European reach until the early twentieth century.[21] Later, at Dolak Island, they tried to communicate with and capture men in canoes:

the men are black, tall and well-built, with coarse and strong limbs, and curly hair like the Caffres, some of them wearing it tied to the neck in a knot, and others letting it fall loose down to the waist. They have hardly any beards; some of them have two, others three holes through the nose, in which they wear fangs or teeth of hogs or sword-fishes. They are stark-naked and have their privities enclosed in a conch-shell, fastened to the waist with a bit of string; they wear no rings of gold, silver, tin, copper, or iron on their persons, but adorn themselves with rings made of tortoise-shell or terturago from which it may be inferred that their land yields no metals or wood of any value . . . The people are cunning and suspicious, and no stratagems on our part availed to draw them near enough to us to enable us to catch one or two with nooses that we had prepared for the purpose . . .[22]

The *Pera* returned along the New Guinea coast while the *Arnhem* crossed the Gulf of Carpentaria to the edge of what is now Arnhem Land, just missing Torres Strait. Aborigines had armed clashes with Carstensz' crew, and during landings in February at Cape Debelle in west New Guinea, ten of the crew were killed, including the *Arnhem*'s skipper. Carstensz named the local river "Moordenaars" (Murderer's River). As with the *Duyfken*'s expedition, the general reports were unenthusiastic, the violent incidents having soured impressions. Carstensz later described the New Guineans as malicious, and he was convinced that they were cannibals because of the strings of human teeth and bones exhibited with great relish to his cabin boys.[23]

After a century of European trading around Maluku, so many extra spice trees had been planted to cope with the boom that the market was soon glutted. During the 1600s, the Dutch attempted to establish a cultivation monopoly, and they began by asserting control over Banda, still the lynchpin of the trade, and by establishing Ambon as their second base. The Portuguese built forts on Banda in 1602, only to have them captured by the Dutch three years later. By 1607, the Dutch found that the Portuguese and Spanish had allied against them. This caused Ternate's Sultan, who was trying to reestablish his own waning power, to join with the Dutch. By the 1610s, the Portuguese, Spanish, Dutch, and English were all fighting to establish dominance in the Malukan spice trade. A decade later, all but the Dutch were in retreat. In the 1610s and 1620s, the voc enforced their control on Banda with devastating consequences for its people. In the end, only 1,000 survived out of a population of 15,000; the rest were killed, starved, or forced to flee to Seram, Seram-Laut, or Kei and Aru Islands. The Dutch instituted a monopoly that limited spice production to Banda and Ambon, and established small garrisons on other Maluku Islands. After 1648, tens of thousands of nutmeg trees were destroyed throughout east Maluku in order to concentrate cultivation on Banda and Ambon under strict supervision. This altered long-established local barter trades, and probably changed the dynamics of the traditional *sosolot* exchange network, particularly in regard to slaves, many of whom came from New Guinea.

Spanish colonization of Luzon in the Philippines in 1565 slowly turned the kingdom's attention away from the Spice Isles and New Guinea. The Spanish and the Portuguese finally evacuated their factories from Maluku in 1663,[24] leaving the VOC in total control. The Portuguese did maintain a presence in nearby Timor, and continually marauded into Maluku to attack the VOC. The Dutch explored the southwest and northern coast of New Guinea, in the process charting many islands in the eastern Pacific archipelagos and circumnavigating Australia. The VOC was well aware of the existing trade in New Guinea slaves and massoi bark from the Onin and Kowiai Peninsulas, but they judged the profits to be too low to be of interest. Most voyages avoided landing when possible, and contact with New Guineans except as necessary to trade for essentials—water, food, and fuel. They usually also tried to erect markers of occupation to stake vague claims for Holland. After several significant voyages of exploration in the 1640s failed to pass through Torres Strait, the Dutch settled for exploiting west New Guinea, particularly the Onin and Kowiai region.

Dutch voyages to New Guinea in the mid-seventeenth century were motivated by the search for precious metals, or for a southern passage to the east, or the need to regulate the massoi bark trade. When crews came into close contact with New Guineans the results were often disastrous. The attack on Carstensz' crew in 1623 was replicated in 1636 when another expedition came to grief at Moordenaars River:[25]

> Pool with ten other persons, among whom were three musketeers, had gone on shore. A hut standing on the river side had been examined by them, though not damaged. In the meantime, some one hundred wild men attacked them; they were black of skin as Kaffirs of Angola, more coarse, taller and bigger of limbs than Europeans; they had long black hair that hung over their shoulders; they were completely naked with the exception of their privates which were more or less covered. Among them was one who had a hairy beast's skin hanging around his neck. Their arms consisted of darts, with sharp iron points and some of them carried bows and arrows. Although they were fired upon they threw, with small shrill cries and frantic action, their darts and arrows at the small crowd so thickly that it was like hail, and they were forced to flee to the boats. In their escape, Commander Pool and Merchant Schiller were shot in the back so that they fell down. Pool still called out to his men, "Run! Run! Try to save yourselves." But the savages had reached him immediately, taken his broadsword, and chopped him and Merchant Schiller into small pieces, some of which they took back into the bush . . .[26]

Despite the lack of commercial successes, and the distinct absence of gold, the Heeren XVII (the VOC's directorate) were loath to give up their efforts. In 1642, they dispatched Abel Tasman on an ambitious voyage to establish the geographic limits of the southern continent. At Tabar Island, several men in a canoe approached the ships, trading sago for trinkets. Tasman observed: "These men are very brown, Yea as black as any kaffir may be . . . [The] hair [is] of different color, which thus varies by the spreading of the lime, the face smeared with red paint, apart from the forehead. Some had a white bone through the nose below, which had about the thickness of a little finger, having further nothing on the body than some greenery before their private parts."[27]

A sketch of these Islanders has survived: one man is blowing a conch shell, two are paddling and the canoe is equipped with devices for shark-calling, an ancient New Ireland art. The expedition passed along the northeast coast of New Ireland, moved north of New Hanover, then south between the Witu Islands and Willaumez Peninsula on the north coast of New Britain. Despite the importance of the trip in locating Van Diemen's Land and New Zealand, and in establishing limits to the size of *Terra Australia*, no new commercial information was procured, nor was anything added to the observations Le Maire and the Schoutens had made of the Bismarck Archipelago. In 1644 Tasman set off again, instructed to find any southern passage between New Guinea and Australia while also searching for possible commercial ventures. His three ships sailed past the Aru Islands, and across the Arafura Sea almost to Torres Strait. Foxed by the inhospitable reefs and shoals, they turned south to Australia. Maps and globes produced in the Netherlands soon included Tasman's voyages: the reasonably accurate outline of western and northern Australia bears the designation Nova Hollandia (New Holland), although the voyages perpetuated the Dutch belief that there was no southern passage between New Guinea and New Holland.[28]

After half a century of voyages, the VOC judged New Guinea and Australia to be of no great economic value, and their peoples too barbarous to be of concern. Local Indies voyages continued, and the Dutch entered into existing trading patterns. In 1660, the VOC acquired rights from the Sultan of Tidore "to get slaves and other goods of Papua and all the other [nearby] islands,"[29] and this led to several 1660s expeditions solely for this purpose. In August 1662 the first voyage specifically to fetch slaves from Onin set out, but arrived only to find that 136 adult slaves had just been taken away by *perahu* to Makasar in southern Sulawesi and Goram Island near Banda Island. The expedition declined an offer to purchase fifty child-slaves. Another expedition later in the year concluded that the Moslem Seramese and Goramese traders had done as much as they possibly could to disrupt any commerce between the Onin people (some of whom were also Moslems) and the *kafir* Dutch. Nevertheless, thirty-eight slaves were eventually procured and sent to Banda. Fearing violence, Nicholass Vinck left Onin, and set sail for Rumakain, a village at the mouth of the Kamundan River in a region controlled by the Raja of Rumbati. His party were well received and they were able to purchase more slaves.[30]

The next year, Banda's Governor sent Vinck back in an attempt to disrupt the activities of the Moslem traders. The price of Rumakain slaves had risen considerably, possibly at the instigation of the Raja of Onin, and only three were purchased before Vinck departed for the nearby village of Isera. On the following day, warriors armed with bows and arrows and spears attacked the expedition. Vinck retaliated for the deaths of three of his crew with a combination of cannon-fire and landing parties; the village was set afire and 150 of its inhabitants killed. Hostile encounters continued during their exploration along the coast. At Onin itself their reception was friendly, and twenty-one slaves were purchased: "In the evening came aboard them the King of Onin's son, with an oronçay [*orang kaya*, merchant] and forty men from the islands of Goram and Seram. They told

them, that the King had gone to the islands of the Papous, in search of slaves."[31] To safeguard his crew, Vinck only allowed his men ashore when he was holding local hostages
on his ships. The Onin ruler sold them a few slaves and revealed that the three dead
crewmembers had been eaten. In early May, the ships returned to Roemakai, where, confronted by a flotilla of armed *perahu*, they fired a few well-aimed cannon shots and departed for Banda.[32]

The antagonisms between the Onin leaders and the Dutch continued during the 1660s
and 1670s, with further armed resistance against the Dutch and Onin *kora-kora* raids
throughout the islands.[33] In 1664, the governor of Banda described the coastal people of
the Onin Peninsula as "pirates, murderers and villains, crafty, suspicious and only faithful to those they feared."[34] The Heeren XVII failed to authorize any punitive expeditions
against Onin, probably for two reasons. First, in 1667, the VOC had acknowledged Tidore's jurisdiction over Onin and surrounding areas, which meant that the Sultanate was
responsible for dealing with the marauding pirates. As well, the price of massoi bark had
declined on the world market, with lessened commercial incentive for exerting control.
In 1678, they finally sent Johannes Keyts to Onin to obtain a trade treaty with Raja Jeef
and the local merchants, the first to be signed with any New Guinea leaders. The Onin
treaty, enacted on 15 August, covered maintenance of mutual friendship and peace, and
stipulated adjudication by the Governor of Banda of any quarrels between the *orang kaya*
and VOC officials. It also fixed prices for slaves and massoi bark, to be collected by the
local merchants and sold for cash to the VOC each June.[35] The VOC pledged to uphold the
rights of leading *orang kaya* to their *sosolot* exchange networks—areas of jurisdiction that
included trade monopolies on New Guinea. In return, these merchants were able to purchase their spices at Ambon and Banda prices for the duration of the treaty, but they
were bound to a trade monopoly with the VOC.[36]

Onin had several good anchorages but slaves and massoi bark were its only two com-
modities. The people were of average height, very dark skinned, with little body hair.
Their weaponry consisted of all kinds of swords, bows and arrows, spears, and daggers.
Although nominally free, in reality they lived in fear of the Keffing (just off southern
Seram) and Goram Islanders, who preyed on them and treated them as a slave-reserve.
Keyts sailed to close-by ports at Fataga and Kilbatij, then to Karas Island and into Se-
bakor Bay behind, which was the furthest extent of Onin's jurisdiction. Cape Baik was
under the control of the Cani, Batour, and Karas Islands. The inhabitants were much like
those of Onin-Lascar ("slave Onin"), although they were not exposed to Islam. Their
lifestyles were simple, based on fishing, gathering forest products, and agriculture—
fruit, manioc, beans, and red rice were readily available. Moffon, the principal *orang kaya*
at Karas Island, agreed to a treaty with the VOC that gave the company monopoly rights
and set the price of massoi bark, to be collected each March for cash. At Namatotte Island,
Seram and Goram traders held a monopoly over all massoi bark, ebony wood, and slaves.

Onin, part of Seramese territory, was divided into two parts: Onin-Lascar and Onin-
Kowiai. Within this territory were nine small Islamic kingdoms trading mainly in massoi

bark and slaves: Rumbati, Patipi, Wertuar, Sekar, Arguni, Atiati, Fatafar, and Kowiai (Namatota). The most powerful centers during the seventeenth and eighteenth centuries were Aiduma, Rumbati, and Kowiai. The *sosolot* trade monopolies may also have crossed over the narrow isthmus into Wandaman Bay at the bottom of Cenderawasih Gulf.[37] Tidore's claims to suzerainty were weak, because the local Rajas owed no real allegiance beyond Seram and Goram, and the voc had decided that the area's commercial potential was too small to be of concern. Over the next two decades, the voc used the merchants of Banda and Ambon as their agents at Onin, and confined official Dutch activities to distributing flags as a claim of ownership. Domestic unrest continued—kidnappings, piracy, and murder were more the norm than was regulated trade. Fleets of New Guinea *kora-kora,* mainly working out of Misool in the Raja Empat Group, continuously raided the Kei and Aru Islands, with even Seram, Keffing, Goram, and Banda experiencing disruptions. When a new Sultan ascended the Tidore throne in 1689, the Dutch renewed their 1667 treaty, and added a new Article Five stipulating that Papuan robberies were to be curbed at all costs. Little changed, however. Haga, author of the definitive two-volume 1884 history of Malukan relationships with New Guinea, and of early European exploration, believed that the Sultan had no real power over his New Guinea dominions until the 1830s, and even then it was imposed more with punitive raids, backed by Dutch-provided cannons, than through any permanent authority.[38]

Dutch interest in New Guinea was not rekindled until 1699, when the British Admiralty dispatched William Dampier to explore the New Guinea east coast and New Holland. During the first two decades of the eighteenth century, Cenderawasih Gulf and the Raja Empat Group were further explored. The Raja Empat Rajas remained vassals of the Sultan of Tidore. The coastal chiefs, usually originating from Tidore and Seram, were Moslem. The major trade was in slaves from New Guinea, sago, turtle-shell, ambergris, and spices. The original population was outwardly Moslem although local belief systems were maintained. They subsisted mainly on sago, tubers, and fish.[39] By the second half of the century, although there had been a great deal of coastal exploration, the Dutch had still failed to circumnavigate the southern continent and the voc's power was decreasing. Dutch influence in western New Guinea was mainly brokered through Bacan, and increasingly involved Tidore. The Tidore Sultanate remained dominant in eastern Maluku, charged with maintaining some semblance of law and order in west New Guinea, but it remains doubtful if Tidore's direct power ever reached very far past the islands off the Bird's Head Peninsula. We can be certain that any control Tidore had over Onin or areas further east was wielded indirectly at best, through vassals on Bacan, Seram, and Misool.[40]

English and French Exploration and Settlement

English buccaneer Francis Drake purchased a cargo of Malukan cloves in 1579, and a few years later another piratical adventurer, Thomas Cavendish, called on his way to the

Philippines.[41] Almost one hundred years after that, in 1688, William Dampier visited Maluku. Although impressed by the splendor of the Ternate and Tidor courts and the size of the international trading community in Maluku, England stayed out of the spice trade, avoiding direct confrontation with Portugal, Spain, and Holland. The same could not be said for England's attitude toward New Guinea. Portugal's power had declined, Spain's Asian interests had re-centered on the Philippines, and residual Spanish claims over New Guinea had ceased with the 1714 Treaty of Utrecht. England's relationship with the Dutch was less straightforward. That nation's East India Company remained interested in opening up trade in the Malay Archipelago, particularly in spices, and in establishing free ports such as already existed in the Caribbean.

Dampier persuaded the Admiralty to finance a second voyage in 1699–1700. He arrived at Massau and Emirau Islands (part of the St. Matthias Group north of New Hanover) in February 1700, skirted the east coast of New Ireland, and then sailed around the Feni Group and southern New Ireland. Dampier named St. George's Bay (actually the passage between New Ireland and New Britain), before passing around west New Britain, his name remaining on Dampier Strait (between Umboi Island and New Britain). He named the entire area New Britain, not realizing that New Ireland was a separate island, and he proved that New Guinea's north coast did not extend further east than 148° east longitude.[42] Twenty years later, another Dutch voyage also explored around the Bismarcks, but it added little to existing knowledge,[43] and for the next half-century the peoples of the eastern islands were left alone. They certainly knew nothing of Charles de Brosses' 1750s dreams of establishing a French trading colony in the Bismarcks, and utilizing that position in relation to Maluku, the Philippines, and Canton.

In the same way that changes in the Dutch route to Java early in the seventeenth century brought more shipping into the proximity of western Australia and New Guinea, changes in sea traffic in the mid-eighteenth century brought more English ships close to New Guinea. The East Indiaman *Pitt* failed to catch the 1759 southwest monsoon in the China Sea, managing instead to sail south of the equator using alternative winds to pass north to the Philippines and Macao via the Raja Empat Group. After several experimental voyages during the 1760s, the East India Company began using the Eastern Passage —between Obi and Seram, then through Pitt's Strait (between Batanta and Salawati Islands), or New Guinea's second Dampier Strait between Batanta and Waigeo Islands— as an alternative route during the northeast monsoon. More than 150 ships used this passage in the fifty years after the *Pitt*'s voyage, which drew the Raja Empat Group into the world's shipping lanes.[44]

After England declared war on Spain in 1762, the East India Company captured Manila for two years, providing them with prime access to the China Trade. From the Manila archives came a report of Torres's 1606 voyage through Torres Strait, the first confirmation the English had of that passage. English trade with Canton continued to increase, shifting the company's commercial center of gravity to the east, making it just as essential to protect the routes from India to China as the route from Europe to India. The Dutch in Batavia were so sure that the English intended to settle a colony on Salawati Island, to provide a safe haven for their ships traveling through the Eastern Passage, that in 1762 they sent an expedition to destroy the imaginary settlement. Twenty years later the English were still considering establishing a colony in west New Guinea.[45]

Equivalent routes were also developing on the eastern side of New Guinea: St. George's Channel between New Britain and New Ireland; Vitiaz and Dampier Straits between the mainland and New Britain; and Torres Strait. The English Admiralty sponsored extensive voyages in the 1760s. Philip Carteret on the *Swallow* passed through the Solomon Islands and the Bismarck Archipelago in 1767, exploring around Buka, New Ireland's outliers and down its eastern coast, the first voyage to discover that Dampier's St. George's Bay was actually a passage. During September, the *Swallow* spent a week under repair in English Cove, southern New Ireland, the first European visitors to spend extended time in St. George's Channel. Carteret sailed west along north New Guinea, used Dampier's Strait between Umboi Island and New Britain, and then passed by Wuvulu and Aua Islands in the Ninigo Group, close enough to watch the inhabitants running along the beach.[46]

A year after Carteret's voyage through Melanesia, French explorer Louis de Bougainville, having "rediscovered" the New Hebrides, was unable to penetrate the north of Australia's Great Barrier Reef. He instead sailed to the New Guinea coast at Orangerie Bay, and edged around the many reefs of the Louisiade Archipelago before cutting north through the New Georgia Group. Here he passed between Choiseul (named after the French Minister for the Navy) and the large northern island of the Solomon Group that bears his name. Buka gained its name from a word used by the island's inhabitants when they paddled canoes out to inspect the strange sailing vessels.[47] The French again left their names on New Guinea's offshore islands when Joseph-Antoine Brundy d'Entrecasteaux carried out extensive exploratory work in 1791–1793, passing through parts of the Bismarck Archipelago. At Buka Island, canoes drew near the ship, and the people were friendly, in contrast with their reputation from earlier voyages. The ships took on wood and water at Carteret Harbour, New Ireland, before moving on to the Admiralty Group, where, contrary to Carteret's impression, the people were again friendly and willing to trade. They found nothing to confirm information from a voyage out of newly-settled Sydney, in New South Wales, that Manus Islanders in canoes had been seen wearing remnants of French uniforms—possibly from survivors of the lost La Pérouse expedition from some years earlier. On the second leg of the voyage, D'Entrecasteaux came upon the Louisiade Archipelago. His ships skirted its northern side, passing Rossel Island (which Bougainville had encountered), and moved on to the Renard, Misima, Deboyne, and Bonvouloir Islands. On 16 June 1793, D'Entrecasteaux reached the archipelago that now bears his name, and a few days later he sailed on to the Trobriand Group.[48]

Meanwhile, England had been busy with exploration and settlement plans. The first

English voyage to approach New Guinea's southern coast from the east, rather than the west, was that of James Cook. After circumnavigating New Zealand, his ship the *Endeavour* traveled up the east coast of Australia in 1770, and passed through Torres Strait, a feat that finally determined for the English that New Guinea was not joined to New Holland. A small party from the ship landed in Asmat territory west of Dolak Island, but they were repelled by sixty to 100 warriors armed with spears, who also threw lime at them, presumably intending to ward off the unwelcome spirits. Cook retaliated with small and ball shot.[49] The British were already well established in north Sumatra, when in 1772–1774 they attempted to build a settlement on Balambangan Island north of Borneo, and another on Penang Island in the Straits of Malacca in 1786. That same year they decided, based on information from the Cook's voyage, to establish a convict settlement on the east coast of New South Wales. The convict fleet arrived at what is now Sydney, in 1788. Once New South Wales was established, the shortest (but most dangerous to navigate) route to Batavia and Bengal passed through Torres Strait and along southern New Guinea. At the end of the eighteenth century, Britain was actually showing more interest in New Guinea than the Dutch voc. Thomas Forrest and a small crew on the ten-ton galley *Tartar* spent a few weeks at Dorei Bay in the northwest of Cenderawasih Gulf in 1774. In an effort to break the Dutch monopoly they collected nutmeg trees before returning to Balambangan. They reported that the local people "purchase their iron tools, chopping knives, and axes, blue and red bastaes, china beads, plates, basons, &c. from the Chinese. The Chinese carry back Missoy bark, which they get to the eastward of Dory, at a place called Warmasine, or Warapine; it is worth 30 dollars, a pecul [133 lb.] on Java. They trade also in slaves, ambergrease, swallo, or sea slug, tortoiseshell, small pearls, black loories, large red loories, birds of Paradise, and many kinds of dead birds, which the Papua men have a particular way of drying."[50]

During the 1770s and 1780s, the Dutch, in their quest for monopoly control of the spice trade, unsuccessfully tried to halt illicit trading in long nutmegs from Onin, which they recognized as being under the control of Tidore. Usually they relied on the Sultan's forces to keep foreigners out of the region, but they also used small Dutch patrols to destroy spice trees. Forrest, reconnoitering for Britain, had to dodge Dutch ships in waters off the Bird's Head. He found that the Dutch only permitted Chinese merchants, carrying a pass from the Sultan of Tidore and flying Dutch colors, to visit west New Guinea. They trusted the Chinese not to trade independently for spices. Coastal tribes, whom Forrest called "Papuans," controlled the spice trade, in turn bartering iron for the services and produce of the "Haraforas," whom he described as the headhunters of the Arfak Mountains.[51]

The voc was clearly in decline during the second half of the eighteenth century, and by 1780 Holland was once again at war with Britain. The war ended with the 1784 Treaty of Paris, which finally broke the Dutch monopoly over the East Indies, and guaranteed British ships free access to the archipelago. Reverses in Dutch politics at home and in the

Indies changed policy in the empire, leading in 1798–1799 to the heavily indebted VOC being wound up when its charter expired.[52] One of the VOC's last maneuvers in Maluku was to depose Sultan Jamaluddin of Tidore in 1779. Three of his sons escaped to Seram, where one, Nuku, resumed the title, and attempted to restore Tidore's power. After an unsuccessful rebellion against the VOC and Ternate, Nuku retreated to the Raja Empat Islands, fighting a guerrilla war against the Dutch, styling himself Sultan of Jailolo, Seram, and the Papuas. This gave Nuku control over the Pitt and Dampier Straits section of the Eastern Passage.[53]

After Forrest's voyage, the British realized the political advantages of alliance with Nuku. Dutch intelligence heard rumors that Britain was planning to establish a base at Dorei Bay, and that Nuku was willing to dispose of the "Papuan Islands" to the British if they helped him to move against Ternate and the Dutch. In 1791–1792, John MacCluer of the Bombay Marine charted the Gulf of Onin (Berau Bay, renamed MacCluer Gulf) and Onin Peninsula, reporting favorably on New Guinea's potential for exporting nutmeg and massoi bark. MacCluer was made well aware of the dangers of dealing with the coastal people when his ship's doctor was clubbed to death while trading for bird-of-paradise pelts. Returning in 1794, MacCluer accepted the cession of New Guinea to Britain by Nuku's emissary at Gebe Island in the Raja Empat Group. Nuku's power was strengthened through his contact with the ships that used the Eastern Passage, which provided him with war supplies, and through a British port briefly established nearby in 1793. After Holland was occupied by France in 1795, and was therefore at war with Britain, the British could legitimately assist Nuku and their own interests. They captured Maluku in 1796–1797, took Ambon and Banda, and finally drove the Dutch out of Ternate in 1801. When Britain seized Ambon, Nuku sent 3,000 men and 100 boats in support.[54] The ageing Nuku was eventually installed as Sultan of Tidore, an honor the Dutch had denied him for twenty years. His triumph was short-lived, however, as peace was made in Europe in 1802 and all Dutch territory other than Ceylon was restored. He died in 1805.[55]

British Settlements, 1793–1829

Although Nuku's offer to allow annexation of New Guinea was not accepted by the East India Company, it did inspire and give some legitimacy to the earliest European settlement on New Guinea, a private British venture at Dorei Bay.[56] It was founded by John Hayes, a Lieutenant in the Bombay Marine, and financed by merchants in India. They were motivated by Forrest's expedition, the desire to acquire spices to sell in Calcutta, and the chance to establish an *entrepôt* near the new Sydney-to-Canton shipping route. Hayes' two ships took the southern route around Australia and sailed north to the Louisiades in hopes of locating the passage through Torres Strait. Failing that, they headed through St. George's Channel and along the north coast. The ships were by now so unseaworthy, and the crews so badly debilitated, that they had no choice but to land at Dorei Bay, which Hayes renamed Restoration Bay. This became the port for New Albion, a colony that Hayes claimed stretched from Waigeo Island off the Bird's Head to Rossel Island in the Louisiades, 2,500 kilometers west. He attempted to assert a monopoly, and refused access to regular Chinese traders who held permits authorized by Tidore and the Dutch.[57]

Hayes, like Forrest before him, was offered slaves for purchase, and he reported that the coastal people lived in fear of raids from Malay slavers. They also kept slaves themselves, usually prisoners of war from inland tribes.[58] During Forrest's expedition, drawings were made of Dorei village, several local men, and outrigger canoes. There are also illustrations dating from Hayes' 1793 settlement, of local people, the tombs of important leaders (which appear to be Malay-influenced), canoes, and houses built on platforms over the water. These typical New Guinea coastal dwellings, suspended on stilts with walkways to the beach, had changed little by the end of the nineteenth century.[59] Hayes described the local people as "very handsome, being tall and well-made, with well-cut features and large aquiline noses," their deep brown skin color approaching black. Although most wore their hair short, some frizzed theirs out with six-pronged bamboo combs. The inland people, known as "Arfaks," looked quite different—they were darker-skinned, their hair was shorter and more matted, and many were afflicted with skin-diseases.[60] Around 500 local people were employed in establishing Fort Coronation and its surrounding plantations, which contained 1,500 nutmeg and massoi trees. Presumably, Malay forges for smelting metals were operating at Dorei in 1793–1795: they were in use at Triton Bay in 1606, and were sketched at Dorei during Dumont d'Urville's expeditions in the 1820s. Reading from the 1820s sketches, bows and arrows were still in use but metal machetes had replaced other cutting blades. One mealtime scene depicts men dressed in Malay-style *sarung*, while another sketch suggests that loincloths were also normal attire. Sacred buildings were also evident, and one on the water's edge at Dorei was gracefully supported by carved wooden figures.[61]

Hayes, in need of supplies, took a cargo of fragrant barks, turtle-shells, beeswax, ambergris, bêche-de-mer, and bird-of-paradise pelts to sell in Bengal, where he tried unsuccessfully to convince his government to ratify the colony, stressing its potential as a source of spices and as a port on the Sydney-to-Canton route.[62] Without government assistance the colony could not continue. Maluku leaders encouraged the colony: Nuku visited early in 1794, followed in August and September by two north Halmahera leaders, Rato and Oese from Galela. MacCluer, who met Hayes in Canton, took provisions to Fort Coronation in November, but by then many of the twenty-six men left behind had died of fever or had been captured as slaves and sold to Seram. When Hayes' ship returned in May 1795, the settlement was deserted.[63]

Events in Europe also took their toll. France's revolutionary wars of the 1790s limited the availability of English ships for further surveying or settlement in New Guinea. The

Napoleonic wars that followed led to a long battle by the Dutch to defend Java, which they lost to occupational forces from British India between 1811 and 1816. The sojourn of Lieutenant-Governor Thomas Stamford Raffles in Java had one unexpected outcome: he returned to England with a ten-year-old New Guinean purchased from a Bali slave market. During his fifteen-month's stay in London, "Dick Papua" became a minor celebrity, interviewed by linguist William Marsden, medically examined by Sir Everard Home, and drawn by William Daniell. He accompanied Raffles back to his Bencoolen and Singapore postings, but is not mentioned again after 1818.[64]

The 1815 peace treaty restored all previous Dutch colonial possessions. In the same year, new limits to Tidore's influence were determined, including suzerainty of the Numfor settlements on the New Guinea coast. After the interregnum in Java and the establishment of a British base on Singapore Island (1819), British focus shifted to the eastern end of the archipelago and to northern Australia, where there were short-lived settlements at Melville Island (1824–1829), Raffles Bay (1827–1829), and Port Essington (1838–1849).[65] The wars after the French Revolution and the imperial adventures of Napoleon (1792–1814) cut Holland off from its earlier maritime exploration and trading ventures, and provided Britain with a temporary monopoly over trade. For several years, until its huge East Indies territory was finally restored in 1816, the new United Kingdom of the Netherlands received no supplies from its colonial outposts. After the wars, Dutch merchants were fully occupied in the Indies. They showed no interest in the rapidly developing Pacific fur, sandalwood, and sealing trades, and paid little notice to the whaling industry that was slowly opening up the Pacific to European commerce.

The major explorers around New Guinea during the 1810s–1830s were French: De Freycinet on *L'Uranie* (1817–1820), Duperrey on *Coquille* (1823), Dumont d'Urville on the *Astrolabe* (1826–1827), and the *Astrolabe* and the *Zélée* (1837–1839). As had become the usual pattern, explorations around west New Guinea concentrated on the Raja Empat Islands, the Bird's Head, and Onin, while the Bismarck Archipelago became the dominant base in the east. The ports in St. George's Channel, Dorei Bay, and the Raja Empat Group were becoming much-visited haunts. In 1827, Dumont d'Urville found it difficult to obtain enough provisions at Dorei. He noted that the people were no longer as hospitable as when he had first visited three years earlier, and only accepted payment in Spanish piastres which they used to make bracelets: "Ugly, filthy, and badly made, they wore up to three or four bracelets on each arm, depending on their wealth."[66] A better welcome came from the Ayakis, a neighboring group on poor terms with the Dorei Bay people, who readily provided Dumont d'Urville with wallabies, birds-of-paradise, and insects, augmenting his natural history collection.[67]

During the travails of the French occupation of Holland, Stadholder William V and his son, the future William VI (later William I), were forced to flee to England. When William I was restored to his united Dutch-Belgium kingdom, he pursued deliberately expansionist policies, utilizing the industrial strength of Belgium combined with the colonial territories and trading acumen of Holland. William had been influenced by the time that he and his father had spent exiled in England during the Napoleonic years, and he believed that at least partial free trade was a better option than mercantilist monopoly. The Netherlands already knew that there was no great economic gain to be made from extending commerce with New Guinea. The 1824 Treaty of London between Britain and the Netherlands awarded the British rights of free trade in the archipelago, reaffirming the Dutch monopoly over trade around Maluku, but contained no direct reference to New Guinea. Meanwhile, the Dutch were considering the implications of British settlement on the east coast of Australia and its inevitable extension to other regions of the continent. The British settlements at Melville Island, Raffles Bay on the Coburg Peninsula, and Port Essington, all in northern Australia, were part of a much wider jockeying for commercial and strategic advantage between Britain and Holland. But they were also motivated by a British desire to forestall Dutch and French settlements. In turn, they provoked the reluctant Dutch, who were now fearful that the British would attempt to establish another settlement in west New Guinea. For instance, when Melville Island was settled, the Dutch responded by sending an expedition to strengthen political ties with the Aru Islands, and several years after Port Essington was established the Dutch commissioned A. L. Weddick, the Governor of Borneo, to enquire into establishing an administrative post at Aru.[68]

During the mid-1790s, the officers of the New South Wales Corps had become fully-fledged merchants in their own right, establishing commercial trade quite independent of the East India Company. Much of the trade was clandestine, and operated using loopholes in the East India Company's monopoly. Speculators prospered with the increase in the British shipping that was visiting the colony, caused by the successful campaign by British whaling interests to dilute the East India Company's monopoly over all British trade east of the Cape of Good Hope. Many of these whalers operated under Company license, and were thus legally able to engage in "country trade" (British-registered ships of less than 350 tons, trading locally) within the Company's monopoly area. By 1800, several of these "country traders" had established agents in New South Wales. The first colonial sealers, whalers, and sandalwood collectors began operating in the 1790s. Shipbuilders defied the prohibition by constructing substantial vessels in the colony. In 1806, the Grenville Ministry in Britain tabled a bill that would exempt New South Wales from the Company monopoly, and allow colonial ships under Company license to trade directly with Britain. The bill was shelved when the Grenville government fell, although the sentiment that had promoted it continued to grow.[69]

After the British seizure of the Dutch East Indies territory in 1811, the further relaxation of the East India Company monopoly in 1813 and 1819 (when colonial shipping was released from restrictive size limits), and the growth of a trade route between the British colonies in eastern Australia[70] and India and Canton, these trading houses established flourishing networks. After the Dutch regained control of the East Indies, facilities remained available to British traders, although their lives were made difficult by high import duties, and by the lack of customs clearance beyond Batavia or a consular presence even there. While the East India Company still prevented direct access to China, intermediate bases were needed. These factors, and the loss of Java, were exactly the reasons that led Raffles to establish a strategically placed free port on Singapore Island in January 1819, at the foot of Melaka Strait but still within the East India Company's region. They were also why merchants lobbied to establish a port in northern Australia, intended to cover the possible loss of Singapore and create an equivalent British base that could service the eastern end of the archipelago. What they did not stress, but obviously knew, was that the north Australian settlements were within the colony of New South Wales, and beyond the jurisdiction of both the Board of Trade and the East India Company.[71]

A bicameral British parliamentary inquiry with broad terms of reference tabled its findings in 1821, which concentrated on the relationship between the Company and the eastern traders. Over the previous half-century, coinciding with Britain's rapid industrialization, economic philosophy had moved away from mercantilism and toward free trade and laissez-faire attitudes. Although the East India Company's charter remained in force until 1833, continuing its right to control all British shipping to Canton, the minimum weight restriction on "country" shipping was no longer enforced and the right of British subjects to carry out trade between ports under the Company's jurisdiction was affirmed. By 1823, the traders, fearing the total loss of Singapore, or its control by the Company, were lobbying to have the Colonial Office establish a settlement in northern Australia.[72]

During 1823 and early 1824, delicate negotiations were entered into with the Dutch over the ramifications of the Singapore settlement and any future northern Australian ports. The Dutch government in the Indies had made further moves to exclude British traders by imposing a prohibitive duty on all ships arriving in ballast, and searching for a cargo, common practice for ships that had just delivered convicts to eastern Australia. Fearing that the cost of sending convicts to New South Wales would become prohibitive, Britain managed to negotiate the 1824 Treaty of London with the Dutch. Henceforth, Melaka Strait was to be the dividing line between British and Dutch interests in the Malay Archipelago. The Netherlands recognized British rights in Singapore, and it was agreed that neither side would form any new settlements in the east of the archipelago without the permission of their home government. The Dutch allowed reciprocity of trade throughout their Indies, and retained rights to levy a tax rate not exceeding double that which they imposed on their own ships. Against the advice of Governor Pieter Merkus of Maluku, and that of Governor-General Van der Capellen, the Netherlands maintained its monopoly of the spice trade in the east of the archipelago. Although it eventually became moribund, the monopoly was not abandoned until 1863. As a supplementary move to the Treaty of London, and at the behest of Governor Merkus, in 1824 the Dutch also removed their injunction against illegal spice trees in Maluku, made new contracts with the Ternate and Tidore Sultanates, and recognized Tidore control over the Raja Empat Islands.

Dutch Settlements, 1828–1836

Rumors of a British settlement on the New Guinea coast, somewhere east of the Aru Islands, reached the ears of Pieter Merkus, Governor of Maluku in 1826. It was likely the decision to shift from Melville Island to Raffles Bay on the Coburg Peninsula that misled the governor. Because any British settlement in New Guinea would have been contrary to the 1824 treaty, Merkus quickly dispatched D. H. Kolff on the *Dourga* to search the New Guinea coast east as far as Dolak Island. When no British settlement was found, Merkus, still uncertain, advised that Tidore should reaffirm its claim to the "whole island [of New Guinea] as a Tidorese possession," and that a Dutch settlement should be established on New Guinea, posthaste.[73] He reasoned that, based on the precedent of British territorial claims in Australia, one settlement together with the Tidore claims would safeguard Dutch rights in New Guinea. In Batavia, Lieutenant-Governor-General Chassé and his superior, Commissioner-General Du Bus de Gisignies were cautious. They sought advice from The Hague and suggested that Tidore's support would be needed. The Minister for Colonial Affairs, fearing expansion of British trade in the eastern islands, wrote to the king in March 1827, seconding Merkus' concerns.

The final decision was left to Du Bus de Gisignies, who imposed two conditions if Merkus was to go ahead: the base would have to support the development of Dutch whaling interests and other trading ventures, and it would have to be cheap. Merkus needed no further urging, and after an abortive attempt to settle on the coast near Dolak Island, they chose Lobo (renamed Merkus-oord) on Oeroe Langoeroe (renamed Triton Bay), and began building Fort du Bus. Formal annexation took place on 24 August 1828, placing under the control of the Governor of Maluku all of west New Guinea from Cape Bonpland (Saprop Maneh) 140°47' on the north coast, along to the Cape of Good Hope (Cape Yamarsba, or Kain Kain Beba) on the north coast, then around to the 141° east latitude on the south coast, including the interior. This same meridian was used in the Portuguese version of the Pope's 1494 Treaty of Tordesillas. The annexation was carefully phrased so as not to usurp the prior rights of the Sultan of Tidore to four areas of Cenderawasih Gulf and to the Raja Empat Islands. Even though the proclamation carefully acknowledged Tidore rights to the Mansarij, Karondefer, Ambarssura, and Amberpon districts,[74] and though Commissioner A. J. Van Delden was given clear instructions to avoid conflict with Malay traders, he chose a bay in the Onin-Kowiai region that was regularly visited by the Seramese. Indeed, some local people spoke Seramese and were already Moslems. On the shore of the bay was a Malay-style house, once the residence of an Islamic Imaum from Seram who had converted the local people. Leading men dressed in Malay-style, and acted as agents in the slave trade. They in turn feared the New

Guinea pirate-slavers operating out of the MacCluer Gulf. Their canoes had outriggers like those of Maluku and their houses, too, were built in Malay-style.[75]

Contrary to the his instructions, Merkus styled the settlement not as a trading base but as a military garrison. Drawings of the fort at the time of its construction show a square within palisades defended by cannons, a powder-store, and two officer's homes each of two rooms with front verandas. Outside the palisade stood a sentry box, a cookhouse, and the soldiers' barrack, while a Dutch flag fluttered gamely overhead. A second Dutch expedition planned for 1829 did not eventuate until 1835. The inhabitants of the small wooden fort struggled on until 1836, suffering from malaria and other tropical diseases, and regularly attacked by locals provoked by Seramese traders. In the end Fort du Bus was abandoned, a total failure. Merkus-oord never fulfilled its expectations as a trading base, the endeavor's only real gain having been some further exploration of the southern coast as far west as Dolak Island.[76]

Perhaps the most unusual Dutch plan of this period was a relatively unknown one uncovered by historian Jeroen Overwell. In 1829, when the newly appointed Governor-General Van den Bosch was about to leave Holland for Batavia, he received instructions from King William I "to order an investigation of the West Coast of New Holland, with the power, should it be so judged, to take possession of a part of this coast in His Majesty's name." Following the lead of Britain in New South Wales, during the 1820s the Netherlands considered establishing a convict colony in the region, perhaps in Maluku, New Guinea, or western Australia. Toward this end, Van den Bosch received permission to take possession of part of the northwest coast of Australia, but he never proceeded with the plan.[77]

"Pax Neerlandica"—nineteenth-century territorial expansion in the Indies—established colonial troops and administrators at various outposts, but not on mainland west New Guinea. The Dutch were very aware of the major British convict settlement at Sydney in eastern Australia, and its 1820s outposts at Moreton Bay and Melville Island, at Raffles Bay, King George Sound (Albany), and Swan River (Perth). These were supplemented in the 1830s by Adelaide and Port Essington, then Somerset and Palmerston (Darwin) in the 1860s. English expeditions around eastern New Guinea were becoming numerous, particularly those relating to Torres Strait and southeastern New Guinea, but there would be no further permanent Dutch government presence on west New Guinea until the late 1890s. The archival records of the Ministry of Colonial Affairs contain constant reminders to the Governors of Maluku to find a new site for settlement on New Guinea, and they reveal a monitoring of every suggestion for colonization emanating from interests operating on the eastern side of New Guinea. The Netherlands was very suspicious of all non-Dutch "scientific" expeditions, and also feared the potential of the British settlement at Port Essington—from there traders might reach out toward the Maluku-New Guinea trade routes, through Kei, Aru, Goram, and Seram Islands.[78]

In the 1840s and 1850s, the Sultan of Tidore's fleet of *kora-kora* annually raided villages in Cenderawasih Gulf in the guise of tribute missions. Tidore's demands, extracted in the form of slaves, turtle-shell, and bird-of-paradise pelts, and enforced by the Sultan's punitive *kora-kora* fleet, struck terror into his so-called subjects living along the coasts. Fighting *kora-kora* were fast and frightening to behold, and their viciousness was legendry. For instance, in the late 1840s Kurudu village on a small island on the east side of the gulf was destroyed and more than 200 of its inhabitants taken into slavery.[79] A few years later, a Tidore fleet traveling with an 1850 Dutch expedition to Cenderawasih Gulf struck fear into the local people. The *Circe*, charged with placing Dutch coats of arms around the coast as far east as Humboldt Bay (the outer limit of the Tidore's claims of suzerainty),[80] was accompanied by eight of the Sultan's vessels, all ornamented with standards, pendants, and ensigns, and conveying large gongs to create a deafening noise. Two of the *kora-kora* were equipped with cannons. Lieutenant Kops, on board the *Circe*, described the scene:

> On the news of the arrival of the *hongi* [war] fleet, the women and children took to flight with the small canoes, carrying with them everything of the least value. They went to the interior bays and the opposite side, in order to avoid the rapacity of the crews of the *hongi*. The chief at once went to Captain Amir, and took with him, as token of his submission, a great number of birds of paradise and a slave for a present.
>
> It is not to be wondered at that the *hongi* instill so much fear everywhere, for wherever they come, the crews pillage and steal as much as they can; they destroy the plantations and appropriate to themselves all they choose. It is through means of the *hongi* voyages that the Sultan maintains his power, for on failure of obedience or negligence in the execution of orders, such a fleet is sent to murder or to make prisoners of the population, to destroy the kampongs, and thus to punish all in a severe manner.[81]

The important leaders at Dorei dressed in Malay-style when greeting foreigners, wearing loose trousers, calico coats, and head-cloths, reverting to tapa loincloths at other times. The women wore short blue calico skirts or loose trousers. Many men had crossed swords and *kris*-blade tattoos, and both sexes wore armlets of shell, fiber, copper, or silver wire. As noted previously, people here operated iron forges and worked iron, copper, and silver obtained by trade.[82] The Dutch-Tidore fleet continued east, calling at several places along the coast as far as Humboldt Bay. There they investigated the possibility of beginning a Dutch garrison as a convenience for shipping traveling along the north coast. This government base was eventually established sixty years later: Hollandia, now Jayapura, the capital of Indonesia's Papua Province.[83]

The Sultan's writ was only ever strong in Cenderawasih Gulf, where he appointed local chiefs as his officials, called Raja, Singaji, Major, Kapitan, or Kapitan-laut. These local officials or agents in the gulf had little power—real authority remained with the Sultan, or the Singaji and Raja of Gebe: "When one of the principal chiefs dies, information of the event is conveyed to the Sultan by one of the relatives, who at the same time takes him a present of slaves and birds of paradise, as a token of fealty. This person is generally named as the successor of the deceased and is presented with a yellow kabaya, breeches and headkerchief. He is then bound to pay a yearly tax to the Sultan of a slave, and to reinforce the hongi with three vessels and to furnish it with provisions."[84]

During the decade after the settlement at Merkus-oord, the Dutch virtually ignored New Guinea, and relied once more on Tidore's supposed suzerainty to justify their vague control. They were not willing to accept any challenge to their sovereignty over west New Guinea, but refused to safeguard themselves from further British incursions. This attitude continued until 1846, when Britain requested clarification of the exact areas in the eastern Malay Archipelago under Dutch claim. That same year, British naval Lieutenant Charles Yule of HMS *Bramble* landed on the south New Guinea coast, and proclaimed the annexation of eastern New Guinea. A. L. Weddick, the Dutch Governor in Borneo, was asked to assess the extent of Tidore's territorial claims and told to "cover the widest possible area." He asserted that Tidore's rule extended along the north coast to Cape Bonpland near Humboldt Bay, along the south coast to around the 141st meridian, and through the interior. Weddick was also concerned about the commercial consequences of Port Essington, fearing that if the right Dutch trading balance was not created in the east of the Indies, maritime and forest product traders might eventually resort to the north Australian port. Makasar had been made a free port in 1846, and as a result of Weddick's report Ambon, Bandaneira, and Ternate were added to the Dutch list in 1853.[85]

In a decree in July 1848, freshly motivated by Britain's HMS *Rattlesnake* expedition to Torres Strait, the Dutch once more asserted their dormant rights to west New Guinea. The Dutch half of New Guinea was recognized as being within the territory of Tidore. Letters of appointment were issued to New Guinea coastal rulers under the suzerainty of the Sultan of Tidore, supplemented by certificates issued by the Dutch Residency in Banda to local "rulers" not under Tidore control.[86] Ten years after the Dutch re-annexation, the Sultan of Tidore's claims of suzerainty had shrunken to just Ternate, northern Halmahera, and the Numfor settlements in Cenderawasih Gulf. By then half of the settlement at Ternate was owned by Dutch trader Renesse van Duivenboden, who wielded more power than the local Sultan. In 1861, Dutch authorities refused to authorize any further *hongi*-fleet expeditions. At the beginning of the 1870s, Tidore reaffirmed its vassal status to the Dutch East Indies government and allowed Dutch indirect rule to continue, but the ancient greatness of this Spice Island capital was by the mid-nineteenth century a shadow of the trading Mecca that had so impressed Francis Drake in 1579.[87] Tidore finally collapsed in the 1900s. There was no Sultan after 1905, and in 1907 the Dutch took away Tidore's Sulawesi territories. Two years later they forced the Sultanate to relinquish all right to independence. The same fate was imposed on Ternate and Bacan in 1910, and the Sultan of Ternate was banished to Java in 1914.[88]

On the other side of the Bird's Head, where the Onin Peninsula was also a center for slave-trading, the focus of power was not Tidore but Seram. Coastal peoples captured slaves from inland, and sold them to traders from Seram and other islands in the Banda Sea within the *kain timur* trade.[89] In the eighteenth century, two centers on the west of Onin Peninsula, Roemakai and Fatage, were much visited by slavers from Banda and Seram.[90] At the small Seram-Laut Archipelago, in the mid-1820s New Guinea male and female slaves could be seen in the depot, awaiting sale and used as rowers on Seramese galleys, which traveled as far as Bali and Singapore to engage in trading and piracy. New Guinea slaves were held in high esteem and were more highly valued than slaves from Bali, Lombok, or Sumbawa. Women from Koby, Ay, and Karas were considered the most attractive, and they often became secondary wives of traders and chiefs in Seram. New Guinea middlemen arranged the procurement of slaves.[91]

The 1828 and 1848 New Guinea claims were further clarified in 1875, when the eastern boundary was fixed as a straight line joining the two points on opposite coasts, and the territory attached to the Ternate Residency.[92] Occasionally, the Dutch were rather vague about how far east their territory stretched. Expeditions sailed east as far as modern-day Wewak, and in 1879 it was suggested that the border should be extended to the 145th meridian, as far as Bogia in present-day Madang Province of Papua New Guinea.[93] A decade later, the Berlin Conference agreed that direct rule had to be established to validate a territorial claim. Even so, it took the Netherlands until 1898 to establish its first permanent government centers on the New Guinea mainland. West New Guinea was governed through the Dutch navy until the 1890s: the captains acted as policing and diplomatic officers, as well as collectors of ethnographic information along the coast. Dutch use of steamboats in the second half of the century made it easier to control the excesses of the Sultans and Rajas, the *sosolot* trade, and piracy. This was similar to the way the British Royal Navy Australia Station operated as a floating government in the southwest Pacific Islands. Tours of duty visited main ports along the coast, investigating complaints. Hostile New Guineans who had transgressed against the European presence were punished with bombardment and calculated destruction of property. French, Spanish and German warships also patrolled the coasts, and mounted punitive bombardments and destroyed property if there was an attack on their citizens.[94]

Indigenous reactions to the decline of Ternate and Tidore, balanced by the increasing Dutch presence, were varied. Coastal trade became safer and more regulated, but few inland people had any direct knowledge of the encroachments by Malays and Europeans. Foreign trade goods found their way into the Highlands, although to a far lesser extent than along the coast. Despite the extensive contact in areas like the Bird's Head, inland cultural spheres remained extremely isolated. As a useful comparison we can look to Australia's Aborigines—they also had extensive communications through trade routes, and information about European arrival around the coast in the south and east made its way ahead of the advancing frontier, even to the north coast.[95] We can be fairly sure that this also occurred in New Guinea.

Dutch government records show a considerable amount of local resistance along the coast onwards from the 1850s, and provide tantalizing evidence of social upheavals in Cenderawasih Gulf, brought on by intensified contact with outsiders. Two prophetic leaders emerged in 1852. One was transported to Ternate, only to be replaced by another from the Schouten Islands above Cenderawasih Gulf. Two more appeared in the next two years, and they had many followers. These prophets predate the arrival of evangelical missionaries at Dorei in 1855, but presumably the incidents they described were earlier events in the same prophetic sequence.[96] Missionaries first heard the story in 1857 involving Mansren, a messenger whose role was to establish a state of salvation through prosperity. The cult was based on Biak Island, and extended to areas around the huge gulf. The hero of this prophetic movement was Manarmakeri, who was supposed to be in communication with the morning star and to have accumulated great wealth. Rebuffed by his own people, who did not believe his claims, Manarmakeri went away, some said to the west, which explained the great abundance and dominance the people saw emanating from the Malay Islands. Others said that Manarmakeri was waiting near the Mamberamo River. All believed that when he returned a golden age would arrive. Today the morning star remains a potent symbol of contemporary west New Guinea independence movements.

Prophetic practices continued. In 1867, one of the many *konoors* (prophets) had a vision and led his people against their enemy. Another prophet in 1883 gained influence beyond his own Biak district and was officially recognized by the Sultan of Tidore. Twenty years later his cult stories had incorporated a cargo ship that would bring goods, and he held meetings, parades, and military exercises, which were concealed from the Dutch. One song said "Lord, we wish to come to you, but we cannot; the strange Dutch birds are closing the door." This prophet remained powerful for at least twenty years, and his daughter married Lan Sen, an official of Chinese origin. In 1910, the prophet was still influential enough to journey east to the Mamberamo River to investigate Moszkowski, a German physician and explorer, to see if he could be Mansren returned. In the same year, when the Corps of the Topographical Engineers began work at the Mamberamo, Biak people decided that Mansren had drawn them to the seat of his power. The cult movement still existed into the 1940s.[97] Just as must have been occurring for centuries when new migrants arrived and disturbed previous patterns, events had to be explained and newcomers were incorporated into local circumstances.

This chapter has concentrated on the Bird's Head, Onin, and Cenderawasih regions of west New Guinea, the three core cultural spheres most in contact with Asia and early European colonial ventures in Southeast Asia, regions alive with foreign influences that increased rapidly in the second half of the nineteenth century. We should not, however, conclude that the populous remainder of west New Guinea was unaffected by the changes further west. There are several other core cultural spheres in west New Guinea: the Asmat of lower Baliem River, the peoples of the upper Digul River and the Trans-Fly, Humboldt Bay and the Lake Sentani area, and Paniai Lakes and Baliem Valley in the Highlands. The west New Guinea Highlands are not as populous as the mountain valleys in the east, but even so there was a considerable population living there, the largest number in the Baliem Valley, neighboring valleys to the northwest, and around the Paniai Lakes. These areas had no direct contact with Malay or European intruders until well into the twentieth century. They may have received occasional foreign artifacts via trade routes, but these would have been so detached from their origins as to have been no more than mysterious treasures, unexplained but useful.

The north coast was more regularly visited by foreigners than the south coast, the latter being much more swampy and less hospitable to European occupation, and sparsely populated from Dolak Island to the border with what became British territory. But even the north coast was fairly uninviting to European maritime and trading interests, with no major harbors between Cenderawasih Gulf and Humboldt Bay. Similar studies need to be made of the effect of introduced goods on local trade systems around Humboldt Bay—a whaling, trading, and scientific base in the nineteenth century, and a missionary and government settlement from the first decade of the twentieth century—or of Merauke, the southern government base established in the 1900s. In both cases, because of their proximity to the east New Guinea settlements, there are difficulties in separating out the effect of changes introduced from the west and those hailing from the east. The Dutch-German-British border that cut through the middle of New Guinea did not coincide with the preexisting cultural spheres, long-held traditions, trade routes, and marriages that figuratively and physically crisscrossed the area. While Europeans' coastal markers indicated where the border began, the interior remained unknown to them.

The scholarly fascination with the Bird's Head region focuses on the way established indigenous Melanesian and Malay trading ventures blend with the more recent commercial interests of European and Chinese traders. Asian contact built up gradually over hundreds of years, possibly a millennium, supplemented by a shorter period of European involvement. This Malay and European presence may well have had a similar effect on local communities as the Lapita migrants once had, three thousand years earlier. As Ian Lilley suggests, the Lapita trade diaspora probably established settlements of spatially dispersed trader communities quite culturally distinct from the communities in which they lived.[98] This is clearly the case with traders of Maluku, and to a lesser extent their European counterparts—whalers, traders, and missionaries—who established bases through the Raja Empat Islands and around the coast of west New Guinea.

The fringes of west New Guinea—mainly Cenderawasih Gulf, the Bird's Head, and Onin Peninsulas, the Raja Empat Islands, Seram, Kei, and Aru Islands—were drawn into the periphery of the world economy, but this region was always as much a part of Maluku as of New Guinea. The earlier Dutch annexations, and the 1884 partition of east New Guinea between Britain and Germany, created three colonial New Guinea spheres of influence, hardly noticed by the wider world until well into the twentieth century. In reality, the huge island remained a setting of many cultural spheres, limited zones of colonial control, and still unknown and unmapped communities.

The Nineteenth Century
Trade, Settlement, and Missionaries

As a consequence of European industrialization and the expansion of empires, contact between New Guineans and the outside world intensified throughout the nineteenth century. Tentative Dutch moves to claim west New Guinea during the first half of the century were in part a reaction to British interest in the region, but their justification was substantially in terms of Malukan suzerainty. As the century progressed, the elements involved grew more diverse and led inexorably to formal, but ultimately superficial and lightly-felt colonization. This chapter and the next are an attempt to encapsulate these changes. Of substantial importance to foreign interest in New Guinea was the establishment of British, French, and German colonies in Australia, New Zealand, Fiji, New Caledonia, and Samoa, which introduced settler societies into the southwest Pacific region. As these grew, they necessitated the establishment of shipping routes, initially skirting Melanesia and New Guinea but, as navigation knowledge improved, coming ever closer to the islands, eventually passing through them and establishing favored ports.

At the same time, maritime trade was becoming more diverse. The initial products Europeans sought in west New Guinea were fragrant and medicinal barks, spices, bird pelts, and slaves, really an extension of Malay commerce. As the nineteenth century progressed, Europeans diversified their interests to include trade in a larger range of marine and land products, and whaling. Commercial extraction also progressed, from the simple gathering of luxury items to processing them—whale oil, pearls, pearlshell, and bêche-de-mer. As well as trading with passing ships and working in these processing industries, coastal New Guineans began to receive visits by scientific expeditions. As a consequence of this intensified contact, some foreign visitors began to stay longer, first castaways and beachcombers, then Christian missionaries, naturalists, bird-pelt collectors, gold miners, settlers, planters, and eventually government officials. New Guinean labor was used in the east, harnessed to plantation economies in the surrounding colonies. Some coastal land began to be alienated and tentative attempts were made to impose European laws and authority. The eventual result was the division of the Melanesian islands into European colonial possessions.

Coastal New Guineans and Islanders in the surrounding archipelagos forged new relationships with the outside world and each other, adapting their ways to either exploit or

The expansion of trade and even a moderate increase in production cannot fail to lead to the development of large-scale shipping in the Bismarck Archipelago. Situated as it is right in the middle of the shortest route between China and Australia, in Blanche Bay it possesses a harbor unsurpassed in respect of safety, size and ease of navigation. Soon we will be able, by connecting with our new steamship lines in the East, to complete the chain destined to achieve for us Germans our place in the Pacific Ocean and to hold it forever.
—Eduard Hernsheim, 1886 (1983, 194).

accommodate the foreigners and their demands. The great majority, particularly inland and Highlands' communities, experienced relatively little change until well into the twentieth century.

The Australasian Colonies' Influence on Shipping Routes around New Guinea

In the 1870s, Eduard Hernsheim, a German trader, centered his commercial interests on New Britain's Gazelle Peninsula, capitalizing on the trading potential of the islands off eastern New Guinea, and their position on the Australia-Asia shipping route. Contact with and commercial exploitation of east New Guinea was altogether different from that in the west, where harnessing of resources was an extension of Malay patterns that had begun two thousand years before. The main exports from west New Guinea were slaves, bird-of-paradise pelts, and massoi bark, and woven cloths and metal goods were the major imports. The Portuguese, Spanish, Dutch, and English all tapped into this established trade network between the sixteenth and nineteenth centuries, dominating, extending, and refining it to their purposes. Exploitation of the east came later—largely in the nineteenth century—after the foundation of British settlement in Australia and New Zealand, and French and German settlement in the South Pacific. These plantation-based and settler societies had a different modus operandi. No longer was New Guinea at the "end of the line," an outpost of Asia. The island now became part of a "South Seas" sphere, as traders reached out to all of the Pacific Islands, seeking economic resources to exploit. Whalers roamed the seas seeking their prey, traders in natural products made forays around the coasts, beginning to establish permanent settlements, and Christian missionaries saw New Guinea as the new Pacific Islands challenge. Many of the commercial developments on the eastern side were outgrowths of Australian-based capitalism. For instance, Queensland's colonial frontier extended out into Torres Strait, the underbelly of New Guinea and the islands around the Coral Sea, where companies harvested natural products and harnessed human labor. This colonization process initially took place through private ventures around the coasts, and later through formal territorial claims by European powers.

The decision to begin a British convict settlement on the east coast of New Holland (Australia) was part of wider British government and East India Company strategies that included the 1772–1774 free port at Balambangan Island off north Borneo, and the opening of another base on Penang Island off the Malay Peninsula in Melaka Strait in 1776. Both were staging posts for improving access to the China trade. If John Hayes had been successful in his 1793–1794 attempts to establish a safe port within Cenderawasih Gulf, along with the use of the Eastern Passage, west New Guinea would have become part of this British network of Asia-Pacific ports.

In 1788 the first British convict fleet reached Port Jackson (Sydney), the headquarters

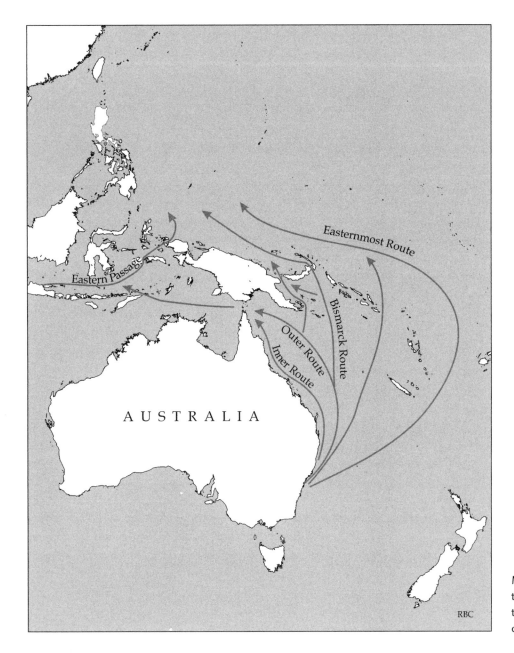

Major trade routes in the western Pacific, eighteenth and nineteenth centuries

of the huge colony of New South Wales—half the continent—which soon also included a small outpost on Norfolk Island, right on the new Pacific shipping route. The original northern border of the colony was set at 10°37' south latitude, running through Muralag (Prince of Wales) Island in Torres Strait. The western boundary cut through the center of Australia. The southern boundary included Van Diemen's Land (Tasmania).

The eastern boundary was so vague that it was sometimes interpreted as the west coast of South America. From 1824 in New South Wales, and 1829 in Van Diemen's Land, Supreme Courts had the power to deal with offences committed by British subjects anywhere in the Pacific Islands not governed by a European state.[1] In 1855, when New South Wales was granted representative government, the Governor's commission gave him jurisdiction over all islands out to 154° east longitude, including most of the Louisiade Archipelago but cutting through Rossel Island. No northern limit was ever declared. New South Wales' area of authority was extended further in 1868, to the annoyance of the newly established colony of Queensland. The senior colony was given the right to grant mining and occupational leases west of 154° east longitude, and to regulate the guano trade on islands on and inside the Great Barrier Reef off Queensland.[2]

Once a port was established at Sydney on the east coast, shipping routes to Asia developed, north along the Australian east coast, then either northeast through the Melanesian and Micronesian islands, or west through Torres Strait. After depositing their human cargo, most of the early convict transport ships left for China under the East India Company's charter, or went whaling under its license. The names of these ships and their captains remain attached to the many islands they encountered. By the second quarter of the nineteenth century most of the outline of New Guinea was mapped, although the southeast coast and the Louisiades were still only vaguely known. Merchants contracted their vessels for use to transport convicts to Australia as a way of breaching the Company's monopoly over the China trade, particularly the rapidly expanding tea trade to Europe. The Chinese preferred silver in exchange for tea, but cotton from India was also an acceptable trade item. Sydney merchants resented the monopoly hold of the East India Company that remained in force until the 1830s, and were persistent in seeking ways around it.

As Maluku and its spices brought west New Guinea into contact with the rest of the world, so the British colonies on Australia's east coast connected the east. The year before Sydney was settled, an American merchantman pioneered the easternmost passage from Australia, hoping to develop a new tea-trade route to China, sailing 320 kilometers off the east coast, past New Caledonia, through the Solomon Sea and up between New Ireland and Buka, then north to Ponape.[3] Of the transport ships in the "First Fleet" that arrived at what became Sydney in 1788, two were merchantmen bound for China which passed north past Melanesia and through southern Micronesia, another left for Tahiti, while *Alexander* and the *Friendship*, both under command of John Shortland, passed through the western islands of the New Georgia Group. Some well-constructed canoes came out to Shortland's ships, and the people indicated "Simboo" as the name of their island. They wore shells and feathers as head-ornaments, and white bone bracelets on their wrists. The Islanders, of friendly disposition, exchanged gifts with the visitors. The ships passed through Bougainville Strait and around north New Guinea, then through Pitt Strait in the Raja Empat Group and west to Batavia. Five convict transports from the

"Second Fleet" also sailed to Canton to take onboard cargo for the East India Company.[4]

Ex-convict transports and British and American merchants began regularly taking routes north out of Sydney that passed east and west of New Caledonia, then either east of the New Hebrides, or between the New Hebrides and the Solomon Islands and north through Micronesia. Over the next two decades these voyages mapped the remainder of the islands off New Guinea. For instance, John Hunter on the Dutch ship *Waaksamheyd* in 1791 headed north to obtain supplies from Batavia. While passing through the Solomon Islands, Hunter's ship located Sikaiana and Ontong Java, before sailing along Bougainville and Buka and through St. George's Channel, taking on water at a bay in the Duke of York Islands, later known as Port Hunter. Despite the many ships that had passed through St. George's Channel, few had called at the Duke of York Islands, as was clear during Hunter's visit when the people appeared not to recognize iron or muskets and wanted only cloth in barter trade. Other voyages located isolated outliers inhabited by Polynesians in northern Melanesia: Bellona, named for a ship in 1793; and the Mortlock Atolls (Etal, Lukunor, and Satawan) east of Buka, named after the captain of the *Young William*.[5]

American merchants began to call at Sydney onwards from 1792, carrying general cargos for the colony, or sea otter and seal skins from South America, Bass Strait and New Zealand. They often passed through Melanesia and Micronesia as they continued on their way north to China or back to North America.[6] Charts drawn in the 1790s record a variety of voyage tracks through the Pacific taken by ships out of Port Jackson. One chart from 1792 marked the best easternmost route from Port Jackson as passing north of the New Hebrides and the Santa Cruz Groups, east of the Solomon Islands, west of Nauru, and south of Guam, before turning toward Asia. Two new recommended routes to Asia eventually emerged from the various voyages, both of them through the Bismarck Archipelago: ships passed east of the Louisiades, then either sailed through the straits between New Britain and New Guinea, or up St. George's Channel.[7] From early in the nineteenth century ships were weaving through the Louisiade and the D'Entrecasteaux Archipelagos off east New Guinea (although these routes were not regarded as safe alternatives to that skirting Melanesia until the 1820s), or they were taking the already established "Outer Route" through Torres Strait.[8] The route through China Strait off the eastern tip of New Guinea and north through the D'Entrecasteaux Archipelago and the Solomon Sea, which cut almost 500 kilometers off voyages, was not safely charted until the explorations of John Moresby on HMS *Basilisk* in the early 1870s.

The Torres Strait route was always the quickest but most dangerous path from eastern Australia to Asia. In 1770, Captain Cook on the *Endeavour* had passed along the Queensland coast from Fraser Island to Lizard Island, the passage later known as the Inner Route. After 1788, sea traffic along the east coast of Australia increased constantly. Three favored passages developed, all using Torres Strait: the Inner Route, through the Capricorn Channel at Gladstone and inside the Barrier Reef for its entire length; the Outer

Route, round the northern end of the Great Barrier Reef; and the Middle Route, passing through the reef at several points opposite Capes Grenville and Direction. Merchant ships usually avoided the dangerous Inner Route, and most opted for the Outer Route, although it too claimed many victims who were lost negotiating the narrow entrances to passages between the Great Barrier Reef and Torres Strait.

Voyages and surveys around Torres Strait and the underbelly of New Guinea during the 1790s increased contact with the peoples of southern New Guinea and its adjacent islands.[9] Naval captains often made territorial claims. Having navigated his way through in a small boat after the *Bounty* mutiny, William Bligh returned to claim the islands of Torres Strait for the British Crown in 1792. The next year, William Bampton on HMS *Shah Hormuzear*, with Matthew Alt on the whaler *Chesterfield*, spent two months investigating Torres Strait and the Gulf of Papua, Bampton claiming the Strait and adjacent areas of the New Guinea coast for Britain. They may also have ventured to Deception Bay in the Gulf of Papua.[10] In 1804, the crew of the 130-ton French privateer *Adèle* was probably the first Europeans to land on the southeast coast of New Guinea since Torres just over two hundred years earlier. Louis Ruault Coutance, returning to Mauritius after trading in South America, touched at several of the southern Solomon Islands before heading west via New Guinea. Coutance sighted Rossel Island in May 1804, named a small island at the western end of its reef after his ship, and continued west, but came up against the Great Barrier Reef. He then sailed into the Gulf of Papua, spending several days there, involved in skirmishes with coastal villagers, before heading west.[11]

One of the most notable European voyages in the Strait was that of Matthew Flinders. A junior officer under Bligh on HMS *Providence*, Flinders returned to Torres Strait on the *Investigator* in 1802 while circumnavigating Australia, making an extensive examination of the waters on both sides of the Great Barrier Reef, also spending several days surveying in the Strait. A decade of exploratory voyages had established Torres Strait, the Arafura Sea, and the Eastern Passage as serviceable shipping routes between New South Wales and Asia. Merchant ships began using the coastal Inner Route as better charts became available. After the East India Company's monopoly was partially lifted in 1813, the route became commercially viable. Abolition of the 350-ton minimum size limit on ships trading between New South Wales and Britain also increased shipping.[12]

By the 1830s, sailing ships passed through Torres Strait from east to west every week of the southeasterly season, April to September, although the wind pattern prevented most west-east traffic until steamships were introduced.[13] The hundreds of wrecks that today litter the Great Barrier Reef and the Strait are indicative of the dangers involved in navigating through the maze of reefs and shoals.[14] The next major surveys of the Inner Passage inside the Great Barrier Reef, Torres Strait, and adjacent coasts of New Guinea were carried out by HMS *Bramble*, *Beagle*, *Fly*, and *Rattlesnake* during 1841–1849.[15] Between the 1840s and the 1870s, settlements were founded all along the coast of Queensland, leading to an enormous increase in shipping using the Inner Route and inevitably placing pressures on the coastal indigenous population. Ships heading north from southern Australian ports entered the reef waters at Capricorn Channel about 130 kilometers north of Fraser Island, giving access to the Queensland ports from Rockhampton north. Those sailing south entered the reefs at Curtis Channel, which allowed access to ports south from Gladstone. This settlement process on the eastern seaboard developed agricultural, pastoral, and mining regions, ports, markets, and navigation beacons and lighthouses. By the 1870s the process had become self-perpetuating, confirming the long-term viability of the Inner Route.

Some Queenslanders viewed the Coral Sea—that area of ocean abutting northeast Australia, including the underbelly of southeast New Guinea, curving north into the Solomon Sea—as a Queensland lake, central to the colony's economic and political development. Queensland's maritime frontier spread in two directions, clockwise and counterclockwise, around New Guinea and into Island Melanesia. Beginning in the earliest decades of the nineteenth century, shipping routes ran up the Queensland coast through Torres Strait, or went further east just skirting the islands off eastern New Guinea. Onwards from the 1860s and 1870s, recruiting of Melanesian labor began in the southeast at the Loyalty Islands and the New Hebrides, and then north to the Solomon Islands. Queensland settlers also entered Melanesia clockwise, moving north through Torres Strait onto the mainland of New Guinea and out into the eastern archipelagos. Explorers, naval hydrographers, traders in exotic Pacific products, whalers, missionaries, timber-getters, pearlshell and bêche-de-mer fishermen, miners, labor recruiters, and government officials proceeded from several east coast ports to the eastern archipelagos, and through Cooktown, Somerset, and Thursday Island to the great "unclaimed" island to the north.[16] Residents of the east coast Australian colonies were conscious of German commercial interests in eastern New Guinea in the 1880s, and they feared that Britain's refusal to annex the region would leave them with a neighboring German colony.

By the 1880s, eastern New Guinea and adjacent islands had become known through shipping routes, and they were already frequented by missionaries, traders, whalers, and the occasional beachcomber. The coastal and island people also became a labor reserve for new Pacific plantation and settler societies, but this operated in a quite different manner to the indigenous slave trade in the west.

Traders

During the nineteenth century, itinerant Chinese, Malay, and European traders began visiting New Guinea with increasing frequency, as did whalers, the occasional escaped convict or shipwrecked mariner, and Islamic and Christian missionaries. Typical of early Pacific trading ships, the *Hound* under Captain Trainer and an unnamed brig captained by a trader named Stewart, visited Cenderawasih and MacCluer Gulfs as well as the southern coast east to Cape Palsu in the late 1830s, trading for bird-of-paradise pelts, pearls, turtle-shells, and ambergris. The *Hound* traveled across the Pacific and along New Guinea's north coast, met up with Stewart's brig, and sailed west to Maluku, then back east into southern Melanesia. Stewart had made several earlier trips to New Britain, New Ireland, and New Guinea, acknowledging that he and others had kidnapped men from eastern New Guinea and sold them as slaves at the Dutch and Chinese settlements further west.[17] John Coulter, on the *Hound,* described the level of contact at MacCluer Gulf: "They all had strings of china beads, variously colored round their necks. The Papuans here seemed to be well provided, by the Chinese and Dutch, with axes, chopping-knives and other iron tools."[18]

Similarly, naturalist Alfred Wallace visited the Kei Islands in January 1857, and described the inhabitants as a mixture of Melanesians, who wore only waist cloths of cotton or bark, and "a mixed race, who are nominally Mahometans, and wear cotton clothing." The latter were said to have been driven out of Banda by early European settlers: "Had I been blind, I could have been certain that these Islanders were not Malays. The loud, rapid, eager tones, the incessant motion, the intense vital activity manifested in speech and action are the very antipodes of the quiet, unimpulsive, unanimated Malay. These Ké men came up singing and shouting, dipping their paddles deep in the water and throwing up clouds of spray; as they approached nearer they stood up in their canoes and increased their noise and gesticulations; and on coming alongside, without asking leave, and without a moment's hesitation, the greater part of them scrambled up on our deck just as if they had come to take possession of a captured vessel. Then commenced a scene of indescribably confusion. These forty black, naked, mop-headed savages seemed intoxicated with joy and excitement."[19]

Wallace's *The Malay Archipelago* contains an etching of Dobo in the Aru Islands during the trading season of 1857. It depicts the Bugi and Chinese trading settlement, showing Europeans, Chinese, and Malays engaged in bargaining with the local people: "We were here two thousand miles beyond Singapore and Batavia, which are themselves emporiums of the "far east" in a place unvisited by, and almost unknown to, European traders; everything reached us through at least two or three hands, often many more; yet English calicoes and American cotton cloths could be bought for 8s. the piece, muskets for 15s., each, and other cutlery, cotton goods, and earthenware in the same proportion. The natives of this out-of-the-way country can, in fact, buy all these things at about the same money price as our workmen at home, but in reality very much cheaper, for the produce of a few hours' labour enables the savage to purchase in abundance what are to him luxuries."[20]

Boats had just returned from the New Guinea side of the island with bundles of firewood, *prahu* were hauled up on the beach being re-caulked for the voyage back to Seram and Goram, sails were being mended, bundles of pearlshell and dried bêche-de-mer made ready for loading. Fattened pigs waited their fates, young cassowaries wandered by, a small tame wallaby caught in the Aru forest hopped about, and bright parrots and cock-

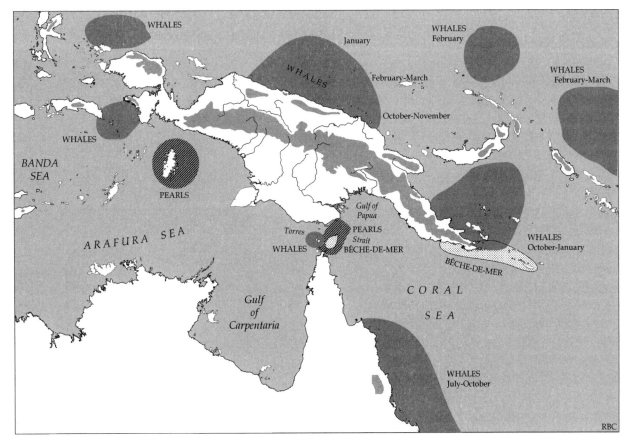

Whale, bêche-de-mer, and pearl grounds

atoos sat on perches. Cockfights were staged daily to amuse the Chinese, Javanese, and other Malay gamblers, tobacco and *arak* were the favored recreational drugs, and drums, Jews' harps and even fiddles provided the musical entertainment. Prosperous Chinese, Javanese, Makasan, and Seramese merchants and ships' crews bargained and loitered. Aru Islanders and New Guineans dressed in loincloths provided labor. All of the products of New Guinea and Aru were on sale, in exchange for manufactured items from the Malay Archipelago, Europe, and America.[21] Wallace declared:

> The trade carried on at Dobbo is very considerable. This year there were fifteen large praus from Macassar, and perhaps a hundred small boats from Ceram, Goram, and Ké. The Macassar cargoes are worth about £1000 each, and the other boats take away perhaps about £3000 worth, so that the whole exports may be estimated at £18,000 per annum. The largest and most bulky items are pearl-shell and tripang, or "bêche-de-mer," with smaller quantities of tortoise-shell, edible birds' nests, pearls, ornamental woods, timber and birds of paradise. These are

purchased with a variety of goods. Of arrack, about equal in strength to ordinary West India rum, 3000 boxes, each containing fifteen half-gallon bottles, are consumed annually. Native cloth from Sulawesi is much esteemed for its durability, and large quantities are sold, as well as white English calico and American unbleached cottons, common crockery, coarse cutlery, muskets, gunpowder, gongs, small brass cannon, and elephants' tusks. These three last articles constitute the wealth of the Aru people, with which they pay for their wives, or which they hoard up as "real property." Tobacco is in immense demand for chewing and it must be very strong, or an Aru will not look at it. Knowing how little these people generally work, the mass of produce obtained annually shows that the islands must be pretty thickly inhabited, especially along the coasts, as nine-tenths of the whole are marine productions.[22]

Anna Forbes described the same village three decades later, when she and her naturalist husband visited Aru in July 1885: "We went on shore early in the day, and found Dobbo a fair-sized village, wonderfully civilized-looking for this out-of-the-world corner. Chinese, Arabs, and Malays bustled in the chief street, where to almost half its breadth, in front of the shops, under great awnings of matting, quantities of trepang or *bêche de mer* were being sewed into bags to ship with us; and piles of oyster-shells, in which the beautiful Aru pearls are found, were being arranged and counted for dispatch to Europe."

The Forbes visited a rich Moslem trader who lived nearby in a bamboo house almost covered with pieces of boxes. The walls were ornamented with old rusty guns and perhaps a dozen pistols. They were served coffee by the trader's New Guinea slave woman.[23] Later in the day, their ship was visited by another important local man, clad in "bright green trousers, a long black coat, and over this a *kabia* or native jacket of bright purple satin, with inch-wide gold-thread stripes and a very dirty and starchless collar." Two of his companions wore "trousers of bright scarlet, with huge butterfly pattern, a faded green silk coat brocaded with large gold flowers, and a shabby grey felt hat," and "a long surtout coat, with a much worn black satin vest, wrong side out, over it."[24]

Gesir Atoll and Goram Island (close to Ceram) were the trading hub for the networks linking west New Guinea with its adjacent islands. Henry Forbes wrote that collectors of birds-of-paradise and other bird pelts from the New Guinea mainland, Salawati, Misool, and Halmahera, and pearl divers from Aru, were all at Gesir in July 1885: "hither the trepang, tortoiseshell, bee's-wax, nutmegs, dammar, and other rich produce from a multitude of islands are brought to be exchanged with the Malay and Chinese traders of Macassar, Singapore, and Ternate—for scarlet, blue, and white cottons and calicoes of the Dutch and English looms, for the yellow-handled hoop-iron knives, which form the universal small change of these regions, and for beads, glass balls, knobs of amber, old keys, scraps of iron, and worthless but gaudy Brummagem manufactures."[25]

At MacCluer Gulf, the chief of the village was dressed in a faded silk *sarung* and wore Asian jewelry. He was supervising the loading of bags of nutmeg purchased by some Moslem traders. The women of the village, whom she claimed had never seen a European woman before, appropriated Anna Forbes: "they gently pushed back my hat to look at my hair, drew back my sleaves, lifted my skirts, and laughed immoderately at my boots."[26]

Foreign traders were not always as welcome. In 1853, the Governor of Maluku took action against trading ships at Ati-Ati, which were operating under the British flag from a business operating out of Sulawesi.[27] Nevertheless, foreign trade of all types intensified in the 1850s, as did attacks on trading vessels and subsequent punitive expeditions by Dutch, British, and French naval ships to punish the aggressors. Captain Deighton, based in Maluku, had been trading with New Guinea for thirty years when Lieutenant G. F. De Bruijn Kops wrote an account of trade at Dorei Bay in 1850. Deighton and his barque *Rembang* seem to have been well regarded in Cenderawasih Gulf, since they acted as a check on the rapacious Tidore tribute-collecting *kora-kora*, although a decade later even he was attacked there.[28]

Traders traveling to and from the central Pacific often passed through islands close to west New Guinea, and visited remote atolls and islands off the north coast. Alfred Tetens, traveling on J. C. Goddefroy and Co.'s *Vesta* on route to Palau, stopped to barter for fruit at one of the Raja Empat Islands. The next year Tetens sailed south from Yap to trade for bêche-de-mer, pearl- and turtle-shells, and coconut oil at the tiny Hermit and Ninigo Groups and Wuvulu Island, 180 kilometers off New Guinea's north coast. Edwin Redlich, another trader, sailed from the Solomon Islands along the north coast of New Guinea, calling at the Salawati and Aru Islands in 1872. The next year, Eduard Hernsheim, who later established a grand permanent base on New Britain, was trading around the same west New Guinea islands, on his way to Hong Kong.[29]

Pamela Swadling's research for *Plumes from Paradise* has for the first time shown the astounding importance of bird-of-paradise pelts and plumes in New Guinea's export trade. Swadling documents early use of the plumes throughout Asia and as far away as Persia and Turkey. Birds-of-paradise were unknown in Europe until the sixteenth century, when the survivors of Magellan's circumnavigation of the world carried five bird-of-paradise pelts, obtained from Maluku, back to the King of Spain. Trade pelts had no feet, wings, or viscera—hunters sealed carcasses with gum or resin, and preserved them through smoking. The taxidermy was so skillful that Europeans initially fancied that the birds always lived in the air, never landing. The Portuguese reported that in Maluku they were called *"bolondinata"* (*burung dewata*, birds of god), and they gave them a name of their own: *"passaros de sol"* (birds of the sun). The Dutch provided the birds with a Latin name, *"avis paradiseus"* (paradise birds). Carolus Linnaeus, the famous Swedish naturalist, perpetuated the myth when he examined and named a bird-of-paradise in 1760, calling it *"paradisaea apoda"* (paradise creature without legs).[30] However, in the 1620s, J. Bruegel and Rubens painted a bird-of-paradise with legs in their "Adam and Eve in Paradise" canvas, which indicates the patchy nature of European knowledge of the birds. René Primevère Lesson, assistant surgeon and pharmacist on Duperrey's expedition on *Coquille* in 1823–

1824, was the first European known to have seen birds-of-paradise in the wild, and he finally dispelled the strange tales.[31]

In 1522, the arrival of the first bird-of-paradise pelts in Europe caused a sensation in the court of Charles V. In the course of the sixteenth century, as more specimens reached Europe, the bird's feathers were rendered by artists in splendid colored images. Between the seventeenth and twentieth centuries, bird-of-paradise pelts and plumes were imported into Europe in enormous quantities, so much so that the whole bird family became endangered. Naturalists vied with each other to discover new species. Fashion-conscious European women decorated their hats with the remarkably beautiful pelts and plumes. It is virtually impossible to calculate the extent of the slaughter. Swadling suggests that approximately 30,000 birds-of-paradise were sold in London each year in the 1900s. The trade peaked just before the First World War with an estimated 80,000 pelts exported from New Guinea in 1913.[32] Batavia and Singapore became major clearing centers for the pelts. Nineteenth- and early twentieth-century prices give us some idea of the values of the trade: Dutch florins (Dfl) 2.50 for a single pelt in Ternate in 1839 or Dfl 50 for a string of pelts; the same string valued at Dfl 100 to Dfl 200 by 1875. The 10,000 pelts exported from German New Guinea in 1913 had an estimated value of about one million marks.[33]

Moves to conserve these and other tropical birds began in the middle of the nineteenth century, gathering pace early in the twentieth century when legislation was introduced by the colonial powers to prohibit hunting and export to supply the European plume industry. This did not save the birds—the Asian export market remained active, and a new one developed: New Guineans themselves began to use modern weapons to hunt the birds, particularly in the Highlands where bird-of-paradise pelts and plumes had become necessary accoutrements in headdresses and stylish armbands.[34]

Dutch statistics for New Guinea from 1845 to 1869 show large-scale exports of birds-of-paradise, bêche-de-mer, turtle-shells, massoi bark, sago, cocoa, wax, tobacco, mother-of-pearl, and wild nutmeg. These exotic items had an added value: they could be traded to China for silks and teas. The statistics do not always differentiate between New Guinea and Maluku, but one set of figures shows exports from New Guinea to Ternate between 1864 and 1869: they were valued at Dfl 111,491, without including slavery or whaling. Bêche-de-mer accounted for 42 percent of the exports to Ternate, massoi bark 25 percent, turtle-shells 21 percent, and sago 9 percent. During the same period imports from Ternate totaled Dfl 86,604: small imports were made of copper, lead, glass, pottery, salt, and *arak*, the major items being linseed oil (55 percent), iron (31 percent) and, peculiarly, coral (7 percent).[35] These statistics do not include Dutch trade with Ambon, Ceram, and neighboring islands, nor with the Aru Islands, which became a major marketplace for pearlshell and pearls.

Itinerant trade with east New Guinea occurred later and was never as extensive as in the west. It usually involved only Europeans, except in the bêche-de-mer and pearling industries, which included some Asians and Pacific Islanders. During the early decades of the nineteenth century, the last great voyages of European exploration in Melanesia coincided with those of Australia-based traders, as well as British and American whalers. We owe our first knowledge of many of the minor islands and atolls to whalers and traders, even though many voyages have been lost from the record because they were "commercial by nature, secret by interest, and outside the mainstream of European hydrographic recording."[36] Traders, as distinct from whalers, were also traveling through the eastern archipelagos onwards from the 1830s and 1840s, part of much wider trading patterns throughout the Pacific. Whalers had always collected large numbers of turtle-shells as well as whale oil, but with the decline of whaling after the 1860s, turtle-shells became the domain of general traders, who also collected copra and ivory palm nuts, bêche-de-mer, pearlshell, artifacts, and bird-of-paradise pelts. In the east, they operated mainly out of Somerset and Thursday Island in far north Queensland, living precariously but profitably.

Early eastern trading ventures were in the hands of individuals and small companies, and one large company, Hamburg-based J. C. Godeffroy and Sons, collecting all types of marine produce, copra, and ivory palm nuts. Godeffroys began its Pacific ventures with trade in Latin America in the 1830s. By the 1850s, the company was operating a ring of trading stations around the Pacific, from Chile to California, including Australia and Southeast Asia.[37] Operations were extended into the South Pacific during the mid-1850s, and in 1871 a station was established on Matupit Island in Simpson Harbour, New Britain, followed two years later by another base nearby. These early New Britain ventures did not last, and the traders were driven off by hostile villagers. Godeffroys managed to establish their first permanent station in the Duke of York Islands in 1875. Four years later, the company's assets were transferred to the Deutsche Handels-und Plantagen-Gesellscaft der Südsee-Inseln zu Hamburg (DHPG), otherwise known as the "Long Handle Company." By then, rival companies had entered the New Guinea market: Thomas Farrell and Co., operated by former employees of DHPG, and Hernsheim and Co. In 1884, just before the German *Schutzgebiet* (Protectorate) was announced, Adolph von Hansemann, a leading German banker previously connected with the creation of the DHPG, formed a consortium that became the Neu Guinea Kompagnie (New Guinea Company), which would operate on the mainland of German New Guinea until the end of the century.[38]

The doyen of private traders in the east was Eduard Hernsheim, who initially used Hong Kong as his northern base, working the central Pacific around Micronesia and the Dutch East Indies. Finding the competition with Godeffroys too great, Hernsheim shifted the headquarters of his operations to New Britain, from where he continued exporting to Europe through Hong Kong. Hernsheim began trading from Makada in the Duke of Yorks in October 1875, and later shifted his head station to Matupit in Blanche Bay, New Britain. He established a web of traders on islands throughout northern Melanesia and

Micronesia, spending his time sailing the Pacific supervising his watery commercial empire, returning to Matupit for several months every year.[39]

Better known were Emma Coe Forsayth, a Samoan-American, and her de facto husband Thomas Farrell, an Australian colonist. They were employed by Godeffroys at their Mioko station in 1878 before establishing their own company. Emma Forsayth foresaw that eventually plantations rather than trading stations would dominate the economy of the Bismarck Archipelago, and she therefore purchased large parcels of land on the Gazelle Peninsula and outlying islands. Known as "Queen" Emma because of the splendid lifestyle at "Gunamtambu," her mansion near Kokopo, she became a legend, surrounded by a Samoan enclave.[40] Forsayth's sister Phoebe and her husband Richard Parkinson joined the commercial venture in 1882,[41] and the family established permanent coconut plantations on the shores of Blanche Bay in the early 1880s. Before this, economic activities between foreigners and local people had revolved around trade in coconuts and marine products. During the 1870s and early 1880s, the Gazelle Peninsula was the center of commercial activity for eastern New Guinea, supplemented from the mid-1880s by Hansemann's Neu Guinea Kompagnie plantations on the New Guinea mainland, considerably enlarging the German commercial presence. In southeast New Guinea, missionaries and traders relied on Queensland's Somerset and Thursday Island for communications and supplies, although later Port Moresby and Samarai too became leading ports.

Smaller itinerant traders constantly moved through the islands. In 1872, O'Dowd and Co. of Sydney had engaged Solomon Islands trader Alexander Ferguson to purchase land for them at Port Hunter, Duke of York Islands, for a trading station.[42] Edwin Redlich, mentioned above, is typical of these smaller traders. During the mid-1870s, he worked in the Torres Strait pearling industry, recruiting his own labor because his Prussian nationality allowed him to ignore the restrictions of the 1872 British *Pacific Islanders' Protection (Kidnapping) Act*. Redlich was a regular visitor to Somerset and traded along the New Guinea coast, opening a store at Port Moresby in 1878. His colorful trading career nearly ended when he mistakenly blew his hand off in 1876, and did four years later when he drowned at Boera.[43]

Botanist and trader Andrew Goldie, born in Ayrshire, Scotland, was one of the more intrepid traders and natural history specimen collectors in the east. Goldie arrived in New Guinea in 1875 at the age of thirty-five. An abstemious hard-working man he was remarkable for traveling more among the southeast coastal people than any other European in his time, the missionaries included, and for being well received in villages. He was initially employed by Holloway and Co. of London to collect medicinal plants, but returned in 1876 as a trader and collector for Sydney's Australian Museum. Goldie traveled the coast in *Alice Meade*, his shallow draft cutter, exploring and trading. He spent several months collecting on Sogeri Plateau and around the Laloki River before he purchased land in Port Moresby and established a trade store there. By 1879, he had collected 1,000 bird pelts from 124 species, other specimens of flora and fauna, as well as many artifacts.

Four years later he was involved in a short-lived and dubious deal to purchase 15,000 acres on the Aroa River inland from Redscar Bay to begin a sugar plantation. Goldie left New Guinea in the late 1880s, far richer than when he arrived.[44]

Whalers

European traders sailed through the islands from the Pacific to Asia and around Australia, in no particular annual pattern, except that they avoided the cyclone season and traveled with the winds, seeking lucrative, diverse exotic commodities. Whalers were more predictable, because they followed the migratory patterns of their prey. Most sought-after were sperm whales on their migration from the Arctic to the tropical South Pacific.[45] Maps based on American whaling logbooks between 1761 and 1920 show sperm whales clustered to the northwest and south of the Bird's Head and across to the Philippines. They moved along the north of New Guinea, roughly from Humboldt Bay to the Huon Peninsula and out to the Admiralties. Sperm whales also migrated through the Louisiade, D'Entrecasteaux, and Bismarck Archipelagos, and around Bougainville, Buka, and down through the Solomon Islands. There were also a few Killer, Bowhead, Humpback, and Southern Right whales.[46] Some whalers used the fields seasonally, hunting the northwest coast during October and November, and the southeast coast—between New Britain and the D'Entrecasteaux Group—from October to January, then moving on to between New Hanover, New Ireland, and Bougainville during February and March.[47] Others seem to have followed no particular pattern. Whalers worked these grounds in conjunction with the more extensive fields in the north and central Pacific. Using prevailing winds, they passed by the Solomons and islands off New Guinea on their way north from New Zealand and Australia, or as they sailed south from Japan and Micronesia at other times of year. Whales seem rarely to have been hunted in the Arafura Sea or anywhere along southern New Guinea, although some may have used Torres Strait and the south coast for their migrations. Confirmation of this is offered by early sources: there were immense numbers of "Noord-Kapers" (North-Capers) off Aru Island in April 1825; and in 1838 Wahaai, a small port on the north coast of Seram, was "much resorted to by English and American whalerships about that time." There are also records of Southern Right whales sighted off Australia's Cape York in 1868 and 1871.[48]

Whaling voyages lasted for three or four years. Whalers needed supplies of wood, water and food, safe havens in storms, and sexual outlets for the crews beyond the male-to-male relationships on the ships. Whalers were a rough and ready group, lacking even the unstable scruples exhibited by government officials, missionaries, and regular traders. While predominantly Europeans, many whalers were of mixed racial origins. Whalers had favorite rendezvous, such as Wahaai, Waigeo, and Batanta in the Raja Empat Group, Humboldt Bay on the north coast, and Buka, the Duke of York Islands, southern New Ireland, and the Trobriands in the east. They must often have been the first Europeans with whom coastal Melanesians had dealings. Their presence led to further suggestions that a permanent European maritime trading base be established on the New Guinea north coast.[49]

The first English whalers arrived in the Pacific in 1789, and as already noted, after New South Wales was established, many of the early convict transports were actually whalers that resumed their trade once their human cargoes were unloaded. Modification to the East India Company charter in the 1790s enabled British whalers to utilize the waters around the Solomon Islands and New Guinea, and during the 1820s and 1830s British whalers based in Australia and New Zealand were the most active in the Pacific. The first of the American whalers entered the Pacific in 1799, but they were not numerous until the 1820s and did not peak until the 1840s. The majority of the North American whalers came from the eastern seaboard—Salem, Nantucket, and New Bedford. Whalers continued to scour the waters around the Bismarck Archipelago until the 1870s and 1880s. The New Guinea and Solomon Islands whaling grounds were an important part of the wider Pacific whaling grounds. Statistics from the 1810s and 1820s show an annual average of forty-four British and fifteen to twenty French whaling vessels in the Pacific, while the *Nautical Magazine* for 1838 recorded 460 American whaling ships there. Judith Bennett's research located 148 whaling voyages that passed through the Solomon Islands between 1799 and 1890, half of them before 1850. Virtually all Pacific whalers spent some months each year working around New Guinea, particularly in the eastern waters.[50]

Buka, Bougainville, and New Ireland (together with its fringing islands) had the earliest contact with whalers around east New Guinea. During the 1810s, the English whaler *Sarah* found north Buka people quite familiar with European trading methods: they understood the uses of glass and iron, presumably indicating contact with intervening voyages since Carteret on the *Swallow* in 1792. The Bismarck Archipelago and particularly New Ireland were favorite hunting grounds for fifty years onwards from the 1820s. Carteret Harbour and Gower's Harbour (Port Praslin) on New Ireland, and the Duke of York Islands in St. George's Channel became the most used rendezvous. Coastal villagers who had contact with beachcombers, or came off in canoes to visit whalers and traders, could often speak broken English. Two decades later, pidgin English was being widely used along the Channel and some local men had served as crews on whalers. When the first Methodist missionary arrived in the Duke of Yorks in 1875, he had with him as interpreter a young man named Teem, who had ended up in Sydney after a spell on a whaling ship. A local bigman, Topulu, had grown wealthy and powerful through his ability to muster 200 to 300 men to cut wood for passing ships, and most of the local men already possessed long-handled iron tomahawks gained through trade or labor.[51]

In the 1830s, whalers were beginning to hunt around the Trobriands and the Louisiades. The *Kent* was whaling off the Lusancay Islands in 1832, and Sydney whaler Captain Grimes of the *Woodlark* visited Woodlark (Murua) Island in the same year. Captain Hunter of the *Marshall Bennett* was another early visitor, in September 1836 to the islands named after his ship, and to Kiriwina in the Trobriand Group, and Murua.[52] But aside from castaways from an 1843 wreck of the whaler *Mary*, there were no early European sojourners in the eastern islands, even as trade with passing vessels flourished. In 1847, the first Catholic missionaries arrived on Woodlark and were befriended by one Pako, who had been to Sydney on a whaling ship and spoke a few words of English. The first Muruan word they heard upon arrival was *"mnoumnou"* (iron).[53]

The average whaler carried twenty-five to thirty men. Most in Melanesia processed their catch at sea in huge vats that boiled the blubber down to oil, but this required large supplies of wood, and particular islands became favorite ports for replenishing wood and other provisions. Other islands were avoided altogether because of past bad experiences. Women were much in demand, and as Bennett points out for the Solomon Islands, often sexual intercourse was the most valuable saleable item any coastal community had to offer.[54] The same ships returned to the same islands, time-after-time, building long-term relationships with local leaders. Even so, most trade took place offshore, the Islanders paddling out to the whaling ships to exchange their foodstuffs for hoop iron and tobacco.

For many coastal New Guineans, whaling was the major early point of contact with Europeans.[55] The putrid glow from whaling ships boiling down blubber to be stored in barrels for a distant market, must have seemed strange to watching villagers, who could not comprehend the capitalist relationship between hunting and manufacture. The whaling industry began to wane in the 1860s, as many American ships were recalled due to the Civil War, and as whale oil became less essential for industry because of easier access to petroleum oil, and technical advances in processing copra for oil.

Alastair Gray's analysis of trading contacts in the Bismarck Archipelago during the whaling period has sharpened our knowledge of the extent of cross-cultural trade, and has important implications for how historians view the trade in labor that developed in the same islands at the tail end of the whaling era. After examining hundreds of whaling logs, Gray drew several conclusions: Trade usually occurred at sea—in liminal space and moments. Whalers were hesitant to go ashore, for reasons of safety and speed, and they were quite circumspect in choosing locations, carefully weighing geographic concerns such as reefs and winds, the reputation of the locals, and the types of trade items available. The fringing islands off New Ireland, Buka, and Bougainville were the earliest areas caught up in the trade. Europeans seem to have avoided dealing with Bukas and Bougainvilleans, however, claiming that they were unpredictable. The feeling may have been mutual. Dr. D. Parker Wilson, surgeon on the *Gypsy* in the 1840s, saw it from the Islanders' perspective: "The natives of Bougainville seldom or ever come off to the ships, afraid to venture near vessels the like of which have vomited forth lightening and death. The natives of Bouka it is, who come off and by treating them fairly a pretty supply of refreshments can be depended on . . ."[56]

Usually, only watering and woodcutting parties needed to spend extended periods on shore. This pattern would have suited the coastal inhabitants, who could thus keep the foreigners at arm's length, exploiting them for their iron, glass, and other exotic items, but not allowing them into their villages or cultures. The exception was the Trobriands, where trade was normally conducted onshore.

Most of the trade was accomplished by men in canoes, who sometimes paddled many kilometers out to whaling ships. By the mid-nineteenth century, ships could be besieged by fifty canoes and hundreds of Islanders, creating a floating market and sometimes scrambling onto the decks with trade items. Some would stay overnight, and even allowed their canoes to be hauled on deck for safety. Although whalers in other areas of the Pacific seem to have added sexual favors to their lists of necessary trade items, sexual codes were generally strict in the Bismarcks. Sex with women was only easily available in the Trobriands and New Ireland. There is no evidence of sex between local and visiting men, but records of this would hardly be expected in any case, given European sexual codes of the day. Homosexuality must have been a constant part of the lives of the men isolated on whaling ships for years at a time, but we will never know if it became common between the visitors and the local men and youths.

Over several years, or sometimes decades, particular bays or islands became prominent in the whalers' trading regimes, only to be then bypassed for another area. A bay or island's popularity could decline due to diminished resources, changing requirements of European industry, European or colonial politics, shifting settlement patterns, or incidents of violence. Two places considered hospitable in east New Guinea waters were Buka Bay at the south of Buka Island, and Port Hunter in the Duke of York Islands in St. George's Channel. Gower's Harbour, just south of Cape St. George at the southern tip of New Ireland, was used to careen ships and their boats, and to barter for supplies. Buka and Bougainville were popular in the 1840s but were avoided by the 1870s, probably because more accommodating contacts had been made along St. George's Channel. Cape Denis at the northeast of the Trobriand Islands was popular over several decades, but after the 1860s the Trobriands were bypassed, perhaps because firewood supplies there had dwindled. The Duke of York Islands ceased to be important as whaling bases after the early 1870s, which may indicate a change in the whalers' focus, but also occurred because resident traders and missionaries were establishing themselves there. After 1860, the main whaling ground off eastern New Guinea was the northeast coast of New Hanover and New Ireland, particularly the smaller islands parallel to New Ireland—the Tabar, Lihir, Tanga, Feni, and Nissan (Green) Groups.[57]

Both sides were bartering items that, generally, each considered of little value. Calculated over eighty years, the Islanders traded just about every imaginable product: coconuts, taro, yams, plantain, bananas, other fruits, Canarium almonds, pigs, fowls, eggs, turtle-shells, many different artifacts, and sexual favors. What was traded was quite particular to each place. The Woodlarks and Trobriands only provided yams, wood, and sex. In the Admiralties and on Nissan Island everything was available except pigs and fruit.

Early in the whaling era Tanga only provided yams. At Feni, one could obtain coconut, yams, and fruit, but not pigs, and most commodities could be gotten from New Ireland.

Typical was the voyage of the whaler *Gypsy*, which lasted three years and five months. Seventy-one whales were caught, yielding 1,773 barrels of oil. When the ship was off New Ireland in 1840, two boats were sent ashore to trade with hoop iron and axes: "They got abundance of taro and yams, bananas, plantains, mangoes and but one pig. The third mate (White) ventured ashore (not deemed altogether safe); he placed himself under the protection of a chief and was introduced to his wife and child and to some other sable damsel with whom he cohabited at the cost of a common clasp knife."[58]

There are indications that as trade became better established, items were produced directly to supply whalers. However, at ceremonial times or periods of shortage the Islanders closed off access to some items. Just as occurred in other areas of the Pacific—Tahiti and its trade in salted pork to New South Wales, Maori provisioning of sealers and timber-getters in New Zealand, or pearl- and turtle-shell collecting in the Aru Islands—the Islanders in the Bismarck and Louisiade Archipelagos began entering into commercial production to obtain the foreign goods they wanted. They were also quite demanding, and their requirements changed as they became more sophisticated over the decades.

If we consider the various accounts from navigators, supplemented by Gray's analysis of the whalers' logs, we see that for a short while after contact began, colored cloth and baubles were sufficient to attract the Islanders. As soon as Islanders realized the qualities of iron and glass, however, these became the most sought after barter items, which suited the ships' crew since they were readily available and expendable. Nails, glass bottles, and hoop iron from old barrels became the most important barter items, the latter being of more value if it was already shaped into crude knives and adzes. There came a saturation point when hoop iron no longer sufficed. In the Duke of Yorks this had occurred by the late 1820s, and on Bougainville by the 1850s. Specialist iron items—wood-planes, axes, knives, and files—had long been given to reward important local leaders. After a few decades of trade all Islanders became more discerning; they refused scrap iron and demanded manufactured tools. Although the items they received were still poor quality (the crews kept the best quality for their own use), the value of the Western trade goods used for barter did increase over time. Tobacco, too, became a much utilized trade commodity in the Pacific. It had the qualities of being divisible into small units, of being totally consumed, and also addictive. There is little evidence that tobacco was an important part of the whalers' trade around eastern New Guinea, probably because betel nut chewing was ubiquitous, and free.

Although Gray uncovered no examples of muskets forming part of the whalers' bartering, nevertheless they had been traded to New Ireland by 1840, perhaps introduced by the first beachcombers. According to Dr. Parker Wilson, by the time he visited Gower Harbour in 1840, twelve or more European "flotsam" had already formed a small settlement there: "There was one Englishman seen ashore. He had left a Sydney vessel along with three more who had since gone away in ships. Some of the natives spoke broken English which they had learnt from runaway sailors, a number of whom (twelve or more) had formed a settlement at Gower's Harbour, where there are few or no natives. . . . Several natives ashore were observed parading the beach with a musket thrown over their shoulder. Already are they stooping before the invincible power of civilized man. They now crave for muskets and powder and tobacco! The last great step is yet to be made. Rum has not, as yet, obtained footing amongst them."[59] The pattern which Gray suggests here for the Bismarck and Louisiade Archipelagos was duplicated by whalers around west New Guinea, a process made easier by the already extensive foreign trade network.

A clear change occurred when the foreigners moved from their ships to the beaches, making relations much more like those that had developed in the west where people from Maluku settled permanently on New Guinea. Temporary camps for processing bêche-de-mer and employing local labor were established in Torres Strait and the Louisiades onwards from the 1860s and 1870s, but were eventually overtaken by pearl-diving ventures. The other key 1870s developments were the arrival of missionaries and permanent traders in the Bismarcks and along the southeast New Guinea coast, and a short gold rush near Port Moresby in 1878. From the mid-1880s government officials were in residence at several Neu Guinea Kompagnie bases and at Port Moresby. At the end of the 1880s, gold miners became an important presence on Sudest, Misima, and Woodlark Islands. The Duke of York Islands, and nearby Simpson Harbour on New Britain's Gazelle Peninsula, became major permanent foreign settlements, as did Thursday Island, Port Moresby, and Samarai. The equivalent bases in the west were Dorei (Manokwari) and Fakfak, with the addition of Merauke and Humboldt Bay in the twentieth century.

While not wanting to present an image of coastal east New Guinea and adjacent archipelagos as peppered with foreigners, their presence within and impact on indigenous society were considerable. One highly significant group was the Christian missionaries.

Christian Missionaries

Foreign religious proselytizing in New Guinea was not new. Since the fifteenth century, Moslems had been spreading their faith around the western coast. It was Christianity, however, which would become the dominant world religion in New Guinea, both in the west and the east, and the first long-term European residents were missionaries.

The earliest Catholic missionary endeavors around New Guinea began in 1606 when Torres and Prado captured fourteen boys and girls aged between six to ten years, taking them from Mailu to Manila and oblivion.[60] Permanent Christian missions were first established in the South Pacific in the 1790s, beginning in Polynesia and moving into southern Melanesia early in the nineteenth century. New Guinea became a missionary goal a hundred years later. Mysterious, unmapped, and unyielding because of the difficult terrain and the high mortality rates suffered by foreigners, the island nevertheless contained huge numbers of souls ready to be saved. The first attempt to establish a permanent mission settlement in east New Guinea waters was by the Catholic Society of Mary, in 1847 on Woodlark Island, and 1848 on Umboi Island, sites chosen upon the advice of whalers. Both islands were on the shipping route north, which meant that the missionaries were not entirely isolated. Even so, the settlements were abandoned in 1856, a year after Protestant missionaries established themselves in the west.[61]

Although the Dutch government did not exert a sustained interest in New Guinea, Dutch missionaries wanted to convert New Guinea's heathens. The first missionaries in the west arrived in 1855 from Germany, and began evangelizing and trading at Mansinam village, Dorei Bay. They were joined in 1862 by three Dutch members of the Utrechtsche Zendingsvereeniging (UZV, Utrecht Protestant Mission Union), which sent eighteen missionaries between 1862 and 1900, establishing a continuous mission presence with four mission stations on the nearby mainland. After five years, the first missionaries had become reasonably fluent in the local language and were beginning to translate the Bible. The first Christian church constructed in the west was at Mansinam in 1864.[62]

The Netherlands Indies' government encouraged missionary work by providing stipends of Dfl 500 to Dfl 1,000 a year, and transport for mission staff working in areas beyond government bases.[63] More missionaries arrived and established missions on the southwest coast in 1863, and then three years later a base at the Aru Islands. In 1870, when the mission stations were taken over by the Zending der Nederlands Hervormde Kerk (Protestant Mission of the Netherlands Reformed Church), part of the Bible had been translated into a local language, but the missionaries had been unable to spread their message much beyond the western shore of Cenderawasih Gulf. Five years later, the UZV announced a plan to begin a colony using Christians from Maluku, but this came to naught. In later years they requested twice-yearly visits from Dutch naval ships to aid in civil administration.[64]

In 1883, Van Hasselt had been a missionary at Dorei Bay for twenty years. Although he was only forty-seven, he looked more than seventy, bent double and enfeebled by fever. His house was on Manokwari Island, built above a pleasant coral beach in a grove of coconut palms, amid flower and vegetable gardens, with a church and schoolroom nearby. During twenty-eight years of work, his mission had lost many missionary lives, but had only managed to convert sixteen adults and twenty-six children. Most of the converts were orphans or the offspring of slaves who had been purchased by the missionaries to establish their flock.[65] Although missionary work moved very slowly, the missionaries were able to make use of the existing extensive network of settlements and trading connections that connected Dorei Bay to Biak and Numfor, as well as the Raja Empat Islands and Tidore.

At the beginning of the twentieth century, there were still only five mission stations in west New Guinea: Mansinam, Kwawe and Andai at Dorei Bay, along with Roon and

Windessi further south. In 1905, the total number of converts in west New Guinea was still no more than 260. Unlike the system of Pacific Islander pastors used so successfully by the London Missionary Society and the Methodists in the east, there were few native teachers available, although some were introduced from Ambon after 1902.[66] The staffing problem was rectified when New Guinea ministers began to be trained, at first at Depok in Java, and then in west New Guinea when the school shifted first to Mansinam in 1916, and then from 1926 at Miei.

Catholic missions entered west New Guinea much later than the Protestants, concentrating their endeavors along the southern coast. Jesuits had first attempted to settle in eastern Seram and on the Kei Islands in 1888. Six years later, one of them set up a base at Kapaur near Fakfak, but he drowned the next year. The next attempt in west New Guinea was by four Sacred Heart missionaries who settled at the newly established government station in Marind-anim territory at Merauke in 1905, and operated as an outpost of their headquarters in Langgur in the Kei Islands. They took a strong, unpopular stand against sexual promiscuity amongst the Marind-anim, in an attempt to stem the spread of granulomatosis, a venereal disease, which had been recently introduced. The Catholics drew on Kei Islanders as mission teachers, but because of cultural differences, and because only one or two generations earlier Kei Islanders had enslaved New Guineans, they were not well suited, and there were many conflicts.[67]

Southeast New Guinea was mainly served by Protestant missions, totally so until the Catholics set up a mission station at Yule Island in 1885. In 1867, a Protestant group, the Society for the Propagation of the Gospel, sent two missionaries funded by the Queensland government to newly established Somerset on Queensland's Cape York. Right from the beginning, they were at odds with the local Police Magistrate and they lasted less than a year, their salaries having been terminated during government financial pruning.[68] The London Missionary Society (LMS) was already well established in Polynesia and southern Melanesia when it moved into Torres Strait in 1871, supported by three European couples and a team of Loyalty, Cook, and Niue Islanders. Their first base was on Murray (Mer) Island. Loyalty Island teachers were placed at Katau and Manumanu in Redscar Bay on New Guinea, but with no mission ship to keep in regular contact, the isolated teachers lacked supplies. Their health suffered, and they were evacuated by Captain John Moresby on HMS *Basilisk*, who scathingly attacked the LMS for risking Pacific Island teachers under conditions no European missionary would endure. Moresby did do the LMS one huge favor: he discovered Halifax Harbour, later the site of Port Moresby, and the first successful LMS base on the mainland.

In December 1874, William and Fanny Lawes settled at Port Moresby, joined by medical missionary William Turner and his wife for several months of the next year. The Lawes received more permanent assistance when the Chalmers (another husband-and-wife team) arrived in October 1877. They opened a new mission at Sua'au on South Cape, extending the eastern LMS mission stations that had begun in the previous year.[69]

Missionaries seldom really understood how the people they contacted perceived them. When James Chalmers arrived at Sua'au, the people feared his ship, and hid women and children inland while Benoma, a magician, went to the beach to spit magic to make the ship go away. Then they decided that Chalmers was Boledau, an ancestral hero returning to help end a four-month drought that had blighted their crops. But why did he no longer speak their language? They searched around the island to see if his was the only ship, then decided to kill him, but he managed to elude them and eventually Sua'au Islanders realized that he was just a man from another country. Benoma was among the first of Chalmers' converts.[70]

Until rudimentary Protectorate government began in 1884, the LMS European missionaries and their Islander teachers were the major traders and explorers on the southeast coast. The mission steamer *Ellengowan* constantly circulated between Somerset, Torres Strait, and the dozen or so LMS stations along the coast around to Milne Bay. Foreigners in trouble always turned to the LMS, but also tended to resent the imperious attitudes of missionaries Lawes, Chalmers, Murray, and MacFarlane, who behaved more like consuls.[71] George Brown was no less imperious in his running of the Wesleyan Methodist mission, begun in the Duke of York Islands in August 1875. He employed similar methods to those of the LMS in southeast New Guinea; the Methodists used European husband-and-wife teams coupled with Fijian, Tongan, and Samoan teachers.[72] They established their headquarters at Kinawanua at Port Hunter, and within a few years they had twenty-three stations scattered throughout the Duke of York Islands, southern New Ireland, and New Britain's Gazelle Peninsula.[73] Local people initially saw the Methodists as useful allies who could support local political and military maneuvers, but instead they disrupted the local power dynamics and dynastic formations based around local leaders.[74]

Catholic priests arrived with the Marquis de Rays' Nouvelle-France settlers in the late 1870s (see the next chapter), but soon moved to Malagunan at Blanche Bay, where they established Our Lady of the Sacred Heart mission. In 1881, Italian-born Father John Cani was sent to explore the south coast of New Guinea, selecting Yule Island, 104 kilometers west of Port Moresby, as the best place to begin evangelizing.[75] Bishop Navarre purchased land on Thursday Island in Torres Strait, establishing his mission station with Italian priests, brothers, and religious sisters. Navarre's plans were strongly discouraged by Magistrate Henry Chester (who was fervently anti-Catholic), but they found favor with Sir Peter Scratchley, the newly appointed but short-lived Special Commissioner for the British New Guinea Protectorate.[76] The Catholic Sacred Heart Mission began work on Yule Island in June 1885, relying on Thursday Island and Cooktown for supplies, but it was in constant conflict with the LMS mission and the administration. The Anglican mission began in Papua in 1891.[77] Society of Divine Word missionaries arrived at Madang in 1896, and Society of Mary missionaries settled on Bougainville in 1897.

The Neuendettelsau Mission Society started Lutheran missionary work around Finsch-hafen in 1886, followed the next year by the Rhenish Lutheran Mission at Madang. Anglican missionaries arrived on the southeast coast in 1891, completing the initial mission pattern in eastern New Guinea. Evidence of this Christian regionalism is still evident amongst Papua New Guinea's population today.[78]

These Christian missions operated as de facto government bases around the coast, providing safe havens for foreign travelers, and acting as sources of information on local conditions. Although their aims were pious, the missionary modus operandi was similar to that of the trader. During at least the first decade of any mission, the indigenous people saw the missionaries more as benevolent traders, and therefore as major sources of European manufactured goods. The pattern noted above with the Methodists in the Bismarck Archipelago occurred more widely as missionaries established themselves in various areas during the nineteenth and twentieth centuries. Often unbeknownst to them, they were regarded as useful allies, since they boosted the opportunities of various local leaders and their descent groups to gain access to foreign goods, trade networks, and political power. When the mission arrived on the Gazelle Peninsula, the already powerful bigmen Topulu, Waruwarum, and Liblib augmented their positions by becoming middlemen for the Methodists, acting as interpreters and food buyers. Ready access to axes, tobacco, glass, fishing hooks, and firearms was revolutionizing Tolai society, and when bigmen accumulated *tambu* or *diwara* (shell currency wealth) through commercial transactions it added to their ritual power. Tobacco became the mission's currency for buying food, favors, copra, and coconuts. Heinz Schütte's analysis holds true more widely:

> It can only be stated that exchange relations between certain Big men and European traders and missionaries (whose demand for land, food and copra grew rapidly), got more and more individualized and that a number of Big men became wealthy through extended trade. The profits they made in their trade ventures with Europeans and with European goods which they sold to inland groups, meant that their social position got consolidated and increased because the Big men depended largely on the ability to distribute presents and to bind have-nots to their households, which they were able to do to a much greater extent than ever before . . . Consequently what we see here is a system based on customs and morals, composed on interests and institutions which are controlled by magico-religious powers and social interests; a system thus, that is based on ideological rather than material principles.[79]

When a Tolai alliance, disturbed by mission inroads on their control of local markets, attacked, killed, and ate a group of mission workers in 1878, Brown resolved to show that "roast missionary is too expensive a dish for them to indulge in." He lead a punitive expedition made up of traders, his Samoan and Fijian staff, and still-friendly Tolai. Brown and his party killed or wounded 90 to 100 Tolai, destroying and confiscating property. The mission proved its superior merit but Brown, wisely, did not humiliate Talili, the defeated bigman, choosing instead to exchange gifts with him. Like many other early missionaries, Brown found that success lay with utilizing local custom for the long-term benefit of the Christian endeavor.

Pearl and Bêche-de-mer Traders

Missionaries, particularly those of the LMS, had a symbiotic relationship with traders. They decried their often less-than-moral ways, but remained linked by the camaraderie that bound all isolated foreigners in Melanesia. The major export industry operating out of east New Guinea waters in the 1860s, 1870s, and 1880s was fishing for and curing bêche-de-mer, the smoke-dried flesh of the several edible species of the class *Holothurioidea*, the sea cumber or trepang, used by Chinese in soups and famed for its supposed aphrodisiac qualities. Although never a rival to the annual Sulawesi-Arnhem Land trade, Maluku bêche-de-mer collecting also occurred around west New Guinea. In Polynesia and southern Melanesia, the bêche-de-mer trade was connected to the sandalwood trade, and provided an alternative income as trees became depleted. In Torres Strait, the bêche-de-mer trade grew up alongside the pearling trade, while amongst New Guinea's most extensive reef system—around the Louisiade Archipelago—it preceded other trades. Bêche-de-mer fishing was a lucrative industry: during the 1870s and 1880s the best species were purchased in Cooktown for more than £100 per ton; lower qualities fetched only £25 to £30.[80]

The earliest European voyager collecting bêche-de-mer in east New Guinea waters was probably the American Benjamin Morell, who worked around Kilinailau, Buka, and Bougainville in 1830 and 1834.[81] Other traders worked out of Sydney, Singapore, Hong Kong, and Port Essington, searching for pearl-, turtle- and trochus-shells, and they were already making voyages as far as Torres Strait in the late 1830s, more significantly so onwards from the 1840s and 1850s.[82] Collecting bêche-de-mer in Torres Strait came later, an extension of trading ventures reaching out of southern Melanesia.[83] As sandalwood reserves were cut out and marine fields became depleted around the New Hebrides and New Caledonia in the late 1850s, traders laid plans to shift their bases to the Queensland coast. The first turtle trading and bêche-de-mer prospecting voyage into Torres Strait was probably in 1861, followed in 1863–1864 by the establishment of a permanent bêche-de-mer station at Darnley Island. This was the beginning of the European occupation of Torres Strait.[84] Over the next few years, bêche-de-mer and pearling vessels began to visit many parts of the New Guinea coast adjacent to Torres Strait.[85] The standard practice was to erect curing houses on beaches in several places, leave a limited staff to supervise operations at each station, and employ local people to gather bêche-de-mer from the reefs and shallows for processing ashore. During the 1860s, indentured Loyalty Islanders were recruited regularly as divers and collectors in Torres Strait, several ships working a circuit between the Loyalty Islands, Sydney, and the Strait. Until the early 1880s, laborers recruited from the New Hebrides and Solomon Islands supplemented them.[86]

In the mid-1870s, the Torres Strait bêche-de-mer reefs were becoming overworked, and Queensland authorities began to regulate the thriving marine industries.[87] This focused interest even more on the rich but uncontrolled New Guinea bêche-de-mer fields: the Louisiade reefs, particularly those surrounding the forty-some islands of the Calvados Chain northwest of Sudest Island, and to a lesser extent along the central coast around Port Moresby.[88] The first Queensland ships ventured to the eastern reefs in 1873.[89] Schooners plied back and forth between north Queensland ports, and whaleboats, cutters, and gigs were used for communication along the reefs and between islands.

In 1885, when the British Protectorate began operating in southeast New Guinea, there were ten ships working in the Louisiades, collecting around 500 tons of bêche-de-mer annually.[90] The appearance of these traders at an island was no longer a novel event. Hugh Romilly, a Western Pacific High Commission official, in 1887 noted a considerable change in the demeanor of the people when dealing with bêche-de-mer traders since his first visit in 1881: "In some parts they are openly hostile and threatening, in others they affect friendship toward the whites, but are equally hostile in their minds. In a few islands only can they be said to be really friendly. In the islands most visited by the shelling boats, they neither interfere with nor assist the shellers, but hold little or no communication with them."[91]

Although the two were intertwined, in the long term it was pearlshell rather than bêche-de-mer that dominated maritime commerce. The change to pearling in Torres Strait began in 1868 when William Banner established a bêche-de-mer station there, which soon changed over to pearling, employing seventy Pacific Islanders on Warrior (Tutu) Island. The next year, James Gascoigne's *Sperwar* began collecting pearlshell in the Strait. The northern Australian pearlshell beds from Broome to Torres Strait are the largest in the world. The shell was highly valued by Europeans for use as buttons and ornamentation. Pearls found in gold-lipped shells were an added but irregular bonus. Early bêche-de-mer traders noted that Torres Strait Islanders used large crescent-shaped pearlshell ornaments, and the divers occasionally brought in pearl oysters. The industry began to grow from the early 1870s, using local Islanders as guides to locate new oyster beds.[92]

In 1877 there were sixteen pearling firms operating 109 vessels in the Strait. When the shallow beds became exhausted, sixty-three ships were equipped with diving apparatus. Most were luggers of about seven tons, and larger schooners up to twenty-five tons were used as mother-ships carrying provisions and men. Some £40,000 was invested in the industry, which showed annual profits averaging £50,000 over 1875–1879. Although pearlshell prices fluctuated greatly—from £200 per ton in 1873–1875, to as low as £80 per ton in late 1877—the Queensland industry was always prosperous. More than fifty Europeans and 700 Asians and Pacific Islanders were employed, some from as far as Hawai'i and New Zealand.[93] Somerset became a Queensland "port of entry" in November 1866, handling exports and imports for Torres Strait, and regulating engagements under the *Merchant Shipping Act*, the *Masters and Servants' Act*, and the *Pacific Islanders' Protection Act of 1872–75*. The Magistrates doubled as immigration and labor officers, and both policed labor contracts and ran a busy court hearing the drunkenness and assault charges of an increasingly unruly community.[94]

Divers worked in teams of ten to fifteen per boat, diving in two to four fathoms (3.6 to 7.3 m) of water. Shells varied in size, from 700 to 2,000 to a ton. The average boat brought up around seven tons per year, of which only five tons were required to pay expenses. It was possible for a ship on a twelve-month voyage to gather twenty-five tons of shell worth £4,000 to £5,000.[95] The best divers were Malays and Loyalty Islanders, and the most skilled often earned wages of up to £12 per month, together with £12 per ton per man from sale profits. Non-divers working on the luggers—mainly Malays and Pacific Islanders—received around £2 per month and a small extra bonus based on the boat's catch. Aborigines and Torres Strait Islanders completed the more menial tasks in the industry, and were paid from ten shillings to £1 or £2 per month. In early years, payment of indigenous divers was often in goods, but as the trade became regulated, payment was in coin. Employees were encouraged to "book up" supplies through their employer, running up considerable debts over years.[96]

Thursday Island became a thriving port with a large fleet of pearl luggers manned mostly by all-Pacific Islander crews. Good divers were scarce, and none earned less than £200 in a year, top men making £300 to £400, almost as much as the Magistrate.[97] When on Thursday Island, captains and divers from luggers paraded up and down the port's single street, dressed as "magnificent swells." They drank heavily, gambled and whored in the northern port, and also took trips to Brisbane and Sydney to further squander their earnings.[98]

In the mid-1880s, pearlshell was worth between £90 and £170 per ton, with the top price going to the gold-lipped variety. The pearling fleet usually worked only in the Strait, but as supplies of shell became depleted, part of the fleet moved to the Louisiade Archipelago for two seasons, 1887–1888. In excess of fifty tons of pearlshell was exported from the Louisiades in 1887. Romilly estimated that pearlshell valued at £50,000 was exported in the first three months of the year. In 1888, there were thirty-two boats and 200 men working in Joanette Harbour. The Louisiade industry did not last, because the shell was of a lesser quality than in Torres Strait and was located too deep for safe diving. Divers had to go down more than twenty fathoms (18.2 m), with the result that some got "the bends" and several died.[99]

Torres Strait pearlers searched for new pearlshell beds west as well as east, and reached the rich Aru beds in the 1870s. When the Indies government established a base at Aru in 1882, it was partly to regulate access by pearlers from the Australian colonies, and certainly an 1893 regulation had this intention. Eventually Aru was so closely linked to Torres Strait commerce that in 1905 part of the Torres Strait pearling fleet moved to the Aru Islands, creating yet another connection between Australia and the islands off New Guinea.[100] Once the "passing trade" era ended in the early 1860s, Europeans developed increasingly sophisticated understandings of Islander customs and encounter protocols, which was crucial to their commercial success. The Torres Strait Islanders, living midway between Aboriginal Cape York and New Guinea, were old hands at negotiating cross-cultural trade encounters. Ceremonies were used to encourage Europeans to trade, and suitable barter items were accumulated. The demand for bows and arrows meant gaining extra wood supplies from the New Guinea mainland; and extra tortoiseshell was also collected.[101] So many ships were wrecked in the Strait (providing metals and other items), and the Islanders accumulated so many trade goods through barter and their labor, that the surplus must have been traded far to the north and south. Torres Strait Islanders, because they became Queenslanders, and then Australians, are often excluded from discussions of New Guinea. However, their intimate involvement in maritime industries and mission endeavors, and their position on a major shipping route, made them the most "modern" of all New Guineans in the nineteenth century.

The Laloki Gold Rush, 1878

In the 1870s, Torres Strait and the southeast coast of New Guinea were firmly part of the commercial outreach of colonial Queensland. When LMS missionary William Lawes went on leave in December 1877, rather unwillingly he took a quartz rock sample, provided by trader Andrew Goldie, to Sydney for analysis. The existence of substantial deposits of gold in Melanesia had long been supposed. Back in the mid-sixteenth century, Mendaña named the Solomon Islands thinking that they were the legendary source of King Solomon's wealth. Much later, Captain Stanley on HMS *Rattlesnake* found a few grains of gold in pottery from Redscar Bay in 1848, and in 1873 Captain Moresby on HMS *Basilisk* thought he found gold quartz at Halifax Bay (later Port Moresby) and at Moresby Island. Henry Chester had obtained a nugget while trading in the early 1870s. The LMS missionaries also discovered gold, but chose to keep their discoveries quiet, and actively discouraged gold-seekers, who they feared would jeopardized their work and change the lives of the people.[102] Their worst fears were confirmed in September 1877, when an Islander employee of Andrew Goldie, Jimmy Caledonia, who had previous mining experience in New Caledonia, New Zealand, and Queensland, found signs of gold at the junction of the Laloki and Goldie Rivers, not far from Port Moresby. He alerted Goldie, who persuaded Lawes to face the inevitable and take the sample south.[103]

Cooktown, on Cape York, was the port for the rich Palmer River goldfields, where a gold rush had begun in 1873. Five years later, the nearby Hodgkinson field had become an even greater magnet than the Palmer. Miners were searching all of north Queensland for new fields, while at the same time European exploration, exploitation of marine resources, and new settlement was moving through the islands of Torres Strait and along the underbelly of New Guinea. The first Queensland-based prospector in New Guinea was probably Carl Thorngren, a Swedish trader based in Torres Strait from 1871, who sailed his eight-ton cutter *Viking* 19 kilometers up Vanapa River at Manumanu in search of gold in late 1872 or early 1873.[104] To the northern miners, a trip to Port Moresby and the new Laloki goldfield was no different from moving from the Herbert River or Cairns to Cooktown and the Palmer. Any new gold rush was worth the risk.

Figure 1. Moa and Jamna Islanders, west New Guinea, sketched during Thomas Forrest's expedition, 1775. (Forrest 1775.)

Figure 2. Dorei Bay in Cenderawasih Gulf, site of John Hayes's New Albion settlement, 1793. (Lee 1912.)

Figure 3. Murray (Mer) Islanders, Torres Strait, offering to barter with Matthew Flinders, 1802. (Flinders 1814.)

Figure 4. Malay Forges for smelting metal in operation at Dorei Bay, in Cenderawasih Gulf, 1826 (Dumont d'Urville 1834–1835.)

Figure 5. (Above) The Dutch Fort Du Bus under construction, at Merkusoord, Triton Bay, 1828. (Müller 1857.)

Figure 6. (Left) Crew of HMS Rattlesnake meeting the people of Redscar Bay, Gulf of Papua, 1840s. (MacGillivray 1852.)

Figure 7. Dobo, main port of the Aru Islands, 1850s. (Wallace 1869.)

Figure 8. Koiari villagers on the Sogeri Plateau inland from Port Moresby, 1885. (Lindt 1887.)

Figure 9. (Above) Warriors from the Orokaiva region of east New Guinea, 1930s. (Clive Moore private collection, University of Queensland.)

Figure 10. (Left) The Kunnuner form of courtship, Mt. Hagen, 1940s. (P. J. Grimshaw Collection, Pacific Manuscripts Bureau, Australian National University.)

Figure 11. (Right) Elevala Island (now within Hanuabada village), Port Moresby viewed from the front of the main London Missionary Society house, 1885. (J. W. Lindt photo 1885, Clive Moore private collection, University of Queensland.)

Figure 12. (Below) The Royal Papuan Constabulary, Kokoda, 1920. (Clive Moore private collection, University of Queensland.)

Figure 13. Father Louis Vangeke, born in Beipa, Mekeo, in Australian Papua's Central District, the first New Guinea Catholic priest (ordained 1937), with students. In 1970 he was consecrated titular bishop of Culusi and auxiliary bishop of Port Moresby. In 1976, he was made bishop of Beraina. (Clive Moore private collection, University of Queensland.)

Figure 14. The labor force on a sisal hemp plantation at Fairfax Harbour, Port Moresby, 1910s. (Murray 1912.)

Figure 15. A family outside their police barracks home in the Highlands, 1950s. (P. J. Grimshaw Collection, Pacific Manuscripts Bureau, Australian National University.)

Figure 16. The first gramophone in Mt. Hagen, 1933. Some Highlanders at first thought that their ancestors were crying out from inside the box. (P. J. Grimshaw Collection, Pacific Manuscripts Bureau, Australian National University.)

Figure 17. An aircraft graveyard on Biak Island after the Second World War. (Max Quanchi private collection, Queensland University of Technology.)

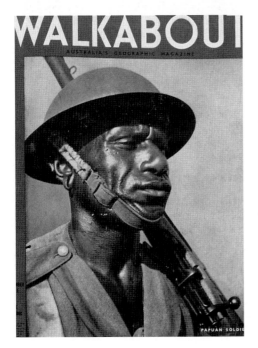

Figure 18. The Papuan Infantry Battalion was formed in Port Moresby in 1940. This soldier was featured on the front cover of Walkabout magazine. (Walkabout: Australia's Geographic Magazine, November 1941.)

Figure 19. Twenty-five members of the Royal Papua and New Guinea Constabulary depart Port Moresby wharf for the coronation of Queen Elizabeth II. (P. J. Grimshaw Collection, Pacific Manuscripts Bureau, Australian National University.)

Figure 20. A District Officer and his carriers set out on patrol, Papua and New Guinea, 1950. (H. C. Morris Collection, Pacific Manuscripts Bureau, Australian National University.)

Figure 21. Women learning to sew, Netherlands New Guinea, 1960. (Max Quanchi private collection, Queensland University of Technology.)

Figure 22. Students at Teachers' Training School, 1950. After the war, teacher training at Sogeri, Kerevat, and Dregerhafen provided general education and technical training in order to provide teachers, medical orderlies, and skilled artisans for the Papua and New Guinea government. (H. C. Morris Collection, Pacific Manuscripts Bureau, Australian National University.)

Figure 23. New Guinea men working in a produce cooperative, 1950. (H. C. Morris Collection, Pacific Manuscripts Bureau, Australian National University.)

Figure 24. An Australian District Officer holds a court hearing in the Highlands, 1950. (H. C. Morris Collection, Pacific Manuscripts Bureau, Australian National University.)

Figure 25. The swearing-in of the only woman in the first Raad, the twenty-eight member New Guinea Council established in Hollandia (Jayapura), 1961. (Max Quanchi, private collection, Queensland University of Technology.)

Figure 26. Crowds at the official opening of Papua New Guinea's new National Parliament at Waigani in August 1984. The building's front is designed after a Sepik Haus Tambaran (ceremonial house). (Clive Moore private collection, University of Queensland.)

Figure 27. Indonesian army soldiers in Papua Province in 1984, at the time that thousands of refugees were fleeing into Papua New Guinea. (Clive Moore private collection, University of Queensland.)

Figure 28. This Highlands man at the 1984 Goroka show has managed to combine the traditional and modern culture of Papua New Guinea. (Clive Moore private collection, University of Queensland.)

Figure 29. Gaunt Goilala women, originally from the Highlands of Australian Papua, scavenging at Port Moresby's Baruni rubbish dump in 2002. Urban poverty is increasingly a feature of modern New Guinea society. (Clive Moore private collection, University of Queensland.)

Figure 30. Hanuabada village in Port Moresby, built on stilts over the water just two kilometers from the center of the business district. (Clive Moore private collection, University of Queensland.)

Figure 31. Razor wire dominates the view from elite houses on Tauaguba hill, overlooking Port Moresby, a reminder that urban crime is a growing problem, in 2002. (Clive Moore private collection, University of Queensland.)

In the early 1870s, the only permanent foreign settlers on the southeast coast of New Guinea were three traders and European and Pacific Islander representatives of the LMS. One of the traders, Englishman William Ingham, a young failed sugar planter from the Herbert River, Queensland, lately of Cairns and Cooktown, had arrived in February 1878. He established a trade store, and managed to get himself appointed as unofficial Government Agent for Queensland. Although this position was legally no more than a confidential correspondent of the colony's Colonial Secretary, Ingham took his shadowy appointment seriously, and attempted to establish rudimentary government services.[105]

The abortive Laloki gold rush of 1878 meant, briefly, that large numbers of Europeans began arriving at Port Moresby, as parties of miners set out from Sydney and Cooktown. Between April and August around 100 miners descended on Port Moresby, ill-equipped for dealing with the environment, malaria, or the indigenous people. Both Thursday Island's Magistrate and Ingham anticipated a large migration from north Queensland, if payable quantities of gold were discovered, and both predicted 10,000 settlers before Christmas. But the rush soon petered out and the miners departed. One short-term legacy was two prostitutes who briefly plied their trade with the miners. The only long-term legacy, a pack of horses, was left roaming the environs of Port Moresby.[106]

Although the failure of the Laloki gold rush discouraged further thought of private colonization, negotiations to establish official British and German spheres of influence continued in London, Berlin, and in the capital cities of the Australian east coast colonies. The European powers were interested in New Guinea for several reasons, one of which was as a source of labor for plantations in the new settler societies of the South Pacific.

· ·

Onwards from the final decades of the eighteenth century, and solidly throughout the nineteenth century, New Guinea's proximity to the Australian colonies meant ever-increasing contact with the outside world, particularly in the east and its adjacent archipelagos. As eastern New Guinea was explored and mapped, the various shipping channels became relatively safe, enabling long distance and local shipping to move around the coasts, exploiting maritime produce, from whales to bêche-de-mer to pearls, pearlshells, and trochus-shells. Gold discoveries in the 1870s and 1880s, and permanent Christian missions—in the west from the 1850s and the east from the 1870s—meant that sooner rather than later European governments would claim the island as protectorates and colonies. Coastal west New Guineans had long been on the edge of the Malay world, linked by commercial and cultural exchanges. In east New Guinea, the same process occurred, though over a much shorter time period and with increasing intensity. Evidence from the Bird's Head, Torres Strait, and the Bismarck Archipelago suggests that coastal communities exploited the new trade situations, managing to accommodate the foreigners and their strange practices into existing ritual pathways and cosmologies. Traditional exchanges, the underlying web that maintained fertility and stability within and between communities, were extended to meet new situations.

In this phase, accommodation did not involve much movement away from the geographic confines of small-scale societies. The next phase would lead to the manipulation of and long-distance movement of the labor reserve, and the eventual full-scale colonization of New Guinea.

The Nineteenth Century

Exploration and Colonization

···

British Authority in the Pacific Islands

The front verandah of the main LMS mission house, overlooking Hanuabada village, Port Moresby, became the favorite site for proclaiming southeast New Guinea as a British territory. As missionary William Lawes remarked in 1888, when British New Guinea ceased being a Protectorate and became a colony, the flag-hoistings and proclamation-readings were becoming monotonous. We do not know what the local Motu people thought about the ceremonies, but since they were always accompanied by distributions of gifts, we can presume the inhabitants of Hanuabada were happy to attend, even if they were oblivious to the international significance of the occasions.

Roving British authority had long been enforced through the Royal Navy Australian Station (RNAS), which began operations based in Sydney in 1821, although until 1872 the station had no jurisdiction above 10° south latitude (which cuts through Timor, Torres Strait, the tail of New Guinea, and the Solomon Islands).[1] Britain had introduced a *Foreign Jurisdiction Act* in 1843, which extended British law to cover its subjects beyond British territory, and utilizing concepts of "sovereignty" and "protectorate" enabled the British Crown to establish a system of jurisprudence in consular courts, without the costs of formal colonization. British settlements in Australia and New Zealand supplemented and succored trade and settlement in the neighboring Pacific Islands. An 1883 report to the Western Pacific High Commission (WPHC), by the High Commissioner and two RNAS Commodores described RNAS activities in keeping order before 1877: "When a British subject was guilty of any serious crime, or became generally obnoxious, he was either taken to Australia for trial, or more often deported to some other island, or to a neighbouring Colony. The powers, such as they were, exercized by British naval officers, had a strong deterrent effect, and the traders were, as a rule, quite ready to bow to their decision in matters of dispute which came before them. In like manner when outrages were committed by the natives the captain of the next ship visiting the place, after a careful investigation on the spot, dealt with the case as he thought best."[2]

The 1870s was an important decade for strengthening British control in the South Pacific. In 1872, the *Pacific Islanders' Protection Act* was passed in an attempt to regulate the labor trade. It extended to all Australasian colonies the power to try British subjects offending against Pacific Islanders. In the same year, Queensland's northern border was

The long-expected proclamation of British sovereignty was duly performed on the 4th instant [November 1888]. British New Guinea is now part of the Queen's dominions . . . There was not much display, and it was well that there was not, for flag-hoisting must seem to the natives to be a white man's amusement. The function of the 4th was the tenth at which I had been present on New Guinea. It is getting monotonous.
—Rev. William Lawes, in James Chalmers: His Autobiography and Letters, 1902, 253

moved north to 96.5 kilometers off Cape York, which enabled regulation of the northerly areas of the bêche-de-mer and pearling trades that had developed in Torres Strait since the late 1860s, although this extension excluded important fishing areas around Saibai Island, Warrior Reef, Darnley (Erub), and Murray (Mer) Islands.[3] The RNAS northern limit was extended to include all of New Guinea north as far as Micronesia and east to 160° longitude. European settlement in Fiji was regularized in 1874, when thirteen chiefs of Fiji, including the well-known Ratu Seru Cakobau, ceded control to Britain.[4] The revised *Pacific Islanders' Protection Act* of 1875 created the position of a High Commissioner, with jurisdiction over all British subjects in the Western Pacific.[5] This was followed in 1877 by an Order-in-Council establishing the Western Pacific High Commission, based at Suva with Fiji's Governor as High Commissioner. The WPHC had certain authority over British subjects in the Pacific, and unclear authority over natives in conflict with British subjects. The new regional government also had an uneasy relationship with the RNAS, the Commodore of which had previously wielded the only real British power in the Pacific beyond the coasts of the Australasian colonies.[6]

Deputy Commissioners were appointed for Samoa and Tonga, but despite plans for roving Deputy Commissioners to be stationed in Melanesia—one in the New Hebrides and one ship-based to cover the Solomon Islands and New Guinea—no permanent appointments were made until 1883. The earliest Deputy Commissioners in Melanesia were RNAS officers whose ships were on patrol through the islands.[7] The High Commissioner's powers were quite restricted, although he was able to make naval commanders members of his court of magistrates and arbitrators, and from 1884 their powers were extended to include extradition. During 1878, Queensland urgently solicited a similar appointment for the Magistrate at Thursday Island in order to circumvent his lack of authority over Murray and Darnley Islands in Torres Strait. The appointment was rescinded in under a year, because Queensland's government doubted the propriety of one of its officers holding an appointment from another British authority.[8] The problem was solved when Britain allowed Queensland to extend its northern boundary to cover all of Torres Strait, to within a few hundred meters of the New Guinea mainland. The 1878 Letters Patent was incorporated into the *Queensland Coast Islands Act* in 1879.[9]

Early in 1883, Hugh Romilly was appointed as Deputy Commissioner of the WPHC, with the brief of establishing a headquarters in northern Melanesia and residing there for at least ten months of each year.[10] Romilly first visited New Guinea's eastern archipelagos in 1881, as a roving Deputy Commissioner on board HMS *Beagle,* to inspect the activities of labor trade vessels.[11] Romilly was in charge of regulating the excesses of the Fijian and Queensland labor trade in New Guinea waters, but was unable to hitch a passage on any passing naval ship, so in July 1883 he hired a Fijian recruiting ship to convey him to Blanche Bay, New Britain. Then, in October, Romilly proceeded to Port Moresby on board HMS *Diamond.* Failing to procure a suitable residence there, he departed in December for Melbourne via Thursday Island and Sydney.[12] When southeast New Guinea became a British Protectorate in November 1884, the process was little more than a re-assertion of existing British authority through the appointment of a Special Commissioner to be based in Port Moresby, answerable to the Governor of Queensland, and financed initially by seven of Britain's Australasian colonies, including Fiji and New Zealand.[13] Later, this limited jurisdiction was found to be unsatisfactory. After the economic impetus given to the Protectorate by the discovery of gold in the Louisiades in 1888, full colonial status was proclaimed for British New Guinea.[14]

The Protectorate concept—an informal extension of Britain's empire—was intended as a loose territorial claim to safeguard and govern British citizens, rather than to govern a colony. The nature of the political and geographic division of east New Guinea into British and German spheres of influence was shaped by the origins of the early European settlers. The area that became British New Guinea in 1884 was an extension of the Queensland colonial frontier, dominated by northern maritime industries and the London Missionary Society.

The Dutch and German territorial claims over New Guinea were just as complicated. The 1828 proclamation of the Dutch New Guinea territory grew out of suzerainty claims emanating from the Tidore sultanate, and was administratively incorporated under the control of the Governor of Maluku. In 1875, administrative control shifted to the Ternate Residency. Southeast New Guinea was dominated by German trading and plantation interests based in the Bismarck Archipelago, with strong commercial ties to Samoa and German concerns in Micronesia and Asia. After the unification of Germany, overseas territories were called *Schutzgebiet,* neither Protectorates nor colonies of the Reich, reflecting that they were protected areas administered by commercial companies.

Efforts to Colonize East New Guinea

Numerous attempts were made to begin settlements in New Guinea. In the west, a private colony established by John Hayes at Dorei Bay in 1793–1794 failed, as had the Dutch try at launching an official settlement at Merkus-oord in Triton Bay between 1828 and 1836. English and French colonization of New Britain was proposed in the 1740s and 1750s, but was never acted upon.[15] Charles de Brosses, President of the Burgundian Parliament, and a shareholder in the French India Company, suggested settling New Britain in 1756, well before James Cook put the east coast of Australia onto the map:

> The island called New Britain is advantageously situated across the fifth parallel south; longitude is 42 degrees . . . neither too close to nor too far from Maluku and the Philippines; within reach of Canton in China, and, perhaps not the least important, within reach of the islands of the Larrones & of numerous islands no longer visited that are to be found in the great Pacific ocean for the opening up of which New Britain is well placed. It would appear a better spot could not be chosen for opening up a trade depot than in these regions, which must promote

useful returns to explore the vast country of Carpentaria and one land Australi du S. Esprit, at a moderate distance to the south. Knowledge of these lands will give successful communication with New Holland, New Zealand, and Diemens land; whether they are continuous lands or whether they are isolated by sea.[16]

The first attempt to form a private Australian colony in east New Guinea seems to have been in 1843,[17] with colonization pursued more seriously in the 1860s and 1870s. Veteran imperialist Rev. Dr. John Dunmore Lang lent his support to several attempts. The year 1862 saw one abortive New Guinea company backed by Lang,[18] and then in 1867 a Sydney-based trading and colonization association headed by A. K. Collins asked to borrow a ship from the New South Wales government to help form a settlement in southeast New Guinea. Also backed by Lang, they had plans to raise £20,000 capital, the intention being to settle the Purari River delta in the Gulf of Papua and trade along the southern coast. The governments of New South Wales and Queensland, however, were not supportive.[19]

The New Guinea Prospecting Expedition of 1872 initially made more progress. Again supported by Lang, a syndicate of gold-miners from Ballarat in Victoria was formed in February 1872, aimed at establishing a private settlement and exploiting supposedly rich gold deposits at Redscar Bay. They chartered the 156-ton brig *Maria,* which left Sydney for Redscar Bay but was wrecked on Bramble Reef off Cardwell, with large loss of life.[20] One year later, Henry Chester, between terms as Magistrate, tried unsuccessfully to float the Queensland Pearl Fishing Company, to begin pearling and trading activities in Torres Strait and along the southern New Guinea coast. The next year he was involved in another failure, the New Guinea Trading Company, which intended to purchase a ship for trading and gold prospecting in New Guinea, following up recent discoveries by HMS *Basilisk.* Chester was to command the expedition, but as with his pearling venture, there were insufficient subscribers to support a company.[21]

In March 1874, Francis Labillere, an Australian colonist visiting London, petitioned the Colonial Secretary, the Earl of Carnarvon, to annex the non-Dutch eastern half. His letter was circulated among the Australian Governors who reacted negatively.[22] Not one to be discouraged, the Rev. Dr. Lang offered his support to an 1875 group planning to form a settlement. A year earlier, Britain reluctantly accepted the cession of Fiji, but did as much as possible to discourage any further extension of its rule in the Pacific, refusing official sanction to any association "brought together by the love of adventure and the desire for profit."[23] Lord Carnarvon received a deputation from the Royal Colonial Institute in April, urging annexation of New Guinea. Next, a British soldier-of-fortune, Brigadier-General H. R. MacIver, began planning a colony for around two hundred people, only to be rebuffed by his government.[24] Also in 1875, William Macleay, a wealthy New South Wales grazier, organized an expedition on the *Chevert* to investigate the scientific and colonizing potential of New Guinea. Three years later, High Commissioner Sir Arthur Gordon discouraged a Melbourne-based colonization scheme seeking a Royal Charter: "the British government disclaim all obligation to protect or interfere on behalf of persons voluntarily placing themselves in positions of danger in a savage country, and that those who enter on such enterprises do so at their own risk and peril."[25]

The Dutch government in the Indies and at home kept a close eye on the progress of British and German initiatives in east New Guinea. When the Melbourne-based Australian Colonization Company negotiated with the Dutch government during 1878–1879 for a ninety-nine-year concession over 150,000 acres along the north coast between Dorei and Humboldt Bays, they never really stood a chance. The same applied to Menotti Garibaldi, the son of the Italian leader, when, in 1879, he mooted plans for an Italian colony in New Guinea.[26]

The most substantial and infamous failed try at colonization occurred in New Ireland during 1879–1882. The scheme, first floated in 1872 by Charles M. B. du Breil, the Marquis de Rays, was to create a permanent settlement at Port Praslin, renamed Port Breton. The whole Nouvelle-France project was an ambitious, unmitigated disaster. Four expeditions totaling 800 French, Belgian, Italian, and German settlers left Europe for Nouvelle-France. A few settlers were landed at the Laughlan Islands but most disembarked at New Ireland in January 1880. Port Breton was judged unsuitable, and the settlers moved to Likiliki on the east coast. They were poorly equipped and fell victim to fever, many dying. Most of the survivors soon departed for Australia and New Caledonia. A few joined the German traders on New Britain; among them were the Catholic priests from Nouvelle-France, who established a mission there.[27] Artifacts of the expedition were scattered around New Britain and Australia. "Queen" Emma Forsayth, who rescued some of the survivors, used a lavish Catholic altar as the liquor bar in her grand mansion at Ralum, Blanche Bay. Some of the survivors founded New Italy on the north coast of New South Wales, and a millstone brought from Europe still decorates the main street of volcano-devastated Rabaul.

Queensland also tried to expand its territory, and in 1883 annexed most of what is now Papua New Guinea, only to be overruled by Britain.[28] The eventual partition of the eastern half of New Guinea between Germany and Britain in 1884 was probably inevitable, given the way in which interest groups had begun to enter the region. British colonists also tried to gain control over areas in west New Guinea after the colonial annexations precluded further action in the east. John Strachan sought a concession over 350,000 acres of southern New Guinea in 1885, with the aim of erecting a sawmill and beginning agricultural activities, and Henry C. Everill applied for one million acres in 1889. Their requests were ignored, but with these colonizing, commercial, and mission interests came an increasing stream of official scientific expeditions attempting to find out more about New Guinea and penetrate the unknown interior.[29]

New Guinea was a huge island seemingly ripe for colonization at the height of the nineteenth-century scramble for colonies. Writers wrote glowing reports on its wonders, although some of their fantastic tales went too far—mountains higher than Everest, sophisticated cities of gold, and men with tails were all included in descriptions by intrepid adventurers making imaginary journeys into New Guinea's interior in the 1870s and 1880s, trading on a gullible Victorian reading public.[30] Yet New Guinea was strange enough without falsification, and even usually reliable observers sometimes made mistakes. For instance, in the 1870s Captain John Moresby recorded seeing rhinoceros tracks at Collingwood Bay. But who would have believed Carstensz and his crew in 1623, when they reported sighting snow-covered mountains in central New Guinea, or travelers who reported, accurately, sighting pigeons the size of small turkeys, and the occasional small dragon (large monitor lizards)? The huge human population, with its astonishing variations of appearances and customs, constantly astounded visitors.[31]

Along with Antarctica, New Guinea was the last unknown region on earth. Its exploration attracted a steady stream of scientific visitors in the second half of the nineteenth century. Some came out of a desire for knowledge, others to exploit its riches. In various ways almost every foreign visitor was an explorer; each whaler, trader, bêche-de-mer fisherman, and missionary made contact with "new" people. Few of them left records, and only those who wrote books and addressed learned societies, made reports to governments, or sold their stories or photos to newspapers, or otherwise were self-publicists, are remembered. Visual records became commonplace in the later decades of the nineteenth century, when sketches by early naturalists and ships' crews were supplemented by photographs from cumbersome cameras on tripods. After 1895, the roll-film hand-held camera made every visitor, and particularly missionaries, capable visual recorders of New Guinea. After the 1890s, their photographic images filled magazines and newspapers, postcards, encyclopedias, and other publications of the day.[32]

Scientific explorers and natural history collectors lived for long periods in isolated parts of New Guinea and were often the first Europeans to travel into inland areas. Science and imperialism combined in New Guinea, with exploration used to assess development prospects and to extend the boundaries of administration. Beginning with the voyages of Bougainville, Carteret, and Cook—which all carried itinerant scientists—botanists, naturalists, and other physical scientists began to supplement their armchair and laboratory work with fieldwork in the Pacific. New Guinea also became influential in the formulation of Western scientific theories. Most of the detailed scientific exploration took place in the final decades of the nineteenth century and early in the twentieth century when Darwinian thought was well established. Learned scientists pontificated on the "Pygmy Question" and the relationship between New Guineans, Africans, and the older mountain-dwelling populations of Southeast Asia, trying to classify the inhabitants into a world hierarchy of Negritos.[33] New Guinea became the center of important scientific expeditions, such as A. C. Haddon's 1898 Cambridge anthropological expedition to Torres Strait, which influenced the whole British social anthropology school, or Bronislaw Malinowski's Trobriands and Mailu research during the First World War, which set international standards for fieldwork, creating a new methodology based on ethnography "in residence," and direct participant-observation.[34]

WEST NEW GUINEA

The Raja Empat Islands and Cenderawasih Bay were the favorite rendezvous of Dutch, Spanish, German, British, French, and Italian explorers and naturalists visiting west New Guinea in the nineteenth century, most of them searching for rare species of the famous birds-of-paradise. The French, the first to annex islands in the South Pacific in the 1840s and 1850s, showed interest in New Guinea earlier than most European powers. The scientific voyages of Freycinet on *L'Uranie* (1817–1820), Duperrey on *Coquille* (1822–1825), Dumont d'Urville on the *Astrolabe* (1826–1829), and the *Astrolabe* and the *Zélée* (1837–1839), all visited New Guinea and neighboring islands, and contributed significantly to scientific knowledge. For instance, during Duperrey's thirty-three month scientific expedition, the *Coquille* was filled with hundreds of geological specimens, 3,000 species of plants, 254 species of birds, twelve new species of quadruped, several human skulls, 63 species of reptiles and amphibians, 298 preserved fish, 1,100 types of insect, and over 1,000 marine invertebrates.[35] Likewise, Dumont d'Urville's 1826–1829 voyage provided huge numbers of specimens for the Museum of Natural History, more than any other French voyage to that date, as well as 6,000 drawings. Even more importantly, Dumont d'Urville's personal observations led to the classification of the Pacific and its peoples into three regions—Melanesia, Polynesia, and Micronesia—a terminology still in use, despite its shortcomings.[36]

The government of the Dutch East Indies allowed a continuous stream of scientific expeditions to visit New Guinea throughout the second half of the nineteenth century, mapping the coast, collecting ethnographic data, and generally "showing the flag," and constantly seeking suitable sites for official settlements. Sometimes the Dutch sponsored foreign expeditions, such as two British ornithological parties between 1910 and 1913, but usually non-Dutch exploration had to be self-contained and self-financed. Most European visitors arriving in west New Guinea headed straight for the missionary settlement at Dorei Bay in Cenderawasih Gulf. A French naturalist, Raffray, arrived there in January 1876, and caused some concern as the Dutch continually suspected other European powers of wanting to establish bases on New Guinea. In the second half of the nineteenth century, the Spanish navy was increasingly present around the islands off west New Guinea, supposedly with plans to establish posts there and in Mindanao in the southern Philippines.[37] Famous British naturalist Alfred Wallace spent nearly six months in Cenderawasih Gulf and on adjacent islands in 1858, although incapacitating illness limited his endeavors. While Wallace was at Dorei Bay, the navy steamer *Etna* arrived on a major interdisciplinary scientific expedition. A son of the Sultan of Tidore and the Dutch Resident of Banda were on board, intending to collect birds-of-paradise. In the 1860s, Dutch naturalist Dr. Heinrich A. Bernstein from Leiden Museum died of malaria while working near Sorong Island, and Count C.B.H. von Rosenberg, a German illustrator and naturalist in the Dutch colonial service, spent some time at Andai, south of Dorei Bay, under the protection of the Sultan of Tidore.[38] German explorer and naturalist, Dr. Adolf B. Meyer, landed at Dorei Bay with a large party in 1873. After skirting around Cenderawasih Gulf, Meyer falsely claimed to have crossed New Guinea. Three years later, Dutch naturalist J. E. Teysmann visited Cenderawasih Gulf and Humboldt Bay, and an expedition led by Dr. F.H.H. Guillemard arrived at Dorei Bay in 1883. The next year a Dutch ship sailed up the Mamberamo River as far as rapids near Havik Island.[39]

Italian interest in New Guinea coincided with the unification of Italy. Giorgio E. Cerruti, an Italian adventurer, chartered a boat at Singapore in 1870, and set off for MacCluer Gulf to investigate founding a colony. He was attacked by the local people, lost his flag and gun, and was wounded in the process. Two of his countrymen, naturalists Luigi Maria d'Albertis and Dr. Odoardo Beccari, pursued birds-of-paradise from April to November 1872 at Sorong Island, Ramoi River on the mainland, Mansinam Island mission near Manokwari, Andai mission opposite on the mainland, and into the Arfak Mountains. Although there had been earlier short trips inland to collect natural history specimens, their Arfak trip was the first substantial European venture into the interior. D'Albertis moved his focus east in 1876, making several voyages up the Fly River in the Gulf of Papua.[40]

EAST NEW GUINEA

Britain concentrated its explorations on the lesser-known coasts around eastern New Guinea. The last voyages of the old era of exploration were the much-documented expeditions of HMS *Sulphur*, *Starling*, *Fly*, *Bramble*, *Rattlesnake*, and *Castlereagh* in the 1830s and 1840s.[41] HMS *Sulphur* and *Starling* were sent to verify and complete data gathered on earlier expeditions, rather than to make new discoveries. During their lengthy voyages (1835–1842), the two ships charted small archipelagos off the northwest coast of New Guinea, locating previously unknown specimens of plants, fish, and birds. More significant were the 1840s voyages that opened up the southeast coast and the Louisiade Archipelago to Europeans, establishing safe shipping routes closer to the mainland. These British naval voyages combined hydrographic surveying with scientific exploration. During 1842–1845, HMS *Fly* and *Bramble* surveyed central and northern Torres Strait and 240 kilometers of the southeast New Guinea coast. HMS *Bramble* and *Castlereagh* in 1846, and HMS *Bramble* in 1848–1849, completed the surveying of the Louisiade Archipelago.[42]

Missionaries and Queensland local government officials also participated in exploration. Henry Chester, the northern Magistrate, borrowed whaleboats from bêche-de-mer schooners to survey the Katau (Binaturi) River on the mainland opposite Daru Island in September 1870, and again at Warrior Reef in Torres Strait in September-October. Chester received a permanent appointment in 1875, which enabled him to continue his explorations, and in late 1877 he traveled up the Mai-Kussa River in two whaleboats.[43] Missionaries MacFarlane and Chalmers used their vessel, the *Ellengowan*, to explore coastal southeast New Guinea while they traveled between LMS stations. Late in 1875, MacFarlane, accompanied by Chester and D'Albertis, used the mission ship to travel 500 kilometers up the Fly River.[44] Chester was with MacFarlane again in 1878 when they voyaged from Port Moresby to Catamaran (Modewa) Bay at South Cape, then crossed the mountains on foot to reach Discovery (Labelabe) Bay within Milne Bay, where they rejoined the *Ellengowan*.[45]

The 1870s also witnessed the arrival of the first long-term European residents, when missionaries settled along St. George's Channel and on the southeast New Guinea coast. The most unusual 1870s resident was Russian scientist Nikolai Miklouho-Maclay, who, accompanied by an assistant, spent fifteen months during 1871–1872 at Astrolabe Bay on the Rai (a corruption of Maclay) coast near present day Madang, an extraordinary stay because of his unusually calm attitude in dealing with the local people. He returned for a second visit from late June 1876 until early November 1877, and again in 1879–1880, when he traveled on Captain Webber's trading schooner through southern Melanesia to the Admiralty Group, southeast New Guinea, Port Moresby, and Torres Strait. He visited the Trobriands and Wari Island, where he joined the *Ellengowan*, calling at stations along the coast to Port Moresby. Miklouho-Maclay returned again in 1881, accompanying Commodore J. C. Wilson in HMS *Wolverine* to Kalo to investigate the deaths of ten LMS teachers and members of their families. He had intended to moderate the retaliatory actions but a series of accidents led to four Kalo men being killed and several wounded. Miklouho-Maclay's last visit to Astrolabe Bay was for one week in March 1883.[46]

Between 1871 and 1874, John Moresby, on the paddle-steamer/sailing ship HMS *Basilisk*, completed the survey work begun in the 1840s, concentrating on the coast from Yule Island to the eastern end of New Guinea. Moresby's was the first expedition to visit what became Port Moresby and China Strait, both later crucial in the development of British New Guinea. The next year Moresby surveyed the D'Entrecasteaux Group, and sailed HMS *Basilisk* around to check on Miklouho-Maclay at Astrolabe Bay. A year later, using Yule Island as his base, Moresby explored the surrounding coast.[47]

During the 1870s and 1880s, east New Guinea received many scientific visitors. Much of the activity was around the south coast, using Somerset, Thursday Island, and Port Moresby as bases from which to explore the sluggish meandering rivers of the Gulf of Papua and the adjacent coast. Some of the visitors were well-to-do dilettantes such as Octavius C. Stone, or Henry and Anna Forbes. Others, like D'Albertis and Andrew Goldie, made a living by collecting natural curiosities and commercial products, or like MacFarlane and Chalmers, added exploration to their missionary activities. Stone was a

[141]

The Nineteenth Century:
Exploration and
Colonization

young geologist with a sufficient personal income to travel the world exploring. His first New Guinea trip was with MacFarlane on the *Ellengowan* in August 1875, when they visited Boigu Island and ventured 100 kilometers up a river they named the Baxter (Mai-Kussa), the eastern boundary of Strachan Island.

New Guinean reactions to these visitors varied, and depended on the approach the foreigners used. D'Albertis traveled a violent path, using explosives and fireworks to intimidate villagers. Trader Andrew Goldie's relations were uniformly amicable, and many of his trips were accomplished with only his dog along for protection. And that most unusual nineteenth-century scientist, Miklouho-Maclay, disarmed one aggressive group by entering a house and falling asleep. His actions caused much consternation, but calmed fears as to his intentions. There were also private scientific ventures, such as those of gentleman-scientist William Macleay in 1875, which failed to live up to expectations, or that of John Strachan to the Mai-Kussa River, which ended in retreat. Macleay's expedition was inspired by the British naval expeditions of the 1840s (particularly naturalist Joseph B. Jukes' speculation that there must be a great river on the south coast at the back of the huge delta which entered the Gulf of Papua), and by Moresby's recent voyage on HMS *Basilisk*. Macleay and his party left Sydney in May 1875 on board the *Chevert*, to explore the Fly River. The expedition reached Darnley Island, where bad weather stopped any further progress toward the Fly. All they managed was a brief exploration of the Binaturi River at Katau on the eastern side of the Gulf, before retreating to Redscar Bay and Somerset, returning with only a few natural history specimens.[48] The next exploration party, assembled by O. C. Stone, intended to cross the southeast tail of New Guinea. After a visit to Yule Island on the LMS vessel, the party moved on to Port Moresby and the neighboring Sogeri Plateau, observing the Koiari people but not managing to penetrate far into the mountains.[49] Other expeditions ended in ignominious disaster. Dr. H. James, a young American scientist (ex-ship's doctor on the *Chevert*), and Swedish trader Carl Thorngreen (who had worked around Torres Strait for several years) were both killed at Yule Island in August 1876.[50]

Volatile Italian Luigi d'Albertis had already made a name for himself in west New Guinea before he shifted his base to Torres Strait. After the preliminary trip up the Fly on the *Ellengowan* in 1875, the next year he mounted his own expedition on the New South Wales government steam-launch *Neva*, a voyage of forty-five days up the Fly River, until forced to retreat by shallow water and a shortage of supplies. His claim, that he traveled 1,062 kilometers upstream as far as the Ok Tedi, was disputed by Governor MacGregor and later explorers, but may well have been accurate. Returning again in 1877, the *Neva* only managed to travel 725 kilometers, and the trip was a disaster. The Chinese crew found D'Albertis so impossible to work with that they deserted him, leading to their certain deaths.[51]

Just before annexation, such a degree of interest was focused on New Guinea that two Melbourne newspapers, the *Age* and the *Argus*, sent rival expeditions of discovery, calculated more to sell papers than enlarge knowledge. Two parties set off inland from

Port Moresby, but their grand plans evaporated when they could proceed no further than Sogeri Plateau, immediately behind the port. Another expedition traveled along the south coast, intending to proceed to the Aru Islands. But hostile warriors stopped them at the Mai-Kussa River, and forced them to desert their boat and retreat overland to the coast opposite Saibai Island, where they eventually signaled LMS teachers to rescue them.[52]

A comparable series of explorations occurred in the Bismarck Archipelago and along the northeast coast, led mainly by German naturalists and scientists, supplemented by missionaries and German traders. The major British expedition in this region arrived in March 1875. The *Challenger*, commanded by Sir George Nares, with a scientific expedition led by Sir Charles Thomson, and accompanied by H. N. Mosley as naturalist, visited the Admiralty Group for several days.[53] The same year, a German expedition on the warship *Gazelle*, under Captain von Schleinitz, visited New Hanover, New Ireland, the Gazelle Peninsula, and Bougainville.[54] German naturalist and ethnographer Dr. F. H. Otto Finsch achieved similar standing to Miklouho-Maclay as an early New Guinea "expert." He first visited east New Guinea and adjacent islands in 1879–1882, collecting scientific specimens, particularly birds, and studying the local peoples. While collecting along the coast of Astrolabe Bay in 1881, he spent time investigating the economic potential of the region on the behalf of German commercial interests. During the next year Finsch based himself at Port Moresby for five months. He returned to New Guinea in 1884, sponsored by Adolph von Hansemann to select sites to establish settlements for the Neu Guinea Kompagnie. From a base in the Duke of York Islands Finsch made five voyages to the northeast mainland of New Guinea. Von Hansemann, head of Disconto-Gesellschaft, one of Europe's largest private banks, had political and commercial motives when in May 1884 his Neu Guinea Kompagnie was given the charter to administer the about-to-be-proclaimed German *Schutzgebiet* (Commercial Protectorate), which although a complete administrative and financial disaster, remained in force until 1899.

Finsch named the northeast coast from east of Humboldt Bay to the Huon Gulf, "Kaiser Wilhelmsland." Late in 1884, Finsch's scientific expedition raised the German flag over what became German New Guinea, followed in November by the official German territorial claim. The next year, Finsch explored the mouth of the huge Sepik River, the existence of which had been surmised by Europeans since the seventeenth century, because of the discoloration of water and debris off the nearby coast. In 1886–1887, three more explorations were carried out along the lower reaches of the Sepik, first by Captain Dallmann on the *Samoa*, then by Von Schleinitz, now a Vice-Admiral and the new High Commissioner for German New Guinea. They were followed in 1887 by a Neu Guinea Kompagnie expedition which managed to ascend more than 600 kilometers. This north coast exploration was expanded when Hugo Zöller and Carl Lauterebach explored the Finnisterre Range and the Ramu Valley, respectively, in the 1880s and 1890s, and Hungarian collector and photographer Lajos Biro traveled along the north coast of German New Guinea between 1896 and 1904.[55]

Finsch's scientific explorations were suitable subterfuge for Von Hansemann. They were also suitable cover for Chancellor Bismarck, who had decided to combine territorial acquisition with German commerce in the annexation of northeast New Guinea. Dr. Finsch's 1879–1882 visit to New Guinea was financed by the Von Humboldt Foundation, and he received assistance in the Bismarck Archipelago from leading traders Franz and Eduard Hernsheim, who invited Finsch with his wife and assistants to travel on their ships. Finsch's extensive reports provided the basis of Von Hansemann's maneuvers to have a German commercial colony established.[56]

European exploration in west New Guinea between 1900 and the First World War far exceeded that in eastern New Guinea. Expeditions penetrated deep into the central mountains, drawn by the magnet of the permanent snowfields, always searching for new species with which to confound the scientific world. The reaction of the New Guineans to these intruders prompted Hendrikus Colijn to report in 1907 that: "In the mind of the Papuan there is no other difference between a Resident [government official] and a native bird of paradise trader than that he understands the presence of the latter, that of the former [is regarded] as a mystery, impossible to elucidate."[57]

As will be further examined in the next chapter, villagers viewed the arrival of Europeans and Asians in complex ways. Initially they seem to have thought of them as returning spirits, or as outsiders to be treated by established etiquettes which fitted the foreigners into existing worldviews. However, more than any other outsiders encountered by the small-scale descent groups, these newcomers brought with them and wanted to trade seemingly unending supplies of new material possessions and technologies. Explorers, naturalists, and scientists traded their way around the coast. Even the missionaries were forced to eke out their small stipends by trading. In the west, when missionaries purchased (and then freed) slaves to create the nucleus of their congregations, inadvertently they were joining themselves to slave-trading networks dating back many centuries. This trading and collecting element linked them to their Malay predecessors, who had exploited the natural and human resources of west New Guinea for several hundred years before European colonial interests arrived, and also to the ceremonial and ultimately cosmological systems that controlled the Melanesian world.

The Labor Reserve and Colonial Partition

We saw in Chapters Three and Four the importance of slavery in western New Guinea, as it was integrated into the social mechanisms incorporating ritual and commodity exchanges. Now we encounter another form of human labor migration, which became the dominant European legal means for procuring an indigenous workforce in the South Pacific. Britain outlawed importation of slaves into any British territory in 1808, and the institution of slavery itself in 1834. Other European nations followed over the next several decades. Indentured labor contracts under *Masters and Servants Acts* were introduced to provide a new legal mechanism—something akin to temporary servitude—for procuring labor in the Pacific and in the settler colonies. Although the contracts were very similar to those used by employers to bind European servants, the unequal knowledge-base and motivations of the employers and the Pacific Islander indentured servants led to even more exploitive relationships. Related to this was the manner of recruitment, which ranged from outright physical kidnapping to what can be best described as "cultural kidnapping," in which trickery and subterfuge were the order of the day.

No accurate estimate can be made of the number of New Guineans who worked informally for Europeans and Asians in eastern New Guinea before 1885. There is little evidence that many Islanders worked directly for whalers, other than through their roles in bartering provisions for the ships.[58] Overall, a figure of several thousand seems fair, if we include those provisioning whaling and trading ships or working for maritime traders, the sexual favors bartered to obtain trade goods, the employees of the Laloki gold rush miners and the missionaries, and local labor used by German settlers on the Gazelle Peninsula in opening up plantations after 1880. This short-term labor was paid for with trade goods, mainly cloth, tobacco, and iron.

Easier to count are the 4,700 mainly male laborers engaged under indenture in Queensland and Fiji between 1878 and 1887, predominantly between 1882 and 1884, from the Bismarck, Louisiade, and D'Entrecasteaux Archipelagos, the shores of Milne Bay, and the northern Solomon Islands. If we add to these the 648 indentured laborers from the Bismarck Archipelago taken to Samoa between 1882 and 1884, then well in excess of 5,000 entered into indenture agreements before formal colonization began. After a Royal Commission into allegations of kidnapping of labor, Queensland ceased recruiting around eastern New Guinea in 1885,[59] the year after the German *Schutzgebiet* was proclaimed, which also closed northeast New Guinea to Fiji recruiters. German recruiting for Samoa continued at around 200 laborers each year. Michel Panoff has calculated that approximately 20,000 inhabitants of the Bismarck Archipelago were recruited between 1887 and 1903: 14,402 working on local plantations and 3,047 traveling to Samoan plantations. He estimated that 50,000 inhabitants of the Bismarck Archipelago provided their labor to German Pacific plantations from 1884–1914.[60]

Much has been written about the place of the labor trade in the colonial partition of Melanesia. Nowhere else in the South Pacific were there such dense populations close to tropical plantation-based settler societies, such as Samoa and Fiji, as well as the broader-based settler societies in New Caledonia and Queensland. When sugar prices were high in the late 1870s and early 1880s, British, German, and French recruiters scrambled to obtain labor, sometimes ruthlessly exploiting indigenous workers and importing Asians. It is significant that the final colonial partition of eastern New Guinea took place at this time. Queensland's bid to control eastern New Guinea certainly had as a primary motivation the desire to monopolize this huge labor supply, and thereby enable development of the tropical north of the colony. Queenslanders saw the Coral Sea as their own oceanic domain. The spacing of Queensland's ports—roughly every 300–400 kilometers along the coast—provided commercial bases along one side of the Coral Sea, with the labor reserve and other resources of the Melanesian islands on the northern and eastern edge, viewed as the outer limits of the Queensland frontier. The Queensland labor trade also brought permanent migrants from other Pacific Islands into New Guinea. During the 1860s and 1870s, many Loyalty Islanders and New Hebrideans drifted north to Torres Strait when their contracts expired, to work as divers. Loyalty Islanders were especially prominent, working as boats' crews and as support staff in New Guinea exploration and trading ventures. Loyalty Islanders, Niue and Cook Islanders, Samoans, Tongans, and Fijians also helped staff the LMS and Methodist missions. All had a substantial effect on coastal communities.[61]

As with slavery in the west, relationships between the labor recruits, the indigenous middlemen who organized the procurement of labor, and the actual labor trade captains and recruiters were never simple, and they are hard to generalize. Historians of the Pacific labor trade accept that substantial kidnapping occurred in the first ten years or so that the labor trade operated in any newly trawled group of islands. There was a moving labor frontier, beginning in the Loyalty Islands and the New Hebrides in the 1860s, moving into the Solomon Islands in the 1870s, and the islands off eastern New Guinea in the first half of the 1880s. Then, repulsed by the Protectorates and fresh allegations of kidnapping (substantiated by Queensland's 1885 Royal Commission), the recruiters concentrated on the Solomons and the New Hebrides (Vanuatu) for the remainder of the century. Recruiters working out of French New Caledonia and German Samoa also exploited these island groups, although, as noted above, the German plantations in Samoa continued to draw labor from the Bismarck Archipelago. Scholars have too quickly written off the first decade of labor recruiting in any island group as totally given over to kidnapping and illegality. There are differences between each island group, reflecting the decade and the degree of previous contact with whalers, traders, and missionaries. And, as Shineberg's study of the New Caledonian labor trade and Panoff's research into the German labor trade shows, scholars are also wrong to infer that after a decade or so of illegal practices, the pattern changed, remaining within legal and reasonable ethical bounds during the following decades. Viewed with the hindsight of more than a century, the Melanesian labor trade was based on cultural exploitation and was thoroughly disreputable. However, it became a Pacific institution, incorporated into the colonial and post-colonial economic fabric. Relying on supporting cultural elements within Melanesian society, labor migration involved coercion, but was also often liberating for the participants.[62]

Did New Guineans who enlisted for Queensland and Fiji, in the late 1870s and the first half of the 1880s, fall totally into the "kidnapped" category? In the 1800s and 1810s, becoming quite regular by the 1850s and 1860s, people of the Louisiades had contact with a few early explorers, and extensive contact with whalers and traders.[63] Then came contact with bêche-de-mer fishermen when, in 1873, Queensland-based ships began to venture away from over-fished Torres Strait to the astonishing array of Louisiade reefs, concentrating on the Calvados Chain northwest of Sudest (Tagula) Island. Bêche-de-mer was collected on the reefs and shallows, but processing required the establishment of smoke-curing huts onshore, since curing, drying, sorting, and bagging operations took several days. Men and women from the islands were employed to gather and cure the bêche-de-mer, and also provided wood, water, provisions, and artifacts. When the British Protectorate began operating, there were ten ships working in the Louisiades, collecting around 500 tons of bêche-de-mer annually. Many of the same islands that provided large numbers of "kidnapped" recruits for the Queensland and Fijian labor trades had already been involved over several decades in large-scale barter trades in commodities and labor with whalers and bêche-de-mer fishermen. Cross-checking the same islands against Gray's excellent maps of whaling contacts in the Bismarck Archipelago, we find a remarkable confluence between whaling and labor recruiting, particularly in St. George's Channel and among New Ireland's eastern outliers. The earliest recruits came from this area, and it is clear that the population had experience in dealing with outsiders.

The most direct evidence we have of Islanders' views on the recruiting process is from Queensland's 1885 Royal Commission into recruiting in New Guinea waters, which interviewed 480 recruits from the Louisiade, D'Entrecasteaux, and Bismarck Archipelagos. Evidence from the interviews varies enormously. The most extreme incidents reported are violent and horrific. Typical elements of the labor trade are quite clear here. Enlistment was peer-influenced, and often occurred away from the control of family members—trade goods were commonly left behind to partially compensate them. A common motivation for enlistment was the pursuit of adventure, but recruits were often ignorant of the actual expectations and duration of the indenture contract. Recruiters seldom bothered to explain contractual details, even in the most voluntary situations.

Analysis of the evidence in the Royal Commission shows clearly that, on the eight voyages examined at least, the Islanders knew more about the ways of the crews than the crews knew of theirs. The Royal Commission and the criminal trials that resulted from it were less about proving the guilt or innocence of the defendants than satisfying the political agenda of the Queensland government and the anti-colored labor lobby, both of which were trying to bring an end to the labor trade.

In one of the more interesting cases, the Commissioners' conclusion that the voyage of one ship, the *Hopeful*, was based on "deliberate kidnapping and cold blooded murder," was true, but part of the evidence was falsely concocted by several of the main recruits and the official interpreter, Cago. The violence at issue was probably more due to the inexperience of the crew and the violent disposition of the recruiter, Neil McNeil, than from an attempt to kidnap. There is compelling evidence that a substantial degree of collusion occurred between the recruits and Cago; something not noticed at the time but quite clear from a close examination of the evidence. The Queensland government remained ignorant that the Islanders had fabricated or rearranged the evidence. The motivations of two of the key players, Cago and Messiah, may have been pecuniary, since both earned quantities of trade goods for their work. Both also bore grudges against some of the *Hopeful*'s crew, and were able to get even with them by manipulating the evidence supplied to the Royal Commission. Cago quite clearly knew the consequences for the ships' crews if the Royal Commission found against them, and he was able to explain to the recruits that they would be returned immediately with large supplies of trade goods, if the evidence suggested that they had been kidnapped.

From this and other cases heard before the Royal Commission we see that Islander agency was operating to their advantage by the 1880s. While it is true that atrocities and kidnapping did occur on some of the voyages examined by the Royal Commission, the New Guinea Islanders sometimes managed to deceive and manipulate the Commissioners, the Government Agents, Police Magistrates, and Inspectors of Pacific Islanders involved.[64]

An unexplained feature of the New Guinea islands recruiting fiasco is the astonishingly high mortality rates the Melanesians suffered in Queensland. The average death rate amongst European males in Queensland, of similar age to the Melanesian laborers (sixteen to thirty-five years), was around nine to ten in every thousand, an acceptable figure by world standards of the time. Over the four decades of the Queensland labor trade, each year on average fifty Melanesian laborers in every thousand died. Earlier historians sought explanations in the poor living conditions on the labor trade vessels, plantations, and farms, and cited malnutrition, cruelty, and overwork as prominent causes. Some Islanders were undoubtedly kidnapped, plucked from their homes, frightened and unable to adapt to wage labor, strange food and surroundings. But they were also ill-equipped to face the new disease environment, one very different from that of their homes. Their exposure to new infectious diseases such as measles, smallpox, chickenpox, influenza, tuberculosis, pneumonia, typhoid, and meningitis, was often catastrophic. At its worst, in 1884, and primarily among the New Guinea islands recruits, Queensland's Melanesian mortality rate was 147 in every 1,000. Between May 1883 and November 1884, 3,000 Islanders from the Bismarck and Louisiade Archipelagos arrived in Queensland. In the Mackay district, the major cane-growing region, 323 Islanders died during 1883, within a total immigrant Melanesian population of 3,845. The next year 823 died, 22 percent of the Melanesian labor force.[65]

The explanation of why the New Guinea Islanders fared worst of all Melanesians in Queensland can only relate to lack of immunity when removed from their reasonably disease-free environment and placed into danger in the colony. The average death rates on recruiting voyages were relatively low, suggesting that the Islanders were usually first exposed to new diseases in the colonies. The average death rate in the first year of indenture was extraordinarily high. Thereafter, the rate declined to levels that were average with other colonists. The main causes of death were bacillary dysentery, pneumonia (often a sequel to influenza), and tuberculosis. Nineteenth-century medical practitioners had only a rudimentary knowledge of disease causation, and although doctors managed to control some epidemics by isolating patients and improving hygiene, generally they failed miserably to understand or stem the high Melanesian mortality rates.[66]

Because of the findings of the Royal Commission, the surviving laborers from the New Guinea islands were compensated with trade goods and quickly repatriated at Queensland government expense, no doubt taking their new diseases home with them. During the whaling era there was no mention in the ships' logs of influenza or dysentery epidemics, nor of measles, chickenpox, or mumps. The only diseases recorded are venereal diseases, pleurisy, "colic," and smallpox, which luckily did not spread far.[67] The return of the ex-Queensland laborers probably caused an increase in the introduction of nonindigenous diseases throughout the eastern archipelagos.

Greed for labor to fuel Pacific and Queensland plantations, and pressure from patriots and expansionists in eastern Australia and New Guinea, brought about the final stages of the partition of New Guinea in 1884. German commercial interests did not want Britain to extend its territorial claims into what they now perceived as their own regions, and the British colonies in Australia did not want German neighbors, possibly as close as across Torres Strait. The gradual buildup of commercial activity during the second half of the nineteenth century led inexorably to the final annexations.[68] Southeast New Guinea remained important, gradually assuming the role of a crucial buffer between British and German interests.

German and British Annexation in 1884

While the Dutch were happy to hoist flags and erect plaques in token demonstration of their control, they were reluctant to get involved in any extensive or permanent administrative role in west New Guinea. The Indies' government was being pressured during the 1890s, by missionaries in the west and the German and British presence in the east, to take more interest in its vast New Guinea territory. Queensland expanded its claims in Torres Strait twice in the 1870s, and in 1883 audaciously attempted to annex a large section of east New Guinea and adjacent islands for Britain, which Britain immediately disallowed. Then, during October and November 1884, Germany and Britain divided the unclaimed eastern area beyond the Dutch boundary into two Protectorates that later (in 1888 for British New Guinea, and in 1899 for German New Guinea) became colonies.[69] The final frontier between the German and British territories was negotiated in 1885. The message this gave to the Dutch East Indies government was perfectly clear: if they wanted to keep their claim over west New Guinea, they had to install a permanent administration and establish settlements of similar style to other Pacific beach communities operating around Christian missions and trading stations.

With subjective vision based on proximity and self-interest, the Australian colonies had seen German intentions take shape in commercial interests in the Bismarck Archipelago, along with German labor recruitment for Samoa in the islands adjacent to eastern New Guinea. With Germany's late but quite clear imperial aspirations, the Australian colonies had no doubt that their (and Britain's) destiny to control eastern New Guinea was about to be preempted. Paradoxically, it was Queensland's 1883 attempt to precipitate British annexation that forced Germany to make its final moves. German New Guinea officially came into existence when the Neu Guinea Kompagnie was granted a charter to govern on 17 May 1884. As Peter Sack reminds us, German New Guinea was not proclaimed a Protectorate or colony, but a *Schutzgebiet*, an overseas mercantile territory.[70] Its first presence, the scientific expedition headed by Dr. Otto Finsch, left Sydney on the *Samoa* on 11 September. Germany had chosen to form a commercial territory, empowering its Neu Guinea Kompagnie to govern northeast New Guinea on its behalf. The mainland was named "Kaiser Wilhelmsland," and the New Britain Archipelago renamed the "Bismarck Archipelago." Sydney gossip at the time suggested that Finsch was about to annex parts of eastern New Guinea, confirmed by his secret instructions—to explore the north coast of New Guinea between the 141st meridian and New Britain, establishing good relations with the natives, "and to acquire as much territory as possible." Between October and December, Finsch traveled along the north coast and around New Britain and New Ireland, hoisting the German flag at more than a dozen places.[71]

Meanwhile, in August, through diplomatic channels Germany had announced its intentions to take possession of areas of New Guinea in which its nationals had commercial interests. On 9 August, Britain responded, that it was planning to make a similar move in regard to areas "of the island which specially interest the Australian colonies." These had already been outlined in 1880: the Solomon Islands, the Bismarck Archipelago, and New Guinea east of the 143rd meridian. On 19 September, Britain redefined its area of interest as east of the 145th meridian, ignoring the section west to the 141st meridian Dutch border. This decision was quite obviously influenced by the advocacy of Miklouho-Maclay, who had sought British protection for the peoples of the Rai coast around present-day Madang.[72] Germany replied on 27 September, displeased, suggesting a compromise along the north coast. By 9 October, Britain had backed off, signaling that its interests could be served by securing only the southern side of eastern New Guinea.

This diplomatic maneuver set the scene for the proclamations that followed. In August 1884, the German government ordered its Sydney consulate to have the German flag raised over northeast New Guinea. This came to fruition on 3 November 1884, when Captain Schering of the *Elisabeth* hoisted the flag in the Bismarck Archipelago, then continued to the mainland, accompanied by the *Hyäne*, to expand the acquisition. Britain, in a comedy of errors, managed to make the initial proclamation twice, first through Hugh Romilly on 23 October, and then again by Commodore John Erskine, on 6 November. Romilly, a Deputy Commissioner of the WPHC, was certain that he would be given charge of British New Guinea. Thus he was delighted to receive a vaguely worded cable while in Cooktown on HMS *Harrier*, ordering him to proceed to New Guinea to proclaim the Protectorate. He cabled the Governor of New South Wales for clarification, but received no immediate reply, and set out for Port Moresby, where he proclaimed a British Protectorate over all of New Guinea from the Dutch boundary at the 141st meridian east to East Cape, along with all islands east to Kosman Island.[73] Erskine had received similar in-

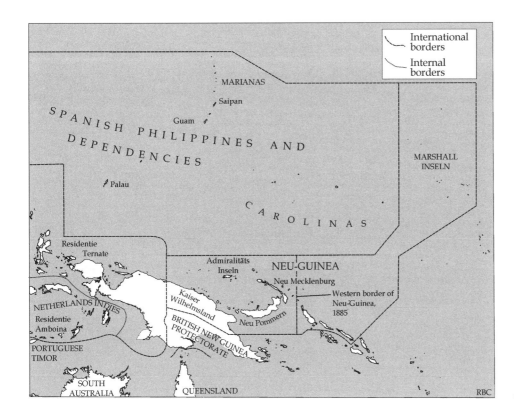

International and administrative boundaries in 1886

structions while in Sydney. He too set off immediately for Port Moresby. Not to be outdone by a lesser-ranking official, Erskine repeated the procedure but used far more restrictive wording, claiming only the "southern shores" from the Dutch border to East Cape, "with all islands adjacent thereto south of East Cape to Kosman Island, inclusive, together with the islands of the Goschen Straits." Neither Romilly's nor Erskine's proclamation included the D'Entrecasteaux Archipelago, which was added later to the newly acquired Protectorate.[74]

On 19 December, Germany officially informed Britain of Finsch and Schering's actions, which led to Erskine's quick return. The Commodore's new orders were to extend the British Protectorate, securing the territory between East Cape and the Huon Gulf, the Louisiade and Woodlark Groups, and Umboi Island in Vitiaz Strait, which ensured that Germany could not extend its territory further south. Erskine also raised the British flag on the Rai coast (close to Fortification Point at 43' south latitude, 147° east longitude), well within German territory, sparking German protests. The jockeying for territory continued until April 1885, when an equitable division was agreed upon, giving Germany about 67,000 square miles and Britain around 63,000 square miles.[75] In April 1886, the final section of what is now Papua New Guinea's border with the Solomon Islands was agreed to. This confirmed the Bismarck Archipelago as German territory, along with Buka and Bougainville, the Shortland Islands (except Mono), Choiseul, Santa Ysabel, and outlying Ontong Java. The remainder of the Solomon Islands were recognized as nominally British, under the loose jurisdiction of the WPHC based in Fiji, although no Protectorate was proclaimed until 1893 and there was no Resident Commissioner until 1896.[76] The Marshall Islands and Palau were acknowledged as within the German sphere, with the Gilbert and Ellice Islands falling into Britain's area of interest.

Several later adjustments were made to the borders. Negotiated over 1893–1895, the boundary between Dutch and British New Guinea was adjusted slightly to include a loop of the Fly River into British territory. The German/British border in the Solomon Islands retreated north in 1899, from between Santa Ysabel and Malaita, to its present position between the Shortland Islands and Bougainville, permanently dividing the Solomon Islands. In the same year, the Micronesian *Inselgebiet* (Island Territory), comprising the Carolines (including Palau) and the Marianas (excluding Guam) was added to German New Guinea. In 1906, the Marshall Islands (a separate German colony in Micronesia since 1885, and including Nauru from 1888) were added to the Island Territory. Finally, in 1910 an agreement was concluded concerning the Dutch-German border. In the same year, German New Guinea and the Island Territory became one financial entity.

These colonially derived boundaries have remained in place, shaping the modern nations of Melanesia, cutting across older cultural connections. New Guinea remains divided; west New Guinea incorporated into Indonesia and the east into Papua New Guinea. Since 1975 the bird-of-paradise flag of Papua New Guinea has flown on Independence Hill in Port Moresby, uniting Australia's New Guinea Trust Territory with the Australian colony of Papua. Papua New Guinea shares a border with, and incorporates the northern islands of, the Solomon Archipelago, the southern section of which achieved independence from Britain in 1978. Modern nations have emerged and the concept of statehood, although still fragile, is no longer foreign.

Onwards from the 1880s, the process and rhetoric of colonialism began to develop a sense of common cultural identity among some indigenous peoples. The process of colonization also created several modern political units, each with its own regional cultural identity. For instance, Australia's Papuans (the peoples of the British and later Australian sphere in southeast New Guinea) came to see their identity as separate from the peoples of west or northeast New Guinea. In the 1970s, Papuans spawned their own nationalist movement, Papua Besena, which opposed Australian moves to unite Australia's colony, Papua, with Australia's New Guinea Trust Territory.[77] Papua Besena's political platform ignored the fact that Australian Papua was not culturally unified, and that any unity was really a construction of recent administrative, missionary, and colonial regimes. Similarly, all of the new nations of Melanesia are artifacts of nineteenth-century European diplomacy and imperial rivalries.

Europeans had never ventured more than a few kilometers from the coast, except up the Fly River and the other major rivers of the Gulf of Papua, or up the Sepik and Mamberamo Rivers on the north coast. Along the southeast coast, Fakfak, Merauke, Thursday Island, Port Moresby, and Samarai emerged as the most important European settlements. The north coast had no central focus for Europeans until the German Neu Guinea Kompagnie arrived in the mid-1880s. Earlier, the German focus was around Blanche Bay on the Gazelle Peninsula and in the nearby Duke of York Islands. The peoples of coastal New Guinea and adjacent islands had already been in substantial contact with Europeans for hundreds of years in the west and fifty in the east. New Guinea had been "colonized," but only in scattered harbors, ports, and along the coasts.

7

Interpreting Early Contact

Liminal Moments and Cautious Coastal Trade

The true privilege of all histories, disciplined and undisciplined, is that they each offer a liminal moment. They offer a "retreat." In-between Past and Present, in-between simulation and invention, in-between conserving and creating, histories are always metonymies of culture in process. In histories we know ourselves as limited by our given experience and liberated by our contrivance. Ultimately, I think that is History's Anthropology.
—Greg Dening,
The Death of William Gooch, 1985, 158.

The cultural history of early contact situations in New Guinea is a study of liminal moments. To approach contact in this way is to understand the uncertainly, role-playing, and theatre of a situation when momentarily two vastly different cultures come into contact. It also reflects the present. We all carry cultural baggage with us, accumulated during a lifetime, that in part shapes our approach to any situation in which presentation and analysis of intercultural conflict occur. Our cultural values and categories suggest we would react in preordained ways. Culture-contact history requires understanding of earlier codes and connections, analysis of complex situations, and a grasp of moral dilemmas. The great attraction, to any historian of first- and early-contact situations, is in dealing with different players in human interactions, each side behaving according to their own understandings. Dilemmas unfold in these dramatic confrontations. Usually, only fragments of evidence remain, created for quite different purposes than our own. Ships' logs, missionaries' letters, lists of trade goods, and government reports inadvertently reveal social actions, gestures in common use, objects described, or patterns of similar reactions in diverse circumstances. And New Guinea contact history has one advantage, almost unique in the world: records of first contact situations exist from the sixteenth century through to the twentieth century, spread from song, story, dance and drama, and the written word, to drawings, etchings, photographs, and film.

Examined in wider context, tempered by contemporary knowledge, we can piece together contact history, but it will always be theatre—a presentation by actors with multiple interpretations possible. There is spontaneous role-playing, out-of-character behaviors, and temporary adoption of new behaviors that were discarded once a semblance of normality returned. As Greg Dening suggests, theatricality is imbedded deep in every cultural action: "Government, law, property, justice, empire, civilisation and God were represented by the strangers in gesture, stylized action, and all the props of flags and weapons. The natives had their theatre too. The intruding strangers were mimicked or mocked or explained away. The ambivalence of the occasion was danced or sung or told in story or painted or carved. My thesis for this ethnographic present of an ethnographic moment is that I must present its theatre and its theatricality if I would represent what actually happened."[1] This chapter is an attempt to present what "actually happened," first around the coast, then throughout the inland areas.

In the north of the Solomon Archipelago, the first Europeans known to have sighted Buka and Bougainville Islands were aboard the *Swallow,* commanded by Philip Carteret in 1767. They did not approach the shore. This was left to French explorer Louis-Antoine de Bougainville the next year, in command of the *Boudeuse* and the *Étoile.* Bougainville's ships sailed along the east coast of both islands, anchoring off Buka on 4 July 1768. Three canoes, each containing five or six men, approached the ships, keeping their distance. Finally, after an hour they were enticed nearer: "Some trifles which were thrown to them, fastened on pieces of planks, inspired them with some confidence. They came along-side of the ship, shewing cocoa-nuts, and crying *bouca, bouca, onelle!* They repeated these words incessantly, and we afterwards pronounced them as they did, which seemed to give them some pleasure. They did not long keep along-side of the vessel. They made signs that they were going to fetch us cocoa-nuts. We applauded their resolution; but they were hardly gone twenty yards, when one of these perfidious fellows let fly an arrow, which happily hit nobody. After that, they fled as fast as they could row; our superior strength set us above punishing them."[2] Another twenty-four years passed before the next European vessels visited Buka, *Recherche* and *Esperance* under the command of D'Entrecasteaux, this time along the west coast. The Buka people would have remembered the previous visit by the huge ships. This time they developed a lively trade, showing more interest in red cloth than in iron, the qualities of which, presumably, they knew nothing.

Usually, the early exchanges were uneven, the Europeans feeling that they and their ships were vastly superior to the Melanesians, but this was not always so. Occasionally, one gets a glimpse of two equal alien groups of humans sighting and inspecting each other, then passing on, puzzled, each side seeing themselves as victors or winners, or merely lucky enough to have experienced something extraordinary. Such a case occurred in 1846 in the Gulf of Papua when HMS *Bramble* encountered a Motuan *lakatoi* on a *hiri* voyage:

Shortly afterwards was seen the strange sail we have figured. This, on being approached within gun-shot, proved to be a gigantic canoe, from 50 to 55 feet in length, kept apart and together by a platform, from 15 to 20 feet broad, which extended nearly the whole length of the canoes, the after end being square with the sterns of the boat; and six or eight feet long paddles over the stern. With the exception of this part of the platform, the whole was covered by a strong well-built house, made of cane; the roof being flat, and about five or six feet above the platform. This roof also answered the purpose of an upper deck. The extraordinary craft was propelled by large mat sails, each spread between two bamboo masts, supported by diagonal poles fore and aft, on either side; the mast-heads being from 20 to 30 feet asunder. Besides these two large sails, the canoe had other smaller square-sails, suspended from the principal masts; and there was likewise a square-sail forward. The spars and rigging were ornamented with flags and streamers. There were about 40 to 50 persons upon the roof, several of whom were stringing their bows, but this was the only indication of hostility. Whence this odd craft came, and wither bound, was not ascertained.[3]

Several patterns emerge from the contacts between New Guineans, Asians, and Europeans over centuries. First, these initial meetings occurred in controlled space on the decks or on the shore. Indigenous protocols already existed for dealing with strangers. These were used to establish rapport with Asians and Europeans, to trade with them, and to control any situation. From an indigenous point of view, these strangers were wanderers, perhaps spirits or ancestors, or like people seen in a dream.[4] Unwittingly, they had entered owned territory and were a worry, but not a harbinger of great change. They were gypsies pleading for food and water, men without women, ships their only homes. Fleetingly, they provided new products and a view of extraordinary technology. From a European point of view, the indigenous people were to be treated with suspicion and condescension, their cooperation necessary if supplies were to be obtained. One or two ships, often in poor condition from sailing around the world, were like weakened wooden fortresses, to be protected at all costs, as their loss or damage would lead to the deaths of their crews and financial loss for the owners or investors. Survival was the most essential part of the exercise. However much crews might regret killing the local people (though sometimes they seem not to have cared much at all), self-preservation came first. First contact seldom involved Europeans on shore, since they were too wary of losing the advantage they had from their ship's decks, but, to obtain water, wood, and food, shore-parties had to be used occasionally. Trips to shore, where they could easily be attacked and overwhelmed, were brief and purposeful. At first contact, Islanders were reluctant to board ships, but they soon began to clamber up, motivated by increasing familiarity with strangers and regularity of trade.

There is a clear repetition of indigenous methods used to deal with strangers, all around the coasts and over a long time period. Several procedures stand out: silent barter of equivalent goods, such as occurred with massoi-bark trading, as described by G. E. Rumphius in west New Guinea in 1685;[5] signaling friendly intentions by waving leafy green tree boughs and making welcoming speeches; and, to a lesser extent, throwing lime or ash, or covering themselves in ash, or performing other ritual acts.

Coastal people from around Dolak Island on the mid-south coast of New Guinea spat lime at James Cook in 1770, using the same technique to ward off Dutch Lieutenant-Commander Kolff fifty years later.[6] In 1791 in the Duke of York Islands, a leader covered himself in white powder when confronting the crew of the *Waaksamheyd*. A party from the ship had gone ashore to collect water, meeting with hostility, as recorded by John Hunter: "An old man, who was powdered all over with a white powder, and who seemed to possess great authority and influence among his countrymen, disposed them to be more and more troublesome; presents were offered him, but he rejected every thing with a very surly and determined air; in short, he seemed resolved that we should not fill water, or remain upon their territory." The Islanders began throwing stones, some launched with great velocity from slingshots. The crew in the boat covering the watering party answered with musket fire, along with a few supporting grape shots from the ship, which probably killed or wounded some Islanders, certainly scaring them all: "at this time there were thirty or forty canoes about the ship, full of people; their terror and consternation at the noise, and probably the effects of the guns, was such, that many leaped from their boats overboard, and swam under water as far as they were able; such guns as were fired from the side on which the canoes were, were pointed well above them, being more intended to intimidate than destroy." Seven tons of water was carted aboard during the first day. Over the next three days, the watering party was very careful about its safety. On the second day:

> many canoes came into the bay . . . but kept at an awful distance, holding up green boughs as a signal of peace and amity; to some we made signs to go away; to others, who ventured a little nearer, we shewed signs of friendship, and made them perfectly understand, that our firing was occasioned by their slinging of stones among our people, who were watering . . . [On] the last evening, as the sailors were coming from the shore, a number of the natives from the woods right above the watering place, came down to the beach with green boughs in their hands, bringing with them cocoa-nuts, yams, plantains, &c. Accompanied by a song of friendship: they seemed earnestly to wish for a reconciliation, and took every means in their power to testify their concern for what had happened; a boat was sent on shore to meet them, with a green branch in the bow, and the boat's crew were desired to spread open their arms when they came near the breach to show they were well disposed to peace. When the boat landed, the natives retired back a little, but not out of sight; having piled up upon the beach their peace-offering, which consisted of yams, cocoa-nuts, plantains, bananas, sugar-cane, and some other articles: on the top of this pile was laid a small living male and female dog, with their mouths and feet tied: (they appeared to be of the small terrier kind) in the middle of the heap was stuck in the sand, a young tree of the palm kind, upon a branch of which were hung a number of braided lines, like what is called by seamen "sennit," and much the same color, being made of the bark of a particular tree: what this could mean we were wholly at a loss to comprehend, unless, as the head of this young tree was designedly bent down by the lines above-mentioned, it was meant as a token of submission.

Harmony, normality, and conventional relationships having been restored, a conch shell sounded from the shore and canoes crowded the bay, each with a green bough, none approaching close to the ship, although all of the occupants had items to trade. Eventually barter began, and Hunter recorded that "they were pleased with such trifles as we had to give them in return." They placed no value on iron, refusing nails, preferring beads, mirrors, and strips of bright white and red cloth.[7]

What actually occurred during first encounters with foreign ships, or during the exchange of goods on the beach, is difficult to establish. Certainly, these situations had ceremonial and ritual aspects. The refusal to accept items from a ship probably signified fear of spirits, and it was wishful thinking on Hunter's part that the intention of the later gifts was to show submission. It is far more likely that they wanted to restore peaceful relations with the strangers, using rituals renewing social equilibrium, showing that they, the residents, were in control of the situation.

Europeans soon began to theorize about Melanesian motives for reacting violently to their intrusion. (They never seemed to think about what their own reactions might be if strange ships had anchored off the Devon or Bordeaux coasts, sending armed parties ashore to collect water, steal crops, and purloin sacred objects from church alters.) There were recurring themes—a superior force holding back (Bougainville at Buka in 1768), and a belief that it would only take a few days for the Islanders to appreciate the foreigners' superiority and submit (Hunter at the Duke of York Islands in 1791). Exchanges of trade trinkets for native valuables and food were expected and usually occurred, and there was always an element of danger and fear of treacherous natives.

Sailors and commanders swapped information in port, and captains read journals from previous voyages, which often meant crews arrived with preordained views on the native population. There was also a difference between west New Guinea, long in contact with the Malay world and visited by Europeans since the sixteenth century, and east New Guinea. Although considered unpredictable, Onin leaders were used to dealing with outsiders. They signed a treaty with the Dutch in 1678, negotiated by Johannes Keyts:

> the elders of the village of Onyn came to us together with an incredible great number of people, and that with such a noise that it was frightening to hear, their proas covered with flags from the front to the back, as many as there are days in the year. I was quite troubled to receive so suddenly so many people, so that I presently ordered that all guns together with hand-granates and firing-pots etc., besides most of the soldiers and some of the courageous sailors were to be placed under cover on the quarter deck, so that only the boatsman and I were to be seen. The natives rowed three times around the ship, wielding their shields and swords . . . After all this had passed, they finally came without any resistance on board, upon which I invited some of the chiefs to come to me which they did and I regaled them with a bottle of Spanish wine and gave them many marks of honor which I thought would be unusual to them.[8]

Europeans in the west often behaved much like Maluku tribute-seekers and raiders. Amasa Delano, an American member of the expedition explained that native duplicity and violence was related to European participation in the Malay enslavement of New Guineans: "When Europeans first visited New Guinea, the natives manifested no spirit of enmity. But Europeans seized and carried them away as slaves, in a most treacherous manner. It was common for them to hook the yard tackles of a ship to a canoe, hoist her on deck with all the crew in her, transport them and sell them for slaves . . . The white people have too often, and to their everlasting disgrace, used their arts and force, as members of civilized society, to betray, to kidnap, or to seize openly and violently, the natives for the most selfish and inhumane purposes. They make reprisals upon us, whenever they can, and are peculiarly inveterate against us in their hostility."[9]

First encounters like these have several dimensions. There is the jolting experience of confronting "otherness"—encountering aliens, recognizably human like oneself, but so different that as Edward Schieffelin and Robert Crittenden suggest, "we momentarily glimpse the epistemological edges of our own social understanding, leaving us in dread and fascination." Although both sides were wary, the Europeans were better prepared, both through previous knowledge of strangers, but also because of their superior technology and ready category for "natives" who occupied a preordained subordinate place. The second dimension is social-cultural, always shaped by the "local social and political structure and framed in the prevailing cultural values, categories, and understandings," leading to: "deeper issues of cultural categories and social organization: the relatively stable system of values, beliefs, and modes of understanding through which human beings live their lives, and the structure of social and political relationships which these values shape and serve."[10]

The third dimension is historical. How do the circumstances behind each incident, the needs of both groups and individual personalities, shape the particular set of events?[11] These dimensions are present when alien groups meet, as well as when individuals, such as beachcombers and castaways, spend long periods of time in a New Guinea host community.

Beachcombers and Castaways

European castaways and beachcombers were at the mercy of their indigenous host societies, able to do little to mediate their situations. Although many beachcombers lived in Polynesia for very extended periods,[12] it was rare for Europeans to spend any great length of time living on New Guinea or the adjacent islands. Voyages of exploration landed only to replenish supplies, and whalers seldom spent more than a few days ashore at favorite bays. Members of crews, inadvertently or purposefully left behind on islands, sometimes survived but more often met a quick death. In 1833 the whaler *Caroline* picked up a man at Port Hunter, Duke of York Islands, who with a companion had been left behind five weeks previously. His friend had been murdered, but he had escaped from the village by swimming out to the *Caroline*. Shipwrecked crews mostly met grisly ends. Melanesian hosts sometimes grew tired of their unwanted guests, who placed strain on limited food supplies, although it was quite usual for villagers to keep one or two of their favorites alive. Typical of shipwrecked mariners were the survivors of the *Charles Eaton*, wrecked in Torres Strait: twenty-one of the crew were killed and decapitated, four sailed an open boat to Timor-Laut, and one of them was taken into slavery. The only survivors kept alive in Torres Strait were two boys, rescued in 1836. They reported that the Meriam people thought "white people always live on ships." Similarly, the twenty-eight castaways from the 1843 wreck of the brig *Mary* at the Laughlan Islands outstayed their welcome. All but one was killed on neighboring Woodlark Island, after nine months of demands on food, accommodation, and women.[13]

Whaling ships brought the first intentional beachcombers: Europeans and Lascars, castaways, deserters from ships, and escaped convicts, who "went native." Beachcombers were living in the Solomon Islands in the 1820s and in the islands off east New Guinea soon after.[14] John Coulter's account of his 1835 voyage on the trader *Hound* gives lengthy descriptions of three early beachcombers, one supposed to have been living in southwest New Guinea, and two more in New Britain and New Ireland.[15] Coulter also describes ex-New South Wales convicts living in southwest New Guinea.[16] It seems likely that parts of Coulter's account are true, with gloss and fictitious details added to titillate his readers. Some substantiation comes from Dr. D. Parker Wilson's 1840 log from the British whaler *Gypsy*, which records that beachcombers were already living on New Ireland. There was a West Indian living in one village; at another there had been four European residents, but three had recently joined a passing ship; while at Port Praslin, near Cape St. George, there were eighteen deserters from Sydney ships that had passed through St. George's Channel.

It is true that escaped convicts, from New South Wales, Norfolk Island, Moreton Bay, and later New Caledonia, were some of New Guinea's earliest European visitors. A remarkable voyage in an open boat in 1791, by nine convicts and two children, from Sydney to Timor through Torres Strait, showed what luck and seamanship could accomplish, as of course does William Bligh's voyage across the Pacific and through Torres Strait two years earlier.[17] In the decade during which transportation of British convicts to Australia ceased, the first convicts arrived in New Caledonia. For thirty years from 1864, French convicts were sent there, occasionally making their escape to Queensland and even New Guinea. For instance, two escapees were killed in the Calvados Group in the early 1880s, and Casmir Gangloff, the sole survivor of four runaway convicts from the 1880s, later became a trader on New Ireland.[18]

Wini, a middle-aged man living on Badu Island in Torres Strait from approximately 1840 to 1864, may also have been of convict origin. In his novel, *The Wild White Man of Badu,* Ion Idriess did Wini the disservice of presenting him as a ruthless killer, when in fact he seems to have been mild-mannered and harmless.[19] Wini arrived on Badu in an open boat with some companions in about 1840, and was adopted by two brothers who found his skills useful in canoe repair. Contemporary sources suggest that he had escaped from an Australian penal colony, or perhaps Norfolk Island. Alternatively, he may have been of Dutch or Indonesian origin, since he appeared not to understand English. The only European known to have seen him was Barbara Thompson, shipwrecked on Prince of Wales (Muralag) Island from 1844–1849.[20] Aged sixteen, Thompson had traveled from Moreton Bay (Brisbane) to Torres Strait with her husband and a crew of three on the cutter *America*, to salvage oil from the wreck of a whaling vessel on Bampton Shoal. The *America* was also wrecked and only Thompson survived, adopted by a local bigman, Peaqui, who accepted her as the reincarnation of his daughter Giom. She was rescued by HMS *Rattlesnake* in 1849, and later provided a substantial account of life in the Strait.[21]

The most memorable of New Guinea's castaways were 324 Chinese from the *St. Paul*, on their way to the Australian goldfields in 1858. The ship was wrecked on Rossel Island, the captain and eight of his crew supposedly leaving to get assistance, but actually abandoning them. Help eventually arrived at Rossel Island months too late, in the form of the French vessel *Styx* from New Caledonia. Only three of the Chinese survived: one remained on Rossel until rescued in 1859; and two traded to neighboring islands were rescued in 1865. The incident was quoted frequently later in the century, giving Rossel Islanders and all New Guineans a reputation for cannibal gluttony. Some of the Chinese died in initial skirmishes, but oral testimony from Rossel Islanders suggests that others built rafts and escaped north, although presumably they too would have perished.[22]

Negotiating with a host community was never easy. Early interpretations of the role of beachcombers and castaways, particularly in Polynesia, often present them as long-staying important middlemen, buffers between encroaching traders and settlers and indigenous leaders, becoming socially prominent in the process. Over a two hundred year period, they were often present in large numbers. The same does not apply to their New Guinea equivalents, who seem to have remained uncertain, often unwelcome guests on the village fringe, or were killed.

Explaining Coastal Violence

All foreign contact with New Guinea between the sixteenth century and the early decades of the twentieth century was limited to the coastal areas. Torres Strait and the eastern archipelagos off New Guinea were really an extension of the Australian frontier even after the Protectorates were proclaimed in 1884, but because the neighboring Melanesian islands were not formally part of the Australian colonies, violence on the Pacific frontier has never been thought of as relating to Australian historical experience in New Guinea.

Queensland newspapers and government records, covering the forty years during which the labor trade operated, provide reasonably complete and accurate details on reported cross-cultural violent incidents.[23] As part of the research for this book, I began to collect examples of early coastal contact incidents involving violence all around New Guinea up until the 1890s. My sources were predominantly in English with a bias toward what became British New Guinea, together with some major incidents gathered from Dutch New Guinea sources. If German and Dutch sources were also combed, the number of violent incidents would expand considerably.[24] Double the figures, and we may be coming close to the actual number of incidents and deaths during the early period of European coastal contact up until the end of the nineteenth century. These figures also take no account of 500 years of Maluku commercial and ritual contact, as well as suzerainty over west New Guinea.

These Melanesian statistics cover 584 violent incidents, accounting for more than 1,400 foreign deaths (Europeans and their employees) and untold numbers of indigenous deaths —presumably at least the same number or more. I have divided the statistics into two parts: incidents from around New Guinea; and incidents from Island Melanesia. My Island Melanesia sample includes the northern archipelagos now part of Papua New Guinea, but excludes Fiji and New Caledonia in the south. New Guinea figures are based on 266 incidents, mainly in the east, which caused more than 724 foreign deaths. Island Melanesia figures are based on 318 incidents with in excess of 684 deaths. While there were several thousand Melanesian deaths due to violent contact with foreigners in this early period, we need also to take into account other deaths from diseases, which should be attributed to contact with Europeans. Some examples will suffice to illustrate a pattern.

In the seventeenth century, Schouten and Le Maire on the *Eendracht* and the *Hoorn* reached New Ireland. On 26 June 1616, the ships were attacked off East Cape by canoes. Four canoes were captured and destroyed, ten of the attackers were killed and three taken prisoner. Two were released the next day when the New Irelanders paid compensation with a pig and a bunch of bananas. The day after, the ships were visited by twenty-one New Irelanders in a large well-appointed canoe. Their manner was friendly, and they brought lime and betel nuts with them, which the Dutch interpreted as signs of friendship. The third prisoner was released and the two ships sailed on.[25] Seven years later, along the southwest New Guinea coast, Carstensz and Van Coiolsteerdt's expedition on the *Arnhem* and *Pera* was attacked when a pinnace went ashore to collect water. The attack came without warning. Eight of the crew were killed with arrows and spears, one was torn apart, a young midshipman was disemboweled, and seven more were wounded.[26]

Another incident occurred in 1791, on the south coast of New Guinea. HMS *Pandora*, commanded by Edward Edwards, was returning from capturing mutineers from William Bligh's ill-fated HMS *Bounty*, when the ship hit a reef and sank near Murray (Mer) Island in Torres Strait. Thirty-one of the crew and four of the *Bounty* mutineers drowned, the remainder escaping in four boats, eventually reaching Timor. On 30 August, the boats were attacked while collecting water at Yorke (Massid) Island in Torres Strait. Their offer of fishhooks and sail-needles in exchange for the water was refused.[27]

There was never a predictable response from either side in early contact situations. New Guineans might attempt to use local etiquette, attack, offer to initiate trade, or attempt compensation after violent behavior. They asserted agency and attempted to control the terms of engagement. Both sides tried to follow their own cultural rules, but also had to resort to temporary role-playing in unorthodox situations. The first 1616 attack was intended to chase away the visitors, but failed. Next, a compensation payment was attempted, which worked, gaining the release of two men. This was followed by a more ceremonial approach, which the Dutch interpreted, correctly, as an attempt at negotiation and friendship, rewarding the New Irelanders by releasing their last prisoner. The military advantage was with the foreigners who never left their ships, but despite suffering casualties in the encounter, the New Irelanders managed to get their three surviving men back from the ships. The 1623 attack was on a beach, a situation where the New Guineans had the advantage. It was sudden, ferocious, and successful, gaining them a bad reputation amongst Europeans, but probably enhancing their reputation among neighboring communities because they chased away the interlopers. In the 1791 case, York Islanders may not have known that the *Pandora* had sunk, nor realized that trade for water was being offered—they were merely repelling an alien group that had landed on their island. The *Pandora*'s crew were in a life-threatening predicament and offered what, to them, were valuable irreplaceable items as trade for water. The fame of Bligh and the *Pandora,* which makes the incident of interest today, meant nothing to the York Islanders.

In 1846, HMS *Bramble* was surveying at Cape Possession in the Maiva district on the southeast coast. Lieutenant Yule and a shore-party were in two boats that capsized in the surf. They were set upon by a large crowd of coastal villagers who plundered everything they had, even stripping them of their clothes, but did nothing to hurt the naked and embarrassed British crew.[28] The advantage was with the Maiva people, since the crew was vulnerable on the beach. Four decades later, another crew working further down the same coast, at Basilaki, were not so lucky to escape unscathed.

The 1885 incident at Basilaki sums up all the difficulties, complexities, motivations, and provocations for the historian retelling the actual story of a violent encounter. The comfortably fitted-out bêche-de-mer schooner *Lallah Rooke*, under Captain Frier (or Fryer), accompanied by John Watwins and several crew members, had been anchored at Hoopiron Bay, Basilaki (Moresby) Island, for three days in July. The local villagers were massing, and Frier's interpreter Billy warned that they intended to attack. Procter, the Mate, was away on a neighboring island at Fucia Augustine's bêche-de-mer station, repairing his cutter. The *Lallah Rooke*'s boats were being used to collect water and wood at Basilaki. Frier stayed on board, while Watkins and Billy Barlow (an Aborigine from the Herbert River, Ingham) and three others went ashore. The local people invited them to share a meal, but they refused. Watkins was killed instantly by a tomahawk blow to the neck, coupled with a knife in his back. A spear went right through Ah Sam's body, which he managed to pull out, surviving the attack. Another member of the crew was caught in the water and beheaded. Francis, a Filipino, had remained in the dingy and was able to fire a warning shot, then picked up one other crew member. Frier had remained on board, sitting on the skylight, trading with a large crowd of local people. At the same time as the attack on land began, his throat was slit from behind.

Billy Barlow rowed to Samarai Island for help, accompanied by Francis and four other crew members, all Queensland Aborigines. Procter returned the next morning with Billy Barlow, finding the schooner completely looted, the deck covered in blood, provisions scattered about and all firearms and tomahawks stolen. The Islanders fired at Procter, saying that they would fight any naval ship sent in retaliation, exclaiming, "white man no good, he gave us too much work along Queensland." The *Lallah Rooke* was reclaimed from the Basilaki people (who were busy gutting her) by an LMS pastor from Samarai, who sailed the vessel back to that port. One crew-member said he had seen Frier's head on top of a heap of yams in a boat. Ah Sam claimed that he had seen Frier's head cooking with yams, and another member of the crew was sure that he had seen Frier's brains eaten. Eventually, Frier's and the carpenter's skulls were recovered. Sir Peter Scratchley, the British New Guinea Special Commissioner, investigated the incident and rewarded the LMS pastor with a silver watch engraved "From the Great Queen Victoria." One month later, HMS *Diamond* arrived to burn down all the villages in the bay.[29]

The *Lallah Rooke* incident shows how difficult it was to be alert to an imminent attack, and that such incidents were not always as unprovoked as Europeans made out. They were often rational attempts on the part of New Guineans to obtain satisfactory compensation for previous wrongs. In the case of the *Arnhem* and *Pera*, at Dolak Island in 1623, the crew had previously been attempting to snare natives from canoes with two nooses, which might well explain the reaction they incurred.[30] Neither was the captain of the *Lallah Rooke* innocent of previous wrongdoing. Frier was working in the bêche-de-mer industry, which over previous years had become a very dangerous occupation, exacerbated by tensions caused by kidnapping of laborers to and their failure to return from Queensland. Bailala, a local leader who had earlier traveled to Sydney with scientist Miklouho-Maclay, told Scratchley that some years previously two Islanders had been recruited at Teste Island on Frier's ship. Both drowned one night while attempting to swim ashore, Frier refusing to offer their families any compensation for the deaths. Laborers had also been taken to Queensland from Hoop-iron Bay. When the survivors returned, compensation was given for two men who had died there, working for Frier, but not for a third. The families of all three had sworn to kill the next European who came to their area. Indeed, when Scratchley visited in October, he was told that men landed from the steamer *Victoria* (chartered to bring back the laborers from Queensland) were busy committing murders. One came on board Scratchley's *Blackall* and confessed to having killed a white man, saying that he had brought some compensatory valuables—four arm shells and a pig's tooth. Scratchley had him put in irons.[31]

In 1885, Diavari and Nagodiri murdered Captain Miller at Laton Island off Normanby Island, where he had gone to erect a bêche-de-mer smokehouse. Diavari surrendered, but Scratchley could not locate Nagodiri, burning his village down as punishment. Diavari actually came to HMS *Dart* to pay compensation in pigs and shell valuables, not understanding that his offer might be refused. Scratchley sentenced Diavari to transportation to Port Moresby for several months, to work on road-building. He wrote to Lord

Derby that: "I believe that such a course will produce a good effect upon the native mind, as it will tend to show that the white man does not act merely in revenge, but in accordance with the principles of law and justice." While in Port Moresby, Diavari divulged the reason for the attack. His cousin and Nagodiri's brother had been taken away by a labor trade vessel some years earlier, and had never returned. When SS *Victoria* brought back the laborers, no compensation was offered, at which the family decided to take a European life in return. Europeans seldom appreciated the protocols and reciprocal obligations of local communities, or that they behaved in a rational manner. Instead, New Guineans were accused of being unpredictable and prone to quick irrational violence.

There are several examples of ex-Queensland laborers from the Louisiades behaving violently toward foreigners after their return, which can be interpreted as payback for past wrongs. Melanesian concepts of reciprocity and demands for compensation are strong cultural elements that could work to the detriment of foreigners; however, those who understood New Guineans used these in their negotiations. Experienced LMS missionary James Chalmers accepted a pig and other gifts in compensation for the death of two naturalists, Thorngren and James, at Yule Island in 1876.[32] On New Britain in 1882, J.B.O. Mouton, an ex-Nouvelle-France colonist who had settled at Kokopo, after the Tolai looted his house and speared him, forced them to pay compensation and return everything they had stolen. His neighbor, Richard Parkinson, also dealt with the Tolai this way, taking canoes in compensation, giving them back when his property was returned.[33] In 1884, WPHC official Hugh Romilly accepted a pig in compensation for the death of William Read, a copra merchant at Tube Tube (Slade) Island in the Engineer Group.[34]

Although violent incidents had occurred from the earliest days of culture contact, they seem to have accelerated in the second half of the nineteenth century and were concentrated around three major areas of maritime industry and permanent settlement: Torres Strait, the tail of east New Guinea and into the Louisiades, and around St. George's Channel between New Britain and New Ireland. Interestingly, among Alastair Gray's 360 examples of contact with whalers, between 1799 and 1884 there are only four violent incidents, aberrant to the pattern of regular violence that followed the bêche-de-mer industry in east New Guinea. The inhabitants of one major area of settlement, Port Moresby, were almost totally peaceful toward foreigners. My statistical sample includes only two incidents from close to Port Moresby, in 1882 and 1884, and neither involved a high number of deaths. One could conclude that the Motuan people were extremely accommodating, a quality learned from being at the center of long-distance trade routes, and that the permanent presence of the LMS after 1874 provided a stabilizing element, injecting enough trade goods into the local economy to satisfy the people.

Several more conclusions can be drawn from the data. Islanders were often willing to accept short-term invasions of their territory, as long as they could see that it was temporary and held some benefit for them. Most attacks were aimed at pinnaces, cutters, and whaleboats used to survey, trade, and collect wood and water, not the large ocean-going ships. These smaller vessels were easier to overwhelm. Europeans were also most vulnerable when they were on shore collecting wood and water, or exploring. Most violence occurred on beaches. Obtaining trade goods was usually the more important objective. The case of Yule in 1846, ignobly stripped of his clothes and belongings, but not injured in any way, suggests it was his possessions, not his presence, that motivated action. While violence came easily to New Guineans, and death was often a very necessary part of compensation, their major prize was typically the trade goods obtained, of which there were usually considerable amounts. Muskets, Snider rifles, tomahawks, tobacco by the hundredweight, glass bottles, metal tools, copper-sheeting from hulls, clothing, and edible supplies were all to be had if a bêche-de-mer camp was overwhelmed, or an ill-defended expedition or trader was killed.

Wrecked or seized European or Chinese vessels were enormous sources of windfall profits for any nearby village. Reefs and waterways around islands were just as much part of indigenous territories as dry land. Fishing for bêche-de-mer occurred on owned reefs, the foreigners involved usually not comprehending that the reefs were the property of nearby villagers. Equally, ships wrecked on reefs, or equipment left on beaches, became the property of the local villagers. There are sixteen examples, all from between 1855 and 1886, of ships wrecked and looted around New Guinea. These do not include the many wrecks in Torres Strait, a dangerous major shipping route and veritable ship's graveyard.[35] For instance, in 1878 when William Ingham foolishly attempted to rescue valuable bêche-de-mer equipment from Brooker (Utian) Island in the Calvados Chain, he was trespassing on an island, the inhabitants of which already had a substantial reputation for killing unwelcome visitors. The Brooker Islanders planned to kill Ingham's party, deciding on an initial show of cooperation to allay any fears. A feast was staged in Ingham's honor before he was allowed to collect firearms and the bêche-de-mer equipment. The attack came on the third day, taking the lives of seven of the crew including Ingham. All were roasted in stone ovens and eaten. Why the Brooker Islanders chose this course is open to interpretation. Were they trying to gain Ingham's mana by eating him, showing distain for Europeans, trying to deter future visitors, or fulfilling customary obligations by staging a cannibal feast?[36]

By the 1880s, there was an interesting polyglot community of visitors working around New Guinea. Chinese, Makasans, Javanese, and people of Maluku had visited and lived around the west coast of New Guinea for hundreds of years, intermarrying with local women. The east became just as diverse. Europeans owned most of the ships and equipment scattered unevenly along the coast, but were in the minority. One has only to list the crew of the *Lallah Rooke*: Englishmen, Australian colonists and Aborigines, a South Sea Islander (from the labor trade), a Chinese, and a Filipino. Or to examine the crew of Ingham's *Voura*: two Englishmen, a Greek, an Australian, two Chinese, three South Sea Islanders, and one Wari Island man. It is also worth noting that not all of the traders were of European origin. Many Chinese traders worked out of north Queensland, sailing junks through to the Louisiades. The most famous was Ah Gim, a Chinese bêche-de-mer fisherman who held a Queensland Ship's Master's certificate and operated out of Cooktown and South Cape. His ketch-rigged thirty-ton junk, the *Wong Hing*, which he replaced with the schooner *Pride of Logan* in 1885 (obtained after its crew were massacred), and finally his lugger *Rarotonga*, were all regulars along the southern New Guinea coast. His crew consisted of Chinese, Malays, Torres Strait Islanders, and South Cape men. Over years, Ah Gim lived with two different women, the first from South Cape, and the second a Rarotongan. In 1886, he was granted a government permit to reside permanently at South Cape.[37] This polyglot presence suggests that analysis of contact situations needs to be refined. The simplistic division between Europeans and New Guineans is misleading, if we assume that the various crew-members could act as mediators in cross-cultural confrontations, and that between them these polyglot crews had considerable experience in dealing with other cultural groups. The presence of these crews of diverse origins and experience might explain the low levels of violence in contact between New Guineans and new arrivals.

During the second half of the nineteenth century, naval retaliation became an inevitable consequence of indigenous attacks. It sometimes took six months before naval ships arrived. Often they could do little to find the real culprits, instead indiscriminately bombarding villages, destroying canoes, houses, coconut trees and gardens, including those belonging to innocent parties. When permanent government arrived, based at Port Moresby, Finchhafen, Kokopo, Samarai, Merauke, Fakfak, and Manokwari, there were the beginnings of an attempt to institute some semblance of Western judicial practice.

While the chronological coverage in this chapter is extensive, and geographically the area examined spreads across more than 3,500 kilometers, the discussion has been limited to events occurring around the coast. Despite occasional expeditions venturing inland during the second half of the nineteenth century, foreigners were really contained around the coast of New Guinea until into the twentieth century. The Highlands did not begin to receive even sporadic contact until the 1910s, followed by major exploration in the 1930s. Outsiders only had access to controlled passages, *porte-cochère* into a cultural fortress which they never entered, all contact mediated through middlemen who became adept at dealing with two cultures. The indigenous people and the foreigners became actors in Greg Dening's theatre of "ethnographic moments."

Contact with Inland Areas during the Twentieth Century

A map of areas explored in the early 1880s would show almost the entire coast, with the Fly and Mamberamo Rivers the only inland area to have been visited. By 1914, many river systems in Australian Papua had been traversed, the same occurring to a more limited extent in German New Guinea. There was still little knowledge of the interior of Dutch

New Guinea. Scientific expeditions had collected physical anthropological data and natural history specimens. The extensive Highlands areas—grand valleys with dense populations—remained virtually unknown until aerial reconnaissance began in the 1920s, along with government expeditions and private parties searching for oil and gold. When the Second World War reached New Guinea, the largest remaining uncontacted areas were those surrounding the Fly and Sepik Rivers and the central Highlands in the west. The concept of liminal moments remains apt to describe interactions with wandering exploration parties made up of a few Europeans, accompanied by large teams of indigenous carriers and police. But when they met the remote peoples, there was a difference from coastal encounters. The outsiders were often at the mercy of the New Guineans they encountered, were dependant on them for food, and often faced violent opposition. They could not up-anchor and sail away, and were often left with little choice other than to barter for peace or kill attackers, if they were to survive.

WEST NEW GUINEA

In the west, nineteenth-century scientific expeditions had provided information from around the Bird's Head Peninsula area, and onwards from the 1880s the Mamberamo River basin, seldom venturing much further. It was not until the 1900s that expeditions, such as that led by Wichmann in 1903, which began in the Bird's Head but eventually concentrated on Humboldt Bay, or the Meyes' expedition of 1904–1905 into the mountains via the southwest coast, began to move through the interior of Dutch New Guinea. Then, between 1907 and 1915, combined army and civilian expeditions were entrusted with a huge exploration and mapping project covering the whole territory, even penetrating some areas of the central mountains in a so-called "race to the snow."

This was largely the doing of Hendrikus Colijn, later a Dutch Prime Minister, who arrived in the Netherlands Indies in 1893 as a second lieutenant, involved in the pacification of Lombok and Acheh. His abilities drew him to the attention of General Van Heutsz. As Van Heutsz' *aide-de-camp* (after the General was appointed Governor-General in 1904), Colijn was involved in writing policy for several regions, and began visiting Maluku, Timor, and New Guinea in 1906. The first permanent Dutch administrative base near New Guinea (beyond Maluku), was in the Aru Islands in 1882. This was followed by a police post on the mainland, briefly, at Sarira, west of present-day Merauke, in 1893, which was abandoned by the middle of the year, having been besieged, leaving one man dead and nine wounded. Discussions toward establishing a permanent base continued during the 1890s, finally gathering pace in 1897, leading the next year to establishment of government posts at Fakfak on Onin Peninsula, and at Manokwari on the west coast of Cenderawasih Gulf (supporting the long-established Protestant mission there). A more substantial well-equipped station was begun at Merauke on the south coast in 1902.[38] All of these early bases were under the control of the Resident at Ternate. Maintaining a Dutch presence became easier when the Koninklijke Paketvaart Maatschappij (KPM, or Royal Packet Steamship Company, formed in 1888), Burns Philp, and other shipping services began regular operations between Australia and Asia in the 1900s, calling at Merauke, Banda, Ambon, and Timor.[39]

Colijn's two 1906 reports on New Guinea doubted the wisdom of making Fakfak on the Onin Peninsula the major Dutch administrative post—he said that it should have been further east—and also suggested that military personnel be used for exploration. Van Heutsz agreed with Colijn's idea, against the advice of the military, who baulked at the thought of answering to civilian authority. The Governor-General funded a series of military expeditions under civilian control. Fakfak and Manokwari, and later Merauke and Humboldt Bay, were used as staging posts for these extensive government expeditions, and for eight private expeditions under military protection. Between 1907 and 1915—by which time the First World War had intervened—the Indies' government spent Dfl 5.5 million in advancing knowledge of west New Guinea. A Royal Dutch Geographical Society expedition, led by Professor A. Wichmann, explored coastal west New Guinea in 1903. The expedition began at Fakfak, moved to Kokas, Sekar, Lakahia, a petroleum well at Horst River, the site of Merkus-Oord, and Namototte Island, and reached the central mountains before being forced to turn back at 2,300 meters. Then, during 1904–1905, Meyers led the Royal Dutch Geographical Society on an unsuccessful attempt to reach the snowfields.[40] Two British expeditions (in 1910–1911 led by Walter Goodfellow, and in 1912–1913 under Alexander F. R. Wollaston) explored the region toward the high mountains around Puncak Jaya (the Carstensz Massif, 5,040 m).[41] In 1907, the same Society that mounted the 1903 expedition sent another team under H. A. Lorentz and J. W. van Nouhuys, unsuccessfully attempting to climb Mt. Trikora (Wilhelmina, 4,700 m). Another expedition in 1909–1910, led by Lorentz, reached an altitude of 4,461 meters. The first successful expedition to the snow line at Puncak Jaya came in 1909–1911, led by Wollaston and C. G. Rawlings, under the auspices of the British Ornithologists' Union, but including representatives from the Royal Geographical Society. Two expeditions also explored around the Mamberamo River: one led by A. Franssen Herderschée in 1909, which failed to reach the snow mountains, followed by another under Dr. Max Moszkowski in 1910–1911. In 1913, Franssen Herderschée led the last great expedition into the central mountains before the War.[42]

The expeditions in the west gathered little information about the inhabitants. The British expedition to Mt. Trikora met mountain people living at altitudes between 1,200 and 1,800 meters, probably Damal speakers, whom they subjected to cranial and body measurement. There are also mysterious reports of people coming to the expedition for food, and the same people being later found dead in shelters. A 1935 report suggests that they were a trading party on their way to the coast, struck down by disease.[43] The 1921 expedition to Mt. Trikora was the first to enter a densely-populated Highland valley. They proceeded upstream along the Toli River, crossing the watershed with the North Baliem before heading for the higher plain north of Mt. Trikora. This area was inhabited by tens of thousands of Western Dani, who impressed the travelers. As in other areas, the Toli Dani seem to have regarded the foreigners as spirits, but they were keen traders of pigs, garden produce, and artifacts for the cowrie shells the expedition arranged to have brought up from the coast for barter. Memories, recounted to anthropologists in the 1960s, record the fear people felt when dealing with the expedition and an epidemic of dysentery that followed their departure. The Dani thought that the sickness had come from trade goods they had received, causing them to throw many of the items into a river. The Dutch judged the Dani to be more sophisticated than the lowlanders, mainly because of their aloofness, and generally peaceful, helpful attitudes. The records of the west New Guinea expeditions show little violence and they seem to have tried to avoid confrontation. However, as the reanalysis of Hides and O'Malley's and the Leahy brothers' expeditions in the east New Guinea Highlands in the 1930s has shown, the violence that occurred was often concealed by Europeans. During the next twenty years, further exploration in the west was slow, largely confined to searching for oil. In the 1930s, aerial mapping followed by geological and geophysical exploration, quickened the pace, with airdrops used to back up land parties. In this way Colijn explored the Carstensz Massif (1936), gold exploration expeditions penetrated the Dugal region (1937–1938), and a third Richard Archbold expedition explored the heavily populated Baliem Valley.[44]

EAST NEW GUINEA

On the German New Guinea mainland, exploration remained largely confined to the Sepik and Markham Rivers and the coastal mountains. Otto Finsch entered the mouth of the Sepik in 1885, the first of a series of expeditions penetrating further inland along the great river. Once the German Neu Guinea Kompagnie was established, settlements began on the mainland, at Finschhafen and Hatzfeldhafen in 1885, the next year at Constantinhafen, and in 1888 at Stephansort, both in Astrolabe Bay. In 1886, German New Guinea's first *Landeschauptmann* (Administrator) Vice-Admiral Georg von Schleinitz, and Dr. C. Schrader, ascended 380 kilometers up the Kaiserin Augusta (Sepik) to just beyond Ambunti, then between 1910 and 1913 Leonard Schultze and Dr. Walter Behrmann ascended to the headwaters, past the point where the river crossed into Dutch New Guinea, almost 1,000 kilometers from the mouth. More mainland settlements were opened over the next two decades: Friedrich Wilhelmshafen (Madang) (1891), Berlinhafen (1897), Aitape (1906), Morobe (1909), and Angoram (1914). Hugo Zöller, a correspondent of the *Kölnische Zeitung*, led a party into the Finisterre Ranges in 1888, a north coast emulation of the *Age* and *Argus* expeditions into Port Moresby's hinterland a few years earlier. Zöller had a clear view of the Bismarck Range and beyond to Mt. Wilhelm (4,509 m), the highest peak in east New Guinea. The Ramu River began to be explored in the 1890s, when botanist Dr. Carl Lauterbach and Ernst Tappenbeck made two trips, up the Gagol River inland from Astrolabe Bay in 1890, and from Stephansort into the Bismarck Ranges in 1896, followed in 1907 by miner Wilhelm Dammköhler, who ascended the Markham and crossed to the Ramu. Missionaries and miners continued to penetrate further inland from the north coast. Lutherans Georg Pilhofer and Leonhardt Flierl went up the Waria in 1913, ascending into the Markham Valley via the Watut Valley, followed by miners. Exploration under the Australian military administration (1914–1921) was limited.[45]

Inland government exploration was managed by creating an outpost, from which influence could spread through the surrounding area, eventually creating other bases and crisscrossing patrols until the whole region was considered to be under control. The two most successful administrators, William MacGregor and Hubert Murray in Papua, both men of enormous energy, were not afraid to take part personally in strenuous exploration work, gathering around them teams of field officers who were immensely capable of carrying out the most taxing patrols. MacGregor twice crossed from Port Moresby to the Mombare River, ascended all of the coastal rivers and climbed the highest mountain in the Owen Stanley Range. He believed in using physical force and punitive raids to establish colonial authority, tactics dictated by limited resources and a belief that Papuan violence should be met by retaliatory force. Even though discontent undoubtedly simmered long after his police and officers had moved on, MacGregor's methods did establish the basic government structure for Papua.[46] His eventual replacement, Hubert Murray, extended government control during his long term as Administrator (1908–1940). Field officers completed much of the early sketchy exploration and applied pacification principles. Several new areas were contacted during the 1910s. Resident Magistrate A. W. Monckton traveled between the Lakekamu River and Kokoda. Acting Administrator M. C. Staniforth-Smith incompetently mistook the upper Kikori for the Strickland, losing one-third of his party plus all notes and supplies. Passing close to Lake Kutubu, his expedition was the first to enter the Southern Highlands. Two years later, in 1913, Patrol Officer Henry Ryan made a short trip up the Kikori, west across country to the Awwora, a tributary of the Bamu.[47] As in the rest of New Guinea, because of the number of government officers away at the First World War, little further exploration took place in the area until after 1918.

During the nineteenth century, the general belief was that the central mountains were precipitous and sparsely populated, but rumors of vast inland valleys had begun in the 1890s. In 1896, Lauterbach sighted and named Mt. Hagen during his ascent of the Sepik and Yuat Rivers. One intrepid German government officer, Captain Hermann Detzner, a surveyor who refused to surrender to the Australian forces in 1914, spent four years roaming the mountains before surrendering and may well have been the first outsider to reach the central high grasslands.[48] A few years later, missionaries began to penetrate the Highlands: Stephen Lehner in 1919 and Georg Pilhofer in 1920 were in contact with villagers south of the Markham River; and in 1926–1927 Leonhardt Flierl made expeditions to the headwaters of the Purari River, west of Kainantu. Two years later, Wilhelm Bergmann and Pilhofer reached the Bina Valley, and the next year Bergmann went again, this time with Leonhardt Flierl's cousin Willie Flierl. At the same time, miners were moving around Kainantu and the Arona Valley. On the Australian Papua side, Charles Karius and Ivan Champion explored the upper Fly and Strickland Rivers in 1927 and 1928, crossing over to the Sepik. William MacGregor, a labor recruiter and gold prospector, probably entered Enga from the Sepik in 1929. In 1930, his group went up the Arrabundie, then across to the Jimi River, prospecting through the Yuat, Tarua, and Maramuni Valleys. Prospectors Michael Leahy and Michael Dwyer entered the eastern Highlands in 1930, and three years later the Leahy brothers, financed by the New Guinea Goldfields Company, built an airstrip at Bena Bena, from which they flew over the Simbu and Wahgi Valleys, proving that huge inhabited valleys existed in the east. The next year, miners Tom and Jack Fox managed to penetrate the Southern Highlands, traveled as far as the Strickland River, Lake Kopiago, and the Tari Basin, then returned via the Mendi Valley and eventually Mt. Hagen.[49]

Aircraft soon began to supplement land exploration parties. The first aircraft to fly over New Guinea reached Australian Papua in 1922, a Curtis flying-boat which traveled west from Port Moresby, to the Purari River and Daru Island, exiting to Thursday Island. The first aerial photographs of New Guinea were taken during the journey. Four years later, over several months a Dutch-American expedition used another sea-plane to fly down the Mamberamo River to the Van Rees Mountains, ferrying supplies to a land party. Soon after, aviation began to be used extensively in the Mandated Territory of New Guinea to carry machinery and supplies into the Bulolo goldfields.[50]

The discovery of gold deposits in the mountains around Wau and Bulolo in the 1920s meant that prospectors were keen to explore further inland. The revenue of the Mandated Territory increased (enabling greater use of aircraft and radio communication) and soon far exceeded that of Papua. Although prospectors like the Leahy and the Fox brothers continued to travel through the Highlands, the most substantial and difficult patrols fell to government officers from both of Australia's territories. In Papua, Murray's few "outside men" were capable bushmen, often from a new generation born in the colony. Jack Hides and Jim O'Malley made a remarkable trip from the Strickland to the Purari in 1935, crossing through the Southern Highlands, followed the next year by Ivan Champion and C. J. Admonson, who traveled east from the Bamu to the Purari. In 1937, Claude Champion and F.W.G. Anderson passed from Kikori to Lake Kutubu, which afterwards became a major base in the Papuan Highlands. Michael and Dan Leahy teamed up with government officer James Taylor in 1933, followed by Taylor and John Black in the 1938–1939 Hagen-to-Sepik patrol.[51]

The arrival of strange white men with their male carriers and police, without women, was a matter of great puzzlement to the Highlanders. Mirani Angil of Endugwa in Simbu explained it this way: "I heard that white men came to Kundiawa. People said they were spirits or *gigl golka* [Simbu "dead spirits"] or dead men who died long time ago coming out of the grave. Might be ancestor. White men and native men came passed through our village, went through Narku clan. The Narku sent a message that this white man and his men had kill a lot of men from Wauga clan so when they come to your place keep away from them. A message was sent from Kamaneku clan there was another ghost or spirit coming from Sumbugu clan. They went to Irpui then to Dimbi and later to Mingende."[52]

As Bill Gammage's *The Sky Travellers* (a history of the 1938–1939 Hagen-Sepik patrol) reveals, the most constantly repeated question voiced by the new peoples with whom Australian exploration parties came into contact in the mountainous Highlands was "Who are you?" Highlanders wanted to know who the strangers were, enabling them to fit the interlopers into existing cosmologies and ultimately to control them. "Highlanders believed that the sky was inhabited by beings in many ways like themselves, who traded, made love and war, and believed in gods. Highlanders varied on whether the sky people were ancestral ghosts or spirits, but most agreed that they were immortal, had wealth, caused thunder, lightning, rain and drought, could take human form and were usually red or white and, although not much interested in people, occasionally descended to earth . . . They were not the only supernatural beings. Sky, earth and underworld held spirits, a hierarchy of deities up to the Creator, and ancestors of different powers depending on when, how and at what age they died. Many beings could take human form, although skin color or strange or ignorant behavior might give them away."[53]

The first Europeans who ventured to New Guinea, in the sixteenth century, were emerging from an era dominated more by religion than science. There were always large differences between the beliefs of the educated leaders of expeditions and those who provided the labor to make ships sail, something still true of those who reached New Guinea in the eighteenth and nineteenth centuries. Europeans who arrived during the twentieth century were different, and tended to believe that the world could be divided into the known, natural world and the unknown, supernatural world. If Europeans believed in supernatural beings, the assumption was that these spirits were beyond human control. As Gammage notes, Highlanders (and *ipso facto* other New Guineans) do not think in this way. In their worldview, the natural and supernatural each balance the other: "Europeans assumed that Highlanders who treated travelers as unearthly therefore thought them powerful and inviolate. They thought being supernatural gave them protection. At best that was only briefly so. Highlanders quickly sought to discover what the travelers were —men, ghosts, spirits or deities—in order to control them. On that depended their well-being, even their lives. Endlessly and universally they asked the newcomers, "Who are you?" That came from clansmen seeing their first white, from carriers on exploring patrols, from village officials, mission helpers and plantation workers touching the European world. The answer mattered because the correct rituals for control depended on it. Amazement, doubt and fear there was at contact, but these only passingly deflected a search for control."[54]

Understandably, at first contact people did not know what to make of their strange visitors. An initial belief that all foreigners were spirits seems to have been widespread and can probably be extrapolated back over the centuries. The film *First Contact*, particularly the interviews with women who had sexual relations with the Leahy brothers, shows that the concept of the foreigners being spirits soon wore off when they were found to perform normal human body functions. New Guineans were not so naive as to continue to believe this after sustained contact. As Ewunga, Michael Leahy's "boss-boy" commented: "There were new fellows, they never fought us the first time they saw us. If we came back a second time we had to watch out, because then they realized we were just ordinary people, not spirits or ancestors."[55]

Jack Hides' account of his and O'Malley's 1935 Strickland-Purari expedition, alongside the 1980s reanalysis presented in Schieffelin and Crittenden's *Like People You See in a Dream*, provide a window into encounters with hitherto unknown populations. Hides, always more innocent and warm than his police (who never trusted any of the newly contacted peoples), offered an expurgated account full of misunderstandings. For example, after a hard struggle across country from the Strickland River, Hides and O'Malley were impressed by the orderly lifestyle of the Huli in the Southern Highlands: "And beyond the gorge, gold and green, reaching as far as the eye could see, lay the rolling timbered slopes and grasslands of the huge valley system. On every slope were cultivated squares, while little columns of smoke rising in the still air revealed to us the homes of the people of this land. I had never seen anything more beautiful. Beyond all stood the heights of some mighty mountain chain that sparkled in places with the colors of the setting sun. As I looked on those green cultivated squares, of such mathematical exactness, I thought of wheatfields, or the industrious areas of a colony of Chinese. Here was a population such as I had sometimes dreamed of finding."[56]

The Huli remembered the violent visit by the Fox brothers a few months earlier, and were not impressed by their visitors.[57] Some Huli were convinced that the patrol members were spirits. One local leader, Puya Indane, thought that he recognized his dead brother, Barina, among the police, which was why he presented Hides with some freshly butchered pork. The expedition made the mistake of carrying steel knives and axes to use for barter, not the much-sought-after cowries or pearlshells. Puya did not allow his people to accept the gifts offered—knives, beads, and mirrors—because he thought that these gifts might prove harmful, not because his people did not want them. Hides misinterpreted Puya's oration as meaning that they lived in a land of plenty and that their stone axes were perfectly satisfactory. A little later, Puya instructed Hides on the direction the party should travel. Hides understood his gesture to the east as advice on the most sensible path, when in fact, according to Telenge Yenape (interviewed in 1986), Puya wanted the patrol to go toward Kerewa, to stop them going further north where there were large populations and gardens which might be affected by these wandering *dama*—powerful nonhuman spirits. Yet, the patrol did go north, much to the concern of the Huli, some of whom decided to kill the *dama*. To Hides, Puya was an arrogant untrustworthy old sorcerer, whereas to the Huli he was behaving in a sensible, moderate manner, attempting to manage a potentially difficult situation, with a possible calamitous spiritual aftermath.[58]

Near the end of the patrol, when the party was weak with exhaustion and starvation in the Kewa area adjacent to the Erave River, Hides ordered his police to obtain food from a garden and shot pigs. Hides' account is diametrically opposed to 1985 testimony gathered from local people. The Kewa thought the expedition of men were ghosts, although they distinguished three types: the carriers, the police, and the "red men" (Hides and O'Malley). Many Kewa were alarmed by their appearances, smell, and clothes, although some were fascinated by the strange group. Ipitango, the owner of the several pigs purloined, shouted out to the patrol not to kill all of his pigs. He was shot dead, through the head. Hides recorded the native as menacing and yodeling a "kill call" to muster others to attack. Hides said they shot at his feet to scare him. Why would Hides forcibly take food from and attack people who had been friendly to the expedition? Exhaustion may have led to confusion, but Hides seems to have been losing control of his police.[59] Confusion, misunderstanding of signs and gestures, fear of attack, and the rapid pace of events were characteristics common to both coastal and Highlands early encounters with outsiders.

Interpreting Early Contact

Four recent books on Papua New Guinea, Edward Schieffelin and Robert Crittenden's *Like People You See in a Dream*, Bill Gammage's *The Sky People*, Bob Connell and Robin Anderson's *First Contact* (and a film of the same name), and August Kituai's *My Gun, My Brother*, provide salutary lessons for anyone relying on eyewitness descriptions to create a picture of early and initial contacts. Ship's captains and government officers were at pains to present themselves in the best possible light. Jack Hides was the master of this. When he wrote his Papuan adventure books, Hides promoted an image of himself as the caring but stern master, handling exuberant, faithful police and carriers, as well as the childlike people they encountered. *Like People You See in a Dream* does not negate the great feat of the Hides-O'Malley patrol, but quite clearly Hides boosted himself, removing or failing to stress any evidence that might show he acted incorrectly.

The Sky People and *My Gun, My Brother* allow us to understand the motivations of the police and carriers in undertaking arduous expeditions, tracing the changes in contact patterns from the initial belief by the indigenous peoples that the patrol members were spirits, to a desire to obtain the new material items the expeditions carried, and to control them. Gammage and Kituai have also shown the impact of what Schieffelin and Crittenden called "accumulated experience" by "historical actors." Put simply, this means that expeditions, patrols, explorers, and others setting off and meeting new people, begin with a set of expected (even official) forms of behavior, but as time passes, these behaviors have to be adjusted and new forms of behavior learnt in order temporarily to manage a situation. These actors therefore accumulate experience and alter their historically determined roles (naval captain, gold-seeker, etc.) to meet situations. By the end of the contact, they are acting differently from when they began. David Chappell's and Ian Campbell's studies of transcultural and early contacts in the Pacific show that early contacts in coastal and Highlands regions of New Guinea have a lot in common with seventeenth- to nineteenth-century contacts in Oceania.[60] Kituai and Gammage also show that the police and carriers had their own agendas, and that "history" was shaped by their actions, as much as by the self-proclaimed European heroes of these encounters. It is clear that, de facto, the police were the real leaders of the expeditions, often using their authority to advance their individual and collective interests.

Although we have little evidence, it is likely that another recurring occurrence was the introduction of diseases by expeditions, with epidemics following their departure. In local explanations, these were usually linked to the expedition that had passed by, and this may well have affected the manner in which the people dealt with the next foreigners they encountered. We know little about the major killer disease, smallpox, although epidemics certainly seem to have reached the north coast around Huon Peninsula in the 1840s, also appearing along the southeast coast in the 1850s and 1860s.[61] The Huon outbreak probably relates to Malay and indigenous traders moving west to east along the north coast, or to whalers, whereas the southeastern epidemic came through Torres Strait, which had become an important shipping route for Australia's east coast colonies. Smallpox was also inadvertently introduced into Kaiser Wilhelmsland (the mainland of German New Guinea) through Javanese laborers during the 1880s. The disease infected a large number of coastal people, and through trade links it was passed to New Britain, where it spread on the south coast as far as South Cape and along the north coast as far as Nakanai. The result was devastating, with the population largely reduced.[62] Governor Albert Hahl described the scene: "The great villages, whose armed men had previously by a show of arms prevented us from entering, now contained only the wretched remnants of their former population."[63]

Recent research into the spread of smallpox among indigenous Australians suggests that a severe and very wide-reaching epidemic was introduced in 1789 through New South Wales, and another in the late 1820s. The evidence on the origins of the latter is unclear. It may have been introduced by the annual seasonal visits of Makasans to Arnhem Land.[64] Given that Makasan contact goes back centuries, unwittingly they probably would have introduced earlier disease epidemics to north Australian Aborigines. A similar argument can be made for west New Guinea. Further, evidence of the spread of European-originated diseases into east New Guinea and the Solomon Islands through the labor trade to Queensland and Fiji, and the devastation caused when measles reached Fiji in the mid-1870s, would suggest that New Guinea must have suffered a similar fate.[65]

Tuberculosis seems to have been introduced along the southeast coast by LMS workers onwards from the 1870s, and by returning laborers from Queensland plantations in the mid-1880s. Bacillary dysentery probably existed before any European presence, but like whooping cough, introduced at the end of the nineteenth century, was devastating

Interpreting
Early Contact

amongst concentrations of plantation or mining laborers. Measles was introduced in 1875 through Torres Strait, where one 1882 estimate suggests the disease killed twenty percent of the Islanders. Lms staff inadvertently spread measles to southeast New Guinea. How New Guineans accounted for these epidemics is not clear. Steve Mullins suggests that the 1875 measles epidemic in Torres Strait was seen as a massive display of supernatural power, interpreted in different ways. On Saibai Island, it led to rejection of Christianity, seen as a gospel of death, while on Boigu Island the people thought it was a sign of the wrath of the Christian god, leading to new conversions.[66]

Ships passing along the coast often did not know what had occurred during previous contacts. In the Highlands, Hides and O'Malley probably both benefited and suffered from the Fox brothers' exploits a few months earlier. As noted earlier, New Guineans reacted to these intrusions using well-established etiquettes for dealing with spirits and strangers. When the visitors did not respond in the expected manner, the reaction—often violent—was again normal in the circumstances. While there were always well-established societal mechanisms to deal with barter, trade, and interpersonal relations, when the situation got out of hand New Guineans reacted in a variety of ways. They asserted their control through physical force, called on supernatural forces, or retreated, remaining distant until the interlopers departed. From the point of view of New Guineans, the strangers were inferior wanderers searching for food and water, and were subject to local customs. Generally, when the meetings took place with some understanding on both sides, they were peaceful and productive.

The changes that followed more regular and sustained contact with exploration parties, missionaries, and government bases, together with use of men's labor on plantations, often led to social adjustment movements expressed through millenarian cults. Onwards from the mid-nineteenth century, these became a regular feature of New Guinea as the colonization process spread through the island. For example, a cult swept through the Huli and Ipili territories in the Papuan Highlands during the 1940s, combining knowledge of the "time of darkness" in the eighteenth century—when a volcanic eruption from Long Island darkened the Highlands—with the arrival of Europeans, and ritual innovation and pacification efforts. Old rituals and taboos were abandoned, replaced with new versions. Promises of prosperity were tied to the coming of the new colonial order. In some places accepting pacification was stressed as necessary to achieve the new wealth.[67]

••

Liminal moments occurred on the ship decks, in canoes alongside, in the distance between ships and canoes, on beaches, in gardens, open spaces, and border zones between language groups, but rarely in villages. Over time, New Guineans became used to the foreign intrusions, relying on missionaries or government officers to deal with some local problems, welcoming new trade items, such as axes and knives that made life easier, accepting some new ideologies relating to religion, health, gender, and other everyday aspects of life. Although first contact situations continued in the Highlands through into the 1950s, most of the coastal people came under the influence of the various colonial administrations seventy years earlier. There was a transition—in some places over hundreds of years and in others only over twenty years—during which an accommodation was reached between continuing local customs and allegiances, and changes imposed as political boundaries were drawn around them, by first colonial administrations and later new nation-states.

The New Guinea colonial frontier did not expand uniformly at any one time, nor was it a fixed geographical space or boundary slowly pushing out through the island. It was more like a mosaic with gaps between the pieces, its existence scattered over decades. It was a cross-cultural encounter, a place of hybridity. As Lynette Russell suggests, in relation to indigenous-European encounters in settler societies: "These are spaces, both physical and intellectual, which are never neutrally positioned, but are assertive, contested, and dialogic. Boundaries and frontiers are sometimes negotiated, contested, sometimes violent and often are structured by convention and protocol that are not immediately obvious to those standing on either one side or the other . . .; the frontier is an intellectual construct which has little if any salience to those people involved in its construction and maintenance."[68]

New Guinea never became a settler society, although there were those that had aspirations to develop the Highland valleys in this way. After the Hagen-Sepik patrol, James Taylor's vision was just that: "I think we should adopt the policy of the government of Kenya and reserve the highlands of New Guinea for Europeans . . . the existence of these highland areas make New Guinea . . . something between a second Java and a second New Zealand."[69]

The development of coffee plantations in the Highlands onwards from the 1950s could have sent Papua New Guinea down this path, but the rush to independence intervened. Instead, coffee planting has become largely an indigenous enterprise. Older Highlanders, who remember when the first Europeans entered their valleys, occupy hybrid space in a manner barely possible amongst coastal communities. However, to varying extents all New Guineans still live in two worlds, that of two modern nations and a thousand tribes.

Cultural Spheres and Refocusing Power

Chapter Two explored the cultural spheres concept, dividing the island into a series of lowland, mid-altitude fringe, and Highland spheres, each with core and fringe areas. It was argued that the relative importance of these cultural spheres was altered when indigenous trade routes and concentrations of indigenous power were inadvertently refocused by the imposed patterns of foreign exploration, exploitation, and settlement. For example, in Torres Strait, always a conduit for trade and exchange between Australia's Cape York and the Trans-Fly, European artifacts were added to existing trade routes in the 1790s, becoming increasingly available onwards from the 1820s, and readily obtainable after bêche-de-mer, pearling, mission, and government bases were established during the 1860s and 1870s. The new artifacts from outside were androgynous: some were earned by women through common labor and trade, and for sexual services, quite independent of their menfolk. But whoever obtained them, or however they were obtained, they enabled exchanges beyond the normal limits associated with long-standing religious and cultural practices. Small quantities of metal and glass objects were available in Torres Strait onwards from the 1790s; it is therefore quite conceivable that occasional foreign items could have been traded into the Highlands by the late 1790s. It is quite probable that some foreign articles were passed up the Fly River and its tributaries and into the southern Highlands by the 1820s and 1830s. This is a certainty by the 1870s, still half a century earlier than is usually supposed. Further, the presence of these foreign artifacts may partly explain the constant raids during the final decades of the nineteenth century by the Marind-Anim people east into the Trans-Fly, and similar western movements by the Kiwaian people.

Applying this hypothesis further, Torres Strait and the surrounding mainland coasts acted like a magnet for other indigenous groups who wanted the new artifacts but had no direct, or only very limited, access to them within their own territories. In the 1880s and 1890s, Torres Strait Islanders, due to concentrated missionary activity and some decades of immersion in intensive maritime industries, were the most "worldly" of all New Guineans. This result of colonial intrusion in the Strait altered the dynamics of power between the Strait's inhabitants and neighboring language-culture groups. At an individ-

I have come from 50,000 years.
So they think.
Others say I was born on 16 September, 1975.
Let my arrows fly another 50,000 years.

—Kumalau Tawali, "Niugini Panorama" mural, University of Papua New Guinea, 1984.

ual level, some precontact bigmen would have been able to enlarge their power bases, and new leaders became prominent based purely on advantages gained from contact with foreigners and their artifacts. Nonindigenous leaders also emerged from among the hundreds of foreign Pacific Islanders who worked in the Strait and married local women, founding dynasties that continue to be influential today.[1]

Similar precolonial scenarios for shifts in the foci of power can be created for areas of the Bismarck Archipelago, the west coast of Cenderawasih Gulf, and the regions around Port Moresby, or Humboldt Bay. The Gazelle Peninsula, the Duke of York Islands, and St. George's Channel between New Britain and New Ireland were on a shipping passage onwards from the late eighteenth century, and became whaling, trading, mission, and government bases during the first several decades of the nineteenth century. This increased the power of the local people vis-à-vis others on the margins of this area. Port Moresby, a mission and trading base from the 1870s, and a government base from the 1880s, was already the center of the *hiri* trade linking coastal and Highland fringe groups from Hula to the Gulf of Papua. In other regions, the reverse applied: they were important before European intervention, then suddenly lost their primacy when faced with new trade systems. An example is the *kula* ring in the Massim region off east New Guinea, which revolved around trade in valuables in a set direction, over an extensive time period before any European presence. What happened when these islands began to receive visits from whalers in the 1840s, or during 1847–1853 when a Marist Mission was established on Woodlark Island, or when they hosted bêche-de-mer fisherman and gold miners in the 1870s–1890s? Were some islands, previously peripheral to the *kula,* thrust into prominence by their new access to foreign trade goods? How was the *kula* affected when Sudest, Misima, the Calvados Chain, and Woodlark became the main European foci in the Massim?[2]

The initial change in New Guinea was largely a shift in power dynamics between the 1790s and 1920s, around the coast and in the mid-altitude fringe. Miners spread colonial influences in the Louisiades and on Woodlark Island in the 1880s and 1890s, amongst the Orokaiva in the northern rivers of British New Guinea in the 1890s, and on the Morobe goldfields at Bulolo and Wau on the northern edge of the Highlands in the 1920s. The Mandated Territory's Eastern Highlands was "opened" in the 1930s, with settlements begun at Mingende, Kundiawa, Goromei, and Goroka. This inland penetration, more complete in east New Guinea than in the west, must have caused changes in central power foci around Goroka and Kundiawa before the 1942–1945 War, and around Mt. Hagen and other nascent Highlands urban settlements (such as Tari and Mendi) in the 1950s. In the same manner as occurred around the coast (at Dorei in the 1850s, Thursday Island, Port Moresby, and Simpson Harbour in the 1870s), or in the Highland fringe (at Wau and Bulolo in the 1920s), in the 1950s Highland clans living closest to the new urban centers had a primary advantage over those further away, even though before colonial contact other groups may have possessed more important assets, or been better situated on key trade routes. Those close to settlements could readily sell their labor or garden produce, thus receiving primary access to trade goods, and also work for missions and the government. Any analysis of the modern New Guinea elite would find that they are often the descendants of early laborers, market-gardeners, carriers, mission staff, police, village constables, interpreters, and other government workers.[3]

Colonial Rule

At the Papua New Guinea Centennial Conference in 1984, Colin Newbury suggested four things that would most strike a resurrected 1884 official, merchant, or missionary. After consternation that the indigenous inhabitants were now governing New Guinea, they would notice an absolute involvement in a cash economy and in consumer spending among the much larger indigenous population (which has increased about three or four fold), and a far larger, more diverse expatriate population than existed a century earlier. They would notice that most of the population are still dependent on agriculture, although there has been a considerable diversification in crops, and that the transport systems have improved. Air travel became important in New Guinea onwards from the 1930s, with Papua New Guineans now using air travel as a standard method of conveyance. The third difference Newbury identified was that wage earning now occurs at all levels, in rural areas often in combination with subsistence activities. A dual economy operates and the public sector has become the largest formal employer. Last, missionaries would rejoice that Christianity has become ubiquitous in east New Guinea, but still feel sad that, despite the spread of education, many children still do not attend school.[4]

East New Guinea became German New Guinea (1884–1914), a *Schutzgebiet*—a mercantile territory (1884–1899), then a colony (1899–1914), and British New Guinea, first a Protectorate (1884–1888) then a colony (1888–1906).[5] Australia gained control of British New Guinea in 1906, renaming it the Territory of Papua.[6] German New Guinea fell to Australia on behalf of the Allies in 1914, the "Old Protectorate" becoming a League of Nations Mandate of Australia in 1921, and the "Island Territory" passing to Japan.[7] Mandated New Guinea became substantially a Japanese territory during the Pacific War, 1942–1945. Only its southern and central regions, and most of Australian Papua, remained under Australian military rule. Australia's two separate administrative units were combined in 1942, with headquarters in Port Moresby, slowly ironing out long-standing tensions between the two Australian administrations. After the war, the Australian New Guinea Administrative Unit was expanded to cover both Territories, the combination formalized by an act of parliament and the 1949 change of status for the Mandated Territory, which became a United Nations Trust Territory. Both Australian Papua and the Trust Territory achieved independence as one nation, Papua New Guinea, on 16 September 1975.[8] West New Guinea became nominally Dutch territory in 1828, a loose claim based on the suzerainty of the Sultan of Tidore. Between the 1890s and World War

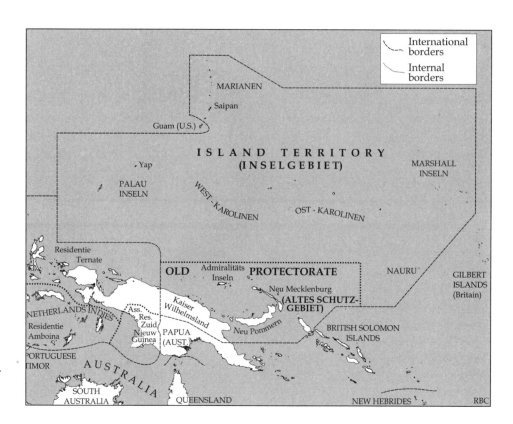

International and administrative boundaries in 1910

Two, Dutch New Guinea was administered through the Maluku Residency, control afterwards transferred to Hollandia, a government base from 1910, now the Indonesian city of Jayapura. The Dutch were forcibly evicted in 1963 following an Indonesian diplomatic and military victory. Control passed formally to Indonesia after a referendum in 1969.

New Guinea and adjacent islands were eventually divided into twenty-six administrative regions: eight in Dutch New Guinea, six in Australian Papua, and thirteen in the Mandated/Trust Territory. The titles of the chief executive varied, from Resident, to Administrator, Governor, or Lieutenant-Governor. Under constant financial limitations, the chief executives attempted to stretch minuscule budgets to cover exploration, extending areas of contact, pacification, and the introduction of legal codes, health, and education. Several of these administrators—men such as Albert Hahl, William MacGregor and Jan van Baal[9]—were of quite exceptional ability, while one—Hubert Murray in Australia Papua—became the longest-serving colonial governor anywhere in the world during the twentieth century.[10] In the main headquarter town of each colony, there was a small group of officials, backed by field-officers, known in east New Guinea as *Kiaps*. Each colony also had a small expatriate population involved largely in mission work, retailing, and running plantations. These expatriates joined Executive Councils, advising the administrators.

There were also indigenous officials at the village level—*Tultul* (interpreters), Village Constables and appointed Headmen (*Luluai*, or *Mamoose* in Torres Strait)—who implemented government orders and mediated between the people and the process of government. As Binandere historian John Waiko records, these were known as the "men who took the government shirt"—the black uniform given to leading Papuan men who became Village Constables. They served as intermediaries between Europeans and villagers, working as guides, interpreters, and messengers between government outstations, keeping local census and record books. In more controlled areas of Australian Papua they also supervised village cash crop production, which was introduced to encourage villagers to participate in the colonial economy, a side product of which was the ability to pay head taxes.[11]

Another interface was through the *Kiaps* based at outstations, patrolling with their colonial police forces. There were many dedicated colonial government officials who worked in New Guinea for long periods, as Resident Magistrates, or District Officers and their deputies. They administered huge populations, often combining their own career advancement and family life with ethnographic interests.[12] One innovation in New Guinea administration was the employment of government anthropologists and ethnographic training for field officers, which produced some very knowledgeable civil servants.[13] As discussed in the last chapter, recent analysis of the roles of the indigenous police indicates that they often were able to pursue their own agendas for power and advancement, well disguised from the officers who thought they were in control.[14] However, the overall administrative apparatus was so minimal that many Highlands areas remained beyond contact until the 1950s. For most villages away from the few patrol posts and towns, the "government" was an annual patrol that might attempt to collect Head Taxes, carry out a rudimentary census, attend to obvious criminal matters, and give very basic attention to health.[15] The *Kiap* then disappeared again for another year, during which time the only administrative presence might be a Village Constable or Government Headman, or (most often) a complete absence of state control.

Edward Said's writings about "Orientalism"—the Western conception of the Middle East and the Orient—have their valid critics, but it is hard to argue against his premise that all cultures tend to shape their representations of foreign cultures in order to master them better, or in some way control them. Any study of how Western knowledge depicted and understood Melanesia must examine the representations and the political power they express. With New Guinea, this is complicated by a Western differentiation between the Malay and Melanesian cultures, and also by Indonesian (mainly Javanese) conceptions of Melanesia as more primitive than the Malay cultural area. Added to this are Australian conceptions of differences between the Aboriginal and New Guinea cultures, even though officials who worked amongst Aborigines in the Northern Territory

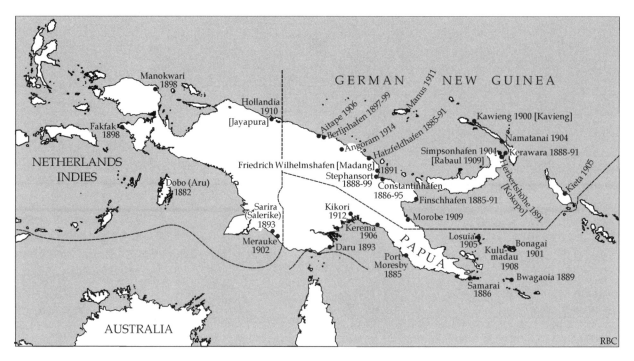

Government towns in
New Guinea, 1885–1914

and in colonial Papua and New Guinea were taught in the same Sydney training institution (known as ASOPA).[16]

In the racist colonial hierarchy, Torres Strait Islanders stood awkwardly between New Guineans and Australian Aborigines. Both Australian Aborigines and Melanesians were seen as doomed races and extinction was predicted, based more on sloppy reasoning and wishful thinking than empirical demographic data.[17] Australia inherited Papua, a British colony that had honored a commitment to preserve indigenous rights, but paradoxically, in the New Guinea Mandated Territory, held as an international trusteeship, Australia was far more severe in its handling of labor recruitment and indigenous living conditions more generally.

While it is easy to find examples of foreigners in New Guinea referring to the indigenous people as barbaric and less than human, the main administrators and field officers tried hard to understand the many different cultures they encountered. But even F. E. Williams, government anthropologist in Papua, explained to literate Papuans in 1930 that white racial superiority was innate, and that "no matter what the reason, these white men seem to be bosses wherever they go."[18] Curfews in towns, laws which forbad wearing clothes above the waist, exploitation of labor, and laws such as the draconian 1926 "White Women's Protection Ordinance" in Papua, were meant to keep the natives in their place—at the bottom of the colonial hierarchy. Urban enclaves like Port Moresby harbored the most racist foreigners, who brimmed with contempt for the natives and irrationally feared their sexuality and violence. The "No Natives, No Dogs" sign, which decorated Port Moresby's Ella Beach up until the 1960s, bluntly stated this deep-seated arrogant racism.[19]

Lewis Lett, private secretary to Hubert Murray, thought it was impossible to "think black," a common phrase in the 1910s and 1920s: "The nearest approach that we can make to it is to appreciate fully the fact that native mentality is not our mentality, that native experience differs totally from ours, and that native moral codes have been evolved through the centuries just as have our own, but differing in texture and pattern owing to the vastly less profuse material that has been presented for their use."[20] Expatriate colonists and responsible politicians in Australia thought that it would take an almost infinite amount of time to bring New Guineans into the modern world. The stress was on slow educational and health changes, left largely in the hands of the Christian missions, which would eventually lead to economic and political change. Up until the 1960s, there was little thought that New Guinea could be self-governing before the twenty-first century.

The Dutch, British, Germans, and Australians deserve no accolades for the manner in which they administered their New Guinea colonies. They made no real financial input until after 1945, and the 1960s push that moved Australian Papua and New Guinea quickly through to independence in 1975 was brought about by international pressures, and at such a forced pace that the exercise was detrimental to balanced development. Nevertheless, even this measures up well against Dutch neglect of the west. The Netherlands did not increase the resources it allocated to west New Guinea until after the Indonesian Revolution (1945–1949), a short-lived benevolence that Indonesia was unable and unwilling to match after 1963. Much of what follows in this chapter is inevitably a comparison of more rapid change in the east than in the west.

Economic Change

Colonial New Guinea was exploited for its ability to produce tropical crops grown on foreign-controlled plantations using indigenous and some imported labor. The first Gazelle Peninsula copra plantations were developed in the 1870s. The German Neu Guinea Kompagnie used an Asian and indigenous labor force to establish tobacco, kapok, and coffee plantations on the mainland of Kaiser Wilhelmsland, but these mainland plantations were never successful. When the Neu Guinea Kompagnie was wound up and the capital of the colony transferred from Finschhafen to Herbertshöhe (Kokopo) in 1899, the center of economic development moved from Kaiser Wilhelmsland to the Bismarck Archipelago. For the remainder of the German period, the island government stations were the real centers of the colony. Kerawara in southern Neu Mecklenburg (New Ireland) operated from 1888 to 1891, replaced by Kaewieng (Kavieng) in the far north in 1900 and Namatanai in 1904. Herbertshöhe on Neu Pommern's (New Britain's) Gazelle

Peninsula began in 1891, supplemented by Simpsonfhafen (1904), renamed Rabaul (1909), which became the third capital. Kieta, on Bougainville, was established in 1905, and the Manus base in 1911. Copra proved to be the main staple, with villagers encouraged to participate in the commercial economy, so that up until 1910 most of the copra exported from German New Guinea was produced from village plantations. A Head Tax was also introduced to force men to earn money, through work on plantations or in government service. The shift to foreign-owned plantations, initiated in the German period, advanced under Australian control of the Mandated Territory. Land alienation and exploitation was much more extensive in the northeast region than in the rest of New Guinea. Plantations in Australian Papua, one-third of the extent of those in the Mandated Territory, were neither as numerous nor as prosperous, and the labor force in Papua was only one-quarter of that indentured in the Mandated Territory. Attempts were made to grow sisal, cotton, and sugarcane, but only copra and rubber proved successful.[21] The agricultural economies of pre-Pacific War Papua and New Guinea depended mainly on copra, with rubber as the extra commodity in Papua.

For much of the colonial period, the main experience New Guineans had with the newly imposed economy was as laborers on plantation and mining ventures. In excess of one million Papua New Guineans worked for wages between 1884 and independence in 1975. This largely male circular-migratory indentured labor system employed far more workers than in all of the other Pacific Islands put together. Approximately 44,000 labor contracts were entered into in British New Guinea, and another 200,000 in the Territory of Papua before the Pacific War. Murray, Papua's Administrator until 1940, despite his desire to further European settlement, ensured that enlistment was voluntary, which meant Papuans never flocked to be laborers. In northeast New Guinea, 100,000 laborer contracts were issued in German New Guinea up until the Australian takeover in 1914, around 130,000 in German New Guinea under Australian military control, and another 280,000 in the Mandated Territory before 1942. If we add to these figures an unknown number of non-indentured wage laborers, it is clear that before the Pacific War three-quarters of a million men and some thousands of women made agreements as wage laborers. When all laborers in Australian Papua and New Guinea were released from their indentures in October 1945, and the indenture system was abolished in 1950, the labor system was thrown into disarray. A new Native Labour Ordinance, which remained in place from 1950 until 1974, replaced indenture and its penal sanctions with written agreements and pecuniary penalties. Although this was an improvement, and allowed more casual labor agreements, some critics labeled the 1950 Ordinance a quasi-indenture system which perpetuated plantation capitalism based on a subservient indigenous labor force. A second major change also began in 1950 and continued until 1974: the Highlands Labour Scheme mobilized 128,000 laborers from the huge labor reserve in the inland valleys, beginning a diaspora that is still expanding today.[22]

In Dutch New Guinea, commercial agricultural development was minimal. Private capital was seldom attracted and the Indies' government was more interested in developing other parts of the archipelago. A few small-scale colonists arrived in the 1920s — *totok-belanda*, ex-Indies public servants; and *indo-belanda,* pure Dutch and Eurasian Dutch — settling around Manokwari and Lake Sentani. They attempted to grow dry rice and bean crops for export. Rather like the Australian Soldier Settlers in the Mandated Territory after the First World War, they were ill-prepared and failed. During the 1930s, west New Guinea's production fell dramatically, export income reduced from Dfl 4,776,000 in 1928 — mostly earned from copra, resin and rattan — to Dfl 796,000 in 1935.[23] The main development was in oil production. In 1951, roughly one-quarter of Netherlands New Guinea's products still came from copra, resins, nutmeg, and mace, with petroleum exports making up the remainder. Gaining sufficient labor to run plantations was deemed a problem, which seems strange, given the extent of labor mobilization by German, British, and Australian planters and miners in east New Guinea.[24] Economic development in the west during the 1950s concentrated on export crops such as copra, nutmeg, cocoa, coffee, and rubber, with the initiative coming from the colonial government, since there were still few privately owned plantations. Sir Paul Hasluck, the Australian Liberal Minister for Territories (1951–1963), disliked anything leading to proletarianization, and ensured that, as far as possible, indigenous households remained attached to their land. Two schemes were developed, the first training indigenous farmers to produce cash crops on their own land, and the second using laborers paid to construct roads and small plantations, doubling up to grow cash crops, using government loans for finance. Cocoa was successfully introduced in many districts and nutmeg production was expanded. Cooperatives, which worked well in east New Guinea, were not as successful in the west.[25]

Papua New Guinea and Indonesia's Irian Jaya Province have remained essentially agricultural, with the majority of the population — seventy-five percent in Papua New Guinea, and a higher figure in Irian Jaya — engaged in subsistence agriculture. In Papua New Guinea, some 97 percent of the land is still communally owned, whereas in Irian Jaya Melanesians have lost large areas of their land to mining and to settlers arriving under Indonesia's transmigration programs *(transmigrasi)*. In villages all over New Guinea, taro, yam, sweet potato, tapioca, and sago form the main bulk in diets, supplemented by greens and small portions of protein. Fruits grow in abundance. Although droughts, floods, and other natural disasters — volcanic eruptions, storms, and tsunami — can regularly devastate regions, overall New Guinea is blessed with a high rainfall, abundant sunlight, and fertile soils. Village life in good times is an experience of natural abundance, however, when anything upsets the delicate balance, there are few reserves to fall back on, given that the bulk of the diet comes from root crops with short storage lives. Most rural people remain semi-subsistence farmers, practicing low intensity shifting cultivation, producing food and some cash crops from their gardens.

New Guinea developed a dual economy that allowed parallel development of a subsistence agricultural economy alongside a capitalist export economy. Village economies subsidized colonial economies, allowing cheaper, more profitable commercial production. The colonial governments manipulated the exploitation of mainly male wage labor, causing considerable hardship for women and children left to maintain subsistence, family, and other social commitments. In Papua and New Guinea, until the beginning of the 1970s commercial agriculture was still mainly confined to plantations, whereas in recent decades there has been rapid development of smallholder production. Once 90 percent of Papua and New Guinea's exports, copra now only accounts for 5 percent of overall production. Today Arabica coffee is the most important cash crop in Papua New Guinea. It has been the major crop in the Highlands since the 1950s, also now found in the Highland fringes of coastal provinces. Similarly, cocoa is grown in north coast and island provinces, and commercial oil palms grown by smallholders began producing in the 1960s. Fresh vegetables and betel nut are also sold for cash.[26]

New Guinea has two major self-regenerating natural economic assets: forests and fish. Tropical forests still cover the major part of the island, although only about one-quarter is accessible commercial forest. Almost all of the forest is on communally owned land. Timber extraction occurred on a large scale during the 1980s and 1990s, involving Asian companies that have acted rapaciously. New Guinea and the Solomon Islands are two of the last areas in the world where whole-log exports of tropical hardwoods continue. Government forest policies in both nations are not adequate to control the exploitation of this major natural resource.[27] Fishing remains a basic part of subsistence for most coastal New Guineans, often mixing age-old methods with modern style outboard motors mounted on fiberglass canoes. Commercial fisheries exist, mainly seeking tuna around the Bismarck Archipelago and off the tail of east New Guinea, using domestic catcher boats supplying mother ships, exporting frozen fish to America and Japan. There are also foreign vessels working on local licenses. Commercial prawn and lobster fisheries flourish in the Gulf of Papua. The only inland fisheries are for two introduced species, tilapia on the Sepik River, and trout at Goroka and other Highlands rivers and lakes.[28]

Exploitation of minerals has provided a huge boost to the economy, but aside from early panning for gold on the Laloki, Massim, and Morobe fields, and the similar 1980s indigenous boom at Mt. Kare in the Highlands, most of the oil, copper, and gold mining has required large capital investments from significant global corporations.[29] Oil seepages were known to exist in New Guinea for more than a century before drilling exploration began in the 1930s, the first oil well moving into production in the Bird's Head in 1936.[30] After the war, oil production continued in the west. Further exploration in the east brought enormous dividends in oil and natural gas generated from the Hides field in Papua New Guinea's Southern Highlands. If political unrest does not unseat the project, Kutubu gas will be linked to Australian industry via a pipeline early in the 2000s. The potential gas and oil wealth in the Southern Highlands is huge, but the province is increasingly crippled and out of control, run by warlords not the government, its future unclear.

Equivalent Irian Jaya gas fields are being developed in the Bintuni Bay region at the base of MacCluer Gulf (Berau Bay), with a planned start-up year of 2006. Vast mineral wealth also lies in copper and gold. Panguna copper mine in Bougainville (1969–1989) contributed 1.17 billion kina to the Papua New Guinea economy before being forced to close. Ok Tedi began by mining gold in 1984, and by 1987 it was the world's third biggest gold mine. Today it remains a significant but environmentally troubled copper mine. Gold is also mined at Misima, Lihir, Porgera, Tolukuma, Hidden Valley, and Wau (all in Papua New Guinea). New Guinea's gold and copper resources are amongst the richest in the world, providing by far the largest revenue export earner for Indonesia and Papua New Guinea. The huge Freeport Grasberg mine in Indonesian Papua began operations in 1967, presently providing 45 percent of Indonesia's tax base and foreign earnings. With an estimated $US54 billion of copper and gold still in reserves, it is probably the world's richest mine.[31]

When the Dutch made their last-ditch stand in west New Guinea between 1949 and 1963, they hurried to upgrade educational and employment opportunities. Papua and New Guinea went through a similar but more substantial metamorphosis between 1946 and 1975, particularly onwards from the 1960s when international pressure forced quick changes. Education systems were expanded rapidly and localization became the catch-cry. In Papua and New Guinea in the mid-1950s, 60 percent of the indigenous workforce was employed in primary production or mining. This percentage fell steadily: to 50 percent ten years later, and just over 30 percent at independence in 1975. Manufacturing, building, and construction grew steadily, while employees in education jumped from 222 in 1955 to 2,202 in 1965. Employees in the finance and property industries tripled between 1955 and 1973, but by far the fastest increase was in the government sector. In 1955 the Australian administration employed 7,763 indigenous workers. A decade later, the number had risen to 28,325. The public service, semi-government authorities, and the professions—particularly health, hospitals, and education—expanded rapidly as the range of services available to the community increased and expatriate positions were localized. Today, Papua New Guinea supports a large, inefficient, national and provincial public service, which is increasingly corrupt and mismanaged, and considerably beyond the nation's financial means.[32] Essential services are disintegrating. In most provinces, roads, postal services, health, education, and law and order are at a lower level in 2002 than at independence in 1975, while expectations in the community and the electorate are much higher. Having learned what is possible, communities are now asking vocally why it has not been achieved.

Social Change

Papua New Guinea glories in the tourist tag "land of the unexpected," which can equally be applied to the whole island. Visitors are always struck by the manner in which New

Guineans manage to combine old and new. While there are urban New Guineans who have never visited their parents' villages and have become alienated from traditional life, most manage to accommodate the two.

In 1968, Albert Maori Kiki, one of the founders of the modern Papua New Guinea nation, called his autobiography *Ten Thousand Years in a Lifetime*, signifying the extent of change that occurred during the decades after the Pacific War.[33] Development of modern states with sophisticated technologies has led to some quite bizarre cultural mixes. Villagers who remember the first time they saw a European can now make phone-calls to relatives living in other towns or overseas. Motuan women with full facial and upper body tattoos can be seen riding the escalators in Port Moresby shopping centers. Old men wearing *as-tanget* (a leaf-garment) and second-hand coats can be seen at domestic air terminals in the Highlands, sitting next to urban-based public servants on their way to finance meetings, swapping *buai* (betel nut) and chatting in *tok pisin*.

Traditional practices have taken on modern significance. In Irian Jaya, where *Bahasa Malay* was used as a trading language long before Indonesia existed, an indigenized form of modern *Bahasa Indonesia* is used, giving New Guineans a private dialect of the national language. In Papua New Guinea, the practice of lopping off finger joints, a traditional sign of mourning among Highlands families, was used to mark the 1986 death of Highlands political leader Sir Iambakey Okuk. As a lecturer at the University of Papua New Guinea in the 1980s, I learnt that when a student came to my office plastered in mud he was in mourning and about to request an extension for an essay deadline. Sir Wiwa Korowi, Papua New Guinea's Governor-General in the 1990s, as his tradition allows, had several wives, but to satisfy British royal etiquette designated only one to be Lady Korowi. In May 2002, while visiting the Goilala settlement behind Port Moresby's Baruni rubbish dump, I was entertained by dancers wearing body ornamentation augmented by glittering Christmas decorations. Such is the blend of the traditional and the modern that exists in contemporary New Guinea, as it does all over the postcolonial world.

Initially, the education system all over New Guinea was left totally to Christian missions, each given an exclusive region in which to proselytize. Over the last forty years the government and church system has expanded at all levels and has been integrated. Primary and secondary education increased rapidly.[34] A few years after independence, 56 percent of Papua New Guinea's school-age children attended community (primary) schools. Early goals of universal primary education have not been reached, due to the government's failure to provide schools in isolated areas and parents' inability to afford basic fees. In 1995–1996, around 20 percent of primary school-age children did not attend school.[35] The emphasis in primary education has been on community based education that relates formal schooling with community life, and on vernacular education. Secondary and tertiary education barely existed before 1960. The number of provincial high schools expanded during the 1960s, with a select number of students continuing on to specialist grade 11–12 schools for matriculation. Even though the upper secondary system expanded during the 1990s, on average the delivery rate falls at about 10 percent each year of the school system, leaving only 10 percent of the initial entry group as matriculants. Growth also came in the form of a great variety of post-secondary training institutions. Universities were established in Jayapura in 1962, Port Moresby in 1966, and Lae in 1974, with four more Papua New Guinea tertiary institutions upgraded to university status in 1996. There are now fifty-five institutions of higher education in Papua New Guinea, catering for a wide range of skill training.[36]

In Dutch New Guinea before the war, education was almost all at the village level, in designated elementary and "civilization" schools, the latter extremely basic. There was one secondary school, and one training school for teachers, at Miei. After 1949, the Dutch government engaged in rapid localization, training indigenous civil servants. The Hollandia public servant training school became the Institute for Administrative and Legal Sciences, part of what became Cenderawasih University in 1962. Elementary schooling and higher vocational training for West New Guineans, in subsidized and non-subsidized schools, increased rapidly, from 26,417 students in 1952 to 40,615 in 1961. Over the same time period, funding for education rose, from Dfl 3,850,900 to Dfl 17,723,100. The village school system expanded rapidly, and by the time the Dutch left, 68 percent of the teachers were indigenous. Under Indonesian rule, the percentage of children not at school is much higher than in Papua New Guinea, probably still around 50 percent.[37]

In the mid-1960s, 5 percent of New Guineans lived in towns. Ten years later, this percentage had doubled. Much of the growth in the workforce was in urban areas. In the late 1960s, Port Moresby increased in size by 10.8 percent per year, Lae increased by almost 16 percent in the same period, and Mt. Hagen, Madang, and Goroka by 12.1, 10.4, and 9.8 percent. Over the same years on Bougainville, the copper mine caused the Panguna-Arawa-Kieta urban area to grow at 78.4 percent per year.[38] In the 2000 census, Port Moresby recorded a population of 252,469, with an overwhelmingly indigenous population. Jayapura is estimated to be of similar size, but eighty percent of Jayapura's population is non-Papuan. Timika, the urban development for the Freeport mine, has a population of 110,000. Workers and their extended families have migrated to urban areas at a very rapid rate, far beyond the speed of infrastructure development, which has led to squatter settlements, high urban unemployment, and large social problems, particularly *raskolism* (criminal gangs) and unrest.[39]

The colonial state ensured the circulation of labor while also maintaining traditional society. Minimal proletarianization has occurred because most workers have eventually returned to their home villages. Since the 1960s, class formation has proceeded at an ever-increasing pace, based initially on the families of elites created in the colonial years —mission workers, police, teachers, public servants, and local politicians.[40] An intermarried ruling class exists in urban areas, particularly in Port Moresby, Jayapura, and provincial towns, based on this early elite and more recent business success. In rural areas, particularly those with a substantial cash crop base in coffee and cocoa, the indigenous elite has accumulated private land and grown rich on commercial agriculture and business ventures. There is a small but ever-expanding urban proletariat, and a developing urban bourgeoisie. Some New Guinea business operators have excelled, notably those from the Papua New Guinea Highlands, where in one generation some families have moved from subsistence to cash-cropping, then to transport and merchant businesses. Papua New Guinea millionaires are increasingly common, but alongside them are another new phenomena—the displaced, homeless poor. During the final decades of the twentieth century in the Papua New Guinea Highlands, a coffee boom led to reliance on "casual" labor, but there were also the beginnings of a landless rural proletariat, dislocated from the precolonial land tenure system that provided access to land for all. In urban centers, many local villagers and squatters (urban fringe-dwellers) rely totally on wage earning. Beggars appeared on Port Moresby's streets for the first time in the late 1980s, signaling that kin-based support systems were breaking down. Violence, bred from desperation, has begun to mar urban centers, to an extent that the elite have fortified themselves, and security services are a fast-growing sector of the economy. The Papua New Guinea government's main responses to *raskolism* have been to introduce States of Emergency, and strengthen the police. However, as Sinclair Dinnen argues, this criminal gang phenomenon partly arises out of traditional culture and bigman roles. It is best combated by church and community organizations, and by the government providing alternative development opportunities, thus generating incomes to redirect gang behavior.[41]

Rural life is also affected, there having been a serious decline in the delivery of services since independence. The 2001 *Papua New Guinea Rural Development Handbook* paints a dismal picture: "The gradual decline of roads, shipping and airlines over the past decade has reduced the delivery of services. This situation has been compounded by smaller government budgets and highly centralized funding programs, which have led to the closure of aid posts and health centers, particularly in remote areas. Those that remain open are often under-stocked with basic supplies, including anti-malaria drugs and antibiotics. The churches are now one of the main providers of health services in rural areas."[42]

Infant and child mortality rates are high and increasing, with rural deaths nearly twice those in urban areas. Despite these serious problems, New Guineans have largely maintained their languages, customs, and value systems, or at least modernized versions of them. Papua New Guinea government policy supports this pride in regional ethnicity while also trying to encourage national sentiments. While a more cynical interpretation would be that the government has been busy constructing a modern national identity, using *kastom* as an ideology of control, and at the same time being buffeted by consumerism and other forces beyond its control, nevertheless the commitment, even if very imperfectly delivered, is more than just rhetoric. This is altogether different from the situation in Irian Jaya, where the Indonesian government shows barely concealed scorn for local culture, advocates the use of Bahasa Indonesia rather than local languages, and inculcates belief in the superiority of Indonesia's Hindu, Buddhist, and Islamic past.

The Second World War

The most significant alteration to the colonial status quo in New Guinea came unexpectedly, in the form of cataclysmic war and invasion. There are no exact demographic statistics concerning New Guinea's population when war began. We do know that there were 1,488 Europeans and three Chinese in Australian Papua, and 4,445 Europeans and 1,838 Asians in the Mandated Territory.[43] Indigenous census details, however, are far from complete: 200,000 indigenous inhabitants were recorded in Papua and 581,000 in the Mandated Territory—the real numbers were probably twice as high. Papua's annual revenue was just over £150,000, one-quarter coming from an Australian government grant. The Mandated Territory's annual revenue was nearly £500,000, all raised within the Territory.[44] There were estimated to have been less than 200,000 indigenous inhabitants and only a very small number of Dutch and Asians in west New Guinea.[45] During the Pacific War (1941–1945) Australian Papua and New Guinea and Netherlands New Guinea were invaded by 300,000 Japanese, more than one million Americans, and several hundred thousand Australians. The burden of war was uneven, falling more heavily on the north coast and adjacent islands. From being a colonial backwater, in 1942 New Guinea suddenly became the center of a crucial phase of the Japanese advance, countered by a huge Allied war effort to force their retreat.[46]

The Dutch seventy-three-man garrison at Manokwari fell immediately, a small force taking to the mountains to conduct guerrilla warfare. Merauke and the upper-Digul regions on the south coast were the only places where the Dutch flag remained flying in the Indies during the war, despite their being bombed from the air. An Assistant Resident carried on limited administration duties from Merauke.

In January, February, and March 1942, the Japanese landed at Rabaul, Finschhafen, Lae, Salamua, and Lorengau, then at Manokwari, Babo, Kokas, and Sorong in April, gaining full control of the north coast and eastern archipelagos. Port Moresby, the key New Guinea base from which an attack could be mounted on Australia, underwent heavy bombardment in April and May. The Japanese advance south was thwarted during the Battle of the Coral Sea (4–8 May), when a Japanese amphibious invasion fleet retreated to Rabaul. The next phase was a Japanese overland assault from Buna across the Owen Stanley Mountains—along the Buna *dala* (road) or Kokoda Track. By August they had managed to get within fifty kilometers of Port Moresby, at the same time attempting (unsuccessfully) to overrun the American base at Milne Bay. During the remainder of 1942, the Allies fought a counterattack along the Kokoda Track. Buna, Gona, and Sananda were finally wrested from the Japanese early in 1943. Later in the year, the Allies regained control of the Huon Peninsula, then jumped over the Japanese bases at Rabaul, Madang, and Wewak to capture Aitape, Hollandia, and Tanah Merah Bay, which were considered more logistically important for retaking the Philippines. Until 1945, Japanese troops remained imbedded around Wewak and the Sepik River, New Ireland, Buka, southern Bougainville, and on New Britain's Gazelle Peninsula. Allied blockades caused severe supply shortages, souring earlier good relations between north coast New Guineans and the Japanese when hungry troops began to loot gardens and villages.[47]

The human impact is almost too great to assess. Papua New Guinea historian, Keimelo Gima, succinctly stated the change that occurred: "For the first time, there was a realization of the true human nature of both races. On the one hand, through their heroic efforts in saving the lives of thousands of Allied soldiers, Papua New Guineans were now seen as friends who could be trusted during times of need. They were more than just 'kanakas' who only waited for orders from the white masters. On the other hand, the myth of White supremacy was erased from the minds of Papua New Guineans who had witnessed white men getting hurt, killed and running away from danger. The Pacific war was the turning point in the history of PNG."[48]

Troops and equipment in unimaginable quantities poured into the islands, multiple airstrips and hospitals were constructed, seemingly overnight. Major airstrips were built in many coastal areas, enabling both sides to use aircraft, leaving New Guinea a legacy which provided the foundation of their postwar air transport system. The Allies built eight strips at Nadzab, seven at Port Moresby, and four at Dobodura. Others were scattered about the eastern islands (Goodenough, Woodlark, and Kiriwina), on New Britain (Cape Gloucester, Talasea, and Hoskins), in the Markham Valley (Kaiapit and Dumpu), on Manus, and at Torokina on Bougainville. The Japanese built four airstrips at Rabaul, two each at Lake Sentani, Wewak, and Alexishafen, and others at Tadji (near Aitape), Bogia, Madang, and Kavieng.[49]

The prewar colonial regimes were carefully constructed edifices with no substance, based on very limited resources and relying on New Guineans not being able to communicate with the outside world. Then came the war and a hasty, ignoble retreat for the ostensibly vastly superior Dutch and Australian "masters" who had lorded it over the local people for so long. These cracks in the colonial edifice suddenly showed just how flimsy it all was, split wide open when literally millions of foreigners with very different agendas passed through. Japanese, American, and Australian soldiers were initially friendly, then increasingly authoritarian in dealing with the local people. New Guineans were unceremoniously forced into supplying labor to both sides. Nevertheless, despite advice not to get too close to the "natives," soldiers at war faced with life-and-death situations operated in a very different way to the prewar "masters." Supplies were shared, close friendships made in the heat of battle, and Black American troops provided inspiration for New Guineans.

The Allies relied on New Guineans as carriers and laborers, and the police became guides and scouts. Local infantry battalions were raised in east and west New Guinea during 1944. The Japanese also conscripted labor and carriers, although they rarely used them as police or soldiers. Along the north coast, the Japanese spent four years in control, replacing Australian and Dutch local administrations with their own version. Wartime children such as Michael Somare—later Papua New Guinea's first Prime Minister and most distinguished citizen—attended Japanese primary schools. Sir Michael retains good memories of the Japanese in his Sepik village.[50] New Guineans traveled widely during the war, both within the islands and to surrounding areas, which facilitated a flow of new ideas and understandings into previously isolated communities. This translated into new indigenous social and economic movements, which were proto-nationalist and forerunners of modern political awareness. It also prepared some New Guineans, despite the lapse from 1945 to the 1960s, for greater political service in local and eventually national government.

Political Change, Decolonization, and Independence

Political activity is a central feature of community and clan relationships among New Guineans. Over tens of thousands of years, debates and political lobbying have been part of village life, involving informal, lengthy, circumlocutory discussions and persuasion, arriving at decisions by consensus, not voting. Males have always held most formal political positions, but there is no doubt that women also exert influence in village-level decision-making. Then, after thousands of years of governance through a thousand different small-scale language-based societies, the people of New Guinea were subjected to a short European colonial intrusion—an interregnum of less than one hundred years. Coastal clans and language groups living near European settlements gained advantages through easy access to new educational and health services. They also enjoyed the dubious pleasures of wage labor and were exposed to Christianity and Islam. Inland peoples, particularly those deep in the mountain fastness of the Highlands, may have had occasional visits from colonial officers each year over decades, or even remained beyond the range of government contacts until after the Second World War. Well over one million Highlanders, a large part of the New Guinea population, lived relatively undisturbed into the 1950s, such was the slowness of evolving contact with colonial administrations and the outside world.

The earliest attempts by New Guineans to try to come to terms with the foreign intrusion were described in Chapter Seven. Later, in the twentieth century, many new religious movements were created that were often messianic and charismatic. Branded by most European observers as irrational "cargo cults," they were based around visionary individuals who, using ritual action and supernatural appeal, explained change and how their people could adjust to new circumstances. There are examples of such leaders and movements in west New Guinea as far back as the 1850s, followed by a continuous string of similar movements all over New Guinea and Island Melanesia up until recent decades. Such "cults" were perfectly rational within the scope of Melanesian cosmology and culture, where economic advantage is often sought through ritual action. Some observers viewed these movements only as proto-nationalist responses to colonialism. Administrators usually deplored them, but they are anchored deep in the Melanesian psyche and are not easily ignored or explained.[51]

The 1929 Rabaul strike, when thousands of laborers walked away from work, de-

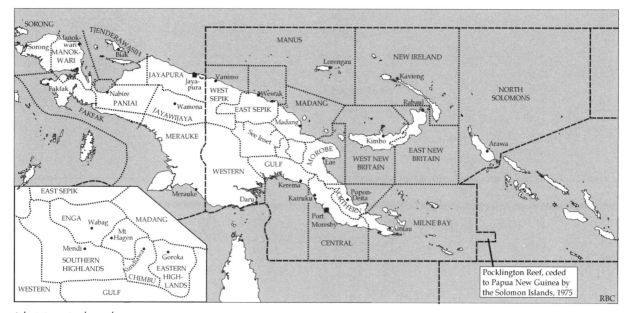

Administrative boundaries in the 1970s: Propinsi Irian Jaya (Indonesia) and Territory of Papua and New Guinea (Australia)

manding better wages and conditions, was the first well-organized attempt to confront colonial control.[52] Australia, by then one of the most unionized nations, was not willing to extend the same rights to its colonial subjects in New Guinea. The indenture system, abolished in Australia, continued in Papua and New Guinea until 1950. After the Pacific War, long before trade unions began to appear, native workers' associations emerged in the form of welfare societies and cooperative movements. Some of their leaders—for instance, Albert Maori Kiki and John Guise—became national political leaders in the 1960s and 1970s. A variety of local church councils and a few informal government councils existed before the Pacific War. *Kiaps* consulted villagers at large meetings called *kivungs*. In 1927, Sir Hubert Murray encouraged the Motu-Koita villagers around Port Moresby to elect councilors, a process repeated in 1929 and 1935. These councilors provided a forum to discuss the problems of semi-urban villagers, individual members acting as assessors for government courts in matters concerning native custom and compensation. Local councils lacked any statutory authority or finances, until Australia enacted the *Papua and New Guinea Act, 1949*, and the *Native Government Councils Ordinances, 1949–60*, which passed to local councils many of the powers formerly exercised by Village Constables in Papua, and *Luluais*, their equivalents in Australian New Guinea. The first village councils were established on the Gazelle Peninsula (New Britain), at Hanuabada village (Port Moresby), and on Baluan Island in Manus District. In 1954, these village councils officially became "local councils," with the intention of fostering economic development as training for future political self-government. Village Constables were attached to council areas, and local councils became responsible for collecting all direct taxes, making regulations on a range of local issues from gambling to community work, control over weapons, diseases, and plant pests. These councils were subject to Department of Native Affairs advisors.

Efforts to introduce universal local government and the council systems were extended after 1963, by a *Local Government Ordinance* that was operational by 1965, with a Director of District Administration appointed in 1967. Although these councils varied enormously in size, level of economic development, and efficiency, by 1967 there were 139 councils covering 82 percent of the Australian Papua and New Guinea population. The 1963 *Ordinance* also removed the word "native," a significant change allowing nonindigenous residents to stand for and vote in elections. Six years later, 111 of the 142 councils were multiracial, amid growing indigenous allegations that Australians were dominating the local-level political process. All of this came to a head in the Gazelle Peninsula, where the Mataungan Association mounted concerted, violent opposition.[53]

Before the Pacific War, the Administrators were advised by small nominated Executive and Legislative Councils. These expanded after the war into one Legislative Council with elected members including the first indigenous representatives. Nominated District Advisory Councils, with expatriate members chaired by the local District Commissioner, began in the 1940s, with indigenous members added in 1956. By the mid-1960s, the majority of its members were indigenous. A Local Government Association was formed in 1968, bolstered in 1971 by a *Local Government (Authorities) Act*, beginning a second level of local government, creating district-level bodies with authority over local councils. In 1961, the Legislative Council was expanded to thirty-seven members. Six elected and six nominated members were indigenous. With moves for greater representation already underway, in 1962 a United Nations mission under Sir Hugh Foot recommended the creation of a 100-seat parliament elected by adult suffrage on a common roll. This came to fruition as the House of Assembly in 1964, which has continued until today as the National Parliament.[54]

The 1964 national election in Papua and New Guinea, based on a 1,028,339-person electoral roll, was the first large-scale exercise in democracy in New Guinea.[55] Since then, Papua New Guinea has had regular democratic elections. A very Melanesian style of politics developed, quite aberrant from the system that Australia designed. This was inevitable in a nation where the many political parties formed since the 1960s lack consistent ideologies, and politicians are very pragmatic and self-seeking, representing their own clans rather than their electorates. Trade unions have never been strong in Papua New Guinea. Individual workers lack class consciousness, and there is no strong labor element in national or provincial politics. Primary identification remains at a clan level, spiraling out without significant allegiance to provincial towns, provinces, and finally the nation. The great triumph is that citizens call the tune and regularly throw out any government or politician of whom they disapprove.[56]

The Papua New Guinea nation that emerged in 1975 was based on a colonial unification of small-scale societies administered as districts, which although they bore some relationship to preexisting cultural spheres had been created piecemeal as government services spread.[57] Right from 1973, when Bougainville, bolstered by the Panguna copper mine, established an interim provincial government, the districts all wanted a measure of autonomy. This move was legitimized by the 1974 *Provincial Government Act* and the 1977 *Organic Law on Provincial Government*, which led to the establishment of nineteen provinces, each with a constitution and an elected Provincial Assembly. The provincial system was not successful: 90 percent of funds came from the national government; there was excessive duplication of government functions; and, at one time or another, most provincial governments were suspended for corruption and incompetence. Reviews in the 1990s led to the abolition of the provincial system in 1995, but conflict existed in Bougainville where rebels had closed the mine in 1989 and were demanding independence. Protracted negations led in 2001 to the renamed North Solomons Province being granted autonomy, with the promise of a future ballot on total independence. This dispute over regional autonomy rocked Papua New Guinea to its foundations all through the 1990s, as a series of inept military campaigns, including actions employing foreign mercenaries, failed to subdue the rebels. The Bougainville dispute exposed the fragile basis of the provincial system and led to national soul-searching about the relationship between the central government and its citizens.[58]

Of the three European nations that once exercised colonial rights over New Guinea, Australia has maintained the closest relationship with its ex-colony. Proximity and continuing large-scale investment will ensure that this connection continues, despite periodic difficulties. Since the 1940s, tens of thousands of Australians have worked in Papua New Guinea, and many Papua New Guineans have been educated in Australia, maintaining a warmth of feeling that extends well beyond the colonial relationship. Australia has given in excess of A$300 million in aid to Papua New Guinea every year since independence, though the aid is now totally "tied," and a degree of resentment is apparent whenever Australia seems to be dictating the terms of the ongoing relationship. Germany has a normal diplomatic relationship with Papua New Guinea, its colonial ties now largely forgotten. After many years of strained relations with its ex-Indies colony, including nationalization of Dutch investments during the 1950s and the breaking of diplomatic relations in 1960, the Netherlands now has an amicable relationship with Indonesia, but does not place any particular stress on connections with Irian Jaya.

Papua New Guinea's volatile but democratic political system contrasts sharply with the sad fate of indigenous politics in Indonesian west New Guinea.[59] At the end of the Pacific War, the Netherlands installed a military administrator, who was replaced in July 1946 by a Resident based at Hollandia. In 1949, as a consequence of the Round Table Conference between the newly victorious Indonesian Republic and the Netherlands, control of the East Indies was transferred, except for the Residency of New Guinea. The Dutch reasoned that by holding onto west New Guinea they maintained some status as a colonial power, and a foothold in the Pacific, and could resettle Indies' Dutch Eurasians around Manokwari. Although hardly consulted, this also suited the few politically-conscious New Guineans, who saw that they could have a better future away from Indonesia.[60] Netherlands New Guinea, administered by a Governor, was divided into four divisions: north, west, south, and central, the latter still beyond administrative "control," aside from the Wissel Lakes which were added to the northern division. The other three divisions had administrative headquarters respectively at Hollandia, Sorong, and Merauke, under Residents with similar powers to the District Commissioners on the Australian side. Divisions were divided into Subdivisions, headed by Controllers, and Districts, supervised by indigenous or Indonesian Assistant Administration Officers. The Dutch established an advisory New Guinea Council of twenty-one members, one of whom was indigenous, nominated by the Governor. From 1951 there was also an Advisory Council for Native Matters for the north, west, and south regions, the majority of whom were indigenous, nominated by the Governor.[61]

Around half of the development expenditure came from the Dutch Treasury. It took many years before local government and mission work spread into more remote areas. As urban centers swelled with the arrival of *indo-belanda* fleeing Indonesia, basic health and educational facilities expanded quickly. The public service was indigenized, to include 19,000 New Guineans by 1962. Young Dutch patrol officers, similar to the Australian *Kiaps* in the east, extended services into rural areas. The first political parties began in the 1950s. In 1961, the *Raad*, a New Guinea Council, was established in Hollandia with twenty-eight elected members. "Papuans" was adopted as the name of the people, and Papua Barat (West Papua) as the name of the future colony and nation. There were a variety of opinions on the length of time the Dutch should remain and the future relationship with Indonesia. Many regional community councils were operating, supporting the *Raad*, and political consciousness was developing among the people. Indonesia, always opposed to Dutch rule, had tried to get United Nations endorsement for its claim over west New Guinea on three occasions during the 1950s, then in 1962 it sent armed troops to wage guerrilla war against the Dutch. The United States, and eventually Australia, supported Indonesia in the dispute. Left with no options, through the New York Agreement of 15 August 1962 the Netherlands transferred sovereignty to the United Nations in October 1962, leading to a handover to Indonesia on 1 May 1963. The essential handover condition was that a plebiscite be held in 1969, allowing the people to decide their own future. When the Dutch withdrew, the indigenous population was estimated to be 487,800, along with 16,600 Asians (Chinese and Indonesians), and 15,500 Europeans (mainly Dutch).

Indonesia acted rapidly to integrate Netherlands New Guinea into Indonesia, changing the name of its new Province to Irian Jaya, stripping out many of the assets the Dutch had assembled, and repressing the indigenous people.[62] The new Governor took his orders directly from President Sukarno. Although a Regional People's Assembly, with an indigenous majority, replaced the *Raad*, it had no power, no control over the provincial budget, and could make no laws independently. Administrative power moved from the public service to the army. In 1968, President Suharto passed a decree placing Irian Jaya under the authority of a section of the Ministry of Domestic Affairs that was controlled by army generals. Although there were nine Regents (*Bupati*) of subdivisions, six of them indigenous, in reality the administration was so tightly controlled from Jakarta that they were allowed no initiative. In 1966, rebels from around Manokwari proclaimed the "Papuan Free State." Rebellion continued through the next few years in several areas and between 1966 and 1969 approximately 2,500 people fled across the border into Papua and New Guinea. The 1969 "Act of Free Choice" became known as the "Act of No Choice," because Indonesia blatantly manipulated the vote to get the result that it wanted, and the international community chose to ignore the disaster. A heavily indoctrinated group of 1,025 "representatives" voted unanimously in open meetings (there were no secret ballots) to remain with Indonesia. This was an unforgivable travesty of democracy, at a time when Australian Papua and New Guinea had more than one million voters on the electoral role for the election of the first representative legislature in 1964.[63]

From the point of view of the Indonesian Republic, the nation had regained territory belonging to the Netherlands East Indies' colony and rightfully part of the new Republic. West New Guinea was a substantial asset, a huge mineral-rich province. Rule by the army and central control are normal in Indonesia. Ignorance of the cultures and rights of the indigenous peoples of the Province, who are seen as primitive and in need of re-education and cultural incorporation within Indonesia, is also normal in an Indonesian context. The mountain peoples of Kalimantan (Borneo) and other outer-island Provinces have fared no differently.

Indonesia was more concerned with conducting military campaigns against the rebels, and establishing the Freeport mine, which began production in 1973, than with furthering the needs of the indigenous population. State school education and health services did expand, but while there were 20,000 secondary school leavers in 1979, most received a general education with no vocational training. This, and the incorporation into Indonesia, means that the majority of technical and public sector jobs went to Indonesians born in other provinces, leaving educated west New Guineans as laborers, or unemployed. Health services remained poorly staffed, lacking essential drugs and equipment. Common diseases, which had begun to decrease in the 1950s, were increasing in the 1970s and 1980s. The military introduced disease-infected pigs into Irian Jaya in 1970, with disastrous results for the herds that were part of the food supply and central to the ceremonial culture of the indigenous people.

The most obvious changes were linked to *transmigrasi*, the government-sponsored transmigration program that resettled Indonesians from overpopulated islands such as Java, into Irian Jaya. More recently, this government scheme has been supplemented by spontaneous migration to the province. Exact figures are difficult to establish, however there are thought to have been around 500,000 voluntary or economic migrants from eastern Indonesia, exceeding the 300,000 who had migrated under government-sponsorship. Many have been resettled in a band along the central border with Papua New Guinea, expanding infrastructure development into once isolated areas, but also forcing the indigenous people off of their communal lands, leaving them as alienated laborers, forced to survive by adopting "Indonesian" values. In 2002, the population of Indonesia's Papua Province is estimated to be approaching 3 million, including in excess of 1.2 million migrants from Indonesia to the west.[64]

Organisasi Papua Merdeka (OPM), the Free Papua Movement, has existed since the 1960s. It is a small guerrilla opposition movement, in reality a number of unconnected guerrilla groups based around specific local communities and areas. For thirty years the OPM groups have fought a stubborn but sporadic campaign, armed with traditional weapons and captured guns. With no overseas military support, the OPM, even though the movement has popular support, has little chance of success, but it remains a thorn in Indonesia's side with a strong international profile and media acknowledgement. The OPM is a constant reminder to the indigenous people of Irian Jaya that they do not have to accept Indonesian rule. Significant problems occurred along the Papua Province/Papua New Guinea border in the 1980s and 1990s, causing tens of thousands of refugees to flee into Papua New Guinea.[65] Elements within the Indonesian army have assassinated important Papuan leaders, such as Arnold Ap in 1984, and the foremost independence leader, Theys Hiu Eluay, in 2001, causing continuing resentment.

Effectively, Papua Province is ruled by the Indonesian armed forces. The state provides only about 25 percent of the military budget, the remainder coming from military business operations. Irian Jaya is a significant source of military wealth, obtained through everything from logging concessions to smuggling, and exports of rare flora and fauna. The current government policy, orchestrated through the army, encourages the growth of militia gangs operating against the Papuans, similar to those Indonesia encouraged in East Timor. Indeed, the 2002 military commander in Papua Province, Simbolan, was previously in charge of Indonesia's military operations in East Timor. The Indonesian government has no idea how to accommodate or quell Papuan nationalism, other than by military suppression and encouragement of unofficial militia gangs. In 2001, Indonesia announced special autonomy status for the Papua Province, aimed at halting moves for succession. Papua New Guineans at all levels feel sympathy for their kin across the border, and, given the instability of Indonesian and Papua New Guinean national and provincial politics, the future is highly uncertain.[66]

. . . .

In 2002, Papua New Guinea and Indonesias Papua Province had a combined population of around 8.2 million people, 5.2 million of them in Papua New Guinea, predominantly

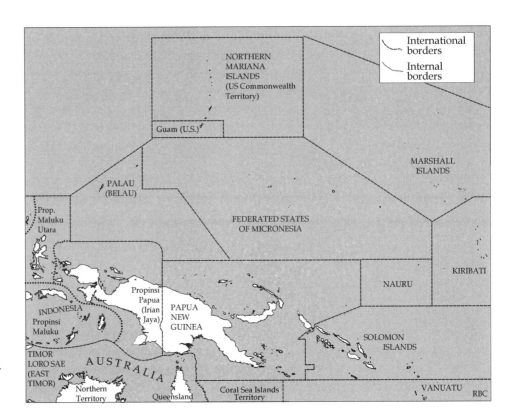

International and administrative boundaries in 2002

of indigenous origin, and 3 million of them in Papua Province, of mixed origins. The rate of population increase is likely to be high. Papua New Guinea's population has doubled in the past thirty years, and is expected to double again by 2030.[67] The same can be expected in Papua Province, where the recent immigrant population is increasing faster than the Papuans. These increases will be tempered by the uncontrolled spread of HIV/AIDS in New Guinea, which may cause the same rate of population decrease as is expected in areas of Africa and Asia.[68] The Indonesianization of west New Guinea—the introduction of a Malay population through *transmigrasi* and casual migration—must eventually, during the next century or two, affect the whole island. Over the next several centuries, the new migrants will cause enormous cultural changes in west New Guinea, the importance of which will outlive the nation-states of Indonesia and Papua New Guinea. At one level, *transmigrasi* is no more than the continuation of a long-established process that was already under way when the Austronesian migrations took place 3,000 to 5,000 years ago, a process merely slowed by the Dutch interregnum. But this has been complicated by the advent of nation-states with firm boundaries. Charles Rowley pointed out at Papua New Guinea's Centennial History Conference that: "Had there been no industrial revolution in Europe, there might well have been paddy fields on the great rivers of New Guinea, in which case those villagers who resisted would, as in the islands east of Java, have been driven into the uplands and the mountains to carry on their shifting slash-and-burn agriculture."[69] Perhaps this is an exaggeration, but the point is worth considering. The export of New Guinea's products west into the Malay Archipelago—humans as slaves, birds, tree bark, and shells—was many centuries old when Europeans arrived in the sixteenth century. Colonization, through trade and the Islamic religion, had already begun. However, the trade between New Guinea and Maluku was a two-way process, and until Europeans provided their weapons to bolster the Sultans' *hongi* raids, New Guineans seem to have been fairly equal partners in the exchanges. Still, over recent centuries, the advantage appears to have been with the people of Maluku, not New Guineans.

The intrusion of British and German colonialism into east New Guinea in 1884, replaced in two stages, 1906 and 1914, by that of the Australian nation, created a much briefer interregnum in the east. Although Australia formally withdrew from Papua New Guinea in 1975, neocolonialism through aid and investment, and the ever-looming proximity of a neighboring highly affluent society of nineteen million people, continue to affect Papua New Guinea. Its boundaries are colonial relics—half a huge island and the northern islands of the Solomon Archipelago. Modern Papua New Guinea missed any chance to establish a "grassroots" sustainable type of development, depending instead on extracting agricultural and mineral resources, and overseas donor aid, to fund the state. While Australia must bear some responsibility for these development choices, a generation of indigenous politicians have now continued down the same economic path.

Modern Indonesia is itself a product of the colonial era—a cobbling together of various diverse peoples from the Malay Archipelago—that developed an industrial infrastructure to exploit light manufacturing, tropical products, and mineral resources for profit. The post-1949 independent state of Indonesia has followed along the same path of resource extraction, valuing the Papua Province's huge expanses and potential wealth of natural resources more than its indigenous inhabitants. One must conclude that the cultures of the west New Guinea people have not been respected by the central government of Indonesia, whereas the cultures in the east are a cornerstone of government policy in Papua New Guinea. If language and culture are the essential components of human development, then the choice of vernacular languages in Papua New Guinea as the main vehicle of education for the masses will preserve the core elements of the New Guinea way of life.

Over one-sixth of the population of the second largest island in the world now consists of recent migrants from further west in the archipelagos. The central border, a dotted line through mountains and swamps, and the present states, are colonial relics. Viewed over the next millennium these nineteenth- and twentieth-century political creations are unlikely to survive in their present form. Regardless of these short-term developments, the *kumul* or *cenderawasih*, the bird-of paradise, the beautiful symbol of New

Guinea recognized worldwide, will continue to fly, no matter who lives or rules there. The people of New Guinea, the greatest equatorial island in the world, have always been an amalgam of those who have passed through over thousands of years. They will continue to absorb change. In the words of Papua New Guinea poet Kumalau Tawali, "Let my arrows fly another 50,000 years."

Notes

Introduction: Interpreting Melanesia

1. An early chart made of the 1606 Torres voyage shows the Bird's Head as "Papuas" and the remainder of the island as "Nova Ginea." The *Duchess of Berry Atlas* (dated at between 1613 and 1615) shows a similar division. Kelly 1966b, plate xii; Jack-Hinton 1969, 179, map xxiv.

2. Forrest 1775, 106; Earl 1853a, 62. I am also indebted to Dr. Robert Cribb for advice.

3. Sollewijn Gelpke 1993, 318–319.

4. Dumont d'Urville's 1832 classification divided the Pacific Islands into Melanesia (the dark islands), Polynesia (the many islands), and Micronesia (the small islands).

5. Codrington 1891; Rivers 1914. The best general studies of Melanesia are by geographers Brookfield with Hart (1971), and anthropologist Chowning (1977).

6. Narokobi 1980.

7. *Post-Courier* (Port Moresby), 29 Dec. 1997.

8. Sahlins 1963; Douglas 1979; Thomas 1989.

9. Originally called the New Britain Archipelago, the name was changed in the 1880s. I call it the Bismarck Archipelago throughout the book.

10. Spriggs 1997, 1.

11. Green 1991.

12. Murray 1932; Rivers 1922; Pitt-Rivers 1927.

13. Said 1978, 2.

14. Mackenzie 1995; Dixon 2001; Douglas 1996.

15. Chappell 1995, 303.

16. Trompf 1991, 14.

17. MacKenzie 1991, 25.

18. Chalmers 1887, 23–24; Allen 1982, 202; Spriggs 1997, 58; Goodman 1998, 43.

19. Clark 1991; Hides 1936, 82, 84, 114, 125–126.

20. Biersack 1995.

21. Talyaga 1977; Moses 1978.

22. Biersack 1995, 8–11; Weiner 1988, 1–2.

23. The best exposition of this is Joël Bonnemaison's analysis of Tannese cultural identity and mobility (1985 and 1994).

24. Lacey 1985a.

25. Ibid., 89.

26. Herdt 1984.

27. Lacey 1985a, 91.

28. Ibid., 205.

29. Hays 1991; Riesenfeld 1951. Certainly by the 1870s and 1880s twist tobacco had become a form of currency.

30. Hughes 1977; Allen 1982.

31. Chalmers 1887, 23.

Chapter 1: Environment and People: 40,000–5,000 B.P.

1. Spriggs 1997, 76.

2. Neumann 1996, 9–11; Spriggs 1997, 215–217; Turner 2001, 267–268; Blong 1982; Brookfield with Hart 1971, 32–35.

3. Braak 1954, 65; Spenceley 1982, 96.

4. Brookfield with Hart 1971, 1–42.

5. Spriggs 1997, 25–45; Gibbons and Clunie 1986; Swadling 1981, 1; Flannery 1995, 182.

6. White and O'Connell 1982, 171.

7. White and O'Connell 1982; Groube 1986; Allen 1988; Wickler and Spriggs 1988; Swadling 1981. Some recent research indicates even older dates for Australia, perhaps back 100,000 years. These dates are still hotly contested, and the evidence is not conclusive.

8. Ironically, when DNA was discovered—providing the only objective criteria for assessing biological differences—the largest genetic variations were found between individuals within the same communities (85 percent), with much smaller genetic variations (6–8 percent) between supposed nations or distinct racial groups. The more obvious variants, such as skin color, may be controlled by as few as four genetic loci. Spriggs 1997, 10.

9. Ibid., 10–11.

10. Ibid., 260–261.

11. Groube 1993.

12. Spriggs 1997, 23.

13. Ibid., ix.

14. Barham and Harris 1983.

15. Mulvaney and Kamminga 1999, 148–162; Ballard 2000.

16. Lilley 1998; Groube, Chappell, Muke, and Price 1986; Bellwood 1998, 958.

17. Irwin 1991; Irwin 1992.

18. Allen 1988; Wickler and Spriggs 1988; White 1997.

19. Spriggs 1992, 282; Lilley 1998.

20. Spriggs 1992, 287–290.

21. Irwin 1992; Spriggs 1997, 23, 28–29; Lilley 1998.

22. Green 1991, 497.

23. Groube, Chappell, Muke, and Price, 1986.

24. Groube 1986.

25. Spriggs 1997, 76–77, 88; Bellwood 1993, 158–159.

26. White and O'Connell 1982, 189–193.

27. Flannery 1995, 108–116.

28. Ibid., 117–124.

29. Ibid., 130.

30. Ibid., 130–134.

31. Mulvaney and Kamminga 1999, 124–129.

32. Flannery 1995, 180–186; Diamond 1997, 42–44.

33. Simanjuntak 1998, 942–943.

34. Lilley 1998.

35. Golson 1977; Golson 1989; Allen 1993; Mulvaney and Kamminga 1999, 174–175.

36. Groube 1989, 298.

37. Golson 1977; 1989; Swadling 1981, 31–39; Spriggs 1997, 61–65.

38. Spriggs 1997, 64–65; Green 1991, 498; White and O'Connell 1982, 177–184.

39. Some archaeologists have suggested that pigs were present in the Highlands between 10,000 and 5,000 years ago. A few pig teeth have been found in New Ireland sites, one associated with a date of around 8,000 years ago, and the other dated at around 6,000 years ago. Recent direct dating suggests that the presence of bones and teeth at these early dates are intrusions from later levels. It is still most likely that domesticated pigs first arrived with Austronesian-speakers. Allen, 1996, 23–24; Groves 1995, 160; Bellwood 1995, 115.

40. Allen 1996, 24.

41. White and O'Connell, 1982, 183–184; Lilley 1998.

42. Yen 1973; 1991; 1995.

43. Silzer and Clouse 1991, 1; Pawley 1998; Wurm 1982b; Foley 1986; Lynch 1998, 27–38.

44. Foley 1986; Pawley 1998.

45. Bellwood 1985, 128; Wurm 1978; 1982a; 1983; Oliver 1989, vol. 1: 67, 69; Foley 1986, 3. I am indebted to Dr. Terry Crowley for advice on the languages of Melanesia.

46. Lilley 1999b.

47. Bellwood 1998, 958–960.

48. Spriggs 1997, 7.

49. Wurm, Laycock, Voorhoeve, and Dutton 1975, 940–943; Tryon 1994.

50. Wurm, Laycock, Voorhoeve, and Dutton 1975; Oliver 1989, vol. 1: 75–76 provides a concise summary. See also Bellwood 1985, 120–121, 128.

51. Pawley 1998.

52. Foley 1986, 277–280.

Chapter 2: Cultural Spheres and Trade Systems: The Last 5,000 Years

1. Waiko 1982, ix.

2. Bellwood 1995; Terrell and Welsch 1997; Terrell 1999; Tryon 1995.

3. Taylor 1981, 155.

4. Spriggs 1997, 1.

5. Andaya 1993, 106.

6. Jonge and van Dijk 1995, 19–21.

7. Spriggs 1998, 934; Bellwood 1998.

8. Laycock and Wurm 1974; Oliver 1989, vol. 1: 67–72; Wurm, Laycock, Voorhoeve, and Dutton 1975, 953–956.

9. Ross 1988, 1; Lynch, Ross and Crowley 2002; Lynch 1998, 45–55; Pawley and Green 1984.

10. Spriggs 1992, 279; Green 1987.

11. Lilley 1999a.

12. Goodenough 1996, 6–9.

13. Spriggs 1993.

14. Diamond 1988.

15. Allen 1996, 12.

16. Spriggs 1992, 280.

17. Flannery 1995, 173–174.

18. Voorhoeve 1982.

19. Ross 1988, 20–21.

20. Monsell-Davis 1981, 36–37.

21. Wurm, Laycock, Voorhoeve, and Dutton 1975, 955–956.

22. Tryon and Hackman 1983; Bennett 1987, 6–7.

23. Lynch 1998.

24. Wurm, Laycock, Voorhoeve, and Dutton 1975, 947; Spriggs 1997, 8.

25. Parkinson 1907, 105–106.

26. I acknowledge Dr. Terry Crowley's attempts to provide guidance in this section.

27. See Akin 1993, 99–110, ch. 7.

28. The nineteenth- and twentieth-century lingua franca are: Dutch and Bahasa Indonesia in Papua Province; Hiri Motu, Tok Pisin, and English in Papua New Guinea.

29. Dutton 1982; 1989; 1996a; 1996b.

30. Hyndman and Morren 1990, 11.

31. Ibid., 10–11.

32. I have provided a more detailed breakdown in west New Guinea than that suggested by Hyndman and Morren.

33. Hyndman and Morren 1990, 12.

34. Ibid., 9–18.

35. See also Knauft's 1993 analysis of the New Guinea south coast from the Asmat to the Elema peoples.

36. Irwin 1978; 1985; Leach and Leach 1983.

37. Lilley 1999a, 29.

38. Spriggs 1997, 165–167; Lilley 1986; 1988.

39. Harding 1970, 99–100; Harding 1967.

40. Burton 1984; White and O'Connell 1982, 189; Lilley 1986, 34–40.

41. Clark 1991, 309–311; Connolly and Anderson 1987, 249–254; A. Strathern 1971.

42. Lawrence 1964, 27.

43. Harding 1970, 96.

44. Spriggs 1997, 165–167.

45. Donohue 1996, 713–717; Dutton 1996a, 213–217; 1985.

46. See Harding 1994 for a neat summary of precolonial New Guinea trade.

47. Bellwood 1985, 272–275, 311–316; Hughes 1977, 16–17.

48. Jonge and van Dijk 1995, 20–21.

49. Spriggs 1998, 935; Simanjuntak 1998, 947.

50. Hughes 1977, 15; Chowning 1977, 19; Ambrose 1988; Spriggs 1997, 164–165; Bellwood 1993, 158–159; Swadling 1996, 51–62.

51. Valdes, Long, and Barbosa 1992, 27.

52. Dunedin Museum, New Zealand exhibit, viewed 10 Dec. 2001.

53. Philippines National Museum exhibits, Manila, viewed 21 Jan. 1996; Spriggs 1997, 91–93, 164–165; Swadling 1996, 51–62; Allen 1996, 25; Hughes 1977, 16. Descriptions and a picture of similar forges on Borneo appear in King 1993, 113–121. See also Ambrose 1988.

54. Hughes 1977, 15–16.

55. Ibid., 19–20; Lee 1912, 103; Whittaker, Gash, Hookey, and Lacey 1975, 200; Spate 1979–1988, vol. 2: 24.

56. Hughes 1977, 23.

57. Forrest 1775, 93–114.

58. Guillemard 1886, vol. 1: 258; Riesenfeld 1951, 77; Hughes 1977, 20.

59. Earl 1853, 69–78.

60. Whittaker, Gash, Hookey, and Lacey 1975, 298–299.

61. Godelier 1986, 181.

62. Guiart 1996.

63. Strathern 1988; Jolly 1987.

64. Lilley 1985, 63.

65. Waiko 1985, 9.

66. Ibid.

67. Green 1991, 494.

68. Hiscock and Attenbrow 1998. McNiven 2000, argues that the tradition may be much older.

69. Green 1991, 498; White and O'Connell 1982, 105–133; Lourandos 1997, 287–295; McNiven 2001.

70. Mulvaney and Kamminga 1999, 68–75; Amery and Bourke 1994; Walsh 1991.

71. Beckett 1987, 25.

72. Golson 1972a. See also Laade 1968; 1979. Laade suggests that, by their own legends, at least part of the population was once a seafaring people who came from the east in large canoes, probably in the seventeenth or eighteenth century.

73. Beckett 1987, 25–26; Golson 1972a, 385–387; Crowley 1983, 309; Sutton 1976.

74. McConnel 1936; Thomson 1933; 1934; Moore 1972; 1978.

75. Rowland 1986; 1987; Haddon 1914; Berck 1995.

76. Thomas 1994, 77.

Chapter 3: West New Guinea and the Malay World

1. Also *janggē* or *zanggē*.

2. Wheatley 1959, 45–47, 122–123.

3. Goodman 1998; Galis 1953, 5, 45; Pigeaud 1960–1963, vol. 1: 12; Souter, 1963, 17.

4. Hall 1985, 20–25.

5. Staden 1998, 692, quoting F. Valentyn's 1724 book.

6. Andaya 1993, 49.

7. Ibid., 71.

8. Leur 1967, 141–143.

9. Jonge and van Dijk 1995, 23.

10. Cloves are the unopened flowering buds of a tree (*Eugenia aromatica*, Kuntze) which grows to 7–12 meters and begins bearing at six to eight years, although before modern cultivation techniques the trees took up to fifteen years to bear. Cloves are the most stimulating and carminative of all aromatics, the medicinal properties residing in the volatile oil. One of the most common uses for cloves is to quell toothaches, but it is also given in powder or infusion for nausea, indigestion, and dyspepsia, and to assist the action of other medicines. Grieve 1931, 208.

11. *Myristica fragrans*, Linn., the round nutmeg, known also as the Banda nutmeg, was highly valued for its seed and its mace (the seed aril or covering). The trees grow to about 7 meters. In medicine, nutmegs have stimulant and carminative properties and were used for a variety of other purposes from tonics in childbirth to cures for malaria, rheumatism, sciatica and various pains. *Myristica fatua*, Houtt., the long nutmeg, was considered inferior and useful only for oil, its mace being of no value. Nutmeg was used medicinally for headaches, as a purgative, as a stimulant to the gastro-intestinal tract, and to conceal the taste of other drugs. Burkill 1935, vol. 2: 1427–1428, 1524–1530; Grieve 1931, 591–592; Lee 1912, 96–97, 133; Earl, 1853, 58. See also Jonge and van Dijk 1995, 24.

12. Andaya 1993, 1–2; Corn 1999, xi, xvii–xxii.

13. Ardika and Bellwood 1991.

14. Hall 1985, 197; Andaya 1993, 1–2; Swadling 1996, 22–27; Wheatley 1959, 45–46.

15. Hall 1985, 209–210; Andaya 1993, 1.

16. Swadling 1996, 23.

17. Information from Philippines National Museum, 31 Jan. 1996. See also Valdes, Long, and Barbosa 1992, particularly Long's section, "History Behind the Jar," pp. 25–69.

18. Hagen 1999.

19. Spriggs 1997, 165; Goodman 1998, 439; Tryon 1984; Capell 1943, 266–276; Sollewijn Gelpke 1993. Rivers first advanced the idea of migration west from the Malay Archipelago at different times and from different places (1914 vol. 1: 572–596).

20. Swadling 1996, 21.

21. Forrest 1775, 145, 147; Earl 1853, 54; Veur 1966a, 6; 1996b; Rowley 1965, 53–57. Andaya 1993, 104, dates this Biak-Tidore connection to around the fifteenth or sixteenth centuries.

22. Andaya 1993, 109.

23. Kolff 1840, 300. This was probably in the Fakfak area.

24. Huizinga 1998, 386–387.

25. Kolff 1840, 329, 330, 341.

26. Whittaker, Gash, Hookey, and Lacey 1975, 203.

27. Ibid., 204.

28. Wallace 1869, 404–405, see also 407.

29. Massoi, massoia, or massoya (*M. aromatica*, Becc., *Cryptocarya massoy*) bark comes from an aromatic tree from the laurel family, and is closely related to the cinnamon tree. It was used as flavoring in food, in cosmetics, tonics, and medicines and for inhaled scents. In 1793 it was worth $30 to $60 a pecul (133 lbs.) in Canton. Pulasari (*Alyxia* R. Br.) is a considerable genus of the family Apocynaceae. The bark is white and maintains its fragrance for upwards of two

years. It is a "hot" bark containing a high content of eugenol, safrol, and turpentine oils. Massoi bark had many uses: during confinement; as an infusion to treat gonorrhea; in curries, liquors, and perfumes; and as a dye fixative in Javanese batik manufacture. Rasamala (*Altingia excelsa,* Noronha) was usually exploited for a liquid storax used for incense and as a tonic. Burkill 1935, vol. 1: 116–121, 123–124, vol. 2: 1427–1428, 1524–1530; Goodman 1998, 441–445.

30. Lee, 1912, 103; Whittaker, Gash, Hookey, and Lacey 1975, 200; Spate 1979–1988, vol. 2: 24.

31. Kolff 1840, 284–301; Earl 1853a, 60, 89, 103–106; Whittaker, Gash, Hookey, and Lacey 1975, 203.

32. Swadling 1996, 51–62; Cribb 1997.

33. Macknight 1976; Gash and Whittaker 1975, 23; Wright 1958, 6–7; Reid 1983, 15, 20, 31; Sutherland 1983, 279, 281; Abeyasekere 1983; Rowley 1965, 53–56, 58; Taylor 1983, 125; Miedema 1994.

34. Wallace 1869, 582–597, provides an early scientific impression of the different racial and ethnic groups of eastern Indonesia and New Guinea. Descriptions by Kolff 1840, Earl 1853, and Forbes 1887 provide a similar picture. Earl's account of population movements in the Aru Islands, Seram, and Halmahera is particularly fascinating (pp. 93–120).

35. Oral testimony from Tarawai, one of the main islands in the Ninigo and Hermit Groups off the Sepik coast of northwest New Guinea, records that Malay traders regularly visited the islands in the nineteenth century, bartering for bêche-de-mer, copra, and tortoiseshell. Masui, an important local bigman in the 1890s, spoke Malay fluently and had traveled back to the Maluku Archipelago with traders. Information from Markus Tanirau, Tarawai Island, told to Dr. John Mackerell, Madang, 1989. Also refer to Sack 2001, 178, 229–232, 295–296; Tuzin 1997, 84–88.

36. Wallace 1869, 532–533.

37. Kolff 1840, 42, 329–330, 341.

38. Pouwer 1999, 161.

39. Cameron 1985, 88; see also Macknight 1976; Sumner 1981.

40. Flinders 1814, vol. 2:172–173.

41. Ibid. vol. 2: 228–231; Eisler and Smith 1988, 221.

42. Macknight 1976, 27–29, 42–45, 84, 96–97; Hughes 1977, 21–22.

43. Williams 1993.

44. Bennett 1987, 13, 30, 70, 89–90, 114; Carter 1990, 6–7; Oliver 1955, 296, 419–420; Hempenstall 1989, 157; Parkinson 1907, 22, 38; Overell 1923, 73; McDougall 2000.

45. Goodman 1998.

46. Reid with Brewster 1983; Warren 1981; Wallace 1869, 319; Huizinga 1998, 400–401.

47. Abeyasekere 1989, 20.

48. See the description of Johannes Keyts' 1678 negotiations at Onin in Chapter Four.

49. Reid 1983, 2–3.

50. Ibid., 8.

51. Taylor 1983, 17.

52. Wallace 1869, 318–319, 587; Earl 1853, 83; see also Haga 1884, vol. 1: 91–96.

53. In 1825, New Guinea slaves were valued at £5 to £6 sterling each (or 60–70 rupees, or 8–10 Spanish dollars). Although the New Guinea middlemen received only a fraction of this

amount, usually in goods such as cloth, metal implements, and attractive baubles, these material items caused a change in Melanesian society quite disproportionate to their actual value. Kolff 1840, 300; Huizinga 1998, 399.

54. Earl 1853, 84.

55. Taylor 1983, 15–18.

56. Feil, 1987, 121.

57. Miedema 1994, 124.

58. Ibid., 1993, 111–112; Barnett 1959, 1014–1015.

59. Miedema 1994, 129.

60. But a compensatory mechanism also developed—allegations of witchcraft against women—which were used to maintain male dominance. Ibid., 140–142; Miedema 1989; Werff 1989.

61. Sir Cecil Abel, born at Kwato mission in British New Guinea in 1902, was an astute observer of New Guinea who spent many decades living in and collecting oral history from eastern New Guinea. Based on a variety of evidence discussed with me, Sir Cecil believed that Asians had visited the Milne Bay region before any sustained European contact. Interview with Sir Cecil Abel, Port Moresby, 16 Apr. 1991.

62. Leur 1967, 175; Veur 1966a, 6.

63. Earl 1853, 57–58; Lee 1912, 180–181.

Chapter 4: West New Guinea: European Trade and Settlement, 1520–1880

1. Gorecki 1985.

2. Galis 1953, 45.

3. Sollewijn Gelpke 1993, 322.

4. Andaya 1993, 116–117; Corn 1999, 24–36.

5. Swadling 1996, 32–33.

6. Sollewijn Gelpke 1993, 321–322.

7. Andaya 1993, 116.

8. Jack-Hinton 1969, 28–29; 1972, 250; Markham 1872, 61–69, 126–128.

9. Galis 1953, 45; Sharp 1960, 29–32; Spate 1979–1988, vol. 1: 97–98.

10. Swadling 1996, 34–37.

11. Amherst and Thompson 1901; Sharp 1960, 42–48, 50–55.

12. Hilder 1980, 48–51; Jack-Hinton 1972; Whittaker, Gash, Hookey, and Lacey 1975, 182–187; Eisler 1995, 47–49, 79; Cortesao 1960, vol. 1: Plates 79, 80, vol. 2: Plates 272, 285, 324, 363; Wroth 1944; Sharp 1960, 63–66; Bayldon 1925.

13. Sollewijn Gelpke 1994, 130–131.

14. Ibid., 127, 131.

15. Ibid., 134–135.

16. Eisler 1995, 11; Eisler and Smith 1988, 19, 97; Thrower 1984, 72; Brosse 1983, 143.

17. Leupe 1875, 3–4; Schumacher 1954, 8; Galis 1953, 12; Eisler 1995, 68–70 (the chart is reproduced); Whittaker, Gash, Hookey, and Lacey 1975, 192–197.

18. Galis 1953, 12, 46, 57, 61; Schumacher 1954, 8; Haga 1884, vol. 1: 29–30; Spate 1979–1988, vol. 2: 22–25; Boogaart 1988; Eisler 1995, 69–73.

19. Jack-Hinton 1972, 254; Eisler and Smith 1988, 23, 27–28. In 1768 Callander recorded them as from the southeast coast. Whittaker, Gash, Hookey, and Lacey 1975, 204.

20. Boogaart 1988, 45.

21. Haga 1884, vol. 1: 32; Gadis 1953, 13; Ballard, Ploeg, and Vink, 2001.

22. Whittaker, Gash, Hookey, and Lacey 1975, 199.

23. Heers 1899, 22–38, 45–47; Spate 1979–1988, vol. 2: 41–42; Gill 1988, 44; Leup 1875, 9–10; Galis 1953, 13; Haga 1884, vol. 1: 37–39, 41; Schumacher 1954, 9; Souter 1963, 6–7; Beaglehole 1966, 118–119; Eisler 1995, 74–77.

24. Hall 1955, 294–311.

25. Schumacher 1954, 9, 112; Haga 1884, vol. 1: 37, 49–50; Galis 1953, 13.

26. Whittaker, Gash, Hookey, and Lacey 1975, 199–200.

27. Eisler 1995, 92.

28. Gill 1988, 57; Spate 1979–1988, vol. 2: 50; Haga 1884, vol. 1: 56; Galis 1953, 14; Schumacher 1954, 10; Eisler 1995, 92–96.

29. Schumacher 1954, 10.

30. Haga 1884, 1: 79–81; Leupe 1875, 58–60; Schumacher 1954, 10–11.

31. Whittaker, Gash, Hookey, and Lacey 1975, 200.

32. Leupe 1875, 62–63; Haga 1884, 1: 81–83.

33. Leupe 1875, 64–65; Haga 1884, 1: 86–87.

34. Leupe 1875, 75.

35. For the text of the treaty, see Whittaker, Gash, Hookey, and Lacey 1975, 202–203.

36. Goodman 1998; Leupe 1875, 68–69; Haga 1884, vol. 1: 87–89, 92–93, 96, 99; Fry 1969, 95; Whittaker, Gash, Hookey, and Lacey 1975, 200–203.

37. Goodman 1998, 436–437.

38. Haga 1884, 1: 126–132, 134.

39. Andaya 1993, 101–104.

40. Galis 1953, 47.

41. Thrower 1984, 70–73.

42. Sharp 1960, 91–92.

43. Ibid., 95–100.

44. Whittaker, Gash, Hookey, and Lacey 1975, 215.

45. Quiason 1966, 139–195; Fry 1969, 23; 1970, 20, 136–137; Andaya 1993, 229–230.

46. Sharp 1960, 109–113; Spate 1979–1988, vol. 3: 92–95; Dunmore 1992, 48–51; Jack-Hinton 1972, 254; Sharp 1960, 111–113.

47. Dunmore 1992, 35–37; 1965–1969, vol. 2: 156–177.

48. Brosse 1983, 84–92; Dunmore 1992, 97–99; Sharp 1960, 173–175.

49. Hawkesworth 1969, 655–659; Whittaker, Gash, Hookey, and Lacey 1975, 97–99; Sharp 1960, 173–175.

50. Forrest 1775, 106, see also 93–117; Bassett 1961; 1964; 1969.

51. Gash and Whittaker 1975, 21; Wright 1958, 19–20; Veur 1966a, 9; Forrest 1775, 106.

52. Hall 1955, 339–342.

53. Nuku assumed the titles of Sultan of Tidore, Seram, and Papua. In 1797, with British assistance, he routed the Dutch-installed Sultan, reclaiming his father's throne. Lee 1912, 162–167; Andaya 1993, 214–239, 230–231.

54. Fry 1969, 96–97; 1970, 156–157; Andaya 1993, 235–236; Hanna and Alwi 1990, 207–237.

55. Veur, 1966a, 8.

56. Ibid., 8.

57. Lee 1912, 180–181.

58. Forrest 1775, 101–102; Lee 1912, 107–108; Haga 1884, vol. 2: 90–91.

59. Forrest 1775; Lee 1912, 65, 81, 97, 101, 105, 173; Gash and Whittaker 1975, 23.

60. Wallace 1869, 496–497, 499–500.

61. Some of these appear in Whittaker, Gash, Hookey, and Lacey 1975, 221, with no source provided. This interpretation is supported by pictures in Broose 1983, 136, 156.

62. The cargo consisted of 1,000 piculs (i.e. 133,000 pounds, or 60,328 kilograms.) of *massoi* bark, expected to sell for $20,000, as well as great quantities of the equally valuable "Cooly Louang" bark, Dammer bark, and six kinds of betel nut and hardwoods. Lee 1912, 112.

63. Veur 1966a, 8; Fry 1970, 154–155; Gordon 1951, 35–42; Lee 1912, 71–185; Griffin 1990; Lee 1912.

64. Hall 1955, 339–342, 473–488; Smithies 1983.

65. Allen 1972.

66. Brosse 1983, 139–151. The same procedure for reworking silver coins was in use during the 1840s. "Australian Islands," in *Colonial Magazine* (Jan. 1842) 7 (2): 59–71. I am indebted to Dr. Marion Diamond for this reference.

67. Whittaker, Gash, Hookey, and Lacey 1975, 227–230; Brosse 1983, 151, 159, 185–194; Dunmore 1992, 89–92.

68. Mullins 2002.

69. Byrnes 1988; Steven 1965; 1983.

70. "Australia," the name for the continent suggested by Matthew Flinders, began to be used instead of "New Holland" in the 1810s, gaining currency through the support of New South Wales Governor Lachlan Macquarie.

71. Cameron 1985, 88–93; Gibson-Hill 1959, 116.

72. Cameron 1985, 93.

73. Veur 1966a, 9; Overweel 1994, 14.

74. Huizinga 1998, 387.

75. Earl 1853, 12–16, 40–56.

76. Müller 1857; Gash and Whittaker 1975, 22; Veur 1966a, 9–11; 1972, 277; Overweel 1994, 14–20.

77. Dutch General State Archives, Ministry of Colonial Affairs, 12 Nov. 1829, no. 72, inv. no. 714, quoted in Overweel 1998b, 12.

78. Overweed 1998a.

79. Earl 1853, 89; Swadling 1996, 29–30.

80. Haga 1884, vol. 2: 92–98.

81. Whittaker, Gash, Hookey, and Lacey 1975, 207.

82. Earl, 1853, 69–82. The forges were also described in 1883 by Guillemard 1886, vol. 1: 285.

83. Earl 1853, 86–92; Overweel 1994, 24–26.

84. Whittaker, Gash, Hookey, and Lacey 1975, 298.

85. Huizinga 1998, 388; Mullins 2002.

86. These were Manokwari Island off Dorei Bay, Numfor (Amberpon or Omberpon) Island in Cenderawasih Gulf, and Karangdifar and Ambarssura (Amberpoera) on the west coast of Cenderawasih Gulf. The Raja Empat Islands contained four Papuan principalities under the suzerainty of the Sultan: Salawati, Waigeo, Misool, and Waigama. Veur 1966a, 2; Lee 1912, 171; Overweel 1994, 23–24.

87. Earl 1853, 86; Galis 1953, 22; Swadling 1996, 118; Wallace 1869, 316–317.

88. Swadling 1996, 119–120.

89. Earl 1853, 69–82; Hughes 1977, 21.

90. Fry 1969, 93–95.

91. Kolff 1840, 299–300; Haga 1884, vol. 1: 13–27.

92. Veur 1966a, 12–13; 1966b, 4–8; Baal, Galis, and Koentjaraningrat 1984, 88; Galis 1953, 48.

93. Veur 1966a, 13.

94. Refer to Overweel 1994 for many references to naval punitive expeditions in west New Guinea.

95. Reynolds 1981, 5–17.

96. Overweel 1994, 26–27.

97. Kamma 1972; Steinbauer 1979, 5–9; Stewart 1998.

98. Lilley 1999b.

Chapter 5: The Nineteenth Century: Trade, Settlement, and Missionaries

1. Report of the Western Pacific Royal Commission, *Queensland Votes and Proceedings (QVP)* 1884, vol. 2: 945.

2. Letters Patent, 10 June 1868. New South Wales had been granting guano leases on islands off Queensland since 1865. Veur 1966a, 21.

3. Jack-Hinton 1972, 255; Richards 1986a, 63–64.

4. Richards 1986b, 104–105; Sharp 1960, 157.

5. Cavanagh 1989; Hunter 1793, 214–244; Jack-Hinton 1972, 256; Richards 1986a, 54–55.

6. Richards 1987, 50–52.

7. Ibid. 1986a.

8. Affleck 1971, 4–5, and Appendix B; Jack-Hinton 1972, 256.

9. Kennedy 1978, 112–125; Gill 1988, 110; Langdon 1966, 185–186; Edwards and Hamilton 1915.

10. Flinders 1814, vol. 1: xxvii; Langdon 1966, 185–186; Jack-Hinton 1972, 256.

11. Langdon 1972, 220–221.

12. Gill 1988, 130; Mather and Bennett, 1993, 232–234.

13. Mullins 1992a; Fraser 1853; Earl 1853; Liddle 1865.

14. Reid 1954, 31–33.

15. Gill 1988, 197, 202, 205, 208, 209, 212, 214.

16. Moore 1997.

17. Forrest 1775, 101, 115.

18. Coulter 1847, vol. 2: 117, and see also 100–142.

19. Wallace 1869, 420.

20. Ibid., 481–482.

21. Ibid., 476–479.

22. Ibid., 485.

23. Forbes 1887, 133.

24. Ibid., 134–135

25. Ibid.

26. Ibid., 124.

27. Overweel 1994, 27.

28. Ibid., 78–79, 87; Whittaker, Gash, Hookey, and Lacey 1975, 237.

29. Tetens 1958, 55, 67–87; Redlich 1874; Hersheim 1983, 12–15.

30. Swadling 1996, 64; Cribb 1997; Eisler and Smith 1988, 87–88; Eisler 1995, 33–36.

31. Brosse, 1983, 149.

32. Swadling 1996, 73–91.

33. Cribb 1997, 383–384, and fn. 10; Sack 2001, 230.

34. Swadling 1996, 98–107.

35. Rosenberg 1875, 145.

36. Jack-Hinton 1972, 257.

37. Spoehr 1963.

38. Firth 1977; 1982, 7–20.

39. Hernsheim 1983; Firth 1978a.

40. Robson 1965; Dutton 1976.

41. Parkinson 1907; Mead 1960.

42. Extract from report by Captain C. H. Simpson of HMS *Blanche*, 11 Dec. 1872, in Whittaker, Gash, Hookey, and Lacey 1975, 251.

43. Goode 1977, 51, 61–64, 107, 161–162, 168, 186–188; Dutton 1985, 183; *Queenslander*, 7 Aug., 21 Oct. 1876, 22 June 1878, 21 Aug. 1880; Gibbney 1972, 290–291; Whittaker, Gash, Hookey, and Lacey 1975, 257.

44. Dutton 1985, 165–166; Bevan 1890, 12–19; *Queenslander*, 13 Jan., 12 Dec. 1877, 12 Jan., 23 Mar. 1878, 13, 27 Sept., 18 Oct., 8 Nov. 1879, 3 Jan. 1880; A. Goldie to Sec. of State, 24 July 1883, Papua New Guinea National Archives (PNGNA) British New Guinea (BNG) G8/85/157; Langmore 1974, 41–43.

45. Jones 1981.

46. Townsend 1935; Morton 1982, 21–29; Dawbin 1972, 274–275.

47. Whittaker, Gash, Hookey, and Lacey 1975, 317, 320–321.

48. Kolff 1840, 318; Earl 1853, 56; *Queenslander*, 20 May 1871.

49. Morton 1982, 63–78; Wallace 1869, 493–508; Overweel 1994, 27.

50. Affleck 1971, Appendix C, 1–2; *Nautical Magazine*, 1838, 302; Bennett 1987, 350–355; Langdon 1984, 184–189; Byrnes 1988; Gray 1999.

51. Oliver 1991, 17–18; Maude 1966, 194; Coulter 1847, vol. 2: 56; Bradley 1860, 78, 81, 125, 127; Schütte 1989b, 54–58. Knowledge of English, or use of sign language, did not always work: on the *Kent*'s 1832 whaling voyage to New Ireland, no amount of broken English, nor even mimicry of fowls and pigs could procure provisions. Beale 1839, 302.

52. Laracy 1976, 22; Jack-Hinton 1972, 257; Affleck 1971, 6–8; Beale 1839, 309.

53. Laracy 1976, 23; Affleck 1971, 10.

54. Bennett 1987, 29–31.

55. Starbuck 1964.

56. Dr. D. Parker Wilson's log, *Gypsy*, in Whittaker, Gash, Hookey, and Lacey 1975, 324.

57. Gray 1999.

58. Wilson log, *Gypsy*, in Whittaker, Gash, Hookey, and Lacey 1975, 325. See also Maude 1966.

59. Ibid., 325.

60. Hilder 1980, 49–51.

61. Wiltgen, 1981, 474–487; Affleck 1971, 13–26; Delbos 1985, 43–55.

62. Galis 1953, 48; Wallace 1869, 494–495; Goode 1977, 34–35; Powell 1883–1884, 14.

63. Overweel 1994, 29.

64. Baal, Galis, and Koentjaningrat 1984, 73; Overweel 1994, 85, 86.

65. Guillemard 1886, 272–275.

66. Kamma 1953, 151; Verschueren 1953, 224.

67. Verschueren 1953; Overweel 1993, 17–19; Pouwer 1999, 162–163.

68. Mullins 1988, 136, 144–146; *QVP* 1867, vol. 2: 993–995; 1868, 519–526; Prideaux 1988, 49–57; Bayton 1964–1965; 1969.

69. Prendergast 1968, 75–88, 104–107, 132, 238; Dutton 1985, 165–166, 189; Gill 1874; 1876, 199–265.

70. Kaniku 1975.

71. Langmore 1974; 1989; Chalmers 1886; 1902; MacFarlane 1888; Murray 1876.

72. Threlfall 1975, 31–62.

73. Whittaker, Gash, Hookey, and Lacey 1975, 362–378.

74. Schütte 1989a; 1989b.

75. Delbos 1985, 43; Maquire 1990, 31.

76. Jackman 1969.

77. Wetherell 1977; 1996.

78. Whittaker, Gash, Hookey, and Lacey 1975, 342–343; Delbos 1985, 75–98; Wagner and Reiner 1986.

79. Schütte 1989b, 65–66.

80. Ward 1972; Munro 1973; 1879–1880 Annual Report, Police Magistrate, Thursday Island, *QVP* 1880, vol. 2: 1158; Pitcairn 1891, 273–274. See also Sumner 1981.

81. Jack-Hinton 1969, 342.

82. Barrett 1948, 101–110; Fraser 1853.

83. MacGillivray 1852, vol. 1: 308; MacGillivray in *Sydney Morning Herald*, 6 Jan. 1862; Mullins 1988, 29; 1992b; Singe 1979, 33; Sumner 1981, 64.

84. MacGillivray in *Sydney Morning Herald*, 14 and 27 Feb. 1862. See also Mullins 1992a; J. Jardine to Col. Sec., 1 Mar. 1865, in Prideaux 1988, 31; Jardine 1866, 84.

85. Mullins 1988, 243; Beckett 1987, 33; H. M. Chester to Col. Sec., 20 Oct. 1870, In letter 3425 of 1870, *QSA* COL/A151; Diary of James Gascoigne, *Queenslander*, 13 Nov. 1869.

86. Shineberg 1967, 107; Howe 1977, 89.

87. Letter to editor, *Cooktown Herald* by eight bêche-de-mer captains, in *Queenslander*, 4 Nov. 1882; In letter 3484 of 1876, *QSA* COL/A231; Capt. Pennefather to H. M. Chester, 10 Oct. 1882,

In letter 5730 of 1882, *QSA* COL/A348; H. M. Chester to Col. Sec., 31 Oct. 1882, In letter 5869 of 1882, *QSA* COL/A349.

88. The *Saucy Jack* from Townsville began fishing for bêche-de-mer around Port Moresby in December 1877. The *Pride of the Logan* was fishing in Hood Bay in 1877 and 1878, joined by the *Annie* in the latter year. *Queenslander*, 12 Jan., 17 Aug., 21 and 28 Sept. 1878.

89. Oram 1976, 16, quoting H. H. Romilly in BNGAR 1889, 29.

90. G. S. Fort, Report on British New Guinea. *QVP* 1886, vol. 2: 953.

91. Report from H. H. Romilly, 26 Oct. 1887, *QVP* 1888, vol. 3: 33–34.

92. *Queenslander*, 18 Aug. 1877.

93. *Queenslander*, 22 Mar. 1873; 10 July 1875; 21 June, 18 Aug. and 6 Oct. 1877; Beckett 1987, 33–34.

94. H. M. Chester to Col. Sec., 7 May 1877, *QVP* 1877, vol. 3: 1123–1124; 1879, vol. 2: 949.

95. The *Three Brothers* gathered twenty-four tons of live shell and four tons of dead shell in fourteen months. *Queenslander*, 10 July 1875.

96. *Queenslander*, 22 Mar. 1873 and 10 July 1875.

97. Commander N.S.F. Digby to Commodore A. H. Hoskins, 19 July 1878, H. M. Chester to Col. Sec. 24 Apr. 1879, J. Merriman et al. petition to Queensland Legislative Assembly, 1 Aug. 1879, *QVP* 1879, vol. 2: 944–949, 953–955; Lieut.-Comm. T. De Houghton to Commodore J. C. Wilson, 22 Sept. 1879, *QVP* 1880, vol. 2: 1163–1166.

98. Romilly 1886, 160–161.

99. Pitcairn 1891, 73–74, 273; Bevan 1890, 108; Romilly 1893, 290; F. Lawes to J. Douglas, 20 Feb. 1888, PNGNA BNG G14 3/88; F. Lawes to H. H. Romilly 21 Feb. 1886, PNGNA BNG G20/12.

100. Mullins 1997; 2002.

101. McNiven 2001.

102. Oram 1976, 17; MacGillivray 1852, 69; *Queenslander*, 28 June, 12 July 1873, 8 May 1874; *Brisbane Courier*, 30 Jan. 1886; Stone 1880, 177; Moresby 1875b, 158; *Queenslander*, 5 Jan. 1878; Gill 1874, 28–30.

103. Letters by W. G. Lawes and A. Goldie, *Queenslander*, 12 Jan. 1878.

104. Crocombe 1972a, 73; Stone 1880, 30–31; Murray 1876, 479.

105. Ingham was killed on Brooker (Utian) Island in the Calvados Group in November 1878.

106. Gibbney 1972; Moore 1992b.

Chapter 6: The Nineteenth Century: Exploration and Colonization

1. Bach 1968; 1986, front map.

2. Report of the Western Pacific Royal Commission, *QVP* 1884, vol. 2: 950.

3. Veur 1966a, 21; *QVP* 1872, 537–539; Mullins 1992a.

4. Young 1984; Scarr 1984, 35–77.

5. 35 and 36 Vic. c. 19 and 38, and 39 Vic. c. 51.

6. Scarr 1967, 38–52; Bach 1986.

7. Report of the Western Pacific High Commission, *QVP* 1884, vol. 2: 948.

8. *Queensland Government Gazette*, 1879, vol. 22: 753, 23 Mar.

9. Veur 1964a, 23–24; Farnfield 1973; Mullins 1988, 240, 263–264, 267–279, 397–401; Mullins 1992a; Griffin 1981; White 1981.

10. Secretary to Lord Derby to H. H. Romilly, 17 Mar. 1883, PNGNA BNG G19/1.

11. *Australasian*, 30 July 1881; Romilly 1886, 109–140.

12. Romilly 1893, 188, 192.

13. These were Queensland, New South Wales, Victoria, South Australia, Tasmania, New Zealand, and Fiji. Several colonies began to default on payments soon after.

14. Newbury 1973.

15. Jack-Hinton 1972, 253; Dunmore 1965–1969, vol. 2: 211.

16. Whittaker, Gash, Hookey, and Lacey 1975, 215.

17. An association was formed in Sydney in the mid-1840s to establish a colony in New Guinea. *Queenslander*, 23 Feb. 1878; Souter 1963, 10–11.

18. Thompson 1980, 37.

19. *Queenslander*, 27 Apr. and 25 May 1867; Secretary to New Guinea Colonisation and Trading Association (Ltd.) to Col. Sec., in letter 1868 of 1867, *QSA* COL\A93.

20. Forty of the seventy-five passengers and crew were saved, thirteen drowned, ten were killed by Aborigines, and twelve disappeared. The Marine Board Inquiry into the wreck attributed it "to the utter incompetence and unfitness of Captain Stratman," because he navigated with inadequate charts and made poor decisions before and after the wreck, leading to his own demise. *Queenslander*, 20 Apr. 1872; see also 9 and 16 Mar., and 6 and 13 Apr. 1872; Prospectus for New Guinea Prospecting Expedition, in Lawrence Hargraves papers, Power House Museum, Sydney; Healy 1965, 106.

21. MacFarlane 1952.

22. Thompson 1980, 37, 100–102.

23. W. R. Malcolm for Lord Derby to Edward Schubert, 30 Oct. 1875, PNGNA BNG G16 4/86; *Queenslander*, 23 Feb. 1876.

24. Gordon 1951, 115–116.

25. Memorandum by Sir Arthur Gordon, 26 Feb. 1881, PNGNA BNG G3 23A/1.

26. Overweel 1994, 67–70.

27. Whittaker, Gash, Hookey, and Lacey 1975, 339–344, 398–408; Biskup 1974.

28. Moore 1984; Overlack 1978–1979.

29. Overweel 1994, 77–80. Everill had also been attempting to begin a substantial settlement in British New Guinea. Bevan 1890, 185; J. Service to J. Douglas, 24 Mar. 1886, Baron von Mueller to Douglas, 24 Mar. 1886, PNGNA BNG G9/86/12; H. C. Everill to Douglas, 3 Mar. 1886, PNGNA BNG G9/61/86.

30. The main works of creative fiction are Beach 1863, Lawson 1875 (thought to have been written by R. H. Armit), and Tregance 1888. See also Armit 1876; *Queenslander*, 23 Dec. 1876, and 14 Jan. 1882; Powell 1883, 275–276, for fanciful tales of natives using gold-tipped spears, and men with monkey-like tails.

31. Souter 1963, 3–15.

32. Quanchi 1996; 1997a; 1997b; 1999; Quanchi and Shekleton 2001.

33. Ballard 2000.

34. Haddon 1901–1935; Young 1988; Ballard 2000; Herle and Rouse 1998; Kuklick 1991; Edwards 1997; 2001.

35. Brosse 1983, 151.

36. Thomas 1989.

37. Overweel 1994, 28, 32.

38. Wallace 1869, 492–512; Baal, Galis, and Koentjaraningrat 1984, 45; Schumacher 1954, 24–26. Bernstein carried an open letter from the Sultan to the "Chiefs of Papua" seeking their cooperation. Rosenberg 1875, 146–148, and passim.

39. Gash and Whittaker 1975, 23; Whittaker, Gash, Hookey, and Lacey 1975, 270–271; Schumacher 1954, 112.

40. Albertis, 1880; *Sydney Mail,* 31 May and 7 June 1873; Goode 1977, 19–52.

41. Dunmore 1992, 17–21, 103–104; Brosse 1983, 168–182; Bassett 1966; Lubbock 1968; Moore 1979.

42. Gordon 1951, 52–55; Jukes 1847; MacGillivray 1852; Huxley 1935.

43. Monteith 1987; *QSA* COL/A151, in Letters 3428 and 3425/1870, H. M. Chester to Col. Sec., Sept. 1870; *Queenslande*r, 2 Feb. 1878; H. M. Chester to Col. Sec., 15 Jan. 1878; *Australian Town and Country Journal (AT&CJ)*, 9 Feb. 1878.

44. Goode 1977, 63–82, 141–154; Wilson 1978; MacFarlane 1875–1876; Albertis, 1880.

45. *Queenslander*, 28 Sept. 1878.

46. Webster 1984, 50–109, 187–208, 223–238; Putilov 1982, 15–40, 78–97, 107–122; Sentinella 1975, 13–224, 235–288, 295–306.

47. Moresby 1875a, 1875b; Inglis and Oram 1973; Moresby 1876.

48. Stone 1880, 13–14; Goode 1977, 63–83, 101–122; Macmillan 1957; Shaw and Ruhen 1977; *AT&CJ*, 11 Dec. 1875.

49. Stone, 1880, 1–8; Goode 1977, 115, 123–137; *Queenslander*, 11, 21, and 28 Apr., 5 May 1883.

50. *QSA* COL/A226, In letter 2447 of 1876, H. M. Chester to Col. Sec., 23 Sept. 1876; Stone 1880, 230–231; Dutton 1985, 182; Whittaker, Gash, Hookey, and Lacey 1975, 257.

51. Goode 1977, 141–207.

52. Pearl 1967; Stuart 1970, 26–29; Dutton 1985, 152; *Queenslander*, 23 June 1884; Strachan 1888, 6–69; Whittaker, Gash, Hookey, and Lacey 1975, 273–274.

53. Mosley 1892.

54. Parkinson 1907, 366.

55. Whittaker, Gash, Hookey, and Lacey 1975, 261–263.

56. Hernsheim 1983, 54, 61, 69, 80, 85–92; Turner 2001, 88–89.

57. Overweel 1998a, 459.

58. Gray 1999, 40.

59. Corris 1968; Jamison 1990.

60. Price with Barker 1976; Siegel 1985; Moses 1977; Panoff 1979; Firth 1976.

61. Mullins 1990; Crocombe 1972a; 1972b; Crocombe and Crocombe 1982.

62. Shineberg 1999; Panoff 1979.

63. Jones 1981; Affleck 1971, Appendices B and C.

64. Jamison 1990.

65. Moore 1985, 244–254.

66. Shlomowitz 1987; 1988; 1990.

67. Gray 1999, 38–39.

68. Newbury 1975.

69. Moore, Griffin, and Griffin 1984.

70. Veur 1966b, 14–17; Sack 2001, 23.

71. Quoted in Veur 1966a, 16; Jacobs 1951a; 1951b.

72. Webster 1984; Sentinella 1975.

73. H. H. Romilly, copy of proclamation, 25 May 1884, PNGNA BNG G9/85/103.

74. [Erskine] 1885; Veur 1966b, 10–12; Legge 1949.

75. The final agreement was to draw a line from the coast near Mitre Rock on the 8th parallel of south latitude through to the 147th meridian east longitude. From there the border went in a straight line northwest to the point of intersection of the 6th parallel with the 144th meridian, and then west-northwest to the intersection with the 5th parallel of south latitude with the 141st meridian of east longitude.

76. British and German Spheres of Influence in Pacific and Reciprocal Freedom of Trade and Commerce Declarations Between the Governments, Berlin, 6 and 10 Apr. 1886, PNGNA BNG G3 23A/-6.; Veur 1966a, 17–20; 1966b, 60–63.

77. Abaijah and Wright 1991; Griffin 1975.

Chapter 7: Interpreting Early Contact

1. Dening 1985, 109–110.

2. Oliver 1991, 17.

3. *Illustrated London News*, 5 Aug. 1848, 67.

4. Schieffelin and Crittenden 1991.

5. Whittaker, Gash, Hookey, and Lacey 1975, 203.

6. Kolff 1840, 326, 332–339; Hunter 1793, 234.

7. Whittaker, Gash, Hookey, and Lacey 1975, 290–291; Salmond 1991, 134. Use of green boughs in contact rituals was ubiquitous throughout the Pacific. Europeans thought that they were peace offerings, but they were probably symbolic of bodies or supernatural powers.

8. Whittaker, Gash, Hookey, and Lacey 1975, 201–203.

9. Ibid., 291.

10. Schieffelin and Crittenden 1991, 4–5.

11. Schieffelin and Crittenden 1991, 4–5.

12. Campbell 1998b.

13. Gray 1999, 35; Barrett 1948, 101–110; *Sydney Herald*, 29 Oct. 1836; Brockett 1836, 12–20; Wemyss 1837, 8–56; McInnes 1983; Howard 1993; Laracy 1976, 22–23; Howard 1993; Beckett 1998, 35.

14. Jack-Hinton 1969, 342; Moore 1985, 35; Bennett 1987, 23, 27, 356–357.

15. Maude 1968, 145. Coulter claimed to have met James Selwin, ex-supercargo and part owner of the brig *Thomas from Bristol* at Willaumez Peninsula, New Britain in 1835. Selwin is supposed to have arrived there around 1815, when his ship was wrecked. All of the crew save the captain, mate, and Selwin were supposed to have been killed and eaten, then his two companions also died, leaving Selwin with his native wife and three children, plus the captain's wife. Coulter also claimed to have met Thomas Manners, an English sailor from a whaling vessel, who had been put ashore on New Ireland at his own request ten years earlier. While Manners

may have existed, a careful reading of the more than forty pages given over to his adventures suggests exaggeration. Selwin's arrival date is too early to be believed. Coulter 1847, vol. 1: 243–288; vol. 2: 1–30, 67–98. Macdonald 1982, 279, fn. 41, indicates inaccuracy in Coulter's depiction of the Micronesian portion of the voyage.

16. Coulter also gives an extensive description of an Irish convict, Terence Connell, and his companion Jim Hutton, said to have escaped from New South Wales with eleven others in the late 1820s or 1830s, then made their way to the southwest coast of New Guinea near Flamingo Bay. There are no exact matches in the convict records from New South Wales. Terence Connell could be Terence Connor, sentenced in 1823, who received a ticket-of-leave in 1835, which is in the same year as the estimated date of Coulter's visit. Why would he want to escape if he was already free? Jim Hutton could be an American James Hodson, sentenced to fourteen years in 1827, who escaped in July 1829. I am indebted to Dr. Jennifer Harrison for obtaining these details.

17. Currey 1963, 22. There is also a report of a whaling ship in the Marshall Islands (presumably in Micronesia) in 1847 that was attacked and looted, the crew brutally murdered. The attack was said to have been organized by an escaped convict from Tasmania, who had been living there for several years. Reid 1954, 21–25, 53. Hezel 1979, 119–120, does not record this incident.

18. *QVP* 1887, vol. 3: 671. See also Thomson 1886–1887; Powell 1883–1884, 29–30; *Mackay Mercury*, 1 Jan. 1891, 28 Jan. 1902, and 23 Jan. 1906; Webster 1898, 284–293.

19. Idriess 1950.

20. In 1867, William Kennett was told on Muralag (Prince of Wales) Island (visited by Wini each year in the turtle season) that Wini had died six years earlier. The crew of *Julia Percy* met one of Wini's daughters in November 1861, who told them that Wini was still alive. Some sources suggest that John Jardine shot Wini in 1865, although a letter written by Jardine indicates that Wini was still alive in March 1865. MacGillivray 1852, vol. 1: 307–308; MacGillivray in *Sydney Morning Herald*, 14 Feb. 1862; Moore 1979, 9, 231; Mullins 1988, 68, 74; Pike 1983, 26; Prideaux 1988, 22, 30; Beckett 1965, 627.

21. Moore 1979, 8–9; MacGillivray 1852, 301–302.

22. Thanks are due to Mr. Glen Tauliso, District Officer, Misima District, for his assistance in collecting oral testimony about the incident. Rochas 1861; *Port Denison Times*, 25 Nov. 1865; Thomson 1886–1887, 145; Pike 1979, 44; Reid 1954, 74–75. "Seventeen Years Among the Savages," Stanmore Perceval Papers, 195–205, British Museum, Item No. 49199-285. Also published in *The Times*, 21 July 1875. The crew abandoned Narcisse Pierne Pellatier (or Pettice), marooned on Cape York for seventeen years. Discovered in April 1875 on Night Island by the crew of a bêche-de-mer vessel, Pellatier did not want to leave his Aboriginal companions. Naked, his skin burnt brown, the young man spoke the local Aboriginal language, carried the scarification marks of initiation, and had an elongated pierced right ear and nasal septum. Initially, he seemed to have forgotten most of his French, but at Somerset the castaway gradually revealed his story. The captain had intended to leave Pellatier with the Chinese, eventually taking him with the rest of the crew, only to desert him on Cape York, never reporting the boy's existence to authorities. Aborigines found the teenager, adopting him into their community.

23. Shineberg 1999; Panoff 1979.

24. See Overweel 1994 for numerous Dutch New Guinea sources.

25. Parkinson 1907, 352.

26. Souter 1963, 6–7; Beaglehole 1966, 118–119.

27. Flinders 1814, vol. 1: xv–xvii; Hughes 1977, 24.

28. MacGillivray 1852, vol. 1: 180; *Illustrated London News*, 5 Aug. 1848.

29. *QVP* 1887, vol. 3: 672, quoting official correspondence; PNGNA BNG G7/47 Scratchley to Derby, Sept. 1885, attachment to Dispatch 47; Fort, Report on British New Guinea with Data, in *QVP* 1886, vol. 2: 32–33; Bevan 1890, 104.

30. Whittaker, Gash, Hookey, and Lacey 1975, 199.

31. Romilly 1893, 269.

32. Chalmers and Gill 1885, 181.

33. Biskup 1974, 72–73; Parkinson 1907, 29.

34. *QVP* 1886, vol. 2: 978, 1887, 3: 671; Bevan 1890, 94–99, 183; Romilly 1893, 229, 235; *Brisbane Courier*, 25 July 1888, quoted in Jamison 1990, 118.

35. Moore 1998a.

36. Many years later, Ingham's skull was returned. Moore 1992b.

37. Dutton 1985, 151; Pitcairn 1891, 75; Bevan 1890, 4–6, 32, 129; Douglas to Ah Gim, 20 Nov. 1886; Forbes to Douglas, 10 Sept. 1886, and postscript 12 Sept. 1886; 8/87, Lawes to Forbes, 21 Feb. 1887, PNGNA BNG G14.

38. Overweel 1994, 99–115.

39. Campo 1991.

40. Velde 1995; Ballard, Vink, and Ploeg 2001, 13.

41. Ballard 2000; Ploeg 1995.

42. Nelson 1982b, 10; Baal, Galis, and Koentjaraningrat 1984, 20–21, 44–45; Overweel 1998a, 474–477; 1994, 99; Ploeg 1995; Ballard, Vink, and Ploeg 2001, 17–23; Souter 1963, 127–141.

43. Ploeg 1995, 234.

44. Ibid., 234–37; Souter 1963, 198–200.

45. Radford 1987; Nelson 1982b, 10; Sack 2001; Souter 1963, 71–78, 110–116.

46. Joyce 1963; 1969; 1971; Souter 1963, 59–69.

47. Schieffelin and Crittenden 1991, 33–40; Souter 1963, 83–109.

48. Schumacher 1954, 113–114; Souter 1963, 120–124.

49. Radford 1987; Nelson 1982b, 10; Allen and Frankel 1991, 97–98; Sinclair 1988; Willis 1969.

50. Souter 1963, 145–156; Specht and Fields 1984; Sinclair 1978.

51. Souter 1963, 157–194; Sinclair 1969; 1988; Fowke 1995; Connolly and Anderson 1987.

52. Brown 1995, 51.

53. Gammage 1998, 1.

54. Ibid., 2.

55. Quoted in Brown 1995, 40.

56. Hides 1936, 77–78.

57. Hides and O'Malley did not know that they were not the first Europeans to enter the area. The Fox brothers, identical twins traveling with sixteen carriers, had crossed the Tari Basin just five months earlier, killing at least forty-five Huli. Biersack 1995, 23.

58. Ibid., 77–91; Allen and Frankel 1991, 88–108.

59. Josephides and Schiltz 1991, 208–215.

60. Chappell 1997; Campbell 1998b.

61. The evidence comes from pox scars still visible in the 1870s and 1880s, their source and dating provided through oral testimony. Bevan 1890, 241; Flierl 1932, 10; Romilly 1886, 67; Stone, 1880, 47–48; *Queenslander*, 28 Apr. 1888.

62. Parkinson 1907, 89–90; Spencer 1999, 28.

63. Hahl 1937, 13–15.

64. Butlin 1993, 102–120.

65. Shlomowitz 1987; 1988; 1989; 1990; Cliff and Haggett 1985.

66. Spencer 1999, 15–32; Stone 1876, 54; 1880, 34, 48, 92; Mullins 1988, 387–388, 391–392; Denoon, Dugan, and Marshall 1989.

67. Biersack 1995, 25–29.

68. Russell 2001, 1.

69. West 1978.

Chapter 8: The Twentieth Century: Colonialism and Independence

1. Moore 1998a; Lawrence 1964.

2. Lepowsky 1983.

3. A counterargument would be that bigmen on the further fringes of urban settlements could also have manipulated the colonial presence to their advantage, possibly using more conventional power structures than leaders who had been severely disrupted by living at the very center of urban developments.

4. Newbury 1989, 38–39.

5. Mayo 1969; 1975.

6. Gibbney 1966.

7. Mackenzie 1927; Rowley 1958; Hiery 1995, 45–115.

8. Mair 1948; Legge 1956; Griffin, Nelson, and Firth 1979; Downs 1980; Waiko 1993.

9. Firth 1978b; Sack 2001; Joyce 1963; 1969; 1971; MacGregor 1889–1890; 1894–1895; 1895; 1898–1899; Baal 1966.

10. Firth 1978b; Joyce 1971; West 1968; Thompson 1986; Murray 1925; Lett 1949.

11. Waiko 1990.

12. Monckton 1921; Sinclair 1969; 1988.

13. For instance, Jan van Baal in Dutch New Guinea, and Francis E. Williams in Australian Papua. Campbell 1998a; 2000.

14. Gammage 1998; Kituai 1998; Hides 1936.

15. Denoon, Dugan, and Marshall 1989.

16. The Australian School of Pacific Administration. Campbell 2000.

17. Rivers 1922.

18. Inglis 1974, 4.

19. Inglis 1974; Wolfers 1975.

20. Lett 1944, 127.

21. Lewis 1996.

22. Moore 1990, 31–36; Munro 1990, xlvi–xlviii; Mair 1948, 159–218; Legge 1956, 155–167; Amarshi, Good, and Mortimer 1979, 38–39; Lewis 1996, 315–318; Newbury 1994–1995.

23. Gogh 1954, 180–184.

24. Ligny and Loenen 1954, 274; Filet 1953, 485–487; Souter 1963, 200.

25. Pouwer 1999, 169–170; Wright 2002b.

26. Sinclair 1995; King and Birge 1982, 52; Hanson, Allen, Bourke, and McCarthy 2001, 11–12.

27. Perry 1982; Bennett 2000.

28. Perry 1982, 58–61; Bottemanne 1954.

29. Nelson 1976; Ryan 1991.

30. Gheyselinck 1953, 347–350.

31. Jackson 1982; Poulgrain 1999; Ryan 1991.

32. Moore 1990, 42–43.

33. Kiki 1968.

34. Duncan 1971.

35. Gibson 2000, 47.

36. Brash 1988; Lynch 1988; Weeks and Gutherie 1982a; 1982b; Moore, Haihuie, and Kema 2001, 4.

37. Pouwer 1999, 169.

38. Moore 1990, 43; Denoon 2000.

39. Oram 1968a; 1968b; M. Strathern 1975; Clifford, Morauta, and Stuart 1984.

40. Gewertz and Errington 1999.

41. Dinnen 2001; Dinnen and Ley 2000.

42. Hanson, Allen, Bourke, and McCarthy 2001, 13.

43. Because Papua was part of Australia, the White Australia Policy applied, stopping Asian migration. Although there were a few Chinese laborers and traders in the nineteenth century, the only Chinese introduced in the first half of the twentieth century worked as tailors.

44. Griffin, Nelson, and Firth 1979, 70.

45. The Dutch had administrative control over only a small portion of their New Guinea territory. Any population estimates are only conjecture.

46. White and Lindstrom 1990; Lindstrom and White 1990; Griffin, Nelson, and Firth 1979, 70–101.

47. Allen 1982; Hoogenband 1954, 369–374.

48. Gima 1998, 75; see also Robinson 1981.

49. Allen 1982.

50. Somare 1975, 4–6.

51. Worsley 1957; Lawrence 1964; Loeliger and Trompf 1985; Trompf 1977; 1991, 188–211.

52. Gammage 1975.

53. Stephen 1972, 104–120; Wright 2002a.

54. Moore 1998b. In writing this section I have benefited from discussions during 1999–2000 with Dr. John Waiko.

55. Bettison, Hughes, and Veur 1965.

56. Turner 1990; Dorney 1990; Moore 1995, covering 1967–1991; Saffu 1996.

57. Downs 1980; Waiko 1993, 108–193; Griffin, Nelson, and Firth 1979, 102–235.

58. May and Spriggs 1990; Quodling 1991; Spriggs and Denoon 1992; Dinnen, May, and Regan 1997; Dorney 1998; O'Callaghan 1999; Wehner and Denoon 2001.

59. Moore with Kooyman 1998.

60. Pouwer 1999, 166–167.

61. Boldingh 1954, 226–230.

62. Budiardjo and Liong 1988.

63. Pouwer 1999, 172; Bettison, Hughes, and Veur 1965; Moore 1998b, xxv.

64. Gietzelt 1989; Pouwer 1999, 174. I have accepted Dr. Greg Poulgrain's estimates of the population, which are higher than the official figures.

65. Osborne 1985; May 1986; Wolfers 1988; Gietzelt 1989.

66. Broek and Szalay 2001.

67. Hanson, Allen, Bourke, and McCarthy 2001, 11.

68. In 2001 the Papua New Guinea National AIDS Council estimated that 15,000 to 22,000 people are infected with the virus. *The National*, 30 Nov. 2001. Also refer to Alley 2001, 16; Ahlburg, Larson, and Brown 1998.

69. Rowley 1989, 446.

Bibliography

General Bibliographies

Baal, J. Van, K. W. Galis, and R. M. Koentjaraningrat. 1984. *West Irian: A Bibliography*. Koninklijk Instituut voor Taal-, Land- en Volkenkunde Bibliographical Series No. 15. Dordrecht, Netherlands and Cinnaminson, N.J.

Butler, Alan, Inge Butler, and Gary Cummings. 1984–1990. *A New Guinea Bibliography*. 5 vols. Waigani: University of Papua New Guinea Press.

Eldridge, Sally. 1985. *Solomon Islands Bibliography to 1980*. Suva, Wellington, and Honiara: Institute of Pacific Studies, University of the South Pacific, Alexander Turnbull Library, and Solomon Islands National Library.

Kaima, Sam, and August Kituai. 1999. *A Bibliography of Madang Province*. Waigani: University of Papua New Guinea.

Kaima, Sam, and Biama Kanasa. 1999. *A Bibliography of Morobe Province*. Waigani: University of Papua New Guinea.

Kanasa, Biama. 1999. *Nova Britannia: An Ethnographic Bibliography of New Britain, 1793–1963*. Kokopo, East New Britain: Historical and Cultural Centre, and War Museum.

Kehoe-Forutan, Sandi. 1987. *A Bibliography of the Torres Strait Islands*. St. Lucia, Queensland: Department of Geographical Sciences, University of Queensland.

Lutton, Nancy. 1980. *Guide to the Manuscripts Held in the New Guinea Collection of the University of Papua New Guinea Library*. Waigani: Library, University of Papua New Guinea.

Moore, Clive. 1992. *New Guinea History: A Bibliography of Journal Articles on Papua New Guinea and Irian Jaya*. Accessing the Past No. 2. St. Lucia, Queensland: Department of History, University of Queensland.

———. 2002. *Torres Strait Bibliography*. Resources. Aboriginal and Torres Strait Islander Unit Webpage, University of Queensland. [http://www.uq.edu.au/ATSIS/index.html]

Nagle, Peter. 1998. *Papua New Guinea Records, 1883–1942*. Microfilm Collections Guide No. 4. Canberra: Australian Archives.

Overweel, Jeroen A., compiler and introduction. 1994. *Archival Sources Relating to Netherlands New Guinea History: The Archives of the Ministry of Colonial Affairs, 19th Century*. Irian Jaya Source Materials No. 8. Leiden/Jakarta: DSALCUL/IRIS.

Sack, Peter, ed. 1980. *German New Guinea: A Bibliography*. Canberra: Department of Law, Research School of Social Science, Australian National University.

Turner, Ann. 2001. *Historical Dictionary of Papua New Guinea*. Asian/Oceanian Historical Dictionaries No. 37. 2d ed. Lanham, Md. and London: Scarecrow Press. [Bibliography, 295–357].

Bibliography

Abaijah, Josephine, and Eric Wright. 1991. *A Thousand Coloured Dreams: The Story of a Young Girl Growing Up in Papua*. Mount Waverley, Victoria: Dellasta Pacific.

Abel, Sir Cecil. 1991 Interview in Port Moresby, 16 April.

Abeyasekere, Susan. 1983. Slaves in Batavia: Insights from a Slave Register. In *Slavery, Bondage and Dependency in Southeast Asia*, edited by Anthony Reid with Jennifer Brewster, 286–314. St. Lucia, Queensland: University of Queensland Press.

———. 1989. *Jakarta: A History*. Singapore: Oxford University Press [rev. ed.].

Affleck, D. A. 1971. Murua or Woodlark Island: A Study of European-Muruan Contact to 1942. B.A. Honors, Australian National University.

Ahlburg, Dennis A., Heidi L. Larson, and Tim Brown. 1998. The Potential Demographic Impact of HIV/AIDS in the Pacific. *Pacific Studies* 21 (4): 67–81.

Akin, David W. 1993. Negotiating Culture in East Kwaio, Malaita. Ph.D. thesis, University of Hawai'i.

Albertis, Luigi Maria d'. 1880. *New Guinea: What I Did and What I Saw*. 2 vols. London: Sampson, Low.

Allen, Bryant J. 1982. The Pacific War, 1941–1945. In *Papua New Guinea Atlas: A Nation in Transition*, edited by David King and Stephen Ranck, 14–15. Port Moresby: Robert Brown and Associates and University of Papua New Guinea.

Allen, Bryant J., and Stephen Frankell. 1991. Across the Tari Furoro. In *Like People You See in a Dream: First Contact in Six Papuan Societies*, by Edward L. Schieffelin and Robert Crittenden, with contributions by Bryant Allen et al. 88–124. Stanford, Calif.: Stanford University Press.

Allen, Jim. 1972. Port Essington—A Successful Limpet Port? *Historical Studies* 15 (59): 341–360.

———. 1982. Pre-Contact Trade in Papua New Guinea. In *Melanesia: Beyond Diversity*, edited by R. J. May and Hank Nelson, vol. 1, 193–205. Canberra: Research School of Pacific Studies, Australian National University.

———. 1993. Notions of the Pleistocene in Greater Australia. In *A Community of Culture: The People and Prehistory of the Pacific*, edited by Matthew Spriggs, 139–151. Canberra: Department of Prehistory, Research School of Pacific Studies, Australian National University.

———. 1996. The Pre-Austronesian Settlement of Island Melanesia: Implications for Lapita Archaeology. In *Prehistoric Settlement of the Pacific*, edited by Ward H. Goodenough, 11–27. Philadelphia: American Philosophical Society.

Allen, Jim, et al. 1988. Pleistocene Dates for the Human Occupation of New Ireland, Northern Melanesia. *Nature* 331: 707–709.

Alley, Roderick. 2001. Identity, Ethnicity and National Loyalty in Oceania: Some Asian Pacific Implications. In *Oceania and Asia: The South Pacific Looks North*, edited by Ralph Pettman, 15–28. Asian Studies Institute Working Paper No.18. Wellington: Victoria University of Wellington.

Amarshi, Azeem, Kenneth Good, and Rex Mortimer. 1979. *Development and Dependency: The Political Economy of Papua New Guinea*. Melbourne: Oxford University Press.

Ambrose, W. R. 1988. An Early Bronze Artefact from Papua New Guinea. *Antiquity* 62 (236): 483–491.

Amery, R., and C. Bourke. 1994. Australian Languages: Our Heritage. In *Aboriginal Australia: An Introductory Reader in Aboriginal Studies*, edited by C. Bourke, E. Bourke and B. Edwards, 102–122. St. Lucia, Queensland: University of Queensland Press.

Amherst, William A. T-A., and Basil Thomson. 1901. *The Discovery of the Solomon Islands by Alvaro de Mendana in 1568*. London: Hakluyt Society. [Facsimile: Nendeln/Liechtenstein, and Millwood, N.Y.: Kraus Reprint, 1967.]

Andaya, Leonard Y. 1993. *The World of Maluku: Eastern Indonesia in the Early Modern Period*. Honolulu: University of Hawai'i Press.

Ardika, I. W., and Peter Bellwood. 1991. Sembiran: the Beginnings of Indian Contact with Bali. *Antiquity* 65: 211–232.

Armit, R. H. 1876. *The History of New Guinea and the Origin of the Negroid Race: A Resume of Past Exploration, Future Capabilities and the Political, Commercial and Moral Aspects of the Island*. London: Trubner.

Baal, Jan van. 1966. *Dema: Description and Analysis of Marind-anim Culture*. KITLV Translation Series No. 9. The Hague: Martinus Nijhoff.

Bach, John. 1968. The Royal Navy in the Pacific Islands. *Journal of Pacific History* 3: 3–20.

———. 1986. *The Australia Station: A History of the Royal Navy in the South Pacific, 1821–1913*. Sydney: University of New South Wales Press.

Ballard, Chris. 2000. Collecting Pygmies: The 'Tapiro' and the British Ornithologists' Union Expedition to Dutch New Guinea, 1910–11. In *Hunting the Gatherers: Ethnographic Collectors, Agents and Agency in Melanesia, 1870s–1930s*, edited by Michael O'Hanlon and Robert L. Welsch, 127–154. Oxford: Berghahn Books.

Ballard, Chris, Anton Ploeg, and Steven Vink. 2001. *Race for the Snow Mountains: Photography in the Early Exploration of Netherlands New Guinea, 1907–1936*. Amsterdam: Royal Tropical Institute.

Barham, A. J., and D. R. Harris. 1983. Prehistory and Palaeoecology of Torres Strait. In *Quaternary Coastlines and Marine Archaeology: Towards the Prehistory of Land Bridges and Continental Shelves*, edited by P. M. Masters and N. C. Flemming, 529–557. London: Academic Press.

Barnett, H. G. 1959. Peace and Progress in New Guinea. *American Anthropologist* 61: 1013–1019.

Barrett, Charles. 1948. *White Blackfellows: The Strange Adventures of Europeans who Lived among Savages*. Melbourne: Hallcraft.

Bassett, D. K. 1961. Thomas Forrest, an Eighteenth-Century Mariner. *Journal of the Malayan Branch of the Royal Asiatic Society* 34 (2): 106–121.

———. 1964. British Commercial and Strategic Interest in the Malay Peninsula during the Late Eighteenth Century. In *Malayan and Indonesian Studies: Essays Presented to Sir Richard Winstedt on His Eighty-fifth Birthday*, edited by J. Bastin and R. Roolvink, 122–140. Oxford: Clarendon Press.

———. 1969. Introduction, Thomas Forrest. In *A Voyage to New Guinea and the Moluccas, 1774–1776*, by Thomas Forrest, 1–22. Kuala Lumpur: Oxford University Press.

Bassett, Marnie. 1966. *'Behind the Picture': H.M.S. Rattlesnake's Australia-New Guinea Cruise, 1846 to 1850*. Melbourne: Oxford University Press.

Bayldon, F. J. 1925. Voyage of Luis Vaez de Torres from the New Hebrides to the Moluccas, June to November, 1606. *Royal Australian Historical Society Journal* 11 (3): 158–194.

Bayton, John. 1964–1965. The Mission to the Aborigines at Somerset. *Journal of the Royal Historical Society of Queensland* 7 (3): 622–633.

———. 1969. Missionaries and Islanders: A Chronicle of Events Associated with the Introduction of the Christian Mission to the People of Torres Strait during the Period 1866–1873. *Queensland Heritage* 1 (10): 16–20.

Beach, Charles. 1863. *Andrew Deverel: The History of an Adventurer in New Guinea.* 2 vols. London: Richard Bentley.

Beaglehole, John C. 1966. *The Exploration of the Pacific.* London: Adam and Black. [3d ed.].

Beale, Thomas. 1839. *The Natural History of the Sperm Whale: To Which Is Added a Sketch of a South Sea Whaling Voyage.* London: John Van Voorst.

Beckett, Jeremy R. 1965. Australia's Melanesian Minority: Political Development in the Torres Strait. *Human Organization* 24 (2): 152–158.

———. 1987. *Torres Strait Islanders: Custom and Colonialism.* Cambridge: Cambridge University Press.

———. 1998. Haddon Attends a Funeral: Fieldwork in Torres Strait, 1888, 1898. In *Cambridge and the Torres Strait: Centenary Essays on the 1898 Anthropological Expedition*, edited by Anita Herle and Sandra Rouse, 23–49. Cambridge: Cambridge University Press.

Bedford, Richard. 1980. *Perceptions, Past and Present, of a Future for Melanesia.* 1979 Macmillan Brown Lectures. Christchurch: Department of Geography, University of Canterbury.

Bellwood, Peter. 1985. *Prehistory of the Indo-Malaysian Archipelago.* Sydney: Academic Press.

———. 1993. Crossing the Wallace Line—With Style. In *A Community of Culture: The People and Prehistory of the Pacific*, edited by Matthew Spriggs et al., 152–163. Canberra: Department of Prehistory, Research School of Pacific Studies, Australian National University.

———. 1995. Austronesian Prehistory in Southeast Asia: Homeland, Expansion and Transformation. In *The Austronesians: Historical and Comparative Perspectives*, edited by Peter Bellwood, James J. Fox, and Darrell Tryon, 97–111. Canberra: Department of Anthropology, Research School of Pacific and Asian Studies, Australian National University.

———. 1998. From Bird's Head to Bird's Eye View. In *Perspectives on the Bird's Head of Irian Jaya, Indonesia. Proceedings of the Conference, Leiden, 13–17 October 1997*, edited by Jelle Miedema, Cecilia Odé, and Rien A. C. Dam, 951–975. Amsterdam, and Atlanta, Ga.: Rodopi.

Bennett, Judith A. 1987. *Wealth of the Solomons: A History of a Pacific Archipelago, 1800–1978.* Honolulu: University of Hawai'i Press.

———. 2000. *Pacific Forest: A History of Resource Control and Contest in Solomon Islands, c. 1800–1997.* Leiden and Cambridge: Brill and White Horse.

Berck, Lionel. 1995. *St. Bees Island: Its History, Life-styles and Tales.* Brisbane: Boolarong.

Bettison, David G., Colin A. Hughes, and Paul W. van der Veur, eds. 1965. *The Papua-New Guinea Elections, 1964.* Canberra: Australian National University.

Bevan, Theodore F. 1890. *Toil, Travel, and Discovery in British New Guinea.* London: Kegan Paul, Trench, Trübner and Co.

Biersack, Aletta. 1995. Introduction: The Huli, Duna and Ipili Peoples Yesterday and Today. In *Papuan Borderlands: Huli, Duna and Ipili Perspectives on the Papua New Guinea Highlands*, edited by Aletta Biersack, 1–54. Ann Arbor: University of Michigan Press.

Biskup, Peter, ed. 1974. *The New Guinea Memoirs of Jean Baptiste Octave Mouton.* Canberra: Australian National University Press.

Blong, Russell J. 1982. *The Time of Darkness: Local Legends and Volcanic Reality in Papua New Guinea.* Canberra: Australian National University Press.

Boldingh, L. G. 1954. Bestuur, Politie en Justitie. In *Nieuw Guinea: De Ontwikkeling op Economisch, Sociaal en Cultureel Gebied, in Nederlands en Australisch Nieuw Guinea*, edited by W. C. Klein, 3: 178–231. 'S-Gravenhage: Staatsdrukkerij-en Uitgeverijbedrijf.

Bonnemaison, Joël. 1985. The Tree and the Canoe: Roots and Mobility in Vanuatu Society. In "Mobility and Identity in the Island Pacific," edited by Murray Chapman, special issue of *Pacific Viewpoint* 26 (1): 30–62.

———. 1994. *The Tree and the Canoe: History and Ethnography of Tanna*, translated by Josée Pénot-Demetry. Honolulu: University of Hawai'i Press.

Boogaart, Ernst van der. 1988. The Mythical Symmetry in God's Creation: The Dutch and the Southern Continent, 1569–1756. In *Terra Australis: The Furthest Shore*, edited by William Eisler and Bernard Smith, 43–50. Sydney: Art Gallery of New South Wales and International Cultural Corporation of Australia.

Bottemanne, C. J. 1954. Zeevisserij. In *Nieuw Guinea: De Ontwikkeling op Economisch, Sociaal en Cultureel Gebied, in Nederlands en Australisch Nieuw Guinea*, edited by W. C. Klein, 2: 357–400. 'S-Gravenhage: Staatsdrukkerij-en Uitgeverijbedrijf.

Braak, C. 1954. Klimaat. In *Nieuw Guinea: De Ontwikkeling op Economisch, Sociaal en Cultureel Gebied, in Nederlands en Australisch Nieuw Guinea*, edited by W. C. Klein, 2: 42–66. 'S-Gravenhage: Staatsdrukkerij-en Uitgeverijbedrijf.

Bradley, J. c.1860. *A Nine Months' Cruise in the 'Ariel' Schooner from San Francisco in Company with the 'Wanderer' of the Royal Yaght Sguadron, Belonging to Benjamin Boyd esq*. Parramatta, New South Wales: J. J. Beukers. [Reissued and annotated by M. D. Cobcroft, Ipswich: Amphion Press, 1991.]

Brash, Elton. 1988. Universitas Cenderawasih (UNCEN). In *Pacific Universities: Achievements, Problems, Prospects*, edited by Ron Crocombe and Malama Meleisea, 167–175. Suva: Institute of Pacific Studies, University of the South Pacific.

Brockett, William E. 1836. *Narrative of a Voyage from Sydney to Torres Strait, in Search of the Survivors of the Charles Eaton: In His Majesty's Colonial Schooner Isabella, C. N. Lewis, Commander*. Sydney: Henry Bull.

Broek, Theo van der, and Alexandra Szalay. 2001. Raising the Morning Star: Six Months in the Developing Independence Movement in West Papua. *Journal of Pacific History* 36 (1): 77–92.

Brookfield, H. C., with Doreen Hart. 1971. *Melanesia: A Geographical Interpretation of an Island World*. London: Methuen and Co.

Brosse, Jacques. 1983. *Great Voyages of Exploration: The Golden Age of Discovery in the Pacific*, translated by Stanley Hochman. Sydney: Doubleday.

Brown, Paula. 1995. *Beyond a Mountain Valley: The Simbu of Papua New Guinea*. Honolulu: University of Hawai'i Press.

Budiardjo, Carmel, and Liem Soei Liong. 1988. *West Papua: The Obliteration of a People*. 2d rev. ed. Surrey, United Kingdom: Tapol.

Burkill, I. H., et al. 1935. *A Dictionary of the Economic Products of the Malay Peninsula*. 2 vols. London: Crown Agents for the Colonies, on behalf of the Governments of the Straits Settlements and the Federated Malay States.

Burton, John. 1984. Quarrying in a Tribal Society. *World Archaeology* 16: 234–247.

Butlin, Noel G. 1993. *Economics and the Dreamtime: A Hypothetical History*. Melbourne: Cambridge University Press.

Byrnes, Dan. 1988. Outlooks for England's South Whale Fishery, 1784–1800, and the Great Botany Bay Debate. *Great Circle* 10 (2): 79–102.

Cameron, J.M.R. 1985. Traders, Government Officials and the Occupation of Melville Island in 1824. *Great Circle* 71 (2): 88–99.

Campbell, Ian C. 1998a. Anthropology and the Professionalisation of Colonial Administration in Papua and New Guinea. *Journal of Pacific History* 33 (1): 69–90.

———. 1998b. *'Gone Native' in Polynesia: Captivity Narratives and Experiences from the South Pacific.* Westport, Conn.: Greenwood Press.

———. 2000. The ASOPA Controversy: A Pivot of Australian Policy for Papua and New Guinea, 1945–49. *Journal of Pacific History* 35 (1): 83–99.

Campo, J. á. 1991. From Far Neighbour to Good Friend: The Birth of the Java Australia Line. *Great Circle* 13 (1): 1–20.

Capell, Arthur. 1943. *The Linguistic Position of South-eastern Papua.* Sydney: Australasian Medical Pub. Co.

Carter, George G. 1990. *Yours in His Service: A Reflection on the Life and Times of Reverend Belshazzar Gina of the Solomon Islands*, edited by Esau Tuza. Honiara: University of the South Pacific Centre.

Cavanagh, A. K. 1989. The Return of the First Fleet Ships. *Great Circle* 11 (2): 1–16.

Chalmers, James. 1887. *Pioneering in New Guinea.* London: Religious Tract Society.

———. 1902. *James Chalmers: His Autobiography and Letters.* London: Religious Tract Society.

Chalmers, James, and W. W. Gill. 1885. *Work and Adventures in New Guinea, 1877 to 1885.* London: Religious Tract Society.

Chappell, David A. 1995. Active Agents versus Passive Victims: Decolonized Historiography or Problematic Paradigm. *Contemporary Pacific* 7 (2): 303–326.

———. 1997. *Double Ghosts: Oceanian Voyagers on EuroAmerican Ships.* New York and London: M. E. Sharpe.

Chowning, Ann. 1977. *An Introduction to the Peoples and Cultures of Melanesia.* 2d ed. Menlo Park, Calif: Cummings.

Clark, Jeffrey. 1991. Pearlshell Symbolism in Highlands Papua New Guinea, with Particular Reference to the Wiru People of Southern Highlands. *Oceania* 61 (4): 309–339.

Cliff, Andrew D., and Peter Haggett. 1985. *The Spread of Measles in Fiji and the Pacific: Spatial Components in the Transmission of Epidemic Waves through Island Communities.* Department of Human Geography Publication No. HG/18. Canberra: Research School of Pacific Studies, Australian National University.

Clifford, William, Louise Morauta, and Barry Stuart. 1984. *Law and Order in Papua New Guinea.* 2 vols. Port Moresby: Institute of National Affairs.

Codrington, Robert H. 1891. *The Melanesians: Studies in Their Anthropology and Folk-lore.* Oxford: Clarendon Press. [Facsimile: New York: Dover, 1972.]

Connolly, Bob, and Robin Anderson. 1987. *First Contact: New Guinea's Highlanders Encounter the Outside World.* New York: Viking Penguin.

Corn, Charles. 1999. *The Scents of Eden: A History of the Spice Trade.* New York: Kodansha International.

Corris, Peter. 1968. 'Blackbirding' in New Guinea Waters, 1883–84: An Episode in the Queensland Labour Trade. *Journal of Pacific History* 3: 85–105.

Cortesao, Armando. 1960. *Portugaliae Monumenta Cartographica*. 6 vols. Lisbon: [n.s].

Coulter, John. 1847. *Adventures on the Western Coast of South America and the Interior of California: Including a Narrative of Incidents at the Kingsmill Islands, New Ireland, New Britain, New Guinea, and Other Islands in the Pacific Ocean; With an Account of the Natural Productions, and the Manners and Customs, in Peace and War, of the Various Tribes Visited*. 2 vols. London: Longman, Brown, Green and Longman.

Cribb, Robert. 1997. Birds-of-Paradise and Environmental Politics in Colonial Indonesia, 1890–1931. In *Paper Landscapes: Explorations in the Environmental History of Indonesia*, edited by Peter Boomgaard, Freek Colombijn, and David Henley, 379–408. Leiden: KITLV Press.

Crocombe, Marjorie T. 1972a. Ruatoka: A Polynesian in New Guinea History. *Pacific Islands Monthly* 43 (11): 69–75.

———. 1972b. Port Moresby's First Missionaries were Pacific Islanders. *Pacific Islands Monthly* 43 (12): 69–76.

Crocombe, Ron, and Marjorie T. Crocombe, eds. 1982. *Polynesian Missions in Melanesia: From Samoa, Cook Islands and Tonga to Papua New Guinea and New Caledonia*. Suva: Institute of Pacific Studies, University of the South Pacific.

Crowley, Terry. 1983. Uradhi. In *Handbook of Australian Langauges*, edited by R.M.W. Dixon and Barry J. Blake, 306–428. Canberra: Australian National University Press.

Curry, Charles H. 1963. *The Transportation, Escape and Pardoning of Mary Bryant (née Broad)*. Sydney: Angus and Robertson.

Dawbin, W. H. 1972. Dolphins and Whales. In *Encyclopaedia of Papua and New Guinea*, edited by Peter Ryan, 1: 270–276. Melbourne: Melbourne University Press in association with the University of Papua New Guinea.

Delbos, Georges. 1985. *The Mustard Seed: From a French Mission to a Papuan Church, 1885–1985*. Port Moresby: Institute of Papua New Guinea Studies.

Dening, Greg. 1980. *Islands and Beaches: Discourse on a Silent Land, Marquesas, 1774–1880*. Honolulu: University of Hawai'i Press.

———. 1985. *The Death of William Gooch: A History's Anthropology*. Melbourne: Melbourne University Press.

———. 1996. *Performances*. Melbourne: Melbourne University Press.

Denoon, Donald. 2000. *Getting under the Skin: The Bougainville Copper Agreement and the Creation of the Panguna Mine*. Melbourne: Melbourne University Press.

Denoon, Donald, with Kathleen Dugan, and Leslie Marshall. 1989. *Public Health in Papua New Guinea: Medical Possibility and Social Constraint, 1884–1984*. Cambridge: Cambridge University Press.

Diamond, Jared M. 1988. Express Train to Polynesia. *Nature* 336: 307–308.

———. 1997. *Guns, Germs and Steel: A Short History of Everybody for the Last 13,000 Years*. London: Vintage.

Dinnen, Sinclair. 2001. *Law and Order in a Weak State: Crime and Politics in Papua New Guinea*. Honolulu: University of Hawai'i Press.

Dinnen, Sinclair, and Allison Ley. 2000. *Reflections on Violence in Melanesia*. Sydney and Canberra: Hawkins and Asia Pacific Press.

Dinnen, Sinclair, Ron May, and Anthony J. Regan, eds. 1997. *Challenging the State: The Sandline Affair in Papua New Guinea*. Canberra: National Centre for Development Studies, and the Department of Political and Social Change, Research School of Pacific and Asian Studies, Australian National University.

Dixon, Robert. 2001. *Prosthetic Gods: Travel, Representation and Colonial Governance*. St. Lucia, Queensland: University of Queensland Press.

Donohue, Mark. 1996. Some Trade Languages of Insular South-east Asia and Irian Jaya. In *Atlas of Languages of Intercultural Communication in the Pacific, Asia, and the Americas*, edited by Stephen A. Wurm, Peter Mühlhäusler, and Darrell T. Tryon, 11.1: 713–716. Berlin and New York: Mouton de Gruyter.

Dorney, Sean. 1990. *Papua New Guinea: People, Politics and History since 1975*. Milsons Point, New South Wales: Random.

———. 1998. *The Sandline Affair: Politics and Mercenaries and the Bougainville Crisis*. Sydney: ABC Books.

Douglas, Bronwen. 1979. Rank, Power, Authority: A Reassessment of Traditional Leadership in South Pacific Societies. *Journal of Pacific History* 14 (1): 2–27.

Douglas, Ngaire. 1996. *They Came for Savages: 100 Years of Tourism in Melanesia*. Lismore: Southern Cross University.

Downs, Ian F. G. 1980. *The Australian Trusteeship: Papua New Guinea, 1945–75*. Canberra: Australian Government Publishing Service.

Dumont d'Urville, Jules S. C. 1834–1835. *Voyage Pittoresque Autour du Monde: Resumé Généal des Voyages de Découvertes de Magellan . . .* Paris: Tenre.

Duncan, Meg. 1971. Native Education in Papua and New Guinea (1884–1970): A Study of Relationships between Education and Policies. B.A. Education honors thesis, University of Queensland.

Dunmore, John. 1965–1969. *French Explorers in the Pacific: Vol. 1, The Eighteenth Century, Vol. 2, The Nineteenth Century*. Oxford: Clarendon.

———. 1992. *Who's Who in Pacific Navigation*, Melbourne: Melbourne University Press.

Dutton, Geoffrey. 1976. *Queen Emma of the South Seas: A Novel*. Melbourne: Macmillan.

Dutton, Tom E. 1982. Languages of Wider Communication (or *Lingua Francas*). In *Papua New Guinea Atlas: A Nation in Transition*, edited by David King and Stephen Ranck, 36–37. Bathurst: Robert Brown and Associates in conjunction with the University of Papua New Guinea.

———. 1985. *Police Motu: Inea Sivarai*. Port Moresby: University of Papua New Guinea Press.

———. 1989. 'Successful Intercourse was had with the Natives': Aspects of European Contact Methods in the Pacific. In *A World of Language: Papers Presented to Professor S. A. Wurm on His 65th Birthday*, edited by D. C. Laycock and W. Winter, 153–171. Pacific Linguistics, Series C, No. 100. Canberra: Department of Linguistics, Research School of Pacific Studies, Australian National University.

———. 1996a. Languages in Contact in Central and South-East Mainland Papua New Guinea. In *Atlas of Languages of Intercultural Communication in the Pacific, Asia, and the Americas*, edited by Stephen A. Wurm, Peter Mühlhäusler and Darrell T. Tryon, 11.1: 215–217. Berlin and New York: Mouton de Gruyter.

———. 1996b. Other Pidgins of Papua New Guinea. In *Atlas of Languages of Intercultural Communication in the Pacific, Asia, and the Americas*, edited by Stephen A. Wurm, Peter Mühlhäusler, and Darrell T. Tryon, 11.1: 215–217. Berlin and New York: Mouton de Gruyter.

Earl, George W. 1853. *The Native Races of the Indian Archipelago: Papuans*. London: Hippolyte Bail-liere.

Edwards, Edward, and George Hamilton. 1915. *Voyage of H.M.S. Pandora: Despatched to Arrest the Mutineers of the 'Bounty' in the South Seas, 1790–91: Being the Narratives of Captain Edward Edwards, R.N. the commander, and George Hamilton the Surgeon, with Introduction and Notes by Basil Thomson*. London: Frances Edwards.

Edwards, Elizabeth. 1997. Making Histories: The Torres Strait Expedition of 1898. *Pacific Studies* 20 (4): 13–34.

———. 2001. *Raw Histories: Photographs, Anthropology and Museums*. Oxford and New York: Berg.

Eisler, Wiliam. 1995. *The Furthest Shore: Images of Terra Australia from the Middle Ages to Captain Cook*. Cambridge: Cambridge University Press.

Eisler, William, and Bernard Smith, eds. 1988. *Terra Australia: The Furthest Shore*. Sydney: Art Gallery of New South Wales and International Cultural Corporation of Australia.

[Erskine, Commodore James, or his secretary H. L. Warren?]. 1885. *Narrative of the Expedition of the Australian Squadron to the South-East Coast of New Guinea, October to December 1884, with Illustrations*. Sydney: Government Printer.

Farnfield, Jean. 1973. Queensland and the Annexation of the Torres Strait Islands. *Australian Outlook* 27 (2): 215–227.

Feil, Daryl K. 1987. *The Evolution of Highland Papua New Guinea Societies*. New York and Melbourne: Cambridge University Press.

Filet, R. E. 1953. Het Arbeidsvraagstuk. In *Nieuw Guinea: De ontwikkeling op economisch, sociaal en cultureel gebied, in Nederlands en Australisch Nieuw Guinea*, edited by W. C. Klein, 1: 451–481. 'S-Gravenhage: Staatsdrukkerij-en Uitgeverijbedrijf.

Firth, Stewart G. 1976. The Transformation of the Labour Trade in German New Guinea, 1899–1914. *Journal of Pacific History* 11 (1): 51–65.

———. 1977. German Firms in the Western Pacific Islands, 1857–1914. *Journal of Pacific History* 8: 10–28.

———. 1978a. Captain Hernsheim: Pacific Venturer, Merchant Prince. In *More Pacific Islands Portraits*, edited by Deryck Scarr, 115–130. Canberra: Australian National University Press.

———. 1978b. Albert Hahl: Governor of German New Guinea. In *Papua New Guinea Portraits*, edited by James Griffin, 28–47, 156–157. Canberra: Australian National University Press.

———. 1982. *New Guinea under the Germans*. Melbourne: Melbourne University Press. [Reprinted, Port Moresby: Webb Books, 1986.]

Flannery, Tim. 1995. *The Future Eaters: An Ecological History of the Australasian Lands and People*. Sydney: Reed New Holland.

Flierl, Johann. 1932. *Christ in New Guinea: Former Cannibals become Evangelists by the Marvelous Grace of God: A Short History of Missionwork done by the Native Helpers and Teachers in the Lutheran Mission in New Guinea*. Tanunda, South Australia: Auricht Printing Office [Lutheran Church].

Flinders, Matthew. 1814. *A Voyage to Terra Australis: Undertaken for the Purpose of Completing the Discovery of that Vast Country in the Years 1801, 1802, and 1803, in His Majesty's Ship the Investigator, and Subsequently in the Armed Vessel Porpoise and Cumberland Schooner with an Account of the Shipwreck of the Porpoise, Arrival of the Cumberland at Mauritius, and Imprisonment of the Commander during Six Years and a Half in that Island*. 3 vols. and charts. London: G. and W. Nicol. [Facsimile: Adelaide: Library Board of South Australia, 1966.]

Foley, William. 1986. *The Papuan Languages of New Guinea*. Cambridge: Cambridge University Press.

Forbes, Anna. 1887. *Insulinde: Experiences of a Naturalist's Wife in the Eastern Archipelago*. Edinburgh and London: William Blackwood and Sons.

Forbes, Henry O. 1885. *A Naturalist's Wanderings in the Eastern Archipelago: A Narrative of Travel and Exploration from 1878 to 1883, with Numerous Illustrations . . . by John B. Gibbs*. York: Harper.

Forrest, Thomas. 1775. *A Voyage to New Guinea and the Moluccas from Balambangan Performed in the Tartar Galley Belonging to the Honourable East India Company during the Years 1774, 1775 and 1776*. London: J. Robson. [New ed., *A Voyage to New Guinea and the Moluccas, 1774–1776*, with Introduction by D. K. Bassett, Kuala Lumpur: Oxford University Press, 1969.]

Fowke, John. 1995. *Kundi Dan: Dan Leahy's Life among the Highlanders of Papua New Guinea*. St. Lucia, Queensland: University of Queensland Press.

Fraser, R. L. 1853. Comparative Routes through Torres Strait. *Nautical Magazine and Naval Chronicle* April: 214–215.

Fry, Howard T. 1969. Alexander Dalrymple and New Guinea. *Journal of Pacific History* 4: 83–104.

———. 1970. *Alexander Dalrymple (1737–1808) and the Expansion of British Trade*. London: Royal Commonwealth Society/Frank Cass & Co.

Galis, Klass W. 1953. Geschiedenis. In *Nieuw Guinea: De Ontwikkeling op Economisch, Sociaal en Cultureel Gebied, in Nederlands en Australisch Nieuw Guinea*, edited by W. C. Klein, vol. 1: 1–65. 'S-Gravenhage: Staatsdrukkerij-en Uitgeverijbedrijf.

Gammage, Bill. 1975. The Rabaul Strike. *Journal of Pacific History* 10: 74–105.

———. 1998. *The Sky Travellers: Journeys in New Guinea, 1938–1939*. Melbourne: Melbourne University Press.

Gash, Noel, and June Whittaker. 1975. *A Pictorial History of New Guinea*. Brisbane: Jacaranda.

George, Margaret. 1966. The Annexation of New Guinea. *Australian National University History Journal* 1 (3): 17–23.

Gewertz, Deborah B., and Frederick K. Errington. 1999. *Emerging Class in Papua New Guinea: The Telling of Difference*. Cambridge: Cambridge University Press.

Gheyselinck, R. F. Ch. R. 1953. Petroleum. In *Nieuw Guinea: De Ontwikkeling op Economisch, Sociaal en Cultureel Gebied, in Nederlands en Australisch Nieuw Guinea*, edited by W. C. Klein, 1: 311–350. 'S-Gravenhage: Staatsdrukkerij-en Uitgeverijbedrijf.

Gibbney, Herbert J. 1966. The Interregnum in the Government of Papua, 1901–1906. *Australian Journal of Politics and History* 12 (3): 341–359.

———. 1972. The New Guinea Gold Rush of 1878. *Journal of the Royal Australian Historical Society* 58 (4): 284–296.

Gibbons, J.R.H., and F.G.A.U. Clunie. 1986. Sea Level Changes and Pacific Prehistory: New Insight into Early Human Settlement of Oceania. *Journal of Pacific History* 21 (2): 58–82.

Gibson, John. 2000. Who's Not in School? Economic Barriers to Universal Primary Education in Papua New Guinea. *Pacific Economic Bulletin* 15 (2): 46–58.

Gibson-Hill, C. A. 1959. George Samuel Windsor Earl. *Journal of the Malayan Branch of the Royal Asiatic Society* 32 (1): 105–153.

Gietzelt, Dale. 1989. The Indonesianization of West Papua. *Oceania* 56 (3): 201–221.

Gill, J.C.H. 1988. *The Missing Coast: Queensland Takes Shape*. Brisbane: Queensland Museum.

Gill, William W. 1874. Three Visits to New Guinea. *Royal Geographical Society Proceedings* 44: 15–31.

———. 1876. *Life in the Southern Isles: Or Scenes and Incidents in the South Pacific and New Guinea*. London: Religious Tract Society.

Gima, Keimelo. 1998. Where are They? The Plight of Papua New Guinea Workers under the Regime of the World Bank and the IMF. In *Labour Organisation and Development: Case Studies*, edited by Michael Hess, 71–90. Canberra: NCDS Asia Pacific Press.

Godelier, Maurice. 1986. *The Making of Great Men: Male Domination and Power among the New Guinea Baruya*. Translated by Rupert Swyer. Cambridge: Cambridge University Press.

Gogh, F. van. 1954. Kleine Landbouw en Kolonisatie. In *Nieuw Guinea: De Ontwikkeling op Economisch, Sociaal en Cultureel Gebied, in Nederlands en Australisch Nieuw Guinea*, edited by W. C. Klein, 2: 106–190. 'S-Gravenhage: Staatsdrukkerij-en Uitgeverijbedrijf.

Golson, Jack. 1972a. Land Connections, Sea Barriers and the Relationship of Australia and New Guinea Prehistory. In *Bridge and Barrier: The Natural and Cultural History of Torres Strait*, edited by David Walker, 375–397. Canberra: Australian National University Press.

———. 1972b. Both Sides of the Wallace Line: New Guinea, Australia, Island Melanesia and Asian Prehistory. In *Early Chinese Art and Its Possible Influence in the Pacific Basin: A Symposium*, edited by H. Barnard, 533–595. New York: Intercultural Arts Press.

———. 1977. No Room at the Top: Agricultural Intensification in the New Guinea Highlands. In *Sunda and Sahul: Prehistoric Studies in South-east Asia, Melanesia and Australia*, edited by Jim Allen, Jack Golson, and Rhys Jones, 601–638. London: Academic Press.

———. 1989. The Origins and Development of New Guinea Agriculture. In *Foraging and Farming: The Evolution of Plant Domestication*, edited by D. R. Harris and G. C. Hillman, 678–687. London: Unwin and Hyman.

Goode, John. 1977. *Rape of the Fly: Exploration in New Guinea*. Melbourne: Nelson and Robert Brown and Associates.

Goodenough, Ward H. 1996. Introduction. In *Prehistoric Settlement of the Pacific*, edited by Ward H. Goodenough, 1–10. Philadelphia: American Philosophical Society.

Goodman, Tom. 1998. The *Sosolot* Exchange Network of Eastern Indonesia during the Seventeenth and Eighteenth Centuries. In *Perspectives on the Bird's Head of Irian Jaya, Indonesia. Proceedings of the Conference, Leiden, 13–17 October 1997*, edited by Jelle Miedema, Cecilia Odé, and Rien A. C. Dam, 421–454. Amsterdam, and Atlanta, Ga.: Rodopi.

Gordon, Donald Craigie. 1951. *The Australian Frontier in New Guinea, 1870–1885*. New York: Columbia University Press. [republished New York: AMS Press, 1968.]

Gorecki, Paul P. 1985. The Documented History of the 'Lost Tribes' of the Schrauder Mountains, 1913–1984. *Research in Melanesia* 8 (1): 47–56.

Gray, Alastair C. 1999. Trading Contacts in the Bismarck Archipelago during the Whaling Era, 1799–1884. *Journal of Pacific History* 34 (1): 23–43.

Green, Roger C. 1987. Obsidian Results from the Lapita Sites of the Reef/Santa Cruz Islands. In *Archaeometry: Further Australasian Studies*, edited by W. Ambrose and J. Mummery, 239–247. Canberra: Australian National University.

———. 1991. Near and Remote Oceania—Disestablishing 'Melanesia' in Culture History. In *Man and a Half: Essays in Pacific Anthropology and Ethnobiology in Honour of Ralph Bulmer*, edited by Andrew Pawley, 491–502. Memoir No. 48. Auckland: The Polynesian Society.

Grieve, Maud. 1931. *A Modern Herbal: The Medicinal, Culinary, Cosmetic and Economic Properties, Cultivation and Folklore of Herbs, Grasses, Fungi, Shrubs and Trees with all their Modern Scientific Uses*, edited and with an introduction by C. F. Leyel. London: Jonathan Cape.

Griffin, Andrew. 1990. London, Bengal, the China Trade and the Unfrequented Extremities of Asia: The East India Company's Settlement in New Guinea, 1793–95. *British Library Journal* 16 (2): 151–173.

Griffin, James. 1975. Papua Besena. *World Review* 14 (3): 3–16.

———. 1981. "Territorial Implications in the Torres Strait; Annex: Possible Motives for Annexing Kawa, Mata Kawa and Kussa, 1878–9"; and "Status of the Islands of Kawa, Mata Kawa and Kussa: A Comment on the paper by Mr. J. Griffin, prepared by the Department of Foreign Affairs and the Attorney General's Department." In *The Torres Strait Treaty: A Symposium*, edited by P. J. Boyce and M.W.D. White, 92–140. Canberra: Australian Institute of International Affairs, Queensland, and Australian National University Press.

Griffin, James, Hank Nelson, and Stewart Firth. 1979. *Papua New Guinea: A Political History*. Richmond, Victoria: Heinemann.

Groube, Les M. 1986. Waisted Axes of Asia, Melanesia and Australia. In *Archaeology at ANZAAS (1984)*, edited by G. K. Ward, 168–177. Canberra: Canberra Archaeological Society, Australian National University.

———. 1989. The Taming of the Rainforests: A Model for Late Pleistocene Forest Exploitation in New Guinea. In *Foraging and Farming: The Evolution of Plant Exploitation*, edited by D. R. Harris and G. C. Hullman, 292–317. London: Unwin and Hyman.

———. 1993. Contradictions and Malaria in Melanesia and Australian Prehistory. In *A Community of Culture: The People and Prehistory of the Pacific*, edited by Matthew Spriggs et al., 64–86. Canberra: Department of Prehistory, Research School of Pacific Studies, Australian National University.

Groube, Les M., John Chappell, John Muke, and David Price. 1986. A 40,000 Year-old Human Occupation Site at Huon Peninsula, Papua New Guinea. *Nature* 324: 453–455.

Groves, Colin P. 1995. Domesticated and Commensal Mammals of Austronesia and Their Histories. In *The Austronesians: Historical and Comparative Perspectives*, edited by Peter Bellwood, James J. Fox, and Darrell Tryon, 152–163. Canberra: Department of Anthropology, Research School of Pacific and Asian Studies, Australian National University.

Guiart, Jean. 1996. Land Tenure and Hierarchies in Eastern Melanesia. *Pacific Studies* 19 (1): 1–29.

Guillemard, Francis H. H. 1886. *The Cruises of the Marchesa to Kamchatka and New Guinea, with Notices of Formosa, Liukiu and Various Islands of the Malay Archipelago; With Maps and Numerous Woodcuts Drawn by J. Keulemans, C. Whymper and Others and Engraved by Edward Whymper*. 2 vols. London: John Murray.

Haddon, Alfred C. et al. 1901–1935. *Reports of the Cambridge Anthropological Expedition to Torres Strait*. Vol. 1: A. C. Haddon, *Ethnography* (1935); vol. 2, Part 1: W.H.R. Rivers (appendix, C. G. Seligman), *Physiology and Psychology, Introduction and Vision*; vol. 2, part 2: C. S. Myers and W. McDougall, (1901), *Physiology and Psychology, Hearing, Smell, Taste etc.* (1903); vol. 3: S. H. Ray (C. G. Seligman, A. Wilkin, G. Pimm, and A. C. Haddon), *Linguistics* (1907); vol. 4: A. C. Haddon, A. Higston Quiggin, W.H.R. Rivers, S. H. Ray, C. S. Myers, and J. Bruce, *Arts and Crafts* (1912); vol. 5: A. C. Haddon, W. H. Rivers, C. G. Seligman, and A. Wilkin, *Sociology, Magic and Religion of the Western Islanders*; vol. 6: A. C. Haddon, W.H.R. Rivers, and A. Wilkin, *Sociology, Magic and Religion of the Eastern Islanders* (1908). Cambridge: Cambridge University Press.

———. 1914. The Outrigger Canoes of Torres Straits and Northern Queensland. In *Essays and Studies Presented to William Ridgeway*, edited by E. C. Quiggin, 609–634. Cambridge: Cambridge University Press.

Haenen, Paul. 1998. History, Exchange, and Myth in the Southeastern Bird's Head of Irian Jaya. In *Perspectives on the Bird's Head of Irian Jaya, Indonesia. Proceedings of the Conference, Leiden, 13–17 October 1997*, edited by Jelle Miedema, Cecilia Odé, and Rien A. C. Dam, 234–256. Amsterdam, and Atlanta, Ga.: Rodopi.

Haga, A. 1884. *Nederlandsch Nieuw Guinea en de Papoesche Eilanden: Historische Bijdrage c. 1500–1883.* Vol. 1 (c. 1500–1817); vol. 2 (1817–1883). Batavia: Bruining's-Hage: Martinus Nijhoff.

Hagen, James M. 1999. The Good behind the Gift: Morality and Exchange among the Maneo of Eastern Indonesia. *Journal of the Royal Anthropological Institute* 5 (3): 361–376.

Hahl, Albert. 1937. *Gouverneursjahre*. Berlin: Frundsberg Verlag. [*Governor in New Guinea*, translated and edited by Peter Sack and Dymphna Clark. Canberra: Australian National University Press, 1980.]

Hall, Daniel G. E. 1955. *A History of South-East Asia*. London: Macmillan.

Hall, Kenneth R. 1985. *Maritime Trade and State Development in Early Southeast Asia*. Honolulu: University of Hawai'i Press.

Hanna, Willard A., and Des Alwi. 1990. *Turbulent Times Past in Ternate and Tidore*. Moluccas: Yayasan Warisan dan Budaya Banda Naira.

Hanson, L. W., B. J. Allen, R. M. Bourke, and T. J. McCarthy. 2001. *Papua New Guinea: Rural Development Handbook*. Canberra: Land Management Group, Department of Human Geography, Research School of Pacific and Asian Studies, Australian National University.

Harding, Thomas G. 1967. *Voyagers of the Vitiaz Strait: A Study of a New Guinea Trade System*. Seattle: University of Washington Press.

———. 1970. Trading in Northeast New Guinea. In *Cultures of the Pacific: Selected Readings*, edited by Thomas G. Harding and Ben J. Wallace, 94–111. New York and London: Free Press and Collier-Macmillan.

———. 1994. Precolonial New Guinea Trade. *Ethnology* 33 (2): 101–125.

Hargraves, Lawrence. Papers, Power House Museum, Sydney.

Hawkesworth, John. 1969. *An Account of a Voyage Round the World with a Full Account of the Voyage of the Endeavour in the Year MDCCLXX along the East Coast of Australia by Lieutenant James Cook, Commander of His Majesty's Bark Endeavour, compiled by D. Warrington Evans*. Brisbane: W. R. Smith and Peterson.

Hays, Terence E. 1991. 'No Tobacco, No Hallelujah': Missions and the Early History of Tobacco in Eastern Papua. *Pacific Studies* 14 (4): 91–112.

Healy, Alan M. 1965. Ophir to Bulolo: The History of the Gold Search in New Guinea. *Historical Studies* 12 (45): 103–118.

———. 1987. Monocultural Administration in a Multicultural Environment: The Australians in Papua New Guinea. In *From Colony to Coloniser: Studies in Australian Administrative History*, edited by J. J. Eddy and J. R. Nethercote, 207–224. Sydney: Hale and Iremonger in association with the Royal Australian Institute of Public Administration.

Heeres, Jan E., ed. 1899. *The Part Borne by the Dutch in the Discovery of Australia, 1606–1765*. London: Luzac & Co.

Hempenstall, Peter. 1989. The Neglected Empire: The Superstructure of the Colonial State in German Melanesia. In *Papua New Guinea: A Century of Colonial Impact, 1884–1984*, edited by Sione Lātūkefu, 133–162. Port Moresby: National Research Institute and the University of Papua New Guinea in association, for the Papua New Guinea Centennial Committee.

Herdt, Gilbert H., ed. 1984. *Ritualized Homosexuality in Melanesia*. Berkeley: University of California Press.

Herle, Anita, and Sandra Rouse, eds. 1998. *Cambridge and the Torres Strait: Centenary Essays on the 1898 Anthropological Expedition*. Cambridge: Cambridge University Press.

Hernsheim, Eduard. 1983. *Eduard Hernsheim: South Sea Merchant*, translated and edited by Peter Sack and Dymphna Clark. Boroko: Institute of Papua New Guinea Studies.

Hezel, Francis X. 1979. *Foreign Ships in Micronesia: A Compendium of Ship Contacts with the Caroline and Marshall Islands, 1521–1885*. Saipan: Trust Territory Historic Preservation Office, Federated States of Micronesia and the U.S. Heritage Conservation and Recreation Service.

Hides, Jack. 1936. *Papuan Wonderland*. Glasgow: Blackie & Son. [Reprinted, Sydney: Angus and Robertson, 1973.]

———. 1938. *Savages in Serge: The Story of the Papuan Armed Constabulary*. Sydney: Angus and Robertson.

Hiery, Herman Joseph. 1995. *The Neglected War: The German South Pacific and the Influence of World War I*. Honolulu: University of Hawaiʻi Press.

Hilder, Brett. 1980. *The Voyage of Torres: The Discovery of the Southern Coastline of New Guinea and Torres Strait by Captain Luis Baez de Torres in 1606*. St. Lucia, Queensland: University of Queensland Press.

Hiscock, Peter, and Val Attenbrow. 1998. Early Holocene Backed Artefacts from Australia. *Archaeology in Oceania* 33: 49–62.

Hoogenband, C. van den. 1954. De Tweede Wereldoorlog. In *Nieuw Guinea: De Ontwikkeling op Economisch, Sociaal en Cultureel Gebied, in Nederlands en Australisch Nieuw Guinea*, edited by W. C. Klein, 3: 346–374. 'S-Gravenhage: Staatsdrukkerij-en Uitgeverijbedrijf.

Howard, M. 1993. The Strange Ordeal of William Valentine. *Journal of the Royal Historical Society of Queensland* 15 (3): 156–166.

Howe, Kerry R. 1977. *The Loyalty Islands: A History of Culture Contacts, 1840–1900*. Canberra: Australian National University.

Hughes, Ian. 1977. *New Guinea Stone Age Trade: The Geography and Ecology of Traffic in the Interior*. Terra Australis No. 3. Canberra: Department of Prehistory, Research School of Pacific Studies, Australian National University.

Huizinga, F. 1998. Relations between Tidore and the North Coast of New Guinea in the Nineteenth Century. In *Perspectives on the Bird's Head of Irian Jaya, Indonesia. Proceedings of the Conference, Leiden, 13–17 October 1997*, edited by Jelle Miedema, Cecilia Odé, and Rien A. C. Dam, 385–419. Amsterdam, and Atlanta, Ga.: Rodopi.

Hunter, John. 1793. *An Historical Journal of the Transactions at Port Jackson and Norfolk Island with the Discoveries which have been Made in New South Wales and in the Southern Ocean, since the Publication of Phillip's Voyage, Compiled for the Official Papers; Including the Journals of Governors Phillip and King, and of Lieut. Ball; and the Voyages from the First Sailing of the Sirius in 1787, to the Return of that Ship's*

Company to England in 1792. London: John Stockdale. [Facsimile: Adelaide: Libraries Board of South Australia, 1968.]

Huxley, J. 1935. *T. H. Huxley's Diary of the Voyage of H.M.S. Rattlesnake.* London: Chatto and Windus.

Hyndman, David, and George E. B. Morren, Jr. 1990. The Human Ecology of the Mountain-Ok of Central New Guinea: A Regional Approach and Inter-regional Approach. In *Children of Afek: Tradition and Change among the Mountain-Ok of Central New Guinea,* edited by Barry Craig and David Hyndman, 9–26. *Oceania Monograph* No. 40. Sydney: Oceania.

Idriess, Ion L.I.L. 1950. *The Wild White Man of Badu: A Story of the Coral Sea.* Sydney: Angus and Robertson.

Inglis, Amirah. 1974. *'Not a White Woman Safe': Sexual Anxiety and Politics in Port Moresby, 1920–1934.* Canberra: Australian National University Press.

Inglis, Ken S., and Nigel D. Oram. 1973. *John Moresby and Port Moresby: A Centenary View.* Port Moresby: Government Printer.

Irwin, Geoff. 1978. The Development of Mailu as a Specialized Trading and Manufacturing Centre in Papuan Prehistory: The Causes and Implications. *Mankind* 11: 406–415.

———. 1985. *The Emergence of Mailu as a Central Place in Coastal Papuan Prehistory.* Terra Australis No. 10. Canberra: Department of Prehistory, Research School of Pacific Studies, Australian National University.

———. 1991. Pleistocene Voyaging and the Settlement of Greater Australia and Its Near Oceanic Neighbours. In *Report of the Lapita Homeland Project,* edited by Jim Allen and C. Gosden, 9–19. Occasional Paper in Prehistory No. 20. Canberra: Research School of Pacific Studies, Australian National University.

———. 1992. *The Prehistoric Exploration and Colonisation of the Pacific.* Cambridge: Cambridge University Press.

Jack-Hinton, Colin. 1969. *The Search for the Islands of Solomon, 1567–1838.* Oxford: Clarendon.

———. 1972. Discovery. In *Encyclopaedia of Papua and New Guinea,* edited by Peter Ryan, 1: 246–257. Melbourne: Melbourne University Press in association with the University of Papua New Guinea.

Jackman, Harry. 1969. Sir Peter Scratchley: Her Majesty's Special Commissioner for New Guinea. *Journal of the Papua New Guinea Society* 3 (1): 46–57.

Jackson, Richard T. 1982. Mineral Resources. In *Papua New Guinea Atlas: A Nation in Transition,* edited by David King and Stephen Ranck, 62–63. Port Moresby: Robert Brown and Associates in conjunction with the University of Papua New Guinea.

Jacobs, M. G. 1951a. The Colonial Office and New Guinea, 1874–84. *Historical Studies,* 5 (17): 106–118.

———. 1951b. Bismarck and the Annexation of New Guinea. *Historical Studies,* 5 (17): 14–26.

Jamison, Bryan. 1990. Blackbirding in New Guinea Waters? The 1884 Voyage of the *Hopeful* and the Queensland Labour Trade, B.A. honors thesis, University of Queensland.

Jardine, John. 1866. Description of the Neighbourhood of Somerset, Cape York, Australia. *Journal of the Royal Geographical Society* 36: 76–85.

Jinks, Brian, Peter Biskup, and Hank Nelson, eds. 1973. *Readings in New Guinea History.* Sydney: Angus and Roberston.

Jolly, Margaret. 1987. The Chimera of Equality in Melanesia. *Mankind* 17 (2): 168–183.

Jones, A.G.E. 1981. The British Southern Whale and Seal Fisheries. *Great Circle* 3 (1): 20–29; 3 (2): 90–102.

Jones, Douglas, ed. 1994. *Michael J. Leahy: Explorations into Highland New Guinea, 1930–1935*. Bathurst: Crawford House.

Jonge, Nico de, and Toos van Dijk. 1995. *Forgotten Islands of Indonesia: The Art and Culture of the Southeast Moluccas*. Hong Kong: Periplus Editions.

Josephides, Lisette, and Marc Schiltz. 1991. Through Kewa Country. In *Like People You See in a Dream: First Contact in Six Papuan Societies*, by Edward L. Schieffelin and Robert Crittenden, with contributions by Bryant Allen et al., 198–224. Stanford, Calif.: Stanford University Press.

Joyce, Roger B. 1963. Sir William MacGregor: A Colonial Governor. *Historical Studies* 11 (41): 18–31.

———. 1969. William MacGregor: The Role of the Individual. In *The History of Melanesia*, edited by Ken K. S. Inglis, 33–44. Canberra: Research School of Pacific Studies, Australian National University and the University of Papua New Guinea.

———. 1971. *Sir William MacGregor*. Melbourne: Oxford University Press.

Jukes, Joseph B. 1847. *Narrative of the Surveying Voyage of H.M.S. Fly Commanded by Captain F. P. Blackwood, R. N. in Torres Strait, New Guinea, and Other Islands of the Eastern Archipelago, during the Years 1842–1846: Together with an Excursion into the Interior of the Eastern Part of Java*. 2 vols. London: T. and W. Boone.

Kamma, Freerk C. 1953. Azending. In *Nieuw Guinea: De Ontwikkeling op Economisch, Sociaal en Cultureel Gebied, in Nederlands en Australisch Nieuw Guinea*, edited by W. C. Klein, 1: 82–159. 'S-Gravenhage: Staatsdrukkerij-en Uitgeverijbedrijf.

———. 1972. *Koreri: Messianic Movements in the Biak-Numfor Culture Area*. The Hague: Martinus Nijhoff.

Kaniku, John. W. 1975. James Chalmers at Sau'au Island. *Oral History* 3 (9): 71–76.

Kelly, Celsus, translation and ed. 1966. *La Australia Del Espíritu Santo: The Journal of Fray Martín de Munilla O.F.M. and Other Documents Relating to the Voyage of Pedro Fernández de Quiros to the South Sea (1605–1606) and the Franciscan Missionary Plan (1617–1627)*. 2 vols. The Hakluyt Society, Second Series, No. 127. Cambridge: Cambridge University Press.

Kennedy, Gavin. 1978. *Bligh*. London: Gerald Duckworth.

Kiki, Albert Maori. 1968. *Kiki: Ten Thousand Years in a Lifetime*. Melbourne: Cheshire.

King, David, and Nancy Birge. 1982. Cash Crops. In *Papua New Guinea Atlas: A Nation in Transition*, edited by David King and Stephen Ranck, 52–53. Port Moresby: Robert Brown and Associates in conjunction with the University of Papua New Guinea.

King, Victor T. 1993. *The Peoples of Borneo*. Oxford: Blackwell.

Kituai, August Ibrum. 1998. *My Gun, My Brother: The World of the Papua New Guinea Colonial Police, 1920–1960*. Pacific Islands Monograph Series No. 15. Honolulu: University of Hawai'i Press.

Klein, Willem C., ed. 1953–1954. *Nieuw Guinea: De Ontwikkeling op Economisch, Sociaal en Cultureel Gebied, in Nederlands en Australisch Nieuw Guinea*. 3 vols. 'S-Gravenhage: Staatsdrukkerij-en Uitgeverijbedrijf.

Knauft, Bruce M. 1993. *South Coast New Guinea Cultures: History, Comparison, Dialectic*. Cambridge: Cambridge University Press.

Kolff, Dirk H. 1840. *Voyages of the Dutch Brig of War Dourga through the Moluccan Archipelago, and along the Previously Unknown Coast of New Guinea, Performed during the Years 1825 and 1826*, translated by G. W. Earl. London: James Madden.

Kuklick, Henrika. 1991. *The Savage Within: The Social History of British Anthropology, 1885–1945*. Cambridge: Cambridge University Press.

Laade, Wolfgang. 1968. The Torres Strait Islanders' Own Traditions on their Origins. *Ethnos*, 33: 141–158.

———, ed. 1979. *Oral Traditions and Written Documents on the History and Ethnology of the Northern Torres Strait Islands*. Wiesbaden: Franz Steiner.

Lacey, Rod J. 1985a. Journeys and Transformations: The Process of Innovation in Papua New Guinea. In "Mobility and Identity in the Island Pacific," edited by Murray Chapman, special issue of *Pacific Viewpoint* 26 (1): 81–105.

———. 1985b. To *Limlimbur*, the 'Wanderers': Reflections on Journeys and Transformations in Papua New Guinea. *Pacific Studies* 9 (1): 83–146.

Langdon, Robert. 1966. Captain Bampton's Journal. *Journal of Pacific History* 1: 185–186.

———. 1972. Coutance, Louis Ruault. In *Encyclopaedia of Papua and New Guinea*, edited by Peter Ryan, 1: 220–221. Melbourne: Melbourne University Press in association with the University of Papua New Guinea.

———. 1984. *Where the Whalers Went: An Index to the Pacific Ports and Islands Visited by American Whalers (and Some Other Ships) in the 19th Century*. Canberra: Pacific Manuscripts Bureau, Research School of Pacific Studies, Australian National University.

Langmore, Diane. 1974. *Tamate—a King: James Chalmers in New Guinea, 1877–1901*. Melbourne: Melbourne University Press.

———. 1989. *Missionary Lives: Papua, 1874–1914*. Pacific Islands Monograph Series No. 6. Honolulu: University of Hawai'i Press.

Laracy, Hugh. 1976. *Marists and Melanesians: A History of the Catholic Missions in the Solomon Islands*. Canberra: Australian National University Press.

Lātūkefu, Sione, ed. 1989. *Papua New Guinea: A Century of Colonial Impact, 1884–1984*. Port Moresby: National Research Institute and the University of Papua New Guinea in association with the Papua New Guinea Centennial Committee.

Lawrence, David. 1989. From the Other Side: Recently Recorded Oral Evidence of Contacts between the Torres Strait Islanders and the Papuan Peoples of the Southwestern Coast. *Aboriginal History* 13 (2): 95–123.

Lawrence, Peter. 1964. *Road Belong Cargo: A Study of the Cargo Movement in the Southern Madang District, New Guinea*. Melbourne: Melbourne University Press.

Lawson, John A. 1875. *Wanderings in the Interior of New Guinea*. London: Chapman and Hall.

Laycock, D. C., and S. A. Wurm. 1974. Languages. In *Papua New Guinea Resource Atlas*, edited by Edgar Ford, 52–53. Brisbane: Jacaranda Press.

Leach, J. W., and E. Leach, eds. 1983. *The Kula: New Perspectives on Massim Exchange*. Cambridge: Cambridge University Press.

Lee, Ida. 1912. *Commodore Sir John Hayes: His Voyage and Life (1767–1831), with Some Account of Admiral D'Entrecasteaux's Voyage of 1792–93*. London: Longmans, Green.

Legge, John D. 1949. Australia and New Guinea to the Establishment of the British Protectorate, 1884. *Historical Studies* 4 (13): 34–47.

————. 1956. *Australian Colonial Policy: A Survey of Native Administration and European Development in Papua.* Sydney: Angus and Robertson.

Leith, Denise. 2002. Freeport and the Suharto Regime, 1965–1998. *Contemporary Pacific* 14 (1): 69–100.

Lepowsky, Maria. 1983. Sudest Island and the Louisiade Archipelago in Massim Exchange. In *The Kula: New Perspectives on Massim Exchange*, edited by J. W. Leach and E. Leach, 467–501. Cambridge: Cambridge University Press.

Lett, Lewis. 1944. *The Papuan Achievement.* Melbourne: Melbourne University Press in association with Oxford University Press.

————. 1949. *Sir Hubert Murray of Papua.* London and Sydney: Collins.

Leupe, P. A. 1875. De Reizen der Nederlanders naar Nieuw-Guinea en de Papoesch Eilanden in de 17de Eeuw. *Bijdragen tot de Taal-, Land- en Volkenkunde* 22: 1–162.

Leur, Jacob C. van. 1967. *Indonesian Trade and Society: Essays in Asian Social and Economic History.* 2d ed. The Hague: W. van Hoeve.

Lewis, David C. 1996. *The Plantation Dream: Developing British New Guinea and Papua, 1884–1942.* Canberra: The Journal of Pacific History.

Liddle, Ralph R. 1865. 'John Temperley'—Sydney to China by Torres Straits, Bligh Entrance. *Nautical Magazine and Naval Chronicle* March: 124–129.

Lilley, Ian. 1985. Chiefs without Chiefdoms? Comments on Prehistoric Sociopolitical Organization in Western Melanesia. *Archaeology in Oceania* 20 (2): 60–65.

————. 1986. Prehistoric Exchange in the Vitiaz Strait, Papua New Guinea. Ph.D. thesis, Australian National University.

————. 1988. Prehistoric Exchange across the Vitiaz Strait, Papua New Guinea. *Current Anthropology* 29 (3): 513–516.

————. 1998. East of Irian: Archaeology in Papua New Guinea. In *Bird's Head Approaches: Irian Jaya Studies—A Programme for Interdisciplinary Research*, edited by Gert-Jan Bartstra, 135–156. Rotterdam and Brookfield: A. A. Balkema.

————. 1999a. Too Good to be True? Post-Lapita Scenarios from Language and Archaeology in West New Britain-North New Guinea. *Indo-Pacific Prehistory Association Bulletin*, No. 18. Melaka Papers 2: 25–34.

————. 1999b. Lapita as Politics. In *Le Pacifique de 5000 á 2000 avant le Présent: Suppléments á l'Histoire d'une Colonisation*, edited by Jean-Christophe Galipaud and Ian Lilley, 21–29. Paris, Éditions de IRD, Institute de Recherche pour le Dévelopment.

Lindstrom Lamont, and Geoffrey White. 1990. *Island Encounters: Black and White Memories of the Pacific War.* Washington and London: Smithsonian Institution Press.

Lindt, John W. 1887. *Picturesque New Guinea: With an Historical Introduction and Supplementary Chapters on the Manners and Customs of the Papuans; Accompanied with Fifty Full-page Autotype Illustrations from Negatives of Portraits from Life and Groups and Landscapes from Nature.* London: Longmans, Green.

Lingny, H. J. de Wilde de, J. Ham, and F. G. van Loenen. 1954. Bevolkingslandbouw. In *Nieuw Guinea: De Ontwikkeling op Economisch, Sociaal en Cultureel Gebied, in Nederlands en Australisch Nieuw Guinea*, edited by W. C. Klein, 3: 259–276. 'S-Gravenhage: Staatsdrukkerij-en Uitgeverijbedrijf.

Loeliger, Carl, and Garry Thompf, eds. 1985. *New Religious Movements in Melanesia.* Suva: Institute of Pacific Studies, University of the South Pacific, and the University of Papua New Guinea.

Lourandos, Harry. 1997. *Continent of Hunter-Gatherers: New Perspectives in Australian Prehistory.* Melbourne: Cambridge University Press.

Lubbock, Adelaide. 1968. *Owen Stanley R. N., 1811–1850: Captain of the Rattlesnake.* Melbourne: Heinemann.

Lynch, John. 1988. The Papua New Guinea System. In *Pacific Universities: Achievements, Problems, Prospects,* edited by Ron Crocombe and Malama Meleisea, 176–187. Suva: Institute of Pacific Studies, University of the South Pacific.

———. 1998. *Pacific Languages: An Introduction.* Honolulu: University of Hawai'i Press.

Lynch, John, Malcolm Ross, and Terry Crowley. 2002. *The Oceanic Languages.* London: Curzon Press.

McCarthy, F. 1939. 'Trade' in Aboriginal Australia, and 'Trade' Relationships with Torres Strait, New Guinea and Malaya. *Oceania* 9 (4): 405–448; 10 (1): 80–104; 10 (2): 171–195.

McConnell, U. H. 1936. Totemic Hero-Cults in Cape York Peninsula, North Queensland. *Oceania* 6 (4): 452–477.

Macdonald, Barry. 1982. *Cinderellas of the Empire: Towards a History of Kiribati and Tuvalu.* Canberra: Australian National University Press.

McDougall, Debra. 2000. Paths of Pinauzu: Captivity and Social Reproductions in Ranongga. *Journal of the Polynesian Society* 109 (1): 99–113.

MacFarlane, Samuel. 1875–1976. Ascent of the Fly River, New Guinea. *Proceedings of the Royal Geographical Society* 20: 253–266.

———. 1888. *Among the Cannibals of New Guinea: Being the Story of the New Guinea Mission of the London Missionary Society.* London: London Missionary Society.

MacFarlane, W. H. 1952. Queen's Representative at an Outpost. *Cummins & Campbell's Monthly Magazine* February, 17, 25, 27; March, 19–22; April, 17–20, 25; May, 17–20; June, 7, 37–39; July, 7, 37–39; August, 7, 37–39; September, 9, 34–35; October, 9, 33–35; November, 7, 37–41; December, 7, 37–39.

MacGillivray, John. 1852. *Narrative of the Voyage of H.M.S. Rattlesnake, Commanded by the Late Captain Owen Stanley, R. N., F.R.S. &c. during the Years 1846–1850. Including Discoveries and Surveys in New Guinea, the Louisiade Archipelago, etc. To which Is Added the Account of Mr. E. B. Kennedy's Expedition for the Exploration of the Cape York Peninsula.* 2 vols. London: T. and W. Boone. [Facsimile: Adelaide: Libraries Board of South Australia, 1967.]

MacGregor, William. 1889–1890. Upper Fly River Exploration, British New Guinea. *Proceedings of the Queensland Branch of the Royal Geographical Society of Australia* 5 (2): 94–100.

———. 1894–1895. British New Guinea. *Proceedings of the Royal Colonial Institute* 26: 193–239.

———. 1895. British New Guinea. *Manchester Geographical Society* 11: 1–15.

———. 1898–1899. British New Guinea. *Proceedings of the Royal Colonial Institute* 30: 238–270.

McInnes, A. 1983. The Wreck of the 'Charles Eaton.' *Journal of the Royal Historical Society of Queensland* 11 (4): 21–50.

MacKenzie, John M. 1995. *Orientalism: History, Theory and the Arts.* Manchester: Manchester University Press.

MacKenzie, Maureen A. 1991. *Androgynous Objects: String Bags and Gender in Central New Guinea.* Chur, Switzerland: Harwood Academic Publishers.

Mackenzie, Seaforth Simpson. 1927. *The Australians at Rabaul: The Capture and Administration of the German Possessions in the South Pacific. Vol. 10, The Official History of Australia in the War of 1914–1918.* [Facsimile of the Angus and Robertson edition, Sydney, 1942, with Introduction by Hank Nelson and Michael Piggott.] St. Lucia, Queensland: University of Queensland Press, in association with the Australian War Memorial, 1987.

Macknight. Charles Campbell. 1972. Macassans and Aborigines. *Oceania* 42 (4): 283–321.

———. 1976. *The Voyage to Marege': Macassan Trepangers in Northern Australia.* Melbourne: Melbourne University Press.

Macmillan, David S. 1957. *A Squatter Went to Sea: The Story of Sir William Macleay's New Guinea Expedition (1875) and His Life in Sydney.* Sydney: Currawong.

McNiven, Ian J. 2000. Backed to the Pleistocene. *Archaeology in Oceania* 35: 48–52.

———. 2001. Torres Strait and the Sea Frontier in Early Colonial Australia. In *Colonial Frontiers: Indigenous-European Encounters in Settler Societies,* edited by Lynette Russell, 175–197. Manchester and New York: Manchester University Press.

Maguire, John. 1990. *Prologue: A History of the Catholic Church as Seen from Townsville, 1863–1983.* Toowoomba: Church Archivists' Society.

Mair, Lucy P. 1948. *Australian in New Guinea.* Melbourne: Melbourne University Press.

Markham, Clements, ed. 1872. *Reports of the Discovery of Peru.* London: Hakluyt Society, Series I, No 47.

Mather, Patricia, and Isobel Bennett, eds. 1993. *A Coral Reef Handbook: A Guide to the Geology, Flora and Fauna of the Great Barrier Reef.* 3d ed. Surrey: Beatty & Sons.

Maude, Harry E. 1966. The Cruise of the Whaler 'Gypsy.' *Journal of Pacific History* 1: 193–194.

———. 1968. *Of Islands and Men: Studies in Pacific History.* Melbourne: Oxford University Press.

May, Ron, and Matthew Spriggs, eds. *The Bougainville Crisis.* Bathurst: Crawford House.

May, Ron J., ed. 1986. *Between Two Nations: The Indonesia-Papua New Guinea Border and West Papuan Nationalism.* Bathurst: Robert Brown and Associates.

Mayo, John. 1969. The Protectorate of British New Guinea, 1884–1888: An Oddity of Empire. In *The History of Melanesia,* edited by Ken S. Inglis, 17–31. Canberra: Research School of Pacific Studies, Australian National University, and the University of Papua New Guinea.

———. 1975. From Protectorate to Possession: British New Guinea, 1884–88. *Australian Journal of Politics and History* 21 (3): 54–69.

Mead, Margaret. 1960. Weaver of the Border (New Britain). In *In the Company of Men,* edited by J. C. Casagrande, 76–210. New York: Harper.

Miedema, Jelle. 1989. History, Demography and Genealogy: Inter-Tribal Marriage Relations in the Bird's Head of New Guinea. In *Peoples on the Move: Current Themes of Anthropological Research in New Guinea, Papers of the New Guinea Workshop, 1987,* edited by Paul Haenen and Jan Pouwer, 137–164. Nijmegen: Centre for Australian and Oceanic Studies, University of Nijmegen.

———. 1993. Akari Survival Strategies: An Account of a Small-scale Irian Jaya Community. In *Vrienden en Verwanten. Liber Amicorum Alex van der Leeden,* edited by Paul Haenen and Albert Trouwborst, 103–116. Leiden and Jakarta: Projects Division, DSALCUL, Leiden University.

———. 1994. Trade, Migration and Exchange: The Bird's Head Peninsula of Irian Jaya in a Historical and Structural Comparative Perspective. In *Migration and Transformations: Regional*

Perspectives on New Guinea, edited by Andrew J. Strathern and Gabriele Stürzenhofecker, 121–153. Pittsburgh and London: University of Pittsburgh Press.

Miedema, Jelle, Cecilia Odé, and Rien A. C. Dam, eds. 1998. *Perspectives on the Bird's Head of Irian Jaya, Indonesia. Proceedings of the Conference, Leiden, 13–17 October 1997*, edited by Jelle Miedema, Cecilia Odé, and Rien A. C. Dam. Amsterdam, and Atlanta, Ga.: Rodopi.

Monckton, Charles A. W. 1921. *Some Experiences of a New Guinea Resident Magistrate*. London: John Lane, The Bodely Head.

Monsell-Davis, Michael. 1981. Nabuapaka: Social Change in a Roro Community. Ph.D. thesis, Macquarie University.

Monteith, G. B. 1987. History of Biological Collecting at Cape York, Queensland, 1770–1970. *Queensland Naturalist* 28 (1–4): 42–51.

Moore, Clive R. 1984. Queensland's Annexation of New Guinea in 1883. *Journal of the Royal Queensland Historical Society* 12 (1): 26–50.

———. 1985. *Kanaka: A History of Melanesian Mackay*. Port Moresby: Institute of Papua New Guinea Studies and the University of Papua New Guinea Press.

———. 1990. Workers in Colonial Papua New Guinea, 1884–1975. In *Labour in the South Pacific*, edited by Clive Moore, Jacqueline Leckie, and Doug Munro, 30–46. Townsville: Department of History and Centre of Melanesian Studies, James Cook University.

———. 1992a. A Precious Few: Melanesian and Asian Women in Northern Australia. In *Gender Relations in Australia: Domination and Negotiation*, edited by Kay Saunders and Raymond Evans, 59–81. Sydney: Harcourt Brace Jovanovich.

———. 1992b. The Life and Death of William Bairstow Ingham: Papua New Guinea in the 1870s. *Journal of the Royal Queensland Historical Society* 14 (10): 414–431.

———. 1995. Politics the Melanesian Way: A Collective Biography of the Members of Papua New Guinea's House of Assembly, 1964–1994. In *Messy Entanglements: Proceedings of the 10th Pacific History Association Conference, Tarawa, Kiribati, July 1994*, edited by Alaima Talu and Max Quanchi, 37–48. Brisbane: Pacific History Association.

———. 1997. Queensland and Its Coral Sea: Implications of Historical Links between Australia and Melanesia. In *Northern Exposures*, edited by Malcolm Gillies, 79–102. Occasional Paper No. 19. Canberra: Australian Academy of the Humanities.

———. 1998a. Toree: The Dynamics of Early Contact and Trade in Torres Strait, Cape York and the Trans-Fly to 1890. In *Lasting Fascinations: Essays on Indonesia and the Southwest Pacific to Honour Bob Hering*, edited by Harry A. Poeze and Antoinette Liem, 257–279. Edisi Sastra Kabar Seberang Sulating Maphilindo No. 28/29, Monograph No. 2 of the Yayasan Soekarno Monograph Series, Stein, Netherlands.

———. 1998b. Papua and New Guinea's Political Development to 1967. In *A Papua New Guinea Political Chronicle, 1967–1991*, edited by Clive Moore with Mary Kooyman, xv–xxxiv. Bathurst and London: Crawford House Publishing and C. Hurst & Co.

Moore, Clive, Jacqueline Leckie, and Doug Munro, eds. 1990. *Labour in the South Pacific*. Townsville: Department of History and Politics, and the Centre of Melensian Studies, James Cook University of North Queensland.

Moore, Clive, James Griffin, and Andrew Griffin. 1984. *Colonial Intrusion: Papua New Guinea, 1884*. Port Moresby: Papua New Guinea Centennial Committee.

Moore, Clive, Samuel Haihuie, and Dikana Kema. 2001. *Report on the Feasibility Study on Distance Education and Flexible Learning in Papua New Guinea*. Office of Higher Education, Papua New Guinea.

Moore, Clive, with Mary Kooyman, eds. 1998. *A Papua New Guinea Political Chronicle, 1967–1991*. Bathurst and London: Crawford House Publishing and C. Hurst & Co.

Moore, David R. 1972. Cape York Aborigines and Islanders of Western Torres Strait. In *Bridge and Barrier: The Natural and Cultural History of Torres Strait*, edited by D. Walker, 327–343. Canberra: Australian National University.

———. 1978. Cape York Aborigines: Fringe Participants in the Torres Strait Trading System. *Mankind*, 11 (3): 319–325.

———. 1979. *Islanders and Aborigines at Cape York: An Ethnographic Reconstruction Based on the 1848–1850 'Rattlesnake' Journals of O. W. Brierly and Information He Obtained from Barbara Thompson*. Canberra: Australian Institute of Aboriginal Studies and New Jersey: Humanities Press.

Moresby, John. 1875a. Recent Discoveries at the Eastern End of New Guinea. *Journal of the Royal Geographical Society* 44: 1–14.

———. 1875b. Discoveries in Eastern New Guinea, by Captain Moresby and the Officers of H.M.S. *Basilisk. Journal of the Royal Geographical Society* 45: 153–170.

———. 1876. *New Guinea and Polynesia: Discoveries and Surveys in New Guinea and the D'Entrecasteaux Islands . . . HMS Basilisk*. London: John Murray.

Morton, Harry. 1982. *The Whale's Wake*. Dunedin: University of Otago Press.

Moses, John A. 1977. The Coolie Labour Question and German Colonial Policy in Samoa, 1900–14. In *Germany in the Pacific and Far East, 1870–1914*, edited by John A. Moses and Paul M. Kennedy, 234–261. St. Lucia, Queensland: University of Queensland Press.

Moses, Richard Rusoto. 1978. Traditional Salt Making in the Enga Province. *Oral History* 6 (6): 82–98.

Mosley, H. N. 1892. *Notes by a Naturalist: An Account of Observations Made during the Voyage of H.M.S. Challenger Round the World in the Years 1872–1876, under the Command of Capt. Sir G. S. Nares, R. N., K.C.B., F.R.S. and Capt. F. T. Thomson, R. N.* London: John Murray.

Müller, Salomon. 1857. *Reizen en Onderzoekingen in der Indischen Archipel Gedaan op Last de Nederlandsche Indische Regering, Tusschen de Jaren, 1822 en 1836*. Amsterdam: Frederik Müller.

Mullins, Steve. 1988. Torres Strait 1864–1884: A History of Occupation and Culture Contact. Ph.D. thesis, University of New England.

———. 1990. 'Heathen Polynee' and 'Nigger Teachers': Torres Strait and the Pacific Islander Ascendancy. *Aboriginal History* 14 (2): 152–167.

———. 1992a. Queensland's Quest for Torres Strait. *Journal of Pacific History* 27 (2): 165–180.

———. 1992b. The Torres Strait Bêche-de-Mer Fishery: A Question of Timing. *Great Circle* 14 (1): 21–30.

———. 1997. From TI to Dobo: The 1905 Departure of the Torres Strait Pearl-Shelling Fleets to Aru, Netherlands East Indies. *Great Circle* 19 (1): 30–39.

———. 2001. Australian Pearl-Shellers in the Moluccas: Confrontation and Compromise on a Maritime Frontier. *Great Circle* 23 (2): 3–23.

Mulvaney, John, and Johan Kamminga. 1999. *Prehistory of Australia*. Sydney: Allen and Unwin.

Munro, Doug. 1973. Fijian Sandalwood and Bêche-de-Mer. M.A. Qualifying Thesis, Australian National University.

———. 1990. The Origins of Labourers in the South Pacific: Commentary and Statistics. In *Labour in the South Pacific*, edited by Clive Moore, Jacqueline Leckie, and Doug Munro, xxxix–li. Townsville: Department of History and Centre of Melanesian Studies, James Cook University.

Murray, A. W. 1876. *Forty Years' Mission Work in Polynesia and New Guinea from 1835 to 1875*. London: James Nisbet and Co.

Murray, John Hubert Plunkett. 1925. *Papua of To-day: An Australian Colony in the Making*. London: P. S. King & Son.

———. 1932. Depopulation in Papua. *Oceania* 3: 207–213.

———. 1912. *Papua or British New Guinea*. London: Fisher, Unwin.

Narokobi, Bernard. 1980. *The Melanesian Way*, edited by Henry Olela. Port Moresby: Institute of Papua New Guinea Studies.

Nelson, Hank N. 1976. *Black, White and Gold: Goldmining in Papua New Guinea, 1878–1930*. Canberra: Australian National University Press.

———. 1982a. Looking North. In *New History: Studying Australia Today*, edited by G. Osborne and W. F. Mandle, 142–152. Sydney: Allen and Unwin.

———. 1982b. European Contact and Administrative Control. In *Papua New Guinea Atlas: A Nation in Transition*, edited by David King and Stephen Ranck, 10–11. Port Moresby: Robert Brown and Associates in conjunction with the University of Papua New Guinea.

Neumann, Klaus. 1992. *Not the Way It Really Was: Constructing the Tolai Past*. Pacific Islands Monograph Series No. 10. Honolulu: University of Hawai'i Press.

———. 1996. *Rabaul Yu Swit Moa Yet: Surviving the 1994 Volcanic Eruption*. Port Moresby: Oxford University Press.

Newbury, Colin D. 1973. 'Treaty, Grant, Usage and Suffrage': The Origins of British Colonial Protectorates. In *W. P. Morrell: A Tribute: Essays in Modern and Early Modern History Presented to William Parker Morrell*, edited by E. Wood and P. S. O'Connor, 69–84. Dunedin: University of Otago Press.

———. 1975. Labour Migration in the Imperial Phase: An Essay in Interpretation. *Journal of Imperial and Commonwealth History* 3 (2): 234–256.

———. 1989. Land, Labour, Capital and Colonial Government in Papua New Guinea. In *Papua New Guinea: A Century of Colonial Impact, 1884–1984*, edited by Sione Lātūkefu, 37–48. Port Moresby: National Research and University of Papua New Guinea in association with the Papua New Guinea Centennial Committee.

———. 1994–1995. The Long Apprenticeship: Labour in the Political Economy of New Guinea, 1915–1941. *Journal of Pacific Studies* 18: 66–104.

O'Callaghan, Mary-Louise. 1999. *Enemies Within: Papua New Guinea, Australia, and the Sandline Crisis: The Inside Story*. Sydney: Doubleday.

Oliver, Douglas L. 1955. *A Solomon Island Society: Kinship and Leadership among the Siuai of Bougainville*. Cambridge, Mass.: Harvard University Press.

———. 1989. *Oceania: The Native Culture of Australia and the Pacific Islands*. 2 vols. Honolulu: University of Hawai'i Press.

————. 1991. *Black Islanders: A Personal Perspective of Bougainville, 1937–1991*. Honolulu: University of Hawai'i Press.

Oram, Nigel D. 1968a. Culture Change, Economic Development and Migration among the Hula. *Oceania* 38 (4): 243–275.

————. 1968b. The Hula in Port Moresby. *Oceania* 39 (1): 1–35.

————. 1976. *Colonial Town to Melanesian City: Port Moresby, 1884–1974*. Canberra: Australian National University Press.

Osborne, Robin. 1985. *Indonesia's Secret War: The Guerilla Struggle in Irian Jaya*. Sydney: Allen and Unwin.

Overell, Lilian. 1923. *A Woman's Impression of German New Guinea*. London: John Lane, Bodley Head.

Overlack, Peter. 1978–1979. Queensland's Annexation of Papua: A Background to Anglo-German Friction. *Journal of the Royal Historical Society of Queensland* 10 (4): 123–138.

Overweel, Jeroen A. 1993. *The Marind in a Changing Environment: A Study on Social-Economic Change in Marind Society to Assist in the Formulation of a Long Term Strategy for the Foundation for Social, Economic and Environmental Development (YAPSEL)*. Merauke/Amsterdam: YAPSEL.

————. 1998a. 'A Systematic Activity': Military Exploration in Western New Guinea, 1907–1915. In *Perspectives on the Bird's Head of Irian Jaya, Indonesia. Proceedings of the Conference, Leiden, 13–17 October 1997*, edited by Jelle Miedema, Cecilia Odé, and Rien A. C. Dam, 455–478. Amsterdam, and Atlanta, Ga.: Rodopi.

————. 1998b. Keep Them Out! Early Nineteenth-Century English/Dutch Rivalry in Eastern Indonesia and Australia. Amsterdam (manuscript).

Panoff, Michel. 1979. Travailleurs, Recruteurs et Planeurs dans l'Archipel Bismarck de 1885 à 1914. *Journal de la Société des Océanistes* 35 (64): 159–173. [Published in English as: "Workers, Recruiters and Planters in the Bismarck Archipelago, 1885–1914." *Journal of Pacific Studies* 1994–1995, 18: 32–65.]

Parkinson, Richard H. R. 1907. *Dreissig Jahre in der Sudsee: Land und Leute, Sitten und Gebrauche im Bismarckarchipel und auf den Deutschen Salomoinseln*. Stuttgart: Strecker and Schroder. [*Thirty Years in the South Seas: Land and People, Customs and Traditions in the Bismarck Archipelago and on the German Solomon Islands*, translated by John Dennison, and edited by J. Peter White. Bathurst: Crawford House Publishing in association with Oceania Publications, University of Sydney, 1999.]

Pawley, Andrew K. 1998. The Trans New Guinea Phylum Hypothesis: A Reassessment. In *Perspectives on the Bird's Head of Irian Jaya, Indonesia, Proceedings of the Conference, Leiden, 13–17 October 1997*, edited by Jelle Miedema, Cecilia Odé, and Rien A. C. Dam, 655–690. Amsterdam, and Atlanta, Ga.: Rodopi.

Pawley, Andrew, and Roger C. Green. 1984. The Proto-Oceanic Language Community. *Journal of Pacific History* 19 (3): 123–146.

Pearl, Cyril. 1967. *Morrison of Peking*. Sydney: Angus and Robertson.

Perry, K. R. 1982. Forestry. In *Papua New Guinea Atlas: A Nation in Transition*, edited by David King and Stephen Ranck, 60–61. Port Moresby: Robert Brown and Associates in conjunction with the University of Papua New Guinea.

Pigeaud, T.G.T. 1960–1963. *Java in the 14th Century: A Study in Cultural History; The Nagara-*

Kertagama by Rakawi Prapanca of Majapahit, 1365 A.D. 5 vols. The Hague: Martinus Nijhoff. [3d rev. ed.]

Pike, Glenville. 1979. *Queen of the North: A Pictorial History of Cooktown and Cape York Peninsula.* Mareeba: the author.

————. 1983. *The Last Frontier.* Mareeba: Pinevale.

Pires, Tome. 1944. *The Suma Oriental of Tome Pires: An Account of the East, from the Red Sea to Japan: Written in Malacca and India in 1512–1515. . . .* London: The Hakluyt Society.

Pitcairn, W. D. 1891. *Two Years among the Savages of New Guinea.* London: Ward and Downey.

Pitt-Rivers, George Henry Lane-Fox. 1927. *The Clash of Culture and the Contact of Races: An Anthropological and Psychological Study of the Laws of Racial Adaptability, with Special Reference to the Depopulation of the Pacific and the Government of Subject Races.* London: Routledge.

Ploeg, Anton. 1995. First Contact, in the Highlands of Irian Jaya. *Journal of Pacific History* 30 (2): 227–239.

Poulgrain, Greg. 1999. Delaying the 'Discovery' of Oil in West New Guinea. *Journal of Pacific History* 34 (2): 205–218.

Pouwer, Jan. 1999. The Colonisation, Decolonisation and Recolonisation of West New Guinea. *Journal of Pacific History* 34 (2): 157–179.

Powell, W. 1883. *Wanderings in a Wild Country: Or Three Years amongst the Cannibals of New Britain.* London: Sampson Low, Marston, Searle and Rivington.

————. 1883–1884. New Guinea and the Western Pacific. *Proceedings of the Royal Colonial Institute* 15: 7–39.

Prendergast, Patricia A. 1968. History of the London Missionary Society in British New Guinea, 1871–1901. Ph.D. thesis, University of Hawai'i.

Price, Charles, with Elizabeth Baker. 1976. Origins of Pacific Island Labourers in Queensland, 1863–1904: A Research Note. *Journal of Pacific History* 11 (1–2): 106–121.

Prideaux, Peter. 1988. *From Spear to Pearl-Shell: Somerset, Cape York Peninsula, 1864–1877.* Brisbane: Boolarong.

Putilov, Boris N. 1982. *Nikolai Miklouho-Maclay: Traveller, Scientist and Humanist.* Moscow: Progress.

Quanchi, Max. 1996. Photography, Representation and Cross-Cultural Encounters: Seeking Reality in Papua, 1880–1930. Ph.D. thesis, University of Queensland.

————. 1997a. The Invisibility of Gospel Ploughmen: The Imaging of South Sea Pastors in Papua. *Pacific Studies* 20 (4): 77–101.

————. 1997b. Thomas McMahon: Photography as Propaganda in the Pacific Islands. *History of Photography* 21 (1): 42–53.

————. 1999. Tree Houses, Representation and Photography on the Papuan Coast, 1880–1930. In *Art and Performance in Oceania*, edited by B. Craig, B. Kernot and C. Anderson, 218–230. Bathurst: Crawford House.

Quanchi Max, and Max Shekleton. 2001. Disorderly Categories in Postcards from Papua New Guinea. *History of Photography* 25 (4): 315–333.

Queensland. 1885. *Report with Minutes of Evidence Taken before the Royal Commission Appointed to Inquire into the Circumstances under which Labourers have been Introduced into Queensland from New Guinea and Other Islands etc., together with the Proceedings of the Commission etc.* Brisbane: Government Printer.

Quiason, Serafin Danganan. 1966. *English 'Country Trade' with the Philippines, 1644–1765*. Quezon City: University of the Philippines Press.

Quodling, Paul. 1991. *Bougainville: The Mine and the People*. Pacific Papers No. 3. n.p.: Center for Independent Studies.

Radford, Robin. 1987. *Highlanders and Foreigners in the Upper Ramu: The Kainantu Area, 1919–1942*. Carlton, Victoria: Melbourne University Press.

Ralston, Caroline. 1975. 'White Woman with a Towel . . .': A Series of Shabby Episodes. *New Guinea and Australia, the Pacific and South-east Asia* 10 (2): 57–62.

Rannie, Douglas. 1912. *My Adventures among South Sea Cannibals: An Account of the Experiences and Adventures of a Government Official among the Natives of Oceania*. London: Seeley & Service.

Redlich, Edwin. 1874. Notes on the Western Islands of the Pacific Ocean and New Guinea. *The Journal of the Royal Geographical Society* 44: 30–37.

Reid, Anthony. 1983. Introduction: Slavery and Bondage in Southeast Asian History. In *Slavery, Bondage and Dependency in Southeast Asia*, edited by Anthony Reid with Jennifer Brewster, 1–43. St. Lucia, Queensland: University of Queensland Press.

Reid, Anthony, with Jennifer Brewster, eds. 1983. *Slavery, Bondage and Dependency in Southeast Asia*. St. Lucia, Queensland: University of Queensland Press.

Reid, F. [Alec Vannard]. 1954. *The Romance of the Great Barrier Reef*. Sydney: Angus and Robertson.

Reynolds, Henry. 1981. *The Other Side of the Frontier: An Interpretation of the Aboriginal Response to the Invasion and Settlement of Australia*. Townsville: History Department, James Cook University.

Richards, Rhys. 1986a. The Easternmost Route to China and the Robertson Aikman Charts. *Great Circle* 8 (1): 54–67.

———. 1986b. The Easternmost Route to China, 1787–1792. *Great Circle* 8 (2): 104–116.

———. 1987. The Easternmost Route to China. *Great Circle* 9 (1): 48–59.

Riesenfeld, Alphonse. 1951. Tobacco in New Guinea and Other Areas of Melanesia. *Journal of the Royal Anthropological Institute* 81 (1–2): 69–102.

Rivers, William H. R. 1914. *The History of Melanesian Society*. 2 vols. Cambridge: Cambridge University Press. [Facsimile: Oosterhout: Anthropological Pub., 1968.]

———. 1922. *Essays on the Depopulation of Melanesia*, edited by W.H.R. Rivers. Cambridge: Cambridge University Press.

Robinson, Neville K. 1981. *Villagers at War: Some Papua New Guinea Experiences in World War II*. Pacific Research Monograph No. 2. Canberra: Australian National University.

Robson, R. W. 1965. *Queen Emma: The Samoan-American Girl who Founded an Empire in 19th Century New Guinea*. Sydney: Pacific Publications. [1979 edition.]

Rochas, R. de M.V. 1861. Naufrage et Scenes D'Anthropophagie a L'Île Rossel, dans l'Archipel de la Louisiade (Melanesie). *Le Tour Du Monde* 4: 81–94.

Romilly, Hugh Hastings. 1886. *The Western Pacific and New Guinea: Notes on the Natives, Christian and Cannibal, with Some Account of the Old Labour Trade*. London: John Murray.

———. 1889. *From My Verandah in New Guinea: Sketches and Traditions*. London: David Nutt.

———. 1893. *Letters from the Western Pacific and Mashonaland, 1878–1891 . . .*, edited with a memoir by S. H. Romilly. London: David Nutt.

Rosenberg, Carl B. H. von. 1875. *Reistochten naar de Geelvinkbaai op Nieuw-Guinea in de Jaren 1869 en 1870*. 'S-Gravenhage: Martinus Nijhoff.

Ross, Malcolm D. 1988. *Proto Oceanic and the Austronesian Languages of Western Melanesia.* Pacific Linguistics Series C, No. 98. Canberra: Department of Linguistics, Research School of Pacific Studies, Australian National University.

Rouffaer, G. P. 1908. De Javaansche Naam 'Seran' van Z.W. Nieuw-Guinea vöör 1545 … *Tijdschrift Kominklijk Nederlandsch Aardrijkskundig Genootschap,* 2d Series, 25: 310–311.

Rowland, M. J. 1986. The Whitsunday Islands: Initial Historical and Archaeological Observations and Implications for Future Work. *Queensland Archaeological Research* 3: 72–87.

———. 1987. The Distribution of Aboriginal Watercraft on the East Coast of Queensland: Implications for Culture Contact. *Australian Aboriginal Studies* 2: 38–45.

Rowley, Charles D. 1958. *The Australians in German New Guinea, 1914–1921.* Melbourne: Melbourne University Press.

———. 1965. *The New Guinea Villager: A Retrospect from 1964.* Melbourne: F. W. Cheshire.

———. 1989. Some Thoughts on a Seminar Topic. In *Papua New Guinea: A Century of Colonial Impact, 1884–1984,* edited by Sione Lātūkefu, 445–457. Port Moresby: National Research Institute and the University of Papua New Guinea in association, for the Papua New Guinea Centennial Committee.

Russell, Lynette, ed. 2001. *Colonial Frontiers: Indigenous-European Encounters in Settler Societies.* Manchester and New York: Manchester University Press.

Ryan, Peter. 1991. *Black Bonanza: A Landslide of Gold.* South Yarra, Victoria: Hyland.

Sack, Peter. 2001. *Phantom History, The Rule of Law and the Colonial State: The Case of German New Guinea.* Canberra: Division of Pacific and Asian History, Research School of Pacific and Asian Studies, Australian National University.

Saffu, Yaw, ed. 1996. *The 1992 PNG Election: Change and Continuity in Electoral Politics.* Political and Social Change Monograph No. 23. Canberra: Department of Political and Social Change, Research School of Pacific and Asian Studies, Australian National University.

Sahlins, Marshall. 1963. Poor Man, Rich Man, Big Man, Chief: Political Types in Melanesia and Polynesia. *Comparative Studies in Society and History* 5: 285–303.

Said, Edward. 1978. *Orientalism: Western Conceptions of the Orient.* London: Routledge & Kegan Paul. [Republished: Harmondsworth: Penguin, 1991.]

Salmond, Anne. 1991. *Two Worlds: First Meetings between Maori and Europeans, 1642–1772.* Auckland: Viking.

Scarr, Deryck. 1967. *Fragments of Empire: A History of the Western Pacific High Commission, 1877–1914.* Canberra: Australian National University Press.

———. 1984. *Fiji: A Short History.* Sydney: Allen & Unwin.

Schieffelin, Edward L., and Robert Crittenden, with contributions by Bryant Allen et al. 1991. *Like People You See in a Dream: First Contact in Six Papuan Societies.* Stanford, Calif.: Stanford University Press.

Schieffelin, Edward L., and Deborah Gewertz. 1985. Introduction. In *History and Ethnohistory in Papua New Guinea,* edited by D. Gewertz and E. Schieffelin, 1–6. Oceania Monograph No. 28. Sydney: University of Sydney.

Schumacher, C. 1954. Exploratie. In *Nieuw Guinea: De Ontwikkeling op Economisch, Sociaal en Cultureel Gebied, in Nederlands en Australisch Nieuw Guinea,* edited by W. C. Klein, 3: 1–115. 'S-Gravenhage: Staatsdrukkerij-en Uitgeverijbedrijf.

Schütte, Heinz. 1989a. The Six Day War of 1878 in the Bismarck Archipelago. *Journal of Pacific History* 24 (1): 38–53.

——. 1989b. Topulu and His Brothers: Aspects of Societal Transition in the Bismarck Archipelago of Papua New Guinea during the 1870s and 1880s. *Journal de la Société des Océanistes* 88–89 (1–2): 53–68.

——. 1991. '*Stori Bilong Wanpela Man Nem Bilong em Toboalilu*': The Death of Godeffroy's Kleinschmidt, and the Perception of History. *Pacific Studies* 14 (3): 69–96.

Seligman, Charles G. 1910. *The Melanesians of British New Guinea (With a Chapter by F. R. Barton and an Appendix by E. L. Giblin)*. Cambridge: Cambridge University Press. [Facsimile: New York: AMS Press, 1976.]

Sentinella, C. S., translation and ed. 1975. *Mikloucho-Maclay: New Guinea Diaries, 1871–1883*. Madang: Kristen Press.

Sharp, Andrew. 1960. *The Discovery of the Pacific Islands*. Oxford: Clarendon Press.

Shaw, W. Hudson, and Olaf Ruhen. 1977. *Lawrence Hargraves: Aviation Pioneer, Inventor and Explorer*. St. Lucia, Queensland: University of Queensland Press.

Shineberg, Dorothy. 1967. *They Came for Sandalwood: A Study of the Sandalwood Trade in the South-west Pacific, 1830–1865*. Melbourne: Melbourne University Press.

——. 1999. *The People Trade: Pacific Island Laborers and New Caledonia, 1865–1930*. Pacific Island Monograph Series No. 16. Honolulu: University of Hawai'i Press.

Shlomowitz, Ralph. 1987. Mortality and the Pacific Labour Trade. *Journal of Pacific History* 22 (1): 34–55.

——. 1988. Mortality and Indentured Labour in Papua (1884–1941) and New Guinea (1920–1941). *Journal of Pacific History* 23 (1): 70–79.

——. 1989. Epidemiology and the Pacific Labour Trade. *Journal of Interdisciplinary History* 19 (4): 585–610.

——. 1990. Mortality and Workers. In *Labour in the South Pacific*, edited by Clive Moore, Jacqueline Lecki, and Doug Munro, 124–127. Townsville: Department of History and Centre of Melanesian Studies, James Cook University.

Siegel, Jeff. 1985. Origins of Pacific Islands Labourers in Fiji. *Journal of Pacific History* 20 (1): 42–54.

Silzer, Peter J., and Heljä Heikkinen Clouse. 1991. *Index of Irian Jaya Languages*. 2d ed. Jayapura: Program Kerjasama Universitas Cenderawasih and Summer Institute of Linguistics.

Simanjuntak, Truman. 1998. Review of the Prehistory of Irian Jaya. In *Perspectives on the Bird's Head of Irian Jaya, Indonesia. Proceedings of the Conference*, Leiden, *13–17 October 1997*, edited by Jelle Miedema, Cecilia Odé, and Rien A. C. Dam, 941–950. Amsterdam, and Atlanta, Ga.: Rodopi.

Sinclair, James P. 1969. *The Outside Man: Jack Hides of Papua*. Sydney: Angus and Robertson.

——. 1978. *Wings of Gold: How the Aeroplane Developed New Guinea*. Bathurst: Robert Brown and Associates.

——. 1988. *Last Frontiers: The Explorations of Ivan Champion of Papua: A Record of Geographical Exploration in Australia's Territory of Papua between 1926 and 1940*. Gold Coast, Queensland: Pacific Press.

——. 1995. *The Money Tree: Coffee in Papua New Guinea*. Bathurst: Crawford House.

Singe, John. 1979. *The Torres Strait Islanders*. St. Lucia, Queensland: University of Queensland Press.

Smithies, Michael. 1983. A New Guinean and the Royal Society, 1816–1817. *Hemisphere Annual* 4: 365–371.

Sollewijn Gelpke, J.H.F. 1993. On the Origin of the Name Papua. *Bijdragen, Tot de Taal-, Land- en Volkenkunde* 149: 318–332.

———. 1994. The Report of Miguel Roxo de Brito of His Voyage in 1581–1582 to the Raja Ampat, the MacCluer Gulf and Seram. *Bijdragen Tot de Taal-, Land- en Volkenkunde* 150: 123–145.

Somare, Michael. 1975. *Sana: An Autobiography*. Port Moresby: Niugini Press.

Somerset Water Police Log, 1871–1876. Library of the Royal Queensland Historical Society, Brisbane.

Souter, Gavin. 1963. *New Guinea: The Last Unknown*. Sydney: Angus and Robertson.

Spate, Oscar H. K. 1979–1988. *The Pacific since Magellan*, vol. 1, *The Spanish Lake*; vol. 2, *Monopolists and Freebooters*; vol. 3, *Paradise Found and Lost*. Canberra: Australian National University Press.

Specht, Jim, and John Fields. 1984. *Frank Hurley in Papua: Photographs of the 1920–1923 Expeditions*. Bathurst: Robert Brown and Associates in association with the Australian Museum Trust.

Spenceley, A. P. 1982. Climatic Regions. In *Papua New Guinea Atlas: A Nation in Transition*, edited by David King and Stephen Ranck, 96–97. Port Moresby: Robert Brown and Associates in conjunction with the University of Papua New Guinea.

Spencer, Margaret. 1999. *Public Health in Papua New Guinea, 1870–1939*. Brisbane: Australian Center for International and Tropical Health and Nutrition, University of Queensland.

Spoehr, F. M. 1963. *White Falcon: The House of Godeffroy and Its Commercial and Scientific Role in the Pacific*. Palo Alto, Calif.: Pacific Books.

Spriggs, Matthew. 1992. Alternative Prehistories for Bougainville: Regional, National or Micronational. *The Contemporary Pacific* 4 (2): 269–298.

———. 1993. Island Melanesia: The Last 10,000 Years. In *Sauhl in Review: Pleistocene Archaeology in Australia, New Guinea and Island Melanesia*, edited by M. A. Smith, M. Spriggs, and B. Fankhauser, 187–220. Occasional Paper in Prehistory No. 24. Canberra: Research School of Pacific Studies, Australian National University.

———. 1997. *The Island Melanesians*. Oxford: Blackwell.

———. 1998. Archaeology of the Bird's Head in Its Pacific and Southeast Asian Context. In *Perspectives on the Bird's Head of Irian Jaya, Indonesia. Proceedings of the Conference, Leiden, 13–17 October 1997*, edited by Jelle Miedema, Cecilia Odé, and Rien A. C. Dam, 931–939. Amsterdam, and Atlanta, Ga.: Rodopi.

Spriggs, Matthew, and Donald Denoon, eds. 1992. *The Bougainville Crisis: 1991 Update*. Canberra and Bathurst: Department of Political and Social Change, Research School of Pacific Studies, Australian National University in association with Crawford House.

Staden, Miriam van. 1998. Where Does Malay End and Tidore Begin? In *Perspectives on the Bird's Head of Irian Jaya, Indonesia. Proceedings of the Conference, Leiden, 13–17 October 1997*, edited by Jelle Miedema, Cecilia Odé, and Rien A. C. Dam, 691–716. Amsterdam, and Atlanta, Ga.: Rodopi.

Starbuck, Alexander. 1964. *History of the American Whale Fishery from Its Earliest Inception to the Year 1876, with a New Preface by Stuart C. Sherman*. 2 vols. New York: Argosy-Antiquarian.

Steinbauer, Friedrich. 1979. *Melanesian Cargo Cults: New Salvation Movements in the South Pacific*, translated by Max Wohlwill. St. Lucia, Queensland: University of Queensland Press.

Stephen, David. 1972. A History of Political Parties in Papua New Guinea. Melbourne: Lansdowne.

Steven, Margaret. 1965. *Merchant Campbell, 1769–1846: A Study of Colonial Trade*. Melbourne: Oxford University Press in association with the Australian National University.

———. 1983. *Trade, Tactics and Territory: Britain in the Pacific, 1783–1823*. Melbourne: Melbourne University Press.

Stewart, Pamela J. 1998. Ritual Trackways and Sacred Paths of Fertility. In *Perspectives on the Bird's Head on Irian Jaya, Indonesia, Proceedings of the Conference, Leiden, 13–17 October 1997*, edited by Jelle Miedema, Cecilia Odé, and Rien A. C. Dam, 275–289. Amsterdam, and Atlanta, Ga.: Rodopi.

Stone, Octavius C. 1876. Description of the Country and Natives of Port Moresby and Neighbourhood, New Guinea. *Journal of the Royal Geographical Society* 46: 34–62.

———. 1880. *A Few Months in New Guinea*. London: Sampson Low, Marston, Searle and Rivington.

Strachan, John. 1888. *Explorations and Adventures in New Guinea*. London: Sampson Low, Marston, Searle and Rivington.

Strathern, Andrew. 1971. Cargo and Inflation in Mount Hagen. *Oceania* 41: 42–67.

Strathern, Marilyn. 1975. *No Money on Our Skins: Hagen Migrants in Port Moresby*. New Guinea Research Bulletin No. 61. Port Moresby and Canberra: New Guinea Research Unit, Australian National University.

———. 1988. *The Gender of the Gift*. Berkeley: University of California Press.

Stuart, Ian. 1970. *Port Moresby: Yesterday and Today*. Sydney: Pacific Publications.

Sumner, Ray. 1981. A Noisome Business: The Trepang Trade and Queensland. *Journal of Australian Studies* 9: 61–70.

Sutherland, Heather. 1983. Slavery and the Slave Trade in South Sulawesi, 1660s–1800s. In *Slavery, Bondage and Dependency in Southeast Asia*, edited by Anthony Reid with Jennifer Brewster, 263–285. St. Lucia, Queensland: University of Queensland Press.

Sutton, Peter, ed. 1976. *Languages of Cape York*. Canberra: Australian Institute of Aboriginal Studies.

Swadling, Pamela. 1981. *Papua New Guinea's Prehistory: An Introduction*. Boroko: National Museum and Art Gallery.

Swadling, Pamela, with contributions by Roy Wagner and Billai Laba. 1996. *Plumes from Paradise: Trade Cycles in Outer Southeast Asia and their Impact on New Guinea and Nearby Islands until 1920*. Boroko: Papua New Guinea National Museum in association with Robert Brown and Associates.

Taltaga, L. 1977. The Enga Salt Trade. *Oral History* 3 (3): 2–37.

Taylor, Alan. 1981. Lapita Culture. In *Historical Dictionary of Oceania*, edited by Robert D. Craig and Frank P. King, 155. Westport, Conn.: Greenwood Press.

Taylor, Jean Gelman. 1983. *The Social World of Batavia: European and Eurasian in Dutch Asia*. Madison: University of Wisconsin Press.

Terrell, John E. 1999. Pacific Lizards or Red Herrings. *Archaeology* 52 (3): 24–25.

Terrell, John, and Robert L. Welsch. 1997. Lapita and the Temporal Geography of Prehistory. *Antiquity* 71: 548–572.

Tetens, Alfred. 1958. *Among the Savages of the South Seas: Memoirs of Micronesia, 1862–1868*, translated by F. M. Spoehr. Stanford: Stanford University Press.

Thomas, Nicholas. 1989. The Force of Ethnology: Origins and Significance of the Melanesia/ Polynesia Division. With replies by A. Abramson, R. C. Green, M. Sahlins, R. A. Stephenson, F. Valjavec, and R. G. White; and a Rejoinder by N. Thomas. *Current Anthropology* 30 (1): 27– 34, 34–41; 30 (2): 211–213.

———. 1991. *Entangled Objects: Exchange, Material Culture and Colonialism in the Pacific*. Cambridge, Mass.: Harvard University Press.

———. 1994. *Colonialism's Culture: Anthropology, Travel and Government*. Melbourne: Melbourne University Press.

Thompson, Roger C. 1980. *Australian Imperialism in the Pacific: The Expansionist Era, 1820–1920*. Melbourne: Melbourne University Press.

———. 1986. Hubert Murray and the Historians. *Pacific Studies* 10 (1): 79–96.

Thomson, D. F. 1933. The Hero Cult, Initiation and Totemism on Cape York. *Journal of the Royal Anthropological Institute of Great Britain and Ireland* 63: 453–537.

———. 1934. Notes on a Hero Cult from the Gulf of Carpentaria, North Queensland. *Journal of the Royal Anthropological Institute of Great Britain and Ireland* 64: 217–235.

Thomson, W. 1886–1887. History of the North-East Coast of Australia. *Proceedings of the Queensland Branch of the Royal Geographical Society of Australia* 2 (2): 129–152.

Threlfall, Neville. 1975. *One Hundred Years in the Islands: The Methodist/United Church in the New Guinea Region, 1875–1975*. Rabaul: Toksave ne Buk Dipatmen, United Church.

Thrower, Norman J. W. 1984. *Sir Francis Drake and the Famous Voyage, 1577–1580: Essays Commemorating the Quadricentennial of Drake's Circumnavigation of the Earth*. Berkeley: University of California Press.

Townsend, C. H. 1935. The Distribution of Certain Whales as Shown by Logbook Records of American Whaleships. *Zoologica: Scientific Contributions of the New York Zoological Society* 19 (1): 3–50 [and maps].

Tregance, L. 1888. *Adventures in New Guinea: The Narrative of Louis Tregance, a French Sailor: Nine Years in Captivity among the Orangwoks, a Tribe in the Interior of New Guinea*, introduction by H. Crocker. London: Sampson Low.

Trompf, Garry W., ed. 1977. *Prophets of Melanesia: Six Essays*. Port Moresby: Institute of Papua New Guinea Studies.

———. 1991. *Melanesian Religion*. Cambridge: Cambridge University Press.

Tryon, Darrell. 1984. The Peopling of the Pacific: A Linguistic Appraisal. *Journal of Pacific History* 19 (3): 147–159.

———. 1994. Language Contact and Contact-Induced Language Change in the Eastern Outer Islands, Solomon Islands. In *Language Contact and Change in the Austronesian World*, edited by Tom Dutton and Darrell Tryon, 611–648. Berlin and New York: Mouton de Gruyter.

———. 1995. Proto-Austronesians and the Major Austronesian Subgroups. In *The Austrone-*

sians: Historical and Comparative Perspectives, edited by Peter Bellwood, James J. Fox, and Darrell Tryon, 17–38. Canberra: Department of Anthropology, Research School of Pacific and Asian Studies, Australian National University.

Tryon, Darrell T., and B. D. Hackman. 1983. *Solomon Islands Languages: An Internal Classification.* Pacific Linguistics Series C, No 72. Canberra: Department of Linguistics, Research School of Pacific Studies, Australian National University.

Turner, Mark. 1990. *Papua New Guinea: The Challenge of Independence*. Ringwood, Victoria: Penguin.

Tuzin, Donald. 1997. *The Cassowary's Revenge: The Life and Death of Masculinity in a New Guinea Society*. Chicago and London: University of Chicago Press.

Valdes, Cynthia O., Kerry N. Long, and Artemio C. Barbosa. 1992. *A Thousand Years of Stoneware Jars in the Philippines*. Manila: Jar Collectors (Philippines), with support of Eugenio Lopez Foundation, and in cooperation with the National Museum and the Oriental Ceramic Society of the Philippines.

Velde, Paul van der. 1995. The Royal Dutch Geographical Society and the Dutch East Indies, 1873–1914: From Colonial Lobby to Colonial Hobby. In *Geography and Imperialism, 1820–1940*, edited by Morag Bell, Robin Butlin, and Michael Hefferman, 80–92. New York: Manchester University Press, St. Martins Press.

Verschueren, J. 1953. De Katholieke Missie. In *Nieuw Guinea: De Ontwikkeling op Economisch, Sociaal en Cultureel Gebied, in Nederlands en Australisch Nieuw Guinea*, edited by W. C. Klein, 1: 160–229. 'S-Gravenhage: Staatsdrukkerij-en Uitgeverijbedrijf.

Veur, Paul W. van der. 1964a. New Guinea Annexations and the Origin of the Irian Boundary. *Australian Outlook* 18 (3): 313–339.

———. 1964b. Papua Irredenta: Queensland's Northern Boundary and the Territory of Papua. *Australian Journal of Politics and History* 10 (2): 183–195.

———. 1966a. *Search for New Guinea's Boundaries: From Torres Strait to the Pacific*. Canberra: Australian National University.

———. 1966b. *Documents and Correspondence on New Guinea's Boundaries*. Canberra: Australian National University Press.

———. 1972. Dutch New Guinea. In *Encyclopaedia of Papua and New Guinea*, edited by Peter Ryan, 276–283. Melbourne: Melbourne University Press in association with the University of Papua New Guinea.

Voorhoeve, C. L. 1982. The Halmahera Conection: A Case for Prehistoric Traffic through Torres Strait. In *Papers from the Third International Conference on Austronesian Linguistics, Tracking the Travellers*, edited by Amran Halim, Lois Carrington, and Stephen A. Wurm, 217–239. 2 vols. Pacific Linguistics C-75. Canberra: Department of Linguistics, Research School of Pacific Studies, Australian National University.

Wagner, Herwig, and Hermann Reiner. 1986. *The Lutheran Church in Papua New Guinea*. Adelaide: Lutheran Publishing House.

Waiko, John Dadamo. 1982. Be Jijimo: A History according to the Tradition of the Binandere People of Papua New Guinea. Ph.D. thesis, Australian National University.

———. 1985. Na Binandere, Imo Averi? We are Binandere, Who are You? In "Mobility and Identity in the Island Pacific," edited by Murray Chapman, special issue of *Pacific Viewpoint* 26 (1): 9–29.

———. 1990. Binandere Forced Labour: Papua New Guinea. In *Labour in the South Pacific*, edited by Clive Moore, Jacqueline Leckie, and Doug Munro, 181–185. Townsville: Department of History and Center of Melanesian Studies, James Cook University.

———. 1993. *A Short History of Papua New Guinea*. Melbourne: Oxford University Press.

Wallace, Alfred Russel. 1869. *The Malay Archipelago: The Land of the Orang-utan, and the Bird of Paradise*. London: Macmillan. [Repr., with an Introduction by John Bastin, Kuala Lumpur: Oxford University Press, 1986; 3d ed., 1994.]

Walsh, M. 1991. Overview of Indigenous Languages of Australia. In *Language in Australia*, edited by S. Romaine. Cambridge: Cambridge University Press.

Ward, Ralph Gerard. 1972. The Pacific *Beche-de-Mer* Trade with Special References to Fiji. In *Man in the Pacific Islands: Essays on Geographical Change in the Pacific Islands*, edited by R. G. Ward, 91–123. Oxford: Clarendon Press.

Warren, James F. 1981. *The Sulu Zone, 1768–1898: The Dynamics of External Trade, Slavery, and Ethnicity in the Transformation of a Southeast Asian Maritime Economy*. Singapore: Singapore University Press.

Webster, Elsie M. 1984. *The Moon Man: A Biography of Nikolai Miklouho-Maclay*. Melbourne: Melbourne University Press.

Webster, Herbert C. 1898. *Through New Guinea and the Cannibal Countries*. London: T. Fisher Unwin.

Weeks, Sheldon, and Gerard Gutherie. 1982a. First Level Education: Community Schools. In *Papua New Guinea Atlas: A Nation in Transition*, edited by David King and Stephen Ranck, 26–27. Port Moresby: Robert Brown and Associates in conjunction with University of Papua New Guinea.

———. 1982b. Secondary and Third Level Education: High School and Beyond. In *Papua New Guinea Atlas: A Nation in Transition*, edited by David King and Stephen Ranck, 28–29. Port Moresby: Robert Brown and Associates in conjunction with the University of Papua New Guinea.

Wehner, Monica, and Donald Denoon, eds. 2001. *Without a Gun: Australia's Experiences Monitoring Peace in Bouganiville, 1997–2001*. Canberra: Pandanus Books.

Weiner, James F. 1988. Looking at the New Guinea Highlands from Its Edge. *Mountain Papuans: Historical and Comparative Perspectives from New Guinea Fringe Highlands Societies*, edited by J. F. Weiner, 1–38. Ann Arbor: University of Michigan Press.

Wemyss, Thomas. 1837. *Narrative of the Melancholy Shipwreck of the Ship Charles Eaton: And the Inhuman Massacre of the Passengers and Crew; With an Account of the Rescue of Two Boys from the Hands of the Savages, in an Island in Torres Strait*. Stockton: Robinson.

Werff, Hely van der. 1989. Shifting Cultivation, Kain Timur and Suangi in Relation to the Position of Women. In *Peoples on the Move: Current Themes of Anthropological Research in New Guinea, Papers of the New Guinea Workshop, 1987*, edited by Paul Haenen and Jan Pouwer, 165–174. Nijmegen: Centre for Australian and Oceanic Studies, University of Nijmegen.

West, Francis. 1968. *Hubert Murray: The Australian Pro-Consul*. Melbourne: Oxford University Press.

———. 1978. An Australian Moving Frontier in New Guinea. In *The Changing Pacific: Essays in Honour of H. E. Maude*, edited by Niel Gunson, 214–227. Melbourne: Oxford University Press.

Wetherell, David. 1977. *Reluctant Mission: The Anglican Church in Papua New Guinea, 1891–1942.* St. Lucia, Queensland: University of Queensland Press.

———. 1996. *Charles Abel and the Kwato Mission of Papua New Guinea, 1891–1975.* Melbourne: Melbourne University Press.

Wheatley, Paul. 1959. Geographical Notes on some Commodities Involved in Sung Maritime Trade. *Journal of the Malayan Branch of the Royal Asiatic Society* 32 (2): 3–140.

White, Geoffrey, and Lamont Lindstrom, eds. 1990. *The Pacific Theatre: Island Representations of World War II.* Melbourne: Melbourne University Press.

White, J. Peter. 1997. Archaeological Survey in Southern New Ireland. *Journal de la Société des Océanistes* 105: 141–146.

White, J. Peter, and James F. O'Connell. 1982. *A Prehistory of Australia, New Guinea and Sahul.* Sydney: Academic Press.

White, M.W.D. 1981. Establishment of the Queensland Border in Torres Strait. In *The Torres Strait Treaty: A Symposium*, edited by P. J. Boyce and M.W.D. White, 16–25. Canberra: Australian Institute of International Affairs, Queensland, and Australian National University Press.

Whittaker, June L., Noel G. Gash, J. F. Hookey, and Roderick J. Lacey. 1975. *Documents and Readings in New Guinea History: Prehistory to 1889.* Brisbane: Jacaranda.

Wichmann, Arthur. 1909–1912. *Entdeckungsgeschichte von Neu-Guinea. Nova Guinea: Uitkomsten der Nederlandsch Nieuw Guinea Expedities.* 2 vols. Leiden: Brill.

Wickler, Stephen, and Matthew Spriggs. 1988. Pleistocene Human Occupation of the Solomon Islands, Melanesia. *Antiquity* 62 (237): 703–706.

Williams, Louise. 1993. Australia: The Secret Story. *Sydney Morning Herald, Good Weekend*, 2 October, 11–16.

Willis, Ian. 1969. Who Was First? The First White Man into the New Guinea Highlands. *Journal of the Papua New Guinea Society* 3 (1): 32–45.

Wilson, Paul D. 1978. Chester's Report on a Voyage to the Fly River, in December 1875: Introduction and Notes. *Queensland Heritage* 3 (9): 19–24.

Wiltgen, Ralph M. 1981. *The Founding of the Roman Catholic Church in Oceania, 1825 to 1850.* Canberra: Australian National University Press.

Wolfers, Edward P. 1975. *Race Relations and Colonial Rule in Papua New Guinea.* Sydney: Australia and New Zealand Book Company.

———, ed. 1988. *Beyond the Border: Indonesia and Papua New Guinea, South-east Asia and the South Pacific.* Waigani and Suva: University of Papua New Guinea, and Institute of Pacific Studies, University of the South Pacific.

Worsley, Peter. 1957. *The Trumpet Shall Sound: A Study of Cargo Cults in Melanesia.* London: MacGibbon & Kee.

Wright, H.R.C. 1958. The Moluccan Spice Monopoly, 1770–1824. *Journal of the Malayan Branch Royal Asiatic Society* 31 (4): i–iv, 1–127.

Wright, Huntley. 2002a. Economic or Political Development: The Evolution of 'Native' Local Government Policy in the Territory of Papua and New Guinea, 1945–1963. *Australian Journal of Politics and History* 48 (2): 193–209.

———. 2002b. A Liberal 'Respect for Small Property': Paul Hasluck and the 'Landless Proletariat' in the Territory of Papua and New Guinea, 1951–63. *Australian Historical Studies* 119: 55–72.

Wroth, L. C. 1944. Early Cartography of the Pacific. *The Papers of the Bibliographical Society of America* 38 (2): 87–268.

Wurm, Stephen A. 1978. The Emerging Linguistic Picture and Lingusitic Prehistory of the Southwestern Pacific. In *Approaches to Language Anthropological Issues*, by W. C. McCormack and S. A. Wurm, 191–221. The Hague: Mouton.

———. 1982a. *Papuan Languages of Oceania*. Tübingen: Gunter Narr Verlag.

———. 1982b. Indigenous Languages. In *Papua New Guinea Atlas: A Nation in Transition*, edited by D. King and S. Ranck, 34–35. Bathurst: Robert Brown and Associates in conjunction with the University of Papua New Guinea.

———. 1983. Linguistic Prehistory in the New Guinea Area. *Journal of Human Evolution* 12: 25–35.

Wurm, Stephen A., D. C. Laycock, C. L. Voorhoeve, and T. E. Dutton. 1975. Papuan Linguistic Prehistory, and Past Language Migrations in the New Guinea Area. In *New Guinea Languages and Language Study, Vol. 1, Papuan Languages and the New Guinea Linguistic Scene*, edited by S. A. Wurm, 935–960. *Pacific Linguistics*, Series C, No. 38. Canberra: Australian National University.

Yen, Douglas E. 1973. The Origins of Oceanic Agriculture. *Archaeology and Physical Anthropology in Oceania* 8 (1): 68–85.

———. 1991. Domestication: The Lessons from New Guinea. In *Man and a Half: Essays in Pacific Anthropology and Ethnobiology in Honour of Ralph Bulmer*, edited by Andrew Pawley, 558–569. Memoir No. 48. Auckland: Polynesian Society.

———. 1995. The Development of Sahul Agriculture with Australia as Bystander. In "Transitions: Pleistocene to Holocene in Australia and Papua New Guinea." edited by Jim Allen and J. F. O'Connell, special issue of *Antiquity* 69: 831–847.

Young, John. 1984. *Adventurous Spirits: Australian Migrant Society in Pre-cession Fiji*. St. Lucia, Queensland: University of Queensland Press.

Young, Michael W., ed. 1988. *Malinowski among the Magi: The Natives of Mailu*. London and New York: Routledge.

Index

ISSCW   995
M821

MOORE, CLIVE
    NEW GUINEA

CENTRAL LIBRARY
03/07